THE OFFICIAL BLUE BOOK®

H A N D B O O K   O F

UNITED STATES COINS

R.S. YEOMAN

EDITOR

KENNETH BRESSETT

68th Edition
2011

Illustrated Catalog and Prices Dealers
Pay for Coins—1616 to Date

Containing Mint records and wholesale prices for U.S. coins from 1616 to the present time, including colonials, regular issues, commemoratives, territorials, gold, Proof sets, and Mint sets. Information on collecting coins—how coins are produced—mints and mintmarks—grading of coins—location of mintmarks—preserving coins—starting a collection—history of mints—and interesting descriptions of all U.S. copper, nickel, silver, and gold coins. Illustrated.

Handbook of United States Coins™
THE OFFICIAL BLUE BOOK OF UNITED STATES COINS™

THE OFFICIAL BLUE BOOK and OFFICIAL BLUE BOOK OF UNITED
STATES COINS are trademarks of Whitman Publishing, LLC.

WCG™ • OCG™

www.whitman**books**.com

Printed in the United States of America.

The WCG™ pricing grid used throughout this publication is patent pending.

© 2010 Whitman Publishing, LLC
3101 Clairmont Road • Suite G • Atlanta GA 30329

OCG™ Collecting Guide   Whitman®

For a complete listing of numismatic reference
books, supplies, and storage products, visit us at
www.whitman**books**.com

INTRODUCTION

Contributors 7
How to Use This Book 8
Collecting Coins 9

PRE-FEDERAL ISSUES

Colonial Issues 16
Post-Colonial Issues 26

FEDERAL ISSUES

Contract Issues and Patterns 41
Half Cents (1793–1857) 42
Large Cents (1793–1857) 46
Small Cents (1856 to Date) 54
Two-Cent Pieces (1864–1873) 65
Three-Cent Pieces (1851–1889) 66
Nickel Five-Cent Pieces (1866 to Date) 68
Half Dimes (1794–1873) 78
Dimes (1796 to Date) 82
Twenty-Cent Pieces (1875–1878) 95
Quarter Dollars (1796 to Date) 96
Half Dollars (1794 to Date) 116
Silver and Related Dollars (1794 to Date) 132
Gold Dollars (1849–1889) 147
Quarter Eagles (1796–1929) 150
Three-Dollar Gold Pieces (1854–1889) 156
Four-Dollar Gold Pieces or "Stellas" (1879–1880) 157
Half Eagles (1795–1929) 158
Eagles (1795–1933) 166
Double Eagles (1849–1933) 172
Commemoratives (1892 to Date) 178
Proof and Mint Sets (1936 to Date) 218

BULLION

Silver Bullion (1986 to Date) 221
Gold Bullion (1986 to Date) 222
Platinum Bullion (1997 to Date) 228

OTHER ISSUES

Private and Territorial Gold 231
Private Tokens 249

APPENDICES

A: Bullion Values 250
B: Selling Your Coins 252

INDEX

INDEX 254

CONTRIBUTORS TO THE SIXTY-EIGHTH EDITION

Special Consultants: Philip Bressett and Jeff Garrett

Whitman Publishing extends its thanks to these members of the coin-buying community who have contributed pricing for this year's *Handbook of United States Coins*. Their data were compiled and then reviewed by editor Kenneth Bressett and consultants Phil Bressett and Jeff Garrett. This process ensures input from a broad range of dealers and auctioneers from across the country—experts who buy, sell, and trade coins every day and know the market inside and out.

Mark Albarian	Ira M. Goldberg	Stuart Levine	Robert Rhue
Jeff Ambio	Lawrence Goldberg	Denis W. Loring	Maurice Rosen
J.H. Cline	Gene L. Henry	Robert T. McIntire	Gerald R. Scherer Jr.
Alan Cohen	John W. Highfill	Lee S. Minshull	Richard Snow
Gary Cohen	Jesse Iskowitz	Scott P. Mitchell	Steve Tanenbaum
James H. Cohen	Steve Ivy	Michael C. Moline	Troy Thoreson
Sheridan Downey	Donald H. Kagin	Mike Orlando	Ben Todd
Mike Fuljenz	Bradley S. Karoleff	Robert M. Paul	David Wnuck
Chuck Furjanic	Robert Lecce	William P. Paul	Mark S. Yaffe
Jeff Garrett	Julian M. Leidman	Joel Rettew Jr.	

Special credit is due to the following for service in past editions of the Handbook:

Gary Adkins	Adam Crum	John J. Kraljevich Jr.	Greg Rohan
David Akers	John Dannreuther	Richard A. Lecce	Leonard R. Saunders
John Albanese	Tom DeLorey	David Leventhal	Mary Sauvain
Mark Albarian	Silvano DiGenova	Kevin Lipton	Gerald Scherer Jr.
Buddy Alleva	Kenneth Duncan	Andy Lustig	Cherie Schoeps
Richard S. Appel	Steven Ellsworth	Dwight N. Manley	Richard Schwary
Michael Aron	John Feigenbaum	David McCarthy	James A. Simek
Richard M. August	Dennis Gillio	Chris McCawley	Craig Smith
Richard A. Bagg	Ronald Gillio	Harry Miller	William J. Spencer
Mitchell A. Battino	Kenneth M. Goldman	Robert Mish	Lawrence R. Stack
Lee J. Bellisario	J.R. Grellman	Paul Montgomery	David M. Sundman
Jack Beymer	Ron Guth	Charles Moore	Anthony J. Swiatek
Mark R. Borckardt	James Halperin	Richard Nachbar	Anthony Terranova
Q. David Bowers	John Hamrick	Chris Napolitano	Jerry Treglia
H. Robert Campbell	Ash Harrison	Paul Nugget	Frank Van Valen
Elizabeth W. Coggan	Karl D. Hirtzinger	John M. Pack	Fred Weinberg
Alan R. Cohen	James J. Jelinski	William S. Panitch	Douglas Winter
Steve Contursi	A.M. Kagin	Joel Rettew Sr.	
Marc Crane	Mike Kliman	Tom Rinaldo	

Special photo credits are due to the following:

Douglas F. Bird, Steve Contursi, Bill Fivaz, Ira & Larry Goldberg Coins & Collectibles, heritagecoins.com, Tom Mulvaney, the Museum of the American Numismatic Association, Noyes–Lusk DVD Photo Project, Numismatic Guaranty Corporation of America (NGC), Brent Pogue, Sarasota Rare Coin Gallery, the Smithsonian Institution, Rick Snow, Spectrum, Stack's Rare Coins of New York, Superior Galleries, Anthony Swiatek, and the United States Mint.

Since 1942, annually revised editions of the *Official Blue Book of United States Coins™* have aided thousands of people who have coins to sell or are actively engaged in collecting United States coins. The popular coin-folder method of collecting by date has created ever-changing premium values, based on the supply and demand of each date and mint. Through its panel of contributors, the Blue Book has, over the years, reported these changing values. It also serves as a source of general numismatic information to all levels of interest in the hobby.

The values shown are representative prices paid by dealers for various United States coins. These are averages of prices assembled from many widely separated sources. On some issues slight differences in price among dealers may result from proximity to the various mints or heavily populated centers. Other factors, such as local supply and demand or dealers' stock conditions, may also cause deviations from the prices listed. While many coins bring no premium in circulated grades, they usually bring premium prices in Mint State and Proof. Extremely rare and valuable coins are usually sold at public auction, and prices vary according to current demand.

THIS BOOK LISTS PRICES MANY COIN DEALERS WILL PAY.

Premium prices are the average amount dealers will pay for coins (according to condition) if required for their stock. This book is not a retail price list.

IF YOU HAVE COINS TO SELL

Whitman Publishing, LLC, is not in the rare coin business; however, chances are that the dealer from whom you purchased this book is engaged in the buying and selling of rare coins—contact him first. In the event that you purchased this book from a source other than a numismatic establishment, consult your local telephone directory for the names of coin dealers (they will be found sometimes under the heading of "Stamp and Coin Dealers"). If you live in a city or town that does not have any coin dealers, obtain a copy of one of the trade publications (such as *Coin World* or *Numismatic News*) or check the Internet in order to obtain the names and addresses of many of the country's leading dealers. Information or sample copies may be obtained by writing to the individual publisher.

Current average *retail* valuations of all U.S. coins are listed in Whitman's *A Guide Book of United States Coins™* by R.S. Yeoman, edited by Kenneth Bressett, Whitman Publishing, LLC, Atlanta, GA ($29.95 Large Print Edition; $19.95 spiralbound hardcover; $16.95 hardcover; $14.95 coilbound).

HOW TO READ THE CHARTS

A dash in a price column indicates that coins in that grade exist even though there are no current sales or auction records from them. (The dash does *not* necessarily mean that such coins are excessively rare.) Italicized prices indicate unsettled or speculative values. A number of listings of rare coins do not have prices or dashes in certain grades. This indicates that they are not available or not believed to exist in those grades.

Mintages of Proof coins are listed in parentheses.

Italicized mintages are estimates.

Numismatics or coin collecting is one of the world's oldest hobbies, dating back several centuries. Coin collecting in America did not develop to any extent until about 1840, as our pioneer forefathers were too busy carving a country out of wilderness to afford the luxury of a hobby. The discontinuance of the large-sized cent in 1857 caused many people to attempt to accumulate a complete set of the pieces while they were still in circulation. One of the first groups of collectors to band together for the study of numismatics was the American Numismatic Society, founded in 1858 and still a dynamic part of the hobby. Lack of an economical method to house a collection held the number of devotees of coin collecting to a few thousand until Whitman Publishing and other manufacturers placed low-priced coin boards and folders on the market in the 1930s. Since that time, the number of Americans collecting coins has increased many-fold.

THE PRODUCTION OF COINS

To collect coins intelligently it is necessary to have some knowledge of the manner in which they are produced. Coins are made in factories called "mints." The Mint of the United States was established at Philadelphia by a resolution of Congress dated April 2, 1792. The act also provided for the coinage of gold eagles ($10), half eagles, and quarter eagles; silver dollars, half dollars, quarter dollars, dimes (originally spelled "disme"), and half dismes or half dimes; and copper cents and half cents. The first coins struck were one-cent and half-cent pieces, in March of 1793 on a hand-operated press. Most numismatic authorities consider the half disme of 1792 the first United States coinage, quoting the words of George Washington as their authority. Washington, in his annual address, November 6, 1792, said, "There has been a small beginning in the coining of the half dimes, the want of small coins in circulation calling the first attention to them." Though the half disme is considered America's first coinage, it was not the first coinage produced by the Mint; these coins were produced off premises in July of 1792 before the mint was completed. In the new Philadelphia Mint are a number of implements from the original mint, and some coins discovered when the old building was wrecked. These coins included half dismes, and the placard identifying them states that Washington furnished the silver and gave the coined pieces to his friends as souvenirs.

Prior to the adoption of the Constitution, the Continental Congress arranged for the issuance of copper coins under private contract. These are known as the 1787 *Fugio cents* from their design, which shows a sundial and the Latin word "fugio"—"I Fly" or, in connection with the sundial, "Time Flies." The ever-appropriate motto "Mind Your Business" is also on the coin.

In the manufacture of a coin, the first step is die preparation. Dies for early federal coinage were prepared by hand; generally, letters and numbers were added with punches, while portraits and other designs were engraved into the die. Eventually, eagles, Liberty heads, and the like were also added with hubs and punches. After about 1836, many dies were made from masters, which contained all elements except the date and, if applicable, the mintmark. The addition of an element to a master die ensured its consistent placement throughout the life of the die. Today, many design tasks are performed with three-dimensional computer graphics. Mint artists are known as sculptor-engravers, and their work takes place mainly at the Philadelphia Mint. The dies are made of soft steel, which is hardened after the impression is received. The die is then dressed or finished to remove imperfections and make it suitable for coining. A typical die for production coinage can be used to strike hundreds of thousands of pieces. Dies for special issues such as Proofs are replaced more often.

The hand method of cutting dies accounts for the many die varieties of early United States coins. Where the amount of coinage of a given year was large enough to wear out many dies, each new die placed in the coining press created another die variety of that year. The dies being cut by hand, no two were exactly alike in every detail, even though some of the major elements such as the head or wreath, were sunk into the die by individual master punches. Of the cents dated 1794, more than sixty different die varieties have been discovered.

Thousands of dies are now used by the mints of the United States each year, but they are all made from one master die, which is produced in the following manner:

After the design is settled upon, the plaster of paris or wax model is prepared several times the actual size of the coin. When this model is finished an electrotype (an exact duplicate in metal) is made and prepared for the reducing lathe. The reducing lathe is a machine that works on the principle of the pantograph, only in this case the one point traces or follows the form of the model while another much smaller point in the form of a drill cuts away the steel and produces a reduced-size die of the model. The die is finished and details are sharpened or worked over by an engraver with chisel and graver. The master die is used to make duplicates in soft steel which are then hardened and ready for the coining press. To harden dies, they are placed in cast-iron boxes packed with carbon to exclude the air, and when heated to a bright red are cooled suddenly with water.

In the coinage operations the first step is to prepare the metal. Among the alloys that have been used are the following: silver coins, 90% silver and 10% copper; five-cent pieces, 75% copper and 25% nickel; one-cent pieces, 95% copper and 5% zinc. (The 1943 cent consists of steel coated with zinc; and the five-cent piece of 1942–1945 contains 35% silver, 56% copper, and 9% manganese.) Under the Coinage Act of 1965, the composition of dimes, quarters, and half dollars was changed to eliminate or reduce the silver content of these coins. The copper-nickel "clad" dimes, quarters, half dollars, and dollars are composed of an outer layer of copper-nickel (75% copper and 25% nickel) bonded to an inner core of pure copper. The silver clad half dollar and dollar have an outer layer of 80% silver bonded to an inner core of 21% silver, with a total content of 40% silver. Current cents are made from a core of 99.2% zinc, 0.8% copper, with a plating of pure copper. Dollars are composed of a pure copper core with outer layers of manganese-brass.

Alloys are melted in crucibles and poured into molds to form ingots. The ingots are in the form of thin bars and vary in size according to the denomination of the coin. The width is sufficient to allow three or more coins to be cut from the strips.

The ingots are next put through rolling mills to reduce the thickness to required limits. The strips are then fed into cutting presses which cut circular blanks of the approximate size of the finished coin. The blanks are run through annealing furnaces to soften them; next they move through tumbling barrels, rotating cylinders containing cleaning solutions which clean and burnish the metal; and finally into centrifugal drying machines.

The blanks are next fed into a milling machine which produces the raised or upset rim. The blank, now called a *planchet,* is now ready for the coining press.

The planchet is held firmly by a collar, as it is struck under heavy pressure varying from 40 tons for the one-cent pieces and dimes to 170 tons for silver dollars. Upper and lower dies impress the design on both sides of the coin. The pressure is sufficient to produce a raised surface level with that of the milled rim. The collar holding the blank for silver or clad coins is grooved. The pressure forces the metal into the grooves of the collar, producing the "reeding" on the edge of the finished coin.

HOW A PROOF COIN IS MADE

Selected dies are inspected for perfection and are highly polished and cleaned. They are again wiped clean or polished after every 15 to 25 impressions and are replaced frequently to avoid imperfections from wear. Coinage blanks are polished and cleaned to assure high quality in striking. They are then hand fed into the coinage press one at a time, each blank receiving two blows from the dies to bring up sharp, high-relief details. The coinage operation is done at slow speed. Finished Proofs are individually inspected and are handled by gloves or tongs. They also receive a final inspection by packers before being sonically sealed in special plastic cases.

Certain coins, including Lincoln cents, Buffalo nickels, quarter eagles, half eagles, eagles, and double eagles, between the years 1908 and 1916, were made with Matte Proof (nickel and silver) and Sand Blast and Satin Proof (gold) finishes. These later Proofs have a dull frosted surface which was either applied to the dies, or produced by special treatment after striking.

MINTS AND MINTMARKS

In addition to the Philadelphia Mint, the U.S. government has from time to time established branch mints in various parts of the country. At present, branch mints operate in Denver, West Point, and San Francisco. Starting in 1968, Proof sets and some of the regular coins were produced at the San Francisco Mint and Assay Office. The Denver Mint has operated since 1906. A mint was operated at New Orleans from 1838 to 1861 and again from 1879 to 1909. Mints were also in service at Carson City, Nevada, from 1870 to 1893; at Charlotte, North Carolina, from 1838 to 1861; at Dahlonega, Georgia, from 1838 to 1861; and at San Francisco since 1854. The U.S. government also operated a mint in the Philippines in the early 1900s.

Coins struck at Philadelphia before 1979 (except 1942 to 1945 five-cent pieces) do not bear a mintmark. Historically the mintmark was used only for branch mints. Recent exceptions include the Lincoln cent and the Kennedy half dollar, which both use the P for Philadelphia. All coins struck after 1967 have the mintmark on the obverse. The letters signifying the various mints are as follows:

    C—Charlotte, North Carolina (gold coins only; 1838–1861)
    CC—Carson City, Nevada (1870–1893)
    D—Dahlonega, Georgia (gold coins only; 1838–1861)
    D—Denver, Colorado (1906 to date)
    O—New Orleans, Louisiana (1838–1861; 1879–1909)
    P—Philadelphia, Pennsylvania (1793 to date; P not used in early years)
    S—San Francisco, California (1854 to date)
    W—West Point, New York (1984 to date)

The mintmark is of utmost importance to collectors because, historically, coinage of the branch mints has often been much smaller than quantities struck at Philadelphia. Many early coins of the branch mints are very scarce.

DISTINGUISHING MARKS

The illustrations and explanations in this section will help the collector identify certain well-known varieties.

Half Cents of 1795–1796 Showing Location of Pole to Cap

The end of the pole lies parallel with the lines of the bust, which is pointed. On some coins, the pole is missing due either to engraver error (while cutting the die) or to an error in "relapping" (when the die is ground to remove wear, clash marks, etc.).

Pole to Cap   **No Pole to Cap**

Stemless Wreath Variety of Half Cents and Large Cents

For this variety, the difference is on the reverse side. Illustrations below show both Stemless and Stems to Wreath types for comparison—stemless wreath found on the 1804, 1805, and 1806 half cents; and on the 1797, 1802, and 1803 large cents.

Stemless Wreath   **Stems to Wreath**

1864 Bronze Indian Head Cent With "L" on Ribbon

A small "L," the initial of the designer James B. Longacre, was added to the Indian design late in 1864 and was continued through 1909. For coins in less than Fine condition, this small letter will often be worn away. The point of the bust is rounded on the 1864 variety without "L"; the bust is pointed on the

variety with "L." The initial must be visible, however, for the 1864 variety to bring the higher premium. If the coin is turned slightly so that the portrait faces the observer, the highlighted details will usually appear to better advantage.

Designer Initials, Overstrikes, Die-Doublings, and Date Varieties

During 1909, initials appeared on the reverse of the Lincoln cent.
Starting in 1918, they appear below the shoulder.

Prior to 1990, mintmarks for all mints were usually applied directly to working dies at Philadelphia in a hand-punching operation. Occasionally, a die was accidentally marked with one letter on top of another.

Dies are produced by impressing the raised coin design of a hub into the end of a cylinder of steel. In early years the Mint made use of old dies by repunching the dates on their dies with new numbers. That practice was stopped prior to 1909. Since that time, all overdated coins have been the result of errors that occur when two different-dated hubs have been used in die preparation, and one is impressed over the other by accident.

1938-D, D Over S
Buffalo Nickel

1918-S, 8 Over 7
A variety of the kind on this quarter dollar is rarely found in coinage of the 20th century.

1942, 2 Over 1
Mercury Dime

1955, Doubled-Die Obverse
Lincoln Cent

Large Date Cent
(1960)

Small Date Cent
(1960)

Large Date Cent
(1982)

Small Date Cent
(1982)

CONDITIONS OF COINS
Essential Elements of the Official ANA Grading System

Proof—A specially made coin distinguished by sharpness of detail and usually with a brilliant, mirrorlike surface. *Proof* refers to the method of manufacture and is not a condition, but normally the term implies nearly perfect condition unless otherwise noted.

    Gem Proof (PF-65)—Brilliant surfaces with no noticeable blemishes or flaws. A few scattered, barely noticeable marks or hairlines.

    Choice Proof (PF-63)—Reflective surfaces with only a few blemishes in secondary focal places. No major flaws.

    Proof (PF-60)—Surface may have several contact marks, hairlines, or light rubs. Luster may be dull and eye appeal lacking.

Mint State—The terms *Mint State (MS)* and *Uncirculated (Unc.)* are used interchangeably to describe coins showing no trace of wear. Such coins may vary to some degree because of blemishes, toning, or slight imperfections, as described in the following subdivisions:

    Perfect Uncirculated (MS-70)—Perfect new condition, showing no trace of wear. The finest quality possible, with no evidence of scratches, handling, or contact with other coins. Very few circulation-issue coins are ever found in this condition.

    Gem Uncirculated (MS-65)—An above average Uncirculated coin that may be brilliant or lightly toned and that has very few contact marks on the surface or rim. MS-67 through MS-62 indicate slightly higher or lower grades of preservation.

    Choice Uncirculated (MS-63)—Has some distracting contact marks or blemishes in prime focal areas. Luster may be impaired.

    Uncirculated (MS-60)—Has no trace of wear but may show a number of contact marks, and surface may be spotted or lack some luster.

Choice About Uncirculated (AU-55)—Evidence of friction on high points of design. Most of the mint luster remains.

About Uncirculated (AU-50)—Traces of light wear on many of the high points. At least half of the mint luster is still present.

Choice Extremely Fine (EF-45)—Light overall wear on highest points. All design details are very sharp. Some of the mint luster is evident.

Extremely Fine (EF-40)—Light wear on design throughout, but all features sharp and well defined. Traces of luster may show.

Choice Very Fine (VF-30)—Light, even wear on the surface and highest parts of the design. All lettering and major features are sharp.

Very Fine (VF-20)—Moderate wear on high points of design. All major details are clear.

Fine (F-12)—Moderate to considerable even wear. Entire design is bold with overall pleasing appearance.

Very Good (VG-8)—Well worn with main features clear and bold, although rather flat.

Good (G-4)—Heavily worn, with design visible but faint in areas. Many details are flat.

About Good (AG-3)—Very heavily worn with portions of lettering, date, and legend worn smooth. The date may be barely readable.

Important: Damaged coins, such as those that are bent, corroded, scratched, holed, nicked, stained, or mutilated, are worth less than those without defects. Flawless Uncirculated coins are generally worth more than values quoted in this book. Slightly worn coins ("sliders") that have been cleaned and conditioned ("buffed") to simulate Uncirculated luster are worth considerably less than perfect pieces.

Unlike damage inflicted after striking, manufacturing defects do not always lessen values. Examples include colonial coins with planchet flaws and weakly struck designs; early silver and gold with weight-adjustment "file marks" (parallel cuts made prior to striking); and coins with "lint marks" (surface marks due to the presence of dust or other foreign matter during striking).

Brief guides to grading are placed before each major coin type. Grading standards are not scientific and often vary among collectors, dealers, and certification services. For more on grading, consult the *Official ANA Grading Standards for United States Coins*.

PRESERVING AND CLEANING COINS

Most numismatists will tell you to "never clean a coin" and it is good advice! Cleaning coins almost always reduces their value. Collectors prefer coins in their original condition.

Some effort should be made to protect Uncirculated and Proof coins so they won't need cleaning. Tarnish on a coin is purely a chemical process caused by oxygen in the air acting on the metal, or by chemicals with which the coin comes in contact. One of the most common chemicals causing tarnish is sulphur; most paper, with the exception of specially manufactured "sulphur-free" kinds, contains sulphur due to the sulphuric acid that is used in paper manufacture; therefore do not wrap coins in ordinary paper. Also keep Uncirculated and Proof coins away from rubber bands (a rubber band placed on a silver coin for a few days will eventually produce a black stripe on the coin where the band touched). The utmost in protection is obtained by storing the coin in an airtight box, away from moisture and humidity, and by using holders made of inert materials.

Many coins become marred by careless handling. Always hold the coin by the edge. The accompanying illustration shows the right and wrong way to handle numismatic specimens. It is a breach of numismatic etiquette to handle another collector's coin except by the edge, even if it is not an Uncirculated or Proof piece.

Right   **Wrong**

STARTING A COLLECTION

One may start a collection of United States coins with very little expense by systematically assembling the various dates and mintmarks of all the types and denominations that are now in general circulation, using Whitman's many different coin folders and albums, especially those for quarters and dollars with various designs.

With the exception of the price paid for the coin folder, collecting coins received in everyday business transactions entails no expense whatsoever; a Jefferson nickel taken out of circulation, for example, can always be spent for five cents if the occasion arises. Filling an album or two with coins found in circulation is probably the best method of determining whether coin collecting appeals to you. Not everyone can be a successful coin collector. It requires patience, intelligence of a high order, and a certain desire to know the meaning behind a lot of things that at first glance appear meaningless. You may not be cut out to be a collector but you'll never know until you look further into the subject, and if by the time an album or two of coins are collected you have no burning desire to acquire many more different coins, you will probably never be a collector. However, chances are that you will be, because if you have read this far in this book, it shows that you are interested in the subject.

High quality is the goal of every endeavor and coin collecting is no exception. After an album has been filled with circulated specimens, the next step will be to replace them with coins in Uncirculated condition, or perhaps to start collecting an obsolete series; in either case, it will be necessary to purchase some coins from dealers or other collectors. The most logical way to keep abreast of the market, or obtain the addresses of the country's leading dealers, is to subscribe to one or more of the trade publications. These magazines carry advertisements of various dealers listing coins for sale. Moreover, through these sources the beginner may obtain price lists and catalogs from the dealers.

There are several good reference books available at reasonable prices which will be helpful to the collector who wishes to know more about U.S. coins and paper money. R.S. Yeoman's *A Guide Book of United States Coins™* (the "Red Book") lists retail values of all regular U.S. coins and also lists all coins of the U.S. colonial period and private and territorial gold coins, plus tokens, pattern coins, errors, and other numismatic collectibles.

Most coin, book, and hobby dealers can supply the following titles:

The Official Red Book®: A Guide Book of United States Coins™—R.S. Yeoman, edited by Kenneth Bressett

A Guide Book of Morgan Silver Dollars: A Complete History and Price Guide—Q. David Bowers

The Expert's Guide to Collecting and Investing in Rare Coins—Q. David Bowers

Coin Collecting: A Beginner's Guide to the World of Coins—Kenneth Bressett

History of the United States Mint and Its Coinage—David W. Lange

T*he Official ANA Grading Standards for United States Coins*—Kenneth Bressett, et al.

A Guide Book of United States Type Coins—Q. David Bowers

Join a Coin Club

Beginners should join a "coin club" if they live in a city which has one. Associating with more experienced collectors will be of great benefit. Practically all larger cities have one or more clubs and they are being rapidly organized in smaller towns. Trade publications carry information about coin clubs and events such as coin shows and conventions.

The American Numismatic Association is a national organization that collectors can join. The ANA web site (www.money.org) has a list of member coin clubs throughout the United States. Contact the ANA by mail at 818 North Cascade Avenue, Colorado Springs, CO 80903, or by phone at 800-367-9732.

Early American coins are rare in conditions better than those listed and are consequently valued much higher.

BRITISH NEW WORLD ISSUES
Sommer Islands (Bermuda)

This coinage, issued around 1616, was the first struck for England's colonies in the New World. The coins were known as "Hogge Money" or "Hoggies."

The pieces were made of copper lightly silvered, in four denominations: shilling, sixpence, threepence, and twopence, indicated by Roman numerals. The hog is the main device and appears on the obverse side of each. SOMMER ISLANDS is inscribed within beaded circles. The reverse shows a full-rigged galleon with the flag of St. George on each of four masts.

Shilling

	AG	G	VG	F	VF	EF
Twopence	$2,000	$3,000	$4,500	$6,500	$15,000	$30,000
Threepence			65,000			
Sixpence	1,750	2,750	4,000	6,500	15,000	30,000
Shilling	2,500	3,600	5,200	15,000	30,000	45,000

Massachusetts
"New England" Coinage (1652)

In 1652 the General Court of Massachusetts ordered the first metallic currency to be struck in the British Americas, the New England silver threepence, sixpence, and shilling. These coins were made from silver bullion procured principally from the West Indies. Joseph Jenks made the punches for the first coins at his Iron Works in Saugus, Massachusetts, close to Boston where the mint was located. John Hull was appointed mintmaster; his assistant was Robert Sanderson.

NE Shilling (1652)

	G	VG	F	VF
NE Threepence *(unique)*				—
NE Sixpence *(8 known)*	$20,000	$40,000	$50,000	$125,000
NE Shilling	25,000	45,000	70,000	150,000

Willow Tree Coinage (1653–1660)

The simplicity of the design on the N.E. coins invited counterfeiting and clipping of the edges. Therefore, they were soon replaced by the Willow Tree, Oak Tree, and Pine Tree series. The Willow Tree coins were struck from 1653 to 1660, the Oak Trees 1660 to 1667, and the Pine Trees 1667 to 1682. All of them (with the exception of the Oak Tree twopence) bore the date 1652. Many varieties of all of these coins exist. Values shown are for the most common types.

Sixpence

	Fair	G	VG	F	VF
1652 Willow Tree Threepence *(3 known)*			—	—	—
1652 Willow Tree Sixpence *(14 known)*	$6,500	$16,000	$25,000	$50,000	$110,000
1652 Willow Tree Shilling	8,000	18,000	30,000	70,000	130,000

Oak Tree Coinage (1660–1667)

Twopence

Threepence

	G	VG	F	VF	EF	AU
1662 Oak Tree Twopence	$375	$500	$1,500	$2,750	$3,750	$6,000
1652 Oak Tree Threepence	380	650	1,700	3,000	4,900	8,000
1652 Oak Tree Sixpence	400	700	1,800	4,000	7,000	10,000
1652 Oak Tree Shilling	450	750	1,850	4,000	7,000	8,500

Pine Tree Coinage (1667–1682)

The first Pine Tree coins were minted on the same size planchets as the Oak Tree pieces. Subsequent issues of the shilling were narrower and thicker, to conform to the size of English coins.

Shilling, Large Planchet (1667–1674)   **Shilling, Small Planchet (1675–1682)**

See next page for chart.   17

	G	VG	F	VF	EF	AU
1652 Pine Tree Threepence	$350	$550	$1,000	$2,200	$3,300	$5,250
1652 Pine Tree Sixpence	400	600	1,200	2,700	3,400	6,000
1652 Pine Tree Shilling, Large Planchet	450	750	1,600	3,200	5,000	8,000
1652 Pine Tree Shilling, Small Planchet	400	650	1,350	3,000	3,700	6,000

Maryland
Lord Baltimore Coinage

In 1659, Cecil Calvert, Lord Baltimore and Lord Proprietor of Maryland, had coinage struck in England for use in Maryland. There were four denominations: shilling, sixpence, fourpence (groat) in silver, and copper penny (denarium). The silver coins have the bust of Lord Baltimore on the obverse, and the Baltimore family arms with the denomination in Roman numerals on the reverse.

Fourpence (groat)

Lord Baltimore Shilling

	G	VG	F	VF	EF	AU
Penny copper (9 known)	—	—	$30,000	$50,000	—	—
Fourpence	$850	$1,700	3,500	7,500	$12,000	$19,000
Sixpence	725	1,300	2,500	5,000	7,000	10,000
Shilling	1,000	1,700	3,500	7,000	10,000	15,000

New Jersey
St. Patrick or Mark Newby Coinage

Mark Newby, who came to America from Dublin, Ireland, in November 1681, brought copper pieces believed by numismatists to have been struck in England circa 1663 to 1672. These are called St. Patrick coppers. The coin received wide circulation in the New Jersey Province, having been authorized to pass as legal tender by the General Assembly in May 1682. The smaller piece, known as a farthing, was never specifically authorized for circulation in the colonies.

St. Patrick Farthing

	G	VG	F	VF	EF	AU
St. Patrick "Farthing"	$90	$150	$500	$1,625	$3,000	$6,750
St. Patrick "Halfpenny"	170	390	900	1,900	6,000	

COINAGE AUTHORIZED BY BRITISH ROYAL PATENT
American Plantations Tokens

These tokens struck in nearly pure tin were the first royally authorized coinage for the British colonies in America. They were made under a franchise granted in 1688 to Richard Holt. Restrikes were made circa 1828 from original dies.

	G	F	EF	AU	Unc.
(1688) James II Plantation Token Farthing					
1/24 Part Real	$125	$300	$750	$1,000	$2,000
1/24 Part Real, Restrike	60	170	375	550	950

Coinage of William Wood
Rosa Americana Coins

William Wood, an Englishman, obtained a patent from King George I to make tokens for Ireland and the American colonies. The Rosa Americana pieces were issued in three denominations—halfpenny, penny, and twopence—and were intended for use in America.

Penny

	VG	F	VF	EF	AU	Unc.
(No date) Twopence, Motto in Ribbon	$90	$170	$375	$700	$1,500	$2,800
1722 Halfpenny, DEI GRATIA REX UTILE DULCI	55	125	210	450	825	1,750
1722 Penny	55	125	210	450	825	1,750
1722 Twopence	80	160	300	550	1,000	2,200

Halfpenny

	VG	F	VF	EF	AU	Unc.
1723 Halfpenny	$40	$100	$175	$450	$900	$1,775

Entry continued on next page.

Twopence

	VG	F	VF	EF	AU	Unc.
1723 Penny	$40	$110	$200	$400	$650	$1,400
1723 Twopence *(illustrated)*	90	130	300	500	900	1,750

Wood's Hibernia Coinage

The type intended for Ireland had a seated figure with a harp on the reverse side and the word HIBERNIA. Denominations struck were the halfpenny and the farthing with dates 1722, 1723, and 1724. Although these have no association with the Americas, because of the connection with William Wood many American collectors desire to obtain them.

1722, Hibernia Halfpenny	First Type	Second Type

	VG	F	VF	EF	AU	Unc.
1722 Farthing, second type	$125	$220	$400	$750	$1,200	$3,000
1722 Halfpenny (first or second type)	40	55	110	250	400	650

1723, Hibernia Farthing	1724, Hibernia Halfpenny

	VG	F	VF	EF	AU	Unc.
1723 Farthing	$20	$35	$80	$150	$250	$425
1723 Halfpenny	20	30	75	140	225	400
1724 Farthing	40	90	250	400	650	1,200
1724 Halfpenny	32	75	170	325	500	950

Virginia Halfpennies

In 1773, coinage of a copper halfpenny was authorized for Virginia by the British Crown. The style is similar to the regular English coinage. These pieces did not arrive in Virginia until 1775, but after then they did circulate on a limited basis. Most examples known today are Uncirculated, by virtue of a hoard of several thousand pieces that came to light in the 19th century and was distributed in numismatic channels.

	G	VG	F	VF	EF	AU	Unc.
1773 Halfpenny	$10	$30	$50	$125	$225	$350	$600

EARLY AMERICAN AND RELATED TOKENS

Elephant Tokens

London Elephant Tokens

The London Elephant tokens were struck circa 1672 to 1694. Although they were undated, two examples are known to have been struck over 1672 British halfpennies. Most are struck in copper, but one is made of brass. The legend on this piece, GOD PRESERVE LONDON, is probably just a general plea for divine aid and not a specific reference to the outbreak of plague in 1665 or the great fire of 1666.

These pieces were not struck for the colonies, and probably did not circulate widely in America, although a few may have been carried there by colonists. They are associated with the 1694 Carolina and New England Elephant tokens, through a shared obverse die.

	VG	F	VF	EF	AU	Unc.
(1694) Halfpenny, GOD PRESERVE LONDON,						
Thick or Thin Planchet	$160	$300	$550	$900	$1,600	$2,200

Carolina Elephant Tokens

Although no law is known authorizing coinage for Carolina, very interesting pieces known as Elephant Tokens were made with the date 1694. These copper tokens were of halfpenny denomination. The reverse reads GOD PRESERVE CAROLINA AND THE LORDS PROPRIETERS. 1694.

The Carolina pieces were probably struck in England and perhaps intended as advertising to heighten interest in the Carolina Plantation.

	VG	F	VF	EF
1694 CAROLINA	$2,500	$4,000	$7,000	$12,000

New England Elephant Tokens

Like the Carolina Tokens, the New England Elephant Tokens were believed to have been struck in England as promotional pieces to increase interest in the American colonies.

	F	VF	EF
1694 NEW ENGLAND	$30,000	$55,000	$75,000

New Yorke in America Token

Little is known about the origin of this token. The design of a heraldic eagle on a regulated staff with oak leaf finials is identical to the crest found on the arms of William Lovelace, governor of New York, 1663 to 1673. It seems likely that this piece is a token farthing struck by Lovelace for use in New York.

	VG	F
(Undated) Brass or Copper	$3,750	$12,000
(Undated) Pewter	—	—

Gloucester Tokens

This token appears to have been a private coinage by a merchant of Gloucester (county), Virginia. The only specimens known are struck in brass. The exact origin and use of these pieces are unknown.

	F
1714 Shilling, brass *(2 known)*	$70,000

Higley or Granby Coppers

The Higley coppers were private issues. All the tokens were made of pure copper. There were seven obverse and four reverse dies. The first issue, in 1737, bore the legend THE VALUE OF THREEPENCE. After a time the quantity exceeded the local demand, and a protest arose against the value of the piece. The inscription was changed to VALUE ME AS YOU PLEASE.

	G	VG	F	VF
1737 THE VALVE OF THREE PENCE, CONNECTICVT, 3 Hammers	$5,000	$9,000	$16,000	$45,000
1737 THE VALVE OF THREE PENCE, I AM GOOD COPPER, 3 Hammers	5,500	9,500	16,000	45,000
1737 VALUE ME AS YOU PLEASE, I AM GOOD COPPER, 3 Hammers	5,500	9,500	16,000	45,000
(1737) VALUE ME AS YOU PLEASE, J CUT MY WAY THROUGH, Broad Axe	5,500	9,500	16,000	45,000
1739 VALUE ME AS YOU PLEASE, J CUT MY WAY THROUGH, Broad Axe	6,500	11,000	20,000	75,000

Hibernia–Voce Populi Coins

These coins, struck in the year 1760, were made in Dublin. Although these have no connection with America, they have been listed in numismatic publications in the United States for a long time and are collected by tradition.

Farthing (1760)

Halfpenny (1760)

	G	VG	F	VF	EF	AU	Unc.
1760 Farthing	$130	$180	$300	$950	$1,350	$2,100	$4,000
1760 Halfpenny	40	75	115	200	380	800	1,500

Pitt Tokens

William Pitt is the subject of these pieces, probably intended as commemorative medalets. He was a friend to the interests of America. The halfpenny served as currency during a shortage of regular coinage.

	VG	F	VF	EF	AU	Unc.
1766 Farthing		$4,000	$12,000			
1766 Halfpenny	$200	400	850	$1,400	$2,200	$4,750

Rhode Island Ship Medals

Although this medal has a Dutch inscription, the spelling and design indicate an English or Anglo-American origin. It is believed that this token was struck in England circa 1779–1780 as propaganda to persuade the Dutch to sign the Treaty of Armed Neutrality. Specimens are known in brass, copper, tin, and pewter. As with many colonial issues, modern copies exist.

1778–1779, Rhode Island Ship Medal

Values shown are for brass or copper pieces. Those struck in pewter are rare and valued higher.

	VF	EF	AU	Unc.
Rhode Island Ship Medal	$550	$1,000	$1,800	$2,750

John Chalmers Issues

John Chalmers, a silversmith, struck a series of silver tokens at Annapolis in 1783. Certain of the dies were by Thomas Sparrow, who also engraved bank note plates. As most examples show wear today, these pieces seem to have served well in commerce.

	VG	F	VF	EF	AU
1783 Threepence	$900	$1,800	$3,500	$6,500	$12,000

	VG	F	VF	EF	AU
1783 Sixpence	$1,300	$3,000	$6,500	$12,000	$18,000
1783 Shilling	700	1,300	2,200	5,000	9,500

FRENCH NEW WORLD ISSUES

None of the coins of the French regime is strictly American. They were all general issues for the French colonies of the New World. The copper of 1717 to 1722 was authorized by edicts of 1716 and 1721 for use in New France, Louisiana, and the French West Indies.

Copper Sou or Nine Deniers

	VG	F	VF
1721-B (Rouen)	$80	$250	$650
1721-H (La Rochelle)	45	100	275
1722-H	45	100	275

French Colonies in General

Coined for use in the French colonies, these circulated only unofficially in Louisiana, along with other foreign coins and tokens. Most were counterstamped RF (République Française) for use in the West Indies. The mintmark A signifies the Paris Mint.

	VG	VF	EF	AU
1767 French Colonies, Sou	$45	$200	$400	$950
1767 French Colonies, Sou, Counterstamped RF	40	100	225	400

SPECULATIVE ISSUES, TOKENS, AND PATTERNS

Nova Constellatio Coppers

The Nova Constellatio pieces were struck supposedly by order of Gouverneur Morris. Evidence indicates that they were all struck in Birmingham, England, and imported for American circulation as a private business venture.

1783, CONSTELLATIO,
Pointed Rays

1783, CONSTELATIO,
Blunt Rays

1785, CONSTELATIO,
Blunt Rays

1785, CONSTELATIO,
Pointed Rays

	VG	F	VF	EF	AU	Unc.
1783, CONSTELLATIO, Pointed Rays	$50	$110	$250	$500	$825	$1,800
1783, CONSTELLATIO, Blunt Rays	55	125	275	650	1,850	2,500
1785, CONSTELATIO, Blunt Rays	60	125	300	700	1,500	3,000
1785, CONSTELATIO, Pointed Rays	50	120	270	550	850	1,800

Immune Columbia Pieces

Nearly all of these are very rare. Many if not most seem to be unofficial, including pieces produced at the private Machin's Mills mint in Newburgh, New York.

1785, Copper,
Star Reverse

1785, George III
Obverse

	G	VG	F	VF	EF	AU
1785 Copper, Star Reverse			$8,000	$14,000	$17,000	
1785, George III Obverse	$2,500	$4,000	6,000	8,000		

1787, IMMUNIS COLUMBIA, Eagle Reverse

	G	VG	F	VF	EF	AU
1785, VERMON AUCTORI Obverse, IMMUNE COLUMBIA	$3,200	$5,500	$7,500	$18,000		
1787, IMMUNIS COLUMBIA, Eagle Reverse	150	375	800	2,000	$3,000	$5,000

Confederatio Coppers

Some Confederatio coppers may have been patterns, but others seem to have been made in limited numbers for general circulation. This will explain why the die with the CONFEDERATIO legend was combined with other designs such as a bust of George Washington, Libertas et Justitia of 1785, Immunis Columbia of 1786, the New York "Excelsiors," Inimica Tyrannis Americana, and others. In all there were 13 dies struck in 14 combinations. There are two types of the Confederatio reverse. In one instance the stars are contained in a small circle; in the other, larger stars are in a larger circle.

Typical Obverse   **Small Circle Reverse**   **Large Circle Reverse**

	VF
1785, Stars in Small Circle, various obverses	$29,000
1785, Stars in Large Circle, various obverses	26,000

Speculative Patterns

1786, IMMUNIS COLUMBIA   **Eagle Reverse**   **Shield Reverse**

	VF
1786, IMMUNIS COLUMBIA, Eagle Reverse	$30,000
1786, IMMUNIS COLUMBIA, Shield Reverse	25,000

Chart continued on next page.

	VF
(No date) (1786) Washington Obverse, Shield Reverse	—
1786, Eagle Obverse, Shield Reverse	$30,000
1786, Washington Obverse, Eagle Reverse *(2 known)*	—

COINAGE OF THE STATES
New Hampshire

New Hampshire was the first of the states to consider the subject of coinage following the Declaration of Independence.

William Moulton was empowered to make a limited quantity of coins of pure copper, authorized by the State House of Representatives in 1776.

	VG
1776 New Hampshire Copper	$20,000

Massachusetts

The coinage of Massachusetts copper cents and half cents in 1787 and 1788 was under the direction of Joshua Witherle. These were the first coins bearing the denomination "cent" as established by Congress. Many varieties exist, the most valuable being that with arrows in the eagle's right talon (on the left side of the coin).

1787 Half Cent   **1787 Cent**

1788 Half Cent   **1788 Cent**

	G	F	VF	EF	AU	Unc.
1787 Half Cent	$45	$120	$300	$650	$1,000	$1,750
1787 Cent, Arrows in Right Talon	4,200	10,000	25,000			
1787 Cent, Arrows in Left Talon *(illustrated)*	45	120	325	700	1,700	2,750

	G	F	VF	EF	AU	Unc.
1788 Half Cent	$50	$125	$300	$675	$1,500	$1,800
1788 Cent	40	110	275	650	1,500	2,000

Connecticut

Authority for establishing a mint near New Haven was granted by the state to Samuel Bishop, Joseph Hopkins, James Hillhouse, and John Goodrich in 1785. Today, well over 300 different die varieties are known of Connecticut coppers dated from 1785 to 1788. These pieces circulated widely and effectively; most are seen with significant evidence of circulation.

1785, Bust Facing Right

1785, Bust Facing Left

1786–1787, Mailed Bust Facing Right

1786–1787, Mailed Bust Facing Left

1787, Draped Bust Facing Left

1788, Mailed Bust Facing Right

Entry continued on next page.

1788, Mailed Bust Facing Left

1788, Draped Bust Facing Left

	AG	G	VG	F	VF	EF
1785, Bust Facing Right	$12	$35	$45	$95	$300	$800
1785, Bust Facing Left	30	100	175	300	850	1,500
1786, Mailed Bust Facing Right	15	40	50	100	275	950
1786, Mailed Bust Facing Left	12	35	45	100	200	500
1787, Mailed Bust Facing Right	15	42	65	175	475	800
1787, Mailed Bust Facing Left	10	25	35	75	200	475
1787, Draped Bust Facing Left	10	25	35	75	225	500
1788, Mailed Bust Facing Right	10	25	50	100	300	700
1788, Mailed Bust Facing Left	10	25	32	80	210	550
1788, Draped Bust Facing Left	10	25	35	100	250	600

New York and Related Issues

Brasher Doubloons

Perhaps the most famous pieces coined before the establishment of the U.S. Mint at Philadelphia were those produced by a well-known goldsmith and jeweler, Ephraim Brasher of New York.

Brasher produced a gold piece weighing about 408 grains, approximately equal in value to a Spanish doubloon (about $15.00).

The punch-mark EB appears in either of two positions as illustrated. This mark is found on some foreign gold coins as well, and probably was so used by Brasher as evidence of his testing of their value. Many modern forgeries exist.

	EF
1787 New York gold doubloon, EB on Breast	$2,000,000
1787 New York gold doubloon, EB on Wing	1,500,000

Copper Coinage

No coinage was authorized for New York following the Revolutionary War, although several propositions were considered. The only coinage laws passed were those regulating coins already in use.

	G	VG	F	VF
1786, NON VI VIRTUTE VICI	$2,500	$4,250	$8,000	$17,000

	G	VG	F	VF	EF
1787 EXCELSIOR Copper, Eagle on Globe Facing Right	$1,000	$2,000	$4,000	$10,000	$18,000
1787 EXCELSIOR Copper, Eagle on Globe Facing Left	1,000	1,800	3,500	9,000	17,000

1787, George Clinton and New York Arms

1787, Indian and New York Arms

1787, Indian and Eagle on Globe

	G	VG	F	VF	EF
1787, George Clinton and New York Arms	$4,500	$8,000	$14,000	$27,000	$55,000
1787, Indian and New York Arms	3,500	5,500	12,000	20,000	50,000
1787, Indian and Eagle on Globe	6,000	9,000	17,500	31,000	75,000

Nova Eborac Coinage for New York

**1787, NOVA EBORAC Reverse,
Seated Figure Facing Right**

**1787, NOVA EBORAC Reverse,
Seated Figure Facing Left**

	Fair	G	F	VF	EF	AU
1787, NOVA EBORAC, Seated Figure Facing Right ...	$30	$60	$175	$600	$1,500	$2,500
1787, NOVA EBORAC, Seated Figure Facing Left	30	50	150	500	900	1,700

New Jersey

On June 1, 1786, the New Jersey Colonial legislature granted to Thomas Goadsby, Albion Cox, and Walter Mould authority to coin some three million coppers no later than June 1788, on condition that they delivered to the treasurer of the state "one-tenth part of the full sum they shall strike and coin," in quarterly installments. These coppers were to pass current at 15 to the shilling. Produced in significant quantities, these coins are often seen in the market today and are widely collectible, although certain varieties can be rare and especially valuable.

Narrow Shield

Wide Shield

	AG	G	F	VF	EF	AU
1786 Narrow Shield	$10	$25	$100	$280	$600	$1,200
1786, Wide Shield	12	30	125	320	800	1,400

Small Planchet

	AG	G	F	VF	EF	AU
1787, Small Planchet	$12	$30	$100	$300	$550	$1,000
1787, Large Planchet	15	35	110	375	700	1,500

Fox Before Legend

	AG	G	F	VF	EF	AU
1788, Horse's Head Facing Right	$12	$30	$100	$300	$675	$1,400
1788, Similar, Fox in Legend	30	75	275	900	1,800	4,500
1788, Horse's Head Facing Left	100	200	800	2,100	6,000	—

Vermont

Reuben Harmon Jr. was granted permission to coin copper pieces beginning July 1, 1785. The franchise was extended for eight years in 1786. However, in 1787 production was shifted to Machin's Mills, Newburgh, New York, in which Harmon had a proprietary interest. Although the Vermont coins were legally issued there, most other products of Machin's Mills were counterfeits, some dies for which were combined with Vermont pieces, creating several illogical pieces below, including the 1785 Immune Columbia and the 1788 Georgivs III Rex.

1785, IMMUNE COLUMBIA   **1785–1786, Plow Type**   **1786, Baby Head**

	AG	G	VG	F	VF	EF
1785, IMMUNE COLUMBIA	$1,900	$3,200	$5,500	$7,500	$18,000	—
1785, Plow Type, VERMONTS	100	175	350	700	1,600	$3,750
1786, Plow Type, VERMONTENSIUM	75	135	260	500	1,000	2,000
1786, Baby Head	100	175	350	800	2,400	5,000

| 1786–1787, Bust Left | 1787, BRITANNIA | 1787, Bust Right |

	AG	G	VG	F	VF	EF
1786, Bust Left	$25	$85	$200	$450	$1,500	$2,600
1787, Bust Left	1,000	2,500	5,500	15,000	23,000	—
1787, BRITANNIA	12	50	85	160	350	950
1787, Bust Right *(several varieties)*	20	70	135	245	600	1,500

| 1788, Bust Right | 1788, GEORGIVS III REX |

	AG	G	VG	F	VF	EF
1788, Bust right *(several varieties)*	$15	$60	$110	$225	$500	$1,000
1788, GEORGIVS III REX	100	325	600	1,400	2,800	7,500

Note: This piece should not be confused with the common British halfpence with similar design and reverse legend BRITANNIA.

PRIVATE TOKENS AFTER CONFEDERATION
North American Tokens

This piece was struck in Dublin, Ireland. The obverse shows the seated figure of Hibernia facing left. Although dated 1781, it is believed to have been struck early in the next century.

	VG	F	VF	EF
1781, Copper or brass	$30	$75	$170	$425

Bar Coppers

The Bar "Copper" is undated and of uncertain origin. It has 13 parallel and unconnected bars on one side. On the other side is the large Roman letter USA monogram. The design was supposedly copied from a Continental button.

	VG	F	VF	EF	AU
(Undated) (Circa 1785) Bar Copper	$925	$1,750	$3,250	$5,000	$7,500

Auctori Plebis Tokens

This token is sometimes included with the coins of Connecticut as it greatly resembles issues of that state. It was struck in England by an unknown maker, possibly for use in America.

	G	VG	F	VF	EF	AU	Unc.
1787, AUCTORI PLEBIS	$40	$90	$150	$350	$700	$1,200	$3,750

Mott Store Cards

This item has long been considered an early token because of its date (1789). Most scholars believe it was most likely produced circa 1809 as a commemorative of the founding of the Mott Company, and probably served as a business card.

	VG	F	VF	EF	AU	Unc.
1789, Mott Token	$50	$110	$200	$350	$500	$900

Standish Barry Threepence

Standish Barry, a Baltimore silversmith, circulated a silver threepence in 1790. The tokens were believed to have been an advertising venture at a time when small change was scarce.

	VG	F	VF
1790 Threepence	$5,000	$11,000	$25,000

Kentucky Tokens

These tokens were struck in England about 1792 to 1794. Each star in the triangle represents a state, identified by its initial letter. These pieces are usually called Kentucky Cents because the letter K (for Kentucky) happens to be at the top. In the 19th century these were often called "triangle tokens," from the arrangement of the stars. Values are for the normal issue with plain edge; lettered edge varieties exist and are scarcer.

	VG	VF	EF	AU	Unc.
(1792–1794) Copper, Plain Edge	$50	$120	$210	$350	$600

Franklin Press Tokens

This piece is an English tradesman's token but, being associated with Benjamin Franklin, has accordingly been included in American collections.

	VG	VF	EF	AU	Unc.
1794, Franklin Press Token	$60	$150	$225	$400	$700

Talbot, Allum & Lee Cents

Talbot, Allum & Lee, engaged in the India trade and located in New York, placed a large quantity of English-made coppers in circulation during 1794 and 1795. ONE CENT appears on the 1794 issue.

**1794 Cent,
With NEW YORK**

1795 Cent

	G	VG	VF	EF	AU	Unc.
1794 Cent, With NEW YORK	$25	$40	$150	$270	$425	$850
1794 Cent, Without NEW YORK	200	300	1,500	3,000	5,000	
1795 Cent	25	40	125	240	350	700

WASHINGTON PORTRAIT PIECES

An interesting series of coins and tokens dated from 1783 to 1795 bear the portrait of George Washington. The likenesses in most instances were faithfully reproduced and were designed to honor Washington. Many of these pieces were of English origin and made later than the dates indicate.

**1783,
Military Bust**

**1783,
Draped Bust**

	F	VF	EF	AU	Unc.
1783, Military Bust	$40	$100	$235	$500	$1,350
1783, Draped bust	45	110	250	475	1,300

1783, UNITY STATES

	VG	F	VF	EF	AU	Unc.
1783, UNITY STATES	$30	$60	$150	$300	$500	$1,350

Undated Double-Head Cent

	VG	F	VF	EF	AU	Unc.
(Undated) Double-Head Cent	$30	$50	$150	$275	$575	$1,700

Obverse   **Large Eagle Reverse**   **Small Eagle Reverse**

	F	EF	AU	Unc.
1791 Cent, Large Eagle (Date on Obverse)	$225	$450	$700	$1,500
1791 Cent, Small Eagle (Date on Reverse)	250	500	800	1,750

	F	EF	AU
1791 Liverpool Halfpenny, Lettered Edge	$750	$2,300	$3,750

1792, Eagle With Stars, copper		—
1792, Eagle With Stars, silver		—
1792, Eagle With Stars, gold *(unique)*		—

(1792) Undated Cent,
WASHINGTON BORN VIRGINIA

1792 Cent,
WASHINGTON PRESIDENT

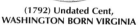

	VG	F	VF
(1792) Undated Cent, WASHINGTON BORN VIRGINIA, copper	$1,200	$2,250	$3,750
1792 Cent, WASHINGTON PRESIDENT, Plain Edge	1,500	3,750	6,000

1792 Getz Pattern

1793 Ship Halfpenny

1795 Halfpenny, Grate Token

	VG	F	VF	EF	AU	Unc.
1792, Getz Pattern, copper	$4,000	$7,000	$14,000	—		
1793 Ship Halfpenny, Lettered Edge	35	110	250	$450	$650	$1,750
1795, Grate Token, Lettered Edge	50	125	250	450	900	1,400
1795, Grate Token, Reeded Edge	30	75	110	250	350	600

	F	VF	EF	AU	Unc.
1795, LIBERTY AND SECURITY Halfpenny, Plain Edge	$75	$200	$400	$800	$1,500
1795, LIBERTY AND SECURITY Halfpenny, Lettered Edge	65	160	325	650	1,700
(1795) Undated, LIBERTY AND SECURITY Penny	165	300	450	850	1,600

	G	F	VF	EF
(1795) NORTH WALES Halfpenny	$60	$150	$385	$850

	F	VF	EF	AU	Unc.
SUCCESS Medal, Large, Plain or Reeded Edge	$135	$275	$500	$800	$1,800
SUCCESS Medal, Small, Plain or Reeded Edge	150	325	600	850	1,900

CONTINENTAL CURRENCY

The Continental Currency pieces probably had some assigned value at their time of issue. The exact nature of their monetary role is uncertain; they might have been experimental, or they might have seen circulation. At any rate, this was the first dollar-sized coin proposed for the United States. They were probably struck in Philadelphia from dies engraved by Elisha Gallaudet. As with many early pieces, modern replicas exist.

	G	F	VF	EF	AU	Unc.
1776, CURENCY, Pewter *(2 varieties)*	$4,000	$7,000	$11,000	$17,000	$25,000	$32,000
1776, CURENCY, Silver *(2 known)*		150,000				
1776, CURRENCY, Pewter	4,000	7,000	12,000	17,500	28,000	37,500
1776, CURRENCY, EG FECIT, Pewter	4,000	7,000	13,000	18,500	28,000	40,000

FUGIO COPPERS

The first coins issued by authority of the United States were the 1787 "Fugio" coppers. The legends have been credited to Benjamin Franklin by many, and the coins, as a consequence, have been referred to as *Franklin cents.*

1787, With Pointed Rays

1787, With Club Rays

	VG	F	VF	EF	AU	Unc.
Pointed Rays, STATES UNITED at Side of Circle *(illustrated)*	$150	$250	$400	$800	$1,000	$2,000
Pointed Rays, UNITED STATES at Side of Circle	150	250	400	800	1,000	2,200
Club Rays, Rounded Ends	250	400	1,000	2,200	3,500	—

The half cent was authorized to be coined April 2, 1792. Originally the weight was to have been 132 grains, but this was changed to 104 grains by the Act of January 14, 1793, before coinage commenced. The weight was again changed to 84 grains January 26, 1796, by presidential proclamation in conformity with the Act of March 3, 1795. Coinage was discontinued by the Act of February 21, 1857. All were coined at the Philadelphia Mint.

LIBERTY CAP (1793–1797)

AG-3 About Good: Clear enough to identify.
G-4 Good: Outline of bust of Liberty clear, no details. Date readable. Reverse lettering incomplete.
VG-8 Very Good: Some hair details. Reverse lettering complete.
F-12 Fine: Most of hair detail visible. Leaves worn, but all visible.
VF-20 Very Fine: Hair near ear and forehead worn, other areas distinct. Some details in leaves visible.
EF-40 Extremely Fine: Light wear on highest parts of head and wreath.
AU-50 About Uncirculated: Only a trace of wear on Liberty's face.

Head Facing Left (1793)

	Mintage	AG-3	G-4	VG-8	F-12	VF-20	EF-40	AU-50
1793 35,334		$900	$1,650	$2,800	$4,200	$7,200	$13,000	$18,000

Head Facing Right (1794–1797)

Pole to Cap	Punctuated Date	No Pole to Cap

	Mintage	AG-3	G-4	VG-8	F-12	VF-20	EF-40	AU-50
1794 81,600		$120	$265	$350	$600	$1,200	$2,800	$5,250
1795, All kinds 139,690								
1795, Lettered Edge, With Pole		80	200	310	525	1,200	2,600	4,200
1795, Lettered Edge, Punctuated Date . .		80	200	310	525	1,200	2,600	4,200
1795, Plain Edge, Punctuated Date		75	160	260	410	1,000	2,400	3,500
1795, Plain Edge, No Pole		75	160	260	410	1,000	2,400	3,500
1796, With Pole 1,390		3,600	6,950	10,000	15,000	24,000	31,000	
1796, No Pole . . . .*		7,000	15,000	19,000	30,000	45,000	75,000	

* Included in number above.

1797, 1 Above 1, Plain Edge   **1797, Plain Edge**

	Mintage	AG-3	G-4	VG-8	F-12	VF-20	EF-40	AU-50
1797, All kinds 127,840								
1797, 1 Above 1, Plain Edge		$75	$210	$300	$450	$900	$2,000	$3,250
1797, Plain Edge		90	220	300	600	1,000	2,100	3,500
1797, Lettered Edge		200	700	1,100	2,750	6,500	14,000	32,000
1797, Gripped Edge		3,500	13,000	27,000				

DRAPED BUST (1800–1808)

AG-3 About Good: Clear enough to identify.
G-4 Good: Outline of bust of Liberty clear, few details, date readable. Reverse lettering worn and incomplete.
VG-8 Very Good: Some drapery visible. Date and legends complete.
F-12 Fine: Shoulder drapery and hair over brow worn smooth.
VF-20 Very Fine: Only slight wear in previously mentioned areas. Slight wear on reverse.
EF-40 Extremely Fine: Light wear on highest parts of head and wreath.
AU-50 About Uncirculated: Wear slight on hair above forehead.

1st Reverse   **2nd Reverse**

	Mintage	AG-3	G-4	VG-8	F-12	VF-20	EF-40	AU-50
1800 202,908		$17	$35	$45	$60	$150	$300	$500
1802, 2 Over 0 20,266		130	360	800	1,850	5,000	13,500	
1803 92,000		17	35	50	70	160	450	700

Plain 4   **Crosslet 4**   **Stemless Wreath**   **Stems to Wreath**

	Mintage	AG-3	G-4	VG-8	F-12	VF-20	EF-40	AU-50
1804, All kinds 1,055,312								
1804, Plain 4, Stems to Wreath		$18	$40	$60	$95	$175	$470	$1,000
1804, Plain 4, Stemless Wreath		17	35	45	70	95	160	300
1804, Crosslet 4, Stemless Wreath		17	35	45	70	95	160	300
1804, Crosslet 4, Stems to Wreath		17	35	45	70	95	160	300

Entry continued on next page.

| | 1804, "Spiked Chin" | Small 5 | Large 5 |

	Mintage	AG-3	G-4	VG-8	F-12	VF-20	EF-40	AU-50
1804, "Spiked Chin" ....*		$18	$40	$50	$75	$110	$200	$350
1805, All kinds 814,464								
1805, Medium 5, Stemless Wreath		17	35	45	70	100	160	300
1805, Small 5, Stems to Wreath		110	375	700	1,500	3,000	5,000	
1805, Large 5, Stems to Wreath		17	35	45	70	100	160	300

* Included in "1804, All kinds" mintage (previous page).

| Small 6 | Large 6 | 1808, 8 Over 7 | Normal Date |

	Mintage	AG-3	G-4	VG-8	F-12	VF-20	EF-40	AU-50
1806, All kinds 356,000								
1806, Small 6, Stems to Wreath		$40	$110	$185	$325	$750	$1,400	$3,750
1806, Small 6, Stemless Wreath		17	35	45	55	75	145	290
1806, Large 6, Stems to Wreath		17	35	45	55	75	145	290
1807 476,000		17	35	45	60	100	225	500
1808, 8 Over 7 ....*		30	70	125	300	700	1,750	5,000
1808, Normal Date 400,000		17	35	45	60	100	225	500

* Included in number below.

CLASSIC HEAD (1809–1836)

G-4 Good: LIBERTY only partly visible on hair band. Lettering, date, and stars worn but visible.
VG-8 Very Good: LIBERTY entirely visible on hair band. Lower curls worn.
F-12 Fine: Only partial wear on LIBERTY, and hair at top worn in spots.
VF-20 Very Fine: Lettering clear-cut. Hair only slightly worn.
EF-40 Extremely Fine: Light wear on highest points of hair and leaves.
AU-50 About Uncirculated: Sharp hair detail with only a trace of wear on higher points.
MS-60 Uncirculated: Typical brown to red surface. No trace of wear.
MS-63 Choice Uncirculated: Well-defined color, brown to red. No traces of wear.

| | 1828, 13 Stars | 1828, 12 Stars |

Brilliant or red Uncirculated coins are worth more than prices shown. Spotted, cleaned, or discolored pieces are worth less.

	Mintage	AG-3	G-4	VG-8	F-12	VF-20	EF-40	AU-50	MS-60	MS-63
1809 1,154,572		$14	$25	$30	$35	$55	$90	$150	$325	$425
1810 215,000		14	25	35	60	110	250	450	900	1,500
1811 63,140		47	115	225	400	950	2,800	3,500	4,500	6,500

	Mintage	G-4	VG-8	F-12	VF-20	EF-40	AU-50	MS-60	MS-63	PF-63
1825	63,000	$25	$30	$35	$50	$90	$150	$450	$750	
1826	234,000	25	30	35	50	85	125	275	450	
1828, 13 Stars	606,000	23	30	35	45	55	120	190	275	
1828, 12 Stars	*	24	35	40	50	125	150	650	900	
1829	487,000	23	30	35	45	65	95	175	325	
1831	2,200									—
1832	51,000	23	28	32	40	55	95	175	250	$2,500
1833	103,000	23	28	32	40	55	95	175	250	2,500
1834	141,000	23	28	32	40	55	95	175	250	2,500
1835	398,000	23	28	32	40	55	95	175	250	2,500
1836										8,000

* Included in number above.

BRAIDED HAIR (1840–1857)

VG-8 Very Good: Beads in hair uniformly distinct. Hair lines visible in spots.
F-12 Fine: Hair lines above ear worn. Beads sharp.
VF-20 Very Fine: Lowest curl worn; hair otherwise distinct.
EF-40 Extremely Fine: Light wear on highest points of hair and on leaves.
AU-50 About Uncirculated: Very slight trace of wear on hair above Liberty's ear.
MS-60 Uncirculated: No trace of wear. Clear luster.
MS-63 Choice Uncirculated: No trace of wear.
PF-63 Choice Proof: Nearly perfect; only light blemishes.

Brilliant or red Uncirculated coins are worth more than prices shown. Spotted, cleaned, or discolored pieces are worth less.

	PF-63			PF-63
1840, Original	$2,700	1845, Original		$3,500
1840, Restrike	2,250	1845, Restrike		3,250
1841, Original	2,600	1846, Original		3,250
1841, Restrike	2,500	1846, Restrike		2,600
1842, Original	2,750	1847, Original		2,600
1842, Restrike	2,500	1847, Restrike		2,600
1843, Original	2,500	1848, Original		2,600
1843, Restrike	2,500	1848, Restrike		2,600
1844, Original	3,500	1849, Original, Small Date		2,900
1844, Restrike	2,600	1849, Restrike, Small Date		2,900

Small Date   **Large Date**

	Mintage	G-4	VG-8	F-12	VF-20	EF-40	AU-50	MS-60	MS-63	PF-63
1849, Large Date	39,864	$17	$23	$30	$40	$75	$100	$225	$300	—
1850	39,812	17	23	30	40	75	100	225	350	$4,000
1851	147,672	15	20	28	35	50	80	135	250	3,000
1852										3,500
1853	129,694	15	20	28	35	50	80	135	250	
1854	55,358	15	20	28	35	50	80	135	250	3,000
1855	56,500	15	20	28	35	50	80	135	250	3,000
1856	40,430	17	22	30	40	60	85	150	275	3,000
1857	35,180	18	25	45	70	85	130	195	320	3,000

Cents and half cents were the first coins struck under the authority of the United States government. Coinage began in 1793 with laws stating that the cent should weigh exactly twice as much as the half cent. Large cents were coined every year from 1793 to 1857 with the exception of 1815, when a lack of copper prevented production. All were coined at the Philadelphia Mint. Varieties listed are those most significant to collectors. Numerous other die varieties may be found, as each of the early dies was individually made.

FLOWING HAIR (1793)

AG-3 About Good: Date and devices clear enough to identify.
G-4 Good: Lettering worn but readable. No detail on bust.
VG-8 Very Good: Date and lettering distinct, some details of head visible.
F-12 Fine: About half of hair and other details visible.
VF-20 Very Fine: Ear visible, most details visible.
EF-40 Extremely Fine: Wear evident on highest points of hair and back of temple.

Chain Reverse (1793)

| Obverse | AMERI. Reverse | | | | AMERICA Reverse | |

	Mintage	AG-3	G-4	VG-8	F-12	VF-20	EF-40
1793, Chain, All kinds	36,103						
1793, AMERI. in Legend		$1,500	$4,500	$8,750	$15,000	$25,000	$44,000
1793, AMERICA		1,300	3,500	6,750	9,500	19,000	34,000

Wreath Reverse (1793)

| Obverse | Wreath Reverse | | | | Strawberry Leaf Variety | |

	Mintage	AG-3	G-4	VG-8	F-12	VF-20	EF-40
1793, Wreath, All kinds	63,353						
1793, Vine and Bars Edge		$325	$1,150	$1,700	$2,750	$4,000	$7,000
1793, Lettered Edge		400	1,350	1,800	3,000	4,200	8,200
1793, Strawberry Leaf	(4 known)	—	—	—			

LIBERTY CAP (1793–1796)

1793, Vine and Bars Edge
Chain and Wreath types only.

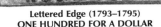

Lettered Edge (1793–1795)
ONE HUNDRED FOR A DOLLAR

Beaded Border (1793)

Head of 1793 (1793–1794)
Head in high, rounded relief.

Head of 1794 (1794)
Well-defined hair;
hook on lowest curl.

Head of 1795 (1794–1796)
Head in low relief;
no hook on lowest curl.

	Mintage	AG-3	G-4	VG-8	F-12	VF-20	EF-40
1793, Liberty Cap 11,056		$950	$2,000	$3,800	$7,000	$17,500	$36,000
1794, All kinds 918,521							
1794, "Head of 1793"		225	700	1,400	1,800	4,250	10,000
1794, "Head of 1794"		50	125	200	400	800	1,750
1794, "Head of 1795"		50	125	200	400	800	1,750
1795, Lettered Edge 37,000		50	130	200	400	900	2,400
1795, Plain Edge 501,500		35	115	225	350	700	1,500
1796, Liberty Cap 109,825		75	180	275	600	1,000	2,300

DRAPED BUST (1796–1807)

AG-3 About Good: Clear enough to identify.
G-4 Good: Lettering worn, but clear; date clear. Bust lacking in detail.
VG-8 Very Good: Drapery on Liberty partly visible. Less wear in date and lettering.
F-12 Fine: Hair over brow smooth; some detail showing in other parts of hair.
VF-20 Very Fine: Hair lines slightly worn. Hair over brow better defined.
EF-40 Extremely Fine: Hair above forehead and left of eye outlined and detailed. Only slight wear on olive leaves.

LIHERTY Error

	Mintage	AG-3	G-4	VG-8	F-12	VF-20	EF-40
1796, Draped Bust 363,375		$40	$70	$150	$300	$700	$1,850
1796, LIHERTY Error ....*		80	135	325	550	1,750	4,200

* Included in number above.

	With Stems	Stemless

Gripped Edge

	Mintage	AG-3	G-4	VG-8	F-12	VF-20	EF-40
1797, All kinds 897,510							
1797, Gripped Edge, 1796 Reverse		$25	$65	$125	$225	$425	$1,550
1797, Plain Edge, 1796 Reverse		25	65	125	230	450	1,700
1797, 1797 Reverse, With Stems		20	50	100	150	235	825
1797, 1797 Reverse, Stemless		25	65	125	250	650	2,300

1798, 8 Over 7	1799, 9 Over 8	1800 Over 1798	1800, 80 Over 79

	Mintage	AG-3	G-4	VG-8	F-12	VF-20	EF-40
1798, All kinds 1,841,745							
1798, 8 Over 7		$25	$65	$135	$225	$800	$2,700
1798		13	35	47	110	225	900
1799, 9 Over 8 . . . .*		700	1,400	2,500	6,000	16,500	
1799, Normal Date . . . .*		650	1,300	2,200	5,600	14,500	
1800, All kinds 2,822,175							
1800 Over 1798		12	28	50	110	350	1,400
1800, 80 Over 79		12	28	50	100	225	1,000
1800, Normal Date		12	28	50	100	225	1,000

* Included in 1798 mintage.

Fraction 1/000	Corrected Fraction	1801 Reverse, 3 Errors

	Mintage	AG-3	G-4	VG-8	F-12	VF-20	EF-40
1801, All kinds 1,362,837							
1801, Normal Reverse		$11	$22	$30	$75	$200	$525
1801, 3 Errors: 1/000, One Stem, and IINITED		25	65	120	325	750	3,200
1801, Fraction 1/000		11	27	40	120	225	800
1801, 1/100 Over 1/000		12	27	42	125	275	925
1802, All kinds 3,435,100							
1802, Normal Reverse		11	24	40	90	175	525
1802, Fraction 1/000		12	30	50	120	250	900
1802, Stemless Wreath		11	24	40	90	175	525

1803, Small Date, Blunt 1	1803, Large Date, Pointed 1	Small Fraction	Large Fraction

	Mintage	AG-3	G-4	VG-8	F-12	VF-20	EF-40
1803, All kinds	3,131,691						
1803, Small Date, Small Fraction	$11	$24	$40	$80	$175	$525
1803, Small Date, Large Fraction	11	24	40	80	175	525
1803, Large Date, Small Fraction	1,000	2,300	4,000	8,250	13,500	
1803, Large Date, Large Fraction	17	33	80	150	425	1,400
1803, 1/100 Over 1/000	11	27	50	100	225	700
1803, Stemless Wreath	11	27	50	100	225	700

Broken Dies

*All genuine 1804 cents have crosslet 4 in date and a large fraction.
The 0 in date is in line with O of OF on reverse.*

	Mintage	AG-3	G-4	VG-8	F-12	VF-20	EF-40
1804 **(a)**	96,500	$350	$750	$1,200	$2,000	$3,000	$6,750
1805	941,116	11	24	40	80	175	500
1806	348,000	11	27	50	95	225	875

a. Values shown are for coins with normal or broken dies.

**Small 1807, 7 Over 6
(Blunt 1)**   **Large 1807, 7 Over 6
(Pointed 1)**

	Mintage	AG-3	G-4	VG-8	F-12	VF-20	EF-40
1807, All kinds	829,221						
1807, Small 7 Over 6, Blunt 1	$410	$1,200	$2,200	$4,500	$8,200	$17,000
1807, Large 7 Over 6	11	24	35	70	175	550
1807, Small Fraction	11	24	35	70	225	600
1807, Large Fraction	11	24	35	70	200	500

CLASSIC HEAD (1808–1814)

AG-3 About Good: Details clear enough to identify.
G-4 Good: Legends, stars, and date worn, but plain.
VG-8 Very Good: LIBERTY all readable. Liberty's ear visible. Details worn but plain.
F-12 Fine: Hair on forehead and before ear nearly smooth. Ear and hair under ear sharp.
VF-20 Very Fine: Some detail in all hair lines. Slight wear on leaves on reverse.
EF-40 Extremely Fine: All hair lines sharp. Very slight wear on high points.

See next page for chart.

	Mintage	AG-3	G-4	VG-8	F-12	VF-20	EF-40
1808	1,007,000	$13	$24	$60	$150	$275	$925
1809	222,867	22	50	110	225	650	1,800

1810, 10 Over 09

1810, Normal Date

1811, Last 1 Over 0

1811, Normal Date

	Mintage	AG-3	G-4	VG-8	F-12	VF-20	EF-40
1810, All kinds	1,458,500						
1810, 10 Over 09		$11	$24	$45	$120	$300	$750
1810, Normal Date		11	24	35	120	260	700
1811, All kinds	218,025						
1811, Last 1 Over 0		16	33	60	210	800	2,500
1811, Normal Date		15	35	70	150	400	850
1812	1,075,500	11	22	35	110	250	650
1813	418,000	13	24	50	125	285	650
1814	357,830	11	22	35	110	250	600

LIBERTY HEAD (1816–1857)

G-4 Good: Details on Liberty's head partly visible. Even wear in date and legends.
VG-8 Very Good: LIBERTY, date, stars, and legends clear. Part of hair cord visible.
F-12 Fine: All hair lines visible. Hair cords uniformly visible.
VF-20 Very Fine: Hair cords only slightly worn. Hair lines only partly worn, all well defined.
EF-40 Extremely Fine: Both hair cords stand out sharply. All hair lines sharp.
AU-50 About Uncirculated: Only traces of wear on hair and highest points on leaves and bow.
MS-60 Uncirculated: Typical brown surface. No trace of wear.
MS-63 Choice Uncirculated: Some distracting contact marks or blemishes in prime focal areas. Impaired luster possible.

Matron Head (1816–1836)

1817, 13 Stars

1817, 15 Stars

Brilliant or red Uncirculated coins are worth more than prices shown. Spotted, cleaned, or discolored pieces are worth less.

	Mintage	G-4	VG-8	F-12	VF-20	EF-40	AU-50	MS-60	MS-63
1816	2,820,982	$8	$11	$16	$32	$70	$125	$250	$375
1817, 13 Stars	3,948,400	8	10	14	27	50	100	200	350
1817, 15 Stars	*	11	13	16	55	225	350	1,100	—
1818	3,167,000	8	10	14	27	50	90	225	325

* Included in number above.

LARGE CENTS

1819, 9 Over 8   **1820, 20 Over 19**

	Mintage	G-4	VG-8	F-12	VF-20	EF-40	AU-50	MS-60	MS-63
1819 2,671,000	$9	$11	$15	$27	$55	$125	$185	$350
1819, 9 Over 8 . . . .*	10	13	18	36	150	175	300	500
1820 4,407,550	8	10	13	30	60	100	200	350
1820, 20 Over 19 . . . .*	10	13	18	45	150	200	500	700
1821 389,000	16	27	60	185	500	1,000	3,600	—
1822 2,072,339	9	12	22	50	100	275	475	775

* Included in number above.

1823, 3 Over 2   **1824, 4 Over 2**   **1826, 6 Over 5**

	Mintage	G-4	VG-8	F-12	VF-20	EF-40	AU-50	MS-60	MS-63
1823, 3 Over 2 . . . .*	$27	$50	$150	$300	$1,000	$1,900	$3,400	—
1823, Normal Date . . . .*	30	55	175	400	1,350	2,400	3,800	—
1824, 4 Over 2 . . . .*	10	18	40	150	550	1,200	2,500	$3,750
1824, Normal Date . .1,262,000	8	10	16	75	210	350	950	1,600
1825 1,461,100	8	10	16	45	150	250	800	1,100
1826, 6 Over 5 1,517,425	12	17	37	110	425	600	1,200	2,300
1826, Normal Date . . . .**	8	10	12	45	110	190	400	650
1827 2,357,732	8	10	12	40	80	150	300	600

* Included in number below. ** Included in number above.

Date Size, Through 1828   **Date Size, 1828 and Later**

	Mintage	G-4	VG-8	F-12	VF-20	EF-40	AU-50	MS-60	MS-63
1828, Large Narrow Date 2,260,624	$8	$10	$14	$40	$70	$150	$400	$650
1828, Small Wide Date . . . .*	8	10	16	50	100	200	500	950
1829 1,414,500	8	10	13	40	70	110	250	525
1830 1,711,500	8	10	13	30	60	100	200	400
1831 3,359,260	7	9	12	22	50	100	200	350
1832 2,362,000	7	9	12	22	50	80	175	325
1833 2,739,000	7	9	12	22	50	↓80	175	325
1834 1,855,100	7	9	12	22	70	100	200	350
1835 3,878,400	7	9	12	22	65	90	200	350
1836 2,111,000	7	9	12	22	55	85	160	300

* Included in number above.

Matron Head Modified (1837–1839)

G-4 Good: Considerably worn. LIBERTY readable.
VG-8 Very Good: Hairlines smooth but visible; outline of ear clearly defined.
F-12 Fine: Hairlines at top of head and behind ear worn but visible. Braid over brow plain; ear clear.
VF-20 Very Fine: All details sharper than for F-12. Only slight wear on hair over brow.
EF-40 Extremely Fine: Hair above ear detailed, but slightly worn.
AU-50 About Uncirculated: Trace of wear on high points of hair above ear and eye and on highest points on leaves and bow.
MS-60 Uncirculated: Typical brown surface. No trace of wear.
MS-63 Choice Uncirculated: Some distracting contact marks or blemishes in prime focal areas. Impaired luster possible.

1839 Over 1836

Brilliant or red Uncirculated coins are worth more than prices shown. Cleaned or discolored pieces are worth less.

	Mintage	G-4	VG-8	F-12	VF-20	EF-40	AU-50	MS-60	MS-63
1837	5,558,300	$7	$9	$12	$22	$65	$90	$160	$240
1838	6,370,200	7	9	12	22	30	85	150	220
1839	3,128,661	7	9	12	22	40	80	150	210
1839, 1839 Over 1836, Plain Cords	........*	110	275	550	1,250	3,500	6,500	—	—
1840	2,462,700	7	9	12	18	40	75	150	275
1841	1,597,367	7	9	12	18	40	75	150	275
1842	2,383,390	7	9	12	18	40	75	150	250

* Included in number above.

Small Letters

Large Letters

"Head of 1840" Petite Head (1839–1843)	"Head of 1844" Mature Head (1843–1857)	

	Mintage	G-4	VG-8	F-12	VF-20	EF-40	AU-50	MS-60	MS-63
1843, Petite, Small Letters	2,425,342	$7	$9	$12	$20	$30	$60	$145	$185
1843, Petite, Large Letters	........*	9	11	20	35	70	125	325	600
1843, Mature, Large Letters	........*	8	10	16	25	50	90	160	400
1844, Normal Date	2,398,752	7	9	12	20	32	65	120	175
1844, 44 Over 81	........*	10	13	20	40	110	235	550	1,250
1845	3,894,804	7	9	12	20	30	70	125	175
1846	4,120,800	7	9	12	20	30	70	125	175
1847	6,183,669	7	9	12	20	30	70	125	175
1847, 7 Over "Small 7"	........*	8	11	17	30	65	160	525	1,000

* Included in number above.

	Mintage	G-4	VG-8	F-12	VF-20	EF-40	AU-50	MS-60	MS-63
1848	6,415,799	$7	$9	$12	$18	$30	$70	$110	$150
1849	4,178,500	7	9	12	18	30	70	125	190
1850	4,426,844	7	9	12	18	30	70	100	150

1844, 44 Over 81   **1851, 51 Over 81**   **1847, 7 Over "Small" 7**

Brilliant or red Uncirculated coins are worth more than prices shown. Spotted, cleaned, or discolored pieces are worth less.

	Mintage	G-4	VG-8	F-12	VF-20	EF-40	AU-50	MS-60	MS-63
1851, Normal Date	9,889,707	$7	$9	$12	$18	$30	$70	$100	$150
1851, 51 Over 81	*	9	11	18	28	70	110	250	435
1852	5,063,094	7	9	12	18	30	70	100	150
1853	6,641,131	7	9	12	18	30	70	100	150
1854	4,236,156	7	9	12	18	30	70	100	150

* Included in number above.

1855, Upright 5's   **1855, Slanting 5's**   **1855, Knob on Ear**

	Mintage	G-4	VG-8	F-12	VF-20	EF-40	AU-50	MS-60	MS-63
1855, All kinds	1,574,829								
1855, Upright 5's		$7	$9	$12	$18	$30	$70	$100	$150
1855, Slanting 5's		7	9	12	18	30	70	115	160
1855, Slanting 5's, Knob on Ear		7	10	14	22	40	90	160	250
1856, Upright 5	2,690,463	7	9	12	18	30	70	100	150
1856, Slanting 5	*	7	9	12	18	30	70	100	150

* Included in number above.

1857, Large Date   **1857, Small Date**

	Mintage	G-4	VG-8	F-12	VF-20	EF-40	AU-50	MS-60	MS-63
1857, Large Date	333,546	$16	$25	$30	$35	$50	$120	$200	$325
1857, Small Date	*	17	27	35	40	55	130	220	350

* Included in number above.

FLYING EAGLE (1856–1858)

The Act of February 21, 1857, provided for the coinage of the small cent. The 1856 Flying Eagle cent was not an authorized Mint issue, as the law governing the new-size coin was enacted after the date of issue. It is believed that nearly 1,000 original strikings and 1,500 or more restrikes were made of the 1856. They are properly referred to as *patterns*.

G-4 Good: All details worn, but readable.

VG-8 Very Good: Details in eagle's feathers and eye evident, but worn.

F-12 Fine: Eagle-head details and feather tips sharp.

VF-20 Very Fine: Considerable detail visible in feathers in right wing and tail.

EF-40 Extremely Fine: Slight wear, all details sharp.

AU-50 About Uncirculated: Slight wear on eagle's left wing and breast.

MS-60 Uncirculated: No trace of wear. Light blemishes.

MS-63 Choice Uncirculated: Some distracting contact marks or blemishes in prime focal areas. Some impairment of luster possible.

PF-63 Choice Proof: Nearly perfect.

| **1858, 8 Over 7** | **1856–1858, Large Letters** | **1858, Small Letters** |

Brilliant Uncirculated and Proof coins are worth more than prices shown. Spotted, cleaned, or discolored pieces are worth less.

	Mintage	G-4	VG-8	F-12	VF-20	EF-40	AU-50	MS-60	MS-63	PF-63
1856	2,000	$4,200	$4,800	$5,200	$6,750	$8,000	$9,000	$11,000	$13,500	$13,250
1857	17,450,000	13	16	20	28	80	100	200	350	
	(485)									4,000
1858, Large Letters	24,600,000	13	16	20	28	80	100	200	350	
	(100)									4,000
1858, 8 Over 7	*		50	110	210	420	725	1,900	5,000	
1858, Small Letters	*	13	16	20	28	80	100	200	350	
	(200)									4,000

* Included in mintage for 1858, Large Letters.

INDIAN HEAD (1859–1909)

The small cent was redesigned in 1859, and a representation of Miss Liberty wearing an Indian war bonnet was adopted as the obverse device. The 1859 reverse was also changed to represent a laurel wreath. In 1860 the reverse was modified to display an oak wreath with a small shield at the top. From 1859 to 1863, cents were struck in copper-nickel. In 1864 the composition was changed to bronze, although copper-nickel cents were also struck during that year.

SMALL CENTS

G-4 Good: No LIBERTY visible.
VG-8 Very Good: At least some letters of LIBERTY readable on head band.
F-12 Fine: LIBERTY mostly visible.
VF-20 Very Fine: Slight but even wear on LIBERTY.
EF-40 Extremely Fine: LIBERTY sharp. All other details sharp. Only slight wear on ribbon end.
AU-50 About Uncirculated: Very slight trace of wear above the ear and the lowest curl of hair.
MS-60 Uncirculated: No trace of wear. Light blemishes.
MS-63 Choice Uncirculated: Some distracting contact marks or blemishes in prime focal areas. Impaired luster possible.
PF-63 Choice Proof: Nearly perfect.

Without Shield at Top of Wreath (1859 Only)

With Shield on Reverse (1860–1909)

Variety 1 – Copper-Nickel, Laurel Wreath Reverse (1859)

Brilliant or red Uncirculated coins are worth more than prices shown. Spotted, cleaned, or discolored pieces are worth less.

	Mintage	G-4	VG-8	F-12	VF-20	EF-40	AU-50	MS-60	MS-63	PF-63
1859 . . . .*(800)* . .36,400,000		$7	$8	$10	$27	$55	$100	$135	$265	$850

Variety 2 – Copper-Nickel, Oak Wreath With Shield (1860–1864)

	Mintage	G-4	VG-8	F-12	VF-20	EF-40	AU-50	MS-60	MS-63	PF-63
1860 . . . . . .*(1,000)* . .20,566,000		$6.00	$7	$8	$10	$32	$65	$100	$150	$550
1861 . . . . . .*(1,000)* . .10,100,000		11.00	13	18	32	65	85	140	190	600
1862 . . . .*(550)* . .28,075,000		5.50	6	7	9	22	40	65	100	475
1863 . . . .*(460)* . .49,840,000		5.50	6	7	9	22	40	65	100	475
1864 . . . .*(370)* . .13,740,000		8.00	10	14	25	38	65	100	140	500

Variety 3 – Bronze (1864–1909)

1864, Indian Head Cent With "L"

	Mintage	G-4	VG-8	F-12	VF-20	EF-40	AU-50	MS-60	MS-63	PF-63
1864, All kinds 39,233,714										
1864, No L *(150)*		$4	$6	$9	$22	$32	$42	$55	$85	$500
1864, With L *(20)*		27	45	70	100	170	190	225	375	—
1865 . . . .*(500)* . .35,429,286		4	5	9	12	20	35	50	85	350
1866 . . . .*(725)* . . .9,826,500		22	25	35	65	100	150	175	275	350
1867 . . . .*(625)* . . .9,821,000		22	25	35	65	100	150	175	275	350
1868 . . . .*(600)* . .10,266,500		22	25	35	65	100	150	175	275	350
1869 . . . .*(600)* . . .6,420,000		35	40	90	150	225	275	300	450	350
1870 . . . . . .*(1,000)* . . .5,275,000		28	35	85	135	200	275	300	350	350
1871 . . . .*(960)* . . .3,929,500		35	45	125	185	225	300	365	500	375
1872 . . . .*(950)* . . .4,042,000		40	60	160	225	300	400	450	650	425
1873 . . . . . .*(1,100)* . .11,676,500		11	14	24	38	80	100	120	220	275
1874 . . . .*(700)* . .14,187,500		9	11	15	30	55	85	110	165	250
1875 . . . .*(700)* . .13,528,000		10	14	20	35	50	75	110	165	250
1876 . . . . . .*(1,150)* . . .7,944,000		15	18	20	60	100	145	185	275	250
1877 . . . .*(900)* 852,500		500	700	850	1,250	1,600	1,900	2,200	2,800	2,800

Brilliant or red Uncirculated coins are worth more than prices shown. Spotted, cleaned, or discolored pieces are worth less.

	Mintage	G-4	VG-8	F-12	VF-20	EF-40	AU-50	MS-60	MS-63	PF-63
1878 . . . . .(2,350) 5,797,500		$14.00	$18.00	$25.00	$65.00	$100	$145	$165	$250	$220
1879 . . . . .(3,200) . . .16,228,000		4.00	6.00	8.00	18.00	40	45	50	80	175
1880 . . . . .(3,955) . . .38,961,000		1.75	2.00	3.00	6.00	15	25	40	70	140
1881 . . . . .(3,575) . . .39,208,000		1.75	2.00	3.00	5.00	10	16	26	37	140
1882 . . . . .(3,100) . . .38,578,000		1.75	2.00	3.00	5.00	10	16	26	37	140
1883 . . . . .(6,609) . . .45,591,500		1.75	2.00	3.00	5.00	10	16	26	37	140
1884 . . . . .(3,942) . . .23,257,800		2.25	2.50	3.50	6.00	14	20	30	60	140
1885 . . . . .(3,790) . . .11,761,594		3.00	4.00	6.00	14.00	35	45	60	95	140
1886 . . . . .(4,290) . . .17,650,000		1.75	3.00	8.00	24.00	65	85	100	125	150
1887 . . . . .(2,960) . . .45,223,523		1.25	1.50	1.75	2.25	8	14	25	35	140
1888 . . . . .(4,582) . . .37,489,832		0.85	1.10	1.80	2.75	8	14	25	40	140
1889 . . . . .(3,336) . . .48,866,025		0.85	1.10	1.80	2.75	6	12	22	35	140
1890 . . . . .(2,740) . . .57,180,114		0.85	1.10	1.80	2.75	6	12	22	35	140
1891 . . . . .(2,350) . . .47,070,000		0.85	1.10	1.80	2.75	6	12	22	35	140
1892 . . . . .(2,745) . . .37,647,087		0.85	1.10	1.80	2.75	6	12	22	35	140
1893 . . . . .(2,195) . . .46,640,000		0.85	1.10	1.80	2.75	6	12	22	35	140
1894 . . . . .(2,632) . . .16,749,500		2.00	3.00	4.75	8.50	25	30	40	50	150
1895 . . . . .(2,062) . . .38,341,574		0.85	1.10	1.30	2.00	6	11	22	28	140
1896 . . . . .(1,862) . . .39,055,431		0.85	1.10	1.30	2.00	6	11	22	28	140
1897 . . . . .(1,938) . . .50,464,392		0.85	1.10	1.30	2.00	6	11	22	28	140
1898 . . . . .(1,795) . . .49,821,284		0.85	1.10	1.30	2.00	6	11	22	28	140
1899 . . . . .(2,031) . . .53,598,000		0.85	1.10	1.30	2.00	6	11	22	28	140
1900 . . . . .(2,262) . . .66,831,502		0.80	1.00	1.10	1.50	5	10	18	25	120
1901 . . . . .(1,985) . . .79,609,158		0.80	1.00	1.10	1.50	5	10	18	25	120
1902 . . . . .(2,018) . . .87,374,704		0.80	1.00	1.10	1.50	5	10	18	25	120
1903 . . . . .(1,790) . . .85,092,703		0.80	1.00	1.10	1.50	5	10	18	25	120
1904 . . . . .(1,817) . . .61,326,198		0.80	1.00	1.10	1.50	5	10	18	25	120
1905 . . . . .(2,152) . . .80,717,011		0.80	1.00	1.10	1.50	5	10	18	25	120
1906 . . . . .(1,725) . . .96,020,530		0.80	1.00	1.10	1.50	5	10	18	25	120
1907 . . . . .(1,475) . .108,137,143		0.80	1.00	1.10	1.50	5	10	18	25	120

Location of Mintmark S on Reverse of Indian Cent (1908 and 1909 Only)

	Mintage	G-4	VG-8	F-12	VF-20	EF-40	AU-50	MS-60	MS-63	PF-63
1908 . . . . . .(1,620) . .32,326,367		$0.80	$1.10	$1.25	$1.50	$5	$10	$18	$25	$120
1908S 1,115,000		40.00	50.00	55.00	65.00	95	120	175	210	
1909 . . . . . .(2,175) . .14,368,470		6.00	7.00	8.00	10.00	12	16	25	32	120
1909S 309,000		275.00	300.00	325.00	350.00	400	450	520	675	

LINCOLN, WHEAT EARS REVERSE (1909–1958)

Victor D. Brenner designed this cent which was issued to commemorate the 100th anniversary of Abraham Lincoln's birth. The designer's initials V.D.B. appear on the reverse of a limited quantity of cents of 1909. Later in the year they were removed from the dies but restored in 1918 as very small incuse letters beneath the shoulder. The Lincoln type was the first cent to have the motto IN GOD WE TRUST.

G-4 Good: Date worn but apparent. Lines in wheat heads missing. Full rims.
VG-8 Very Good: Half of lines visible in upper wheat heads.
F-12 Fine: Wheat lines worn but visible.
VF-20 Very Fine: Lincoln's cheekbone and jawbone worn but separated. No worn spots on wheat heads.
EF-40 Extremely Fine: Slight wear. All details sharp.
AU-50 About Uncirculated: Slight wear on cheek and jaw and on wheat stalks.
MS-60 Uncirculated: No trace of wear. Light blemishes. Brown or red-brown color.
MS-63 Choice Uncirculated: No trace of wear. Slight blemishes. Red-brown color.
MS-65 Gem Uncirculated: No trace of wear. Barely noticeable blemishes. Nearly full red color.
PF-63 Choice Proof: Reflective surfaces with only a few blemishes in secondary focal places. No major flaws.

Location of mintmark S or D on obverse of Lincoln cent.

Designer's Initials V.D.B. (1909 Only)

No V.D.B. on Reverse (1909–1958)

Brilliant Uncirculated coins are worth more than prices shown. Spotted, cleaned, or discolored pieces are worth less.

	Mintage	G-4	VG-8	F-12	VF-20	EF-40	AU-50	MS-60	MS-63	MATTE PF-63
1909, V.D.B.										
. . . .(1,194) . . .27,995,000		$6.00	$6.50	$7.00	$8.00	$9.00	$10.00	$12.00	$15	$1,300
1909S, V.D.B. 484,000		450.00	500.00	550.00	725.00	825.00	975.00	1,150.00	1,400	
1909 . . . . .(2,618) . . .72,702,618		1.00	1.25	1.60	2.00	2.50	6.00	8.50	15	225
1909S 1,825,000		50.00	60.00	70.00	95.00	150.00	165.00	200.00	235	
1910 . . . . .(4,118) . . .146,801,218		0.07	0.10	0.15	0.30	1.00	2.50	9.00	13	150
1910S 6,045,000		7.50	9.00	11.00	12.00	25.00	40.00	55.00	70	
1911 . . . . .(1,725) . . .101,177,787		0.10	0.15	0.30	0.50	1.50	3.50	11.00	25	175
1911D 12,672,000		2.25	3.00	4.50	9.00	21.00	35.00	50.00	70	
1911S 4,026,000		16.00	22.00	28.00	31.00	40.00	55.00	110.00	150	
1912 . . . . .(2,172) . . .68,153,060		0.15	0.25	0.70	2.00	2.50	8.00	17.00	25	150
1912D 10,411,000		2.75	3.50	4.25	10.00	25.00	40.00	75.00	120	
1912S 4,431,000		10.00	12.00	14.00	17.00	33.00	45.00	90.00	125	
1913 . . . . .(2,983) . . .76,532,352		0.15	0.20	0.50	1.50	8.00	12.00	16.00	25	160
1913D 15,804,000		0.75	1.00	1.50	3.50	20.00	26.00	50.00	100	
1913S 6,101,000		5.50	6.75	9.00	12.00	27.00	50.00	85.00	135	
1914 . . . . .(1,365) . . .75,238,432		0.20	0.30	0.75	2.00	6.50	17.00	25.00	37	180
1914D **(a)** 1,193,000		100.00	125.00	200.00	250.00	450.00	800.00	1,100.00	2,000	
1914S 4,137,000		11.00	12.00	14.00	19.00	40.00	90.00	175.00	260	
1915 . . . . .(1,150) . . .29,092,120		0.40	1.00	2.00	6.00	25.00	35.00	46.00	65	275
1915D 22,050,000		0.50	1.00	1.50	2.25	9.00	22.00	45.00	60	
1915S 4,833,000		8.00	9.00	11.00	14.00	30.00	60.00	100.00	150	
1916 . . . . . .(600) . . .131,833,677		0.05	0.08	0.15	0.50	2.00	5.00	10.00	15	450
1916D 35,956,000		0.10	0.20	0.50	1.50	5.50	12.00	35.00	65	
1916S 22,510,000		0.50	0.75	1.50	3.00	10.00	20.00	45.00	90	
1917 196,429,785		0.05	0.07	0.10	0.25	0.60	3.00	10.00	15	
1917D 55,120,000		0.10	0.20	0.40	1.50	14.00	19.00	39.00	70	
1917S 32,620,000		0.08	0.10	0.25	0.50	2.75	12.00	35.00	65	

a. Beware of altered date or mintmark. No V.D.B. on shoulder of genuine 1914-D cent.

Designer's initials placed on Lincoln's shoulder next to rim, starting 1918.

Brilliant Uncirculated coins before 1934 are worth more than prices shown. Spotted, cleaned, or discolored pieces are worth less.

	Mintage	G-4	VG-8	F-12	VF-20	EF-40	AU-50	MS-60	MS-63
1918	288,104,634	$0.04	$0.05	$0.10	$0.20	$1.00	$3.00	$6.00	$15.00
1918D	47,830,000	0.10	0.15	0.60	1.25	6.00	12.00	33.00	68.00
1918S	34,680,000	0.10	0.15	0.50	1.00	4.00	15.00	35.00	75.00
1919	392,021,000	0.04	0.05	0.07	0.15	0.75	1.50	5.00	14.00
1919D	57,154,000	0.05	0.06	0.10	0.40	2.50	15.00	28.00	60.00
1919S	139,760,000	0.05	0.06	0.10	0.30	1.35	7.00	18.00	70.00
1920	310,165,000	0.03	0.05	0.07	0.15	0.50	1.50	6.00	12.00
1920D	49,280,000	0.20	0.40	0.80	2.00	6.00	15.00	35.00	60.00
1920S	46,220,000	0.10	0.20	0.30	0.70	3.50	17.00	45.00	115.00
1921	39,157,000	0.06	0.08	0.15	0.35	1.50	6.00	22.00	40.00
1921S	15,274,000	0.35	0.50	0.70	1.50	15.00	35.00	55.00	100.00
1922D	7,160,000	7.00	8.00	9.00	11.00	17.00	28.00	45.00	75.00
1922, No D **(b)**	*	300.00	375.00	550.00	650.00	1,400.00	2,500.00	4,500.00	16,000.00
1923	74,723,000	0.04	0.05	0.07	0.15	1.00	2.50	7.00	14.00
1923S	8,700,000	0.50	0.60	0.75	2.00	14.00	35.00	100.00	225.00
1924	75,178,000	0.04	0.05	0.07	0.15	1.50	3.50	15.00	25.00
1924D	2,520,000	15.00	19.00	23.00	30.00	55.00	90.00	150.00	225.00
1924S	11,696,000	0.40	0.50	0.80	1.10	9.00	30.00	55.00	110.00
1925	139,949,000	0.03	0.04	0.05	0.15	0.50	2.00	5.00	10.00
1925D	22,580,000	0.04	0.06	0.10	0.30	4.50	11.00	27.00	38.00
1925S	26,380,000	0.04	0.06	0.10	0.25	3.00	14.00	40.00	80.00
1926	157,088,000	0.03	0.04	0.05	0.15	0.50	2.00	5.00	8.00
1926D	28,020,000	0.04	0.06	0.10	0.30	2.50	9.00	35.00	50.00
1926S	4,550,000	3.00	3.50	4.50	6.00	14.00	32.00	65.00	140.00
1927	144,440,000	0.03	0.04	0.05	0.20	0.50	1.00	5.00	10.00
1927D	27,170,000	0.10	0.15	0.50	1.00	2.00	6.00	26.00	42.00
1927S	14,276,000	0.25	0.30	0.50	1.25	4.00	11.00	35.00	70.00
1928	134,116,000	0.03	0.04	0.05	0.15	0.50	1.00	4.50	10.00
1928D	31,170,000	0.04	0.06	0.10	0.25	0.85	4.00	15.00	34.00
1928S	17,266,000	0.06	0.10	0.25	0.50	1.50	5.00	34.00	55.00
1929	185,262,000	0.03	0.04	0.05	0.15	0.35	1.50	4.00	6.00
1929D	41,730,000	0.04	0.06	0.10	0.25	1.00	2.00	12.00	15.00
1929S	50,148,000	0.03	0.05	0.10	0.15	0.60	1.75	7.00	11.00
1930	157,415,000	0.03	0.04	0.05	0.15	0.25	0.75	2.00	3.50
1930D	40,100,000	0.04	0.06	0.10	0.25	0.60	1.00	5.00	10.00
1930S	24,286,000	0.03	0.05	0.10	0.15	0.40	2.00	3.50	5.00
1931	19,396,000	0.15	0.20	0.30	0.40	0.60	2.00	10.00	15.00
1931D	4,480,000	2.00	2.25	3.00	3.50	5.00	14.00	30.00	42.00
1931S	866,000	50.00	60.00	65.00	75.00	80.00	85.00	90.00	100.00
1932	9,062,000	0.40	0.50	0.60	1.00	1.25	3.75	10.00	13.00
1932D	10,500,000	0.25	0.35	0.40	0.50	1.00	3.25	10.00	15.00
1933	14,360,000	0.30	0.40	0.50	0.70	1.25	3.75	10.00	15.00
1933D	6,200,000	1.00	1.25	1.50	2.50	4.25	7.00	13.00	16.00

* Included in number above. **b.** 1922 cents with a weak or missing mintmark were made from extremely worn dies that originally struck normal 1922-D cents. Three different die pairs were involved; two of them produced "Weak D" coins. One die pair (no. 2, identified by a "strong reverse") is acknowledged as striking "No D" coins. Weak D cents are worth considerably less. Beware of removed mintmark.

SMALL CENTS

	Mintage	G-4	VG-8	F-12	VF-20	EF-40	AU-50	MS-60	MS-63	PF-63
1934	219,080,000	$0.03	$0.03	$0.03	$0.03	$0.10	$1.00	$3.00	$4.50	
1934D	28,446,000	0.04	0.06	0.08	0.15	0.50	2.00	9.00	15.00	
1935	245,388,000	0.03	0.03	0.03	0.04	0.06	0.20	2.00	3.00	
1935D	47,000,000	0.03	0.03	0.03	0.04	0.20	0.50	3.00	4.00	
1935S	38,702,000	0.03	0.04	0.04	0.04	0.12	1.25	4.00	6.00	
1936 (5,569)	309,632,000	0.03	0.03	0.03	0.04	0.06	0.25	1.00	3.00	$85
1936D	40,620,000	0.03	0.03	0.03	0.04	0.08	0.20	1.00	3.00	
1936S	29,130,000	0.03	0.03	0.03	0.04	0.10	0.20	1.00	3.00	
1937 (9,320)	309,170,000	0.02	0.03	0.03	0.03	0.05	0.20	0.50	3.00	34
1937D	50,430,000	0.02	0.03	0.03	0.03	0.06	0.30	0.80	4.00	
1937S	34,500,000	0.03	0.03	0.03	0.04	0.06	0.30	0.80	4.00	
1938 (14,734)	156,682,000	0.02	0.03	0.03	0.03	0.05	0.30	0.75	2.00	25
1938D	20,010,000	0.02	0.03	0.04	0.06	0.15	0.50	1.00	5.00	
1938S	15,180,000	0.06	0.08	0.10	0.12	0.15	0.30	1.00	4.00	
1939 (13,520)	316,466,000	0.02	0.03	0.03	0.03	0.03	0.20	0.30	2.50	23
1939D	15,160,000	0.06	0.08	0.10	0.12	0.15	0.35	1.00	4.00	
1939S	52,070,000	0.03	0.03	0.03	0.04	0.10	0.30	1.00	4.00	
1940 (15,872)	586,810,000	0.02	0.03	0.03	0.03	0.03	0.20	0.30	2.00	16
1940D	81,390,000	0.02	0.03	0.03	0.03	0.03	0.20	0.40	2.00	
1940S	112,940,000	0.02	0.03	0.03	0.03	0.04	0.20	0.40	2.75	
1941 (21,100)	887,018,000	0.02	0.03	0.03	0.03	0.03	0.20	0.30	2.00	15
1941D	128,700,000	0.02	0.03	0.03	0.03	0.03	0.40	0.80	3.00	
1941S	92,360,000	0.02	0.03	0.03	0.03	0.04	0.35	1.00	5.00	
1942 (32,600)	657,796,000	0.02	0.03	0.03	0.03	0.03	0.10	0.15	1.00	15
1942D	206,698,000	0.02	0.03	0.03	0.03	0.03	0.10	0.15	2.00	
1942S	85,590,000	0.02	0.03	0.03	0.03	0.10	1.00	2.00	8.00	

Variety 2 – Zinc-Coated Steel (1943)

	Mintage	F-12	VF-20	EF-40	MS-60	MS-63	MS-65
1943	684,628,670	$0.05	$0.10	$0.15	$0.70	$1.25	$3.00
1943D	217,660,000	0.05	0.10	0.15	0.90	2.00	4.50
1943S	191,550,000	0.06	0.12	0.20	1.20	2.75	6.00

Variety 1 (Bronze) Resumed (1944–1958)

1944-D, D Over S

1955, Doubled-Die Error

	Mintage	VF-20	EF-40	MS-63	MS-65	PF-65
1944	1,435,400,000	$0.03	$0.03	$0.15	$0.50	
1944D	430,578,000	0.03	0.03	0.20	0.50	
1944D, D Over S	*	75.00	90.00	225.00	600.00	
1944S	282,760,000	0.03	0.03	0.15	1.50	

* Included in number above.

Chart continued on next page.

	Mintage	VF-20	EF-40	MS-63	MS-65	PF-65
1945	1,040,515,000	$0.03	$0.03	$0.20	$0.50	
1945D	266,268,000	0.03	0.03	0.15	0.50	
1945S	181,770,000	0.03	0.03	0.10	2.00	
1946	991,655,000	0.03	0.03	0.10	0.50	
1946D	315,690,000	0.03	0.03	0.15	1.00	
1946S	198,100,000	0.03	0.03	0.15	1.25	
1947	190,555,000	0.03	0.03	0.25	0.50	
1947D	194,750,000	0.03	0.03	0.12	0.50	
1947S	99,000,000	0.03	0.03	0.15	1.50	
1948	317,570,000	0.03	0.03	0.15	0.50	
1948D	172,637,500	0.03	0.03	0.12	0.60	
1948S	81,735,000	0.03	0.03	0.20	1.50	
1949	217,775,000	0.03	0.03	0.30	0.75	
1949D	153,132,500	0.03	0.03	0.20	0.75	
1949S	64,290,000	0.04	0.05	0.50	2.00	
1950	(51,386) 272,635,000	0.03	0.03	0.25	0.50	$30.00
1950D	334,950,000	0.03	0.03	0.10	0.50	
1950S	118,505,000	0.03	0.03	0.25	0.80	
1951	(57,500) 284,576,000	0.03	0.03	0.25	0.80	35.00
1951D	625,355,000	0.03	0.03	0.10	0.50	
1951S	136,010,000	0.03	0.03	0.30	0.60	
1952	(81,980) 186,775,000	0.03	0.03	0.15	0.60	25.00
1952D	746,130,000	0.03	0.03	0.15	0.60	
1952S	137,800,004	0.03	0.03	0.50	1.50	
1953	(128,800) 256,755,000	0.03	0.03	0.10	0.50	25.00
1953D	700,515,000	0.03	0.03	0.10	0.50	
1953S	181,835,000	0.03	0.04	0.12	0.50	
1954	(233,300) 71,640,050	0.03	0.06	0.10	0.50	10.00
1954D	251,552,500	0.03	0.03	0.05	0.30	
1954S	96,190,000	0.03	0.03	0.05	0.30	
1955	(378,200) 330,958,200	0.03	0.03	0.06	0.30	10.00
1955, Doubled-Die Obverse	*	600.00	800.00 (a)	1,500.00	5,500.00	
1955D	563,257,500	0.03	0.03	0.05	0.25	
1955S	44,610,000	0.10	0.15	0.15	0.50	
1956	(669,384) 420,745,000	0.03	0.03	0.05	0.25	1.75
1956D	1,098,201,100	0.03	0.03	0.05	0.30	
1957	(1,247,952) 282,540,000	0.03	0.03	0.05	0.30	1.75
1957D	1,051,342,000	0.03	0.03	0.05	0.30	
1958	(875,652) 252,525,000	0.03	0.03	0.05	0.30	2.00
1958D	800,953,300	0.03	0.03	0.05	0.30	

* Included in number above. **a.** Value for MS-60 Uncirculated is $1,150.

LINCOLN, MEMORIAL REVERSE (1959–2008)

Small Date Large Date

	Mintage	MS-63	MS-65	PF-65
1959	(1,149,291) 609,715,000	$0.01	$0.10	$1.00

1969-S, Doubled-Die Error — **Small Date, Numbers Aligned at Top** — **Large Date, Low 7 in Date** — **Enlarged Detail of 1972 Doubled-Die Error**

	Mintage	MS-63	MS-65	PF-65
1959D	1,279,760,000	$0.01	$0.10	
1960, Lg Dt	586,405,000	0.01	0.10	
	(1,691,602)			$0.50
1960, Sm Dt	*	1.00	2.50	
	*			9.00
1960D, Lg Dt	1,580,884,000	0.01	0.10	
1960D, Sm Dt	*	0.02	0.10	
1961	753,345,000	0.01	0.10	
	(3,028,244)			0.50
1961D	1,753,266,700	0.01	0.10	
1962	606,045,000	0.01	0.10	
	(3,218,019)			0.50
1962D	1,793,148,140	0.01	0.10	
1963	754,110,000	0.01	0.10	
	(3,075,645)			0.50
1963D	1,774,020,400	0.01	0.10	
1964	2,648,575,000	0.01	0.10	
	(3,950,762)			0.50
1964D	3,799,071,500	0.01	0.10	
1965	1,497,224,900	0.02	0.12	
1966	2,188,147,783	0.04	0.12	
1967	3,048,667,100	0.03	0.12	
1968	1,707,880,970	0.02	0.12	
1968D	2,886,269,600	0.01	0.10	
1968S	258,270,001	0.02	0.10	
	(3,041,506)			0.50
1969	1,136,910,000	0.05	0.20	
1969D	4,002,832,200	0.03	0.10	
1969S	544,375,000	0.03	0.10	
	(2,934,631)			0.50
1969S, DDO	*	—	—	
1970	1,898,315,000	0.05	0.10	
1970D	2,891,438,900	0.02	0.10	
1970S, Sm Dt (High 7)	**	20.00	30.00	
	**			25.00
1970S, Lg Dt (Low 7)	690,560,004	0.03	0.10	
	(2,632,810)			0.25

	Mintage	MS-63	MS-65	PF-65
1971	1,919,490,000	$0.05	$0.20	
1971D	2,911,045,600	0.03	0.20	
1971S	525,133,459	0.03	0.20	
	(3,220,733)			$0.25
1972, DDO	**	190.00	300.00	
1972	2,933,255,000	0.01	0.05	
1972D	2,665,071,400	0.02	0.10	
1972S	376,939,108	0.02	0.10	
	(3,260,996)			0.25
1973	3,728,245,000	0.01	0.10	
1973D	3,549,576,588	0.01	0.10	
1973S	317,177,295	0.02	0.10	
	(2,760,339)			0.25
1974	4,232,140,523	0.01	0.10	
1974D	4,235,098,000	0.01	0.10	
1974S	409,426,660	0.03	0.10	
	(2,612,568)			0.25
1975	5,451,476,142	0.01	0.10	
1975D	4,505,275,300	0.01	0.10	
1975S	(2,845,450)			1.50
1976	4,674,292,426	0.01	0.10	
1976D	4,221,592,455	0.02	0.10	
1976S	(4,149,730)			1.25
1977	4,469,930,000	0.01	0.10	
1977D	4,194,062,300	0.01	0.10	
1977S	(3,251,152)			1.00
1978	5,558,605,000	0.01	0.10	
1978D	4,280,233,400	0.01	0.10	
1978S	(3,127,781)			1.00
1979	6,018,515,000	0.01	0.10	
1979D	4,139,357,254	0.01	0.10	
1979S, Filled S	(3,677,175)			1.75
1979S, Clear S	*			2.00
1980	7,414,705,000	0.01	0.10	
1980D	5,140,098,660	0.01	0.10	
1980S	(3,554,806)			1.00
1981	7,491,750,000	0.01	0.10	
1981D	5,373,235,677	0.01	0.10	
1981S, Filled S	(4,063,083)			1.50
1981S, Clear S	*			18.00

* Included in number above. ** Included in number below.

Large Date **Small Date**

	Mintage	MS-63	MS-65	PF-65
1982,				
Lg Dt	10,712,525,000	$0.01	$0.10	
1982, Sm Dt ....*		0.02	0.12	

	Mintage	MS-63	MS-65	PF-65
1982D,				
Lg Dt ..6,012,979,368		$0.01	$0.10	
1982S ....(3,857,479)				$1.60

* Included in number above.

Copper-Plated Zinc (1982–2008)

1995, Doubled Die showing strong doubling on word LIBERTY.

	Mintage	MS-63	MS-65	PF-65
1982, Lg Dt ....*		$0.01	$0.05	
1982, Sm Dt ....*		0.01	0.05	
1982D, Lg Dt ....*		0.05	0.50	
1982D, Sm Dt ....*		0.01	0.05	
1983 7,752,355,000		0.01	0.05	
1983D 6,467,199,428		0.01	0.05	
1983S ....(3,279,126)		0.01	0.05	$1.10
1984 8,151,079,000		0.01	0.05	
1984, Dbl Ear ....**		50.00	100.00	
1984D 5,569,238,906		0.01	0.05	
1984S ....(3,065,110)				1.10
1985 5,648,489,887		0.01	0.05	
1985D 5,287,339,926		0.01	0.05	
1985S ....(3,362,821)				1.25
1986 4,491,395,493		0.01	0.05	
1986D 4,442,866,698		0.01	0.05	
1986S ....(3,010,497)				2.00
1987 4,682,466,931		0.01	0.05	
1987D 4,879,389,514		0.01	0.05	
1987S ....(4,227,728)				1.10
1988 6,092,810,000		0.01	0.05	
1988D 5,253,740,443		0.01	0.05	
1988S ....(3,262,948)				3.25
1989 7,261,535,000		0.01	0.05	
1989D 5,345,467,111		0.01	0.05	
1989S ....(3,220,194)				3.00
1990 6,851,765,000		0.01	0.05	
1990D 4,922,894,533		0.01	0.05	
1990S ....(3,299,559)				2.00
1990, Pf, No S ....**				—
1991 5,165,940,000		$0.01	$0.05	
1991D 4,158,446,076		0.01	0.05	
1991S ....(2,867,787)				$10.00
1992 4,648,905,000		0.01	0.05	
1992, Close AM (a) ....**		—	—	
1992D 4,448,673,300		0.01	0.05	
1992D, Close AM (a) ....**		—	—	
1992S ....(4,176,560)				1.10
1993 5,684,705,000		0.01	0.05	
1993D 6,426,650,571		0.01	0.05	
1993S ....(3,394,792)				2.00
1994 6,500,850,000		0.01	0.05	
1994D 7,131,765,000		0.01	0.05	
1994S ....(3,269,923)				2.00
1995 6,411,440,000		0.01	0.05	
1995, DblDie Obv ....**		4.00	18.00	
1995D 7,128,560,000		0.01	0.05	
1995S ....(2,797,481)				2.00
1996 6,612,465,000		0.01	0.05	
1996, Wide AM (a) ......**		—		
1996D 6,510,795,000		0.01	0.05	
1996S ....(2,525,265)				1.25
1997 4,622,800,000		0.01	0.05	
1997D 4,576,555,000		0.01	0.05	
1997S ....(2,796,678)				2.00
1998 5,032,155,000		0.01	0.05	
1998, Wide AM (a) ......**		2.00	4.00	
1998D 5,225,353,500		0.01	0.05	
1998S ....(2,086,507)				2.00

* Included in previous section's mintages. ** Included in number above. **a.** Varieties were made using Proof dies that have a wide space between AM in AMERICA. The letters nearly touch on other Uncirculated cents.

Mintage	MS-63	MS-65	PF-65
1999 5,237,600,000	$0.01	$0.05	
1999, Wide AM (a) . . . . . .**		—	
1999D 6,360,065,000	0.01	0.05	
1999S . . . .(3,347,966)			$2
1999S, Close AM (a) . . . .**		—	
2000 5,503,200,000	0.01	0.05	
2000, Wide AM (a) . . . . . .**	2.00	2.50	
2000D 8,774,220,000	0.01	0.05	
2000S . . . .(4,047,993)			1
2001 4,959,600,000	0.01	0.05	
2001D 5,374,990,000	0.01	0.05	
2001S . . . .(3,184,606)			1
2002 3,260,800,000	0.01	0.05	
2002D 4,028,055,000	0.01	0.05	
2002S . . . .(3,211,995)			1
2003 3,300,000,000	0.01	0.05	
2003D 3,548,000,000	0.01	0.05	

Mintage	MS-63	MS-65	PF-65
2003S . . . .(3,298,439)			$1
2004 3,379,600,000	$0.01	$0.05	
2004D 3,456,400,000	0.01	0.05	
2004S . . . .(2,965,422)			1
2005 3,935,600,000	0.01	0.05	
2005D 3,764,450,500	0.01	0.05	
2005S . . . .(3,344,679)			1
2006 4,290,000,000	0.01	0.05	
2006D 3,944,000,000	0.01	0.05	
2006S . . . .(3,054,436)			1
2007 3,762,400,000	0.01	0.05	
2007D 3,638,800,000	0.01	0.05	
2007S . . . .(2,577,166)		0.05	1
2008 2,558,800,000	0.10	0.50	
2008D 2,849,600,000	0.10	0.50	
2008S . . . .(2,180,548)			1

** Included in number above. **a.** Varieties were made using Proof dies that have a wide space between AM in AMERICA. The letters nearly touch on other Uncirculated cents.

LINCOLN, BICENTENNIAL (2009)

One-cent coins issued during 2009 are a unique tribute to President Abraham Lincoln, recognizing the bicentennial of his birth and the 100th anniversary of the first issuance of the Lincoln cent. These coins use four different design themes on the reverse to represent the four major aspects of President Lincoln's life. The obverse of each of these coins carries the traditional portrait of Lincoln that has been in use since 1909.

The special reverse designs, released as quarterly issues throughout 2009, are described as: Birth and Early Childhood in Kentucky (designer, Richard Masters; sculptor, Jim Licaretz); Formative Years in Indiana (designer and sculptor, Charles Vickers); Professional Life in Illinois (designer, Joel Iskowitz; sculptor, Don Everhart); and Presidency in Washington (designer, Susan Gamble; sculptor, Joseph Menna). Those issued for commercial circulation are made of the exact same copper-plated composition used since 1982. Special versions included in collector sets are made of the same metallic composition as was used for the original 1909 cents (95% copper, 5% tin and zinc).

2009 Lincoln cent reverse designs

	Mintage	MS-63	MS-65	PF-65
2009, Birth and Early Childhood	284,400,000	$0.05	$0.10	
2009D, Birth and Early Childhood	350,400,000	0.05	0.10	
2009S, Birth and Early Childhood	(1,994,998)			$2
2009, Formative Years	376,000,000	0.05	0.10	
2009D, Formative Years	363,600,000	0.05	0.10	
2009S, Formative Years	(1,994,998)			2

Chart continued on next page.

	Mintage	MS-63	MS-65	PF-65
2009, Professional Life		$0.05	$0.10	
2009D, Professional Life		0.05	0.10	
2009S, Professional Life	(1,994,998)			$2
2009, Presidency		0.05	0.10	
2009D, Presidency		0.05	0.10	
2009S, Presidency	(1,994,998)			2

LINCOLN, SHIELD REVERSE (2010 TO DATE)

At the conclusion of the 2009 Bicentennial One-Cent Program, future one-cent coins feature a reverse that has "an image emblematic of President Lincoln's preservation of the United States of America as a single and united country."

	Mintage	MS-65	PF-65
2010		$0.10	
2010D		0.10	
2010S			$2

TWO-CENT PIECE (1864–1873)

The Act of April 22, 1864, which changed the weight and composition of the cent, included a provision for the bronze two-cent piece. The weight was specified as 96 grains, the alloy being the same as for the cent. There are two varieties for the first year of issue, 1864: the Small Motto and the Large Motto. The differences are illustrated in the closeups below.

| 1864, Small Motto | 1864, Large Motto |

On the obverse the D in GOD is narrow on the Large Motto variety. The stem to the leaf shows plainly on the Small Motto variety.

G-4 Good: At least part of IN GOD visible.
VG-8 Very Good: WE weakly visible.
F-12 Fine: Complete motto visible. The word WE weak.
VF-20 Very Fine: WE is clear, but not strong.
EF-40 Extremely Fine: The word WE bold.
AU-50 About Uncirculated: Traces of wear visible on leaf tips, arrow points, and the word WE.
MS-60 Uncirculated: No trace of wear. Light blemishes.
MS-63 Choice Uncirculated: Some distracting contact marks or blemishes in prime focal areas. Some impairment of luster possible.
PF-63 Choice Proof: Reflective surfaces with only a few blemishes in secondary focal places. No major flaws.

Brilliant red choice Uncirculated and Proof coins are worth more than prices shown. Cleaned or discolored pieces are worth less.

	Mintage	G-4	VG-8	F-12	VF-20	EF-40	AU-50	MS-60	MS-63	PF-63
1864, Small Motto . . . .*		$60	$75	$125	$225	$325	$400	$550	$800	$10,000
1864, Large Motto . .*(100+)* . .19,847,500		8	9	12	16	23	32	55	90	325
1865 . . . .*(500+)* . .13,640,000		8	9	12	16	23	32	55	90	275
1866 . . . .*(725+)* . . .3,177,000		8	9	12	16	23	32	55	90	275
1867 . . . .*(625+)* . . .2,938,750		8	9	12	16	23	32	55	90	275
1868 . . . .*(600+)* . . .2,803,750		8	9	14	18	25	37	65	110	275
1869 . . . .*(600+)* . . .1,546,500		9	10	14	19	32	60	100	110	275
1870 . . . .*(1,000+)* 861,250		11	13	19	25	45	80	125	150	375
1871 . . . .*(960+)* 721,250		13	15	22	30	65	90	165	190	400
1872 . . . .*(950+)* 65,000		150	200	225	275	400	500	650	950	600
1873 . . . .*(1,000+)*							700			1,000

* Included in number below.

SILVER THREE-CENT PIECES (TRIMES) (1851–1873)

This smallest of United States silver coins was authorized by Congress March 3, 1851. The first three-cent silver pieces had no lines bordering the six-pointed star. From 1854 through 1858 there were two lines, while issues of the last 15 years show only one line. Issues from 1854 through 1873 have an olive sprig over the III and a bundle of three arrows beneath.

G-4 Good: Star worn smooth. Legend and date readable.
VG-8 Very Good: Outline of shield defined. Legend and date clear.
F-12 Fine: Only star points worn smooth.
VF-20 Very Fine: Only partial wear on star ridges.
EF-40 Extremely Fine: Ridges on star points visible.
AU-50 About Uncirculated: Trace of wear visible at each star point. Center of shield possibly weak.
MS-60 Uncirculated: No trace of wear. Light blemishes.
MS-63 Choice Uncirculated: Some distracting contact marks or blemishes in prime focal areas. Some impairment of luster possible.
PF-63 Choice Proof: Reflective surfaces with only a few blemishes in secondary focal places. No major flaws.

Mintmark location.

No Outline Around Star (1851–1853)	**Three Outlines to Star, Large Date** (1854–1858)	**Two Outlines to Star, Small Date** (1859–1873)	**1862, 2 Over 1**

Well-struck specimens command higher prices.

	Mintage	G-4	VG-8	F-12	VF-20	EF-40	AU-50	MS-60	MS-63	PF-63
1851	5,447,400	$13	$16	$18	$24	$33	$70	$90	$150	—
18510	720,000	16	20	25	47	75	110	180	260	
1852	18,663,500	13	16	18	24	33	70	85	150	—
1853	11,400,000	13	16	18	24	33	70	85	150	
1854	671,000	14	17	20	26	55	115	175	325	$6,500
1855	139,000	16	28	30	50	100	135	275	450	2,200
1856	1,458,000	13	16	20	26	50	100	150	320	1,800
1857	1,042,000	13	16	20	26	50	100	150	320	1,800
1858 ...(300+)	1,603,700	13	16	20	26	50	90	150	320	1,200
1859 ...(800)	364,200	13	16	20	26	35	75	90	175	275
1860 ...(1,000)	286,000	13	16	20	26	35	75	90	175	275
1861 ...(1,000)	497,000	13	16	20	26	35	75	90	175	275
1862, 2/1 ...*		13	16	20	26	35	90	110	225	
1862 ...(550)	343,000	13	16	20	26	35	75	90	175	285
1863 ...(460)	21,000				150	200	275	350	550	320
1864 ...(470)	12,000				150	200	275	350	550	310

	Mintage	VF-20	EF-40	AU-50	MS-60	MS-63	PF-63
1865 ...(500)	8,000	$175	$200	$300	$375	$525	$315
1866 ...(725)	22,000	150	175	275	350	500	315
1867 ...(625)	4,000	175	200	300	375	525	315
1868 ...(600)	3,500	175	200	300	375	600	315
1869 ...(600)	4,500	175	200	300	375	500	315
1870 ...(1,000)	3,000	175	200	300	375	500	325
1871 ...(960)	3,400	175	200	300	375	500	325
1872 ...(950)	1,000	200	225	300	375	600	350
1873, Proof only ...(600)			400				700

* Included in number below.

NICKEL THREE-CENT PIECES (1865–1889)

The three-cent pieces struck in nickel composition were designed to replace the silver three-cent coins. Composition is 75% copper and 25% nickel. All were coined at Philadelphia and have plain edges.

G-4 Good: Date and legends complete though worn. III smooth.
VG-8 Very Good: III half worn. Rims complete.
VF-20 Very Fine: Three-quarters of hair details visible.
EF-40 Extremely Fine: Slight, even wear.
AU-50 About Uncirculated: Slight wear on hair curls, above forehead, and on wreath and numeral III.
MS-60 Uncirculated: No trace of wear. Light blemishes.
MS-63 Choice Uncirculated: Some distracting contact marks or blemishes in prime focal areas. Some impairment of luster possible.
PF-63 Choice Proof: Reflective surfaces with only a few blemishes in secondary focal places. No major flaws.

Brilliant choice Uncirculated and Proof coins are worth more than prices shown. Spotted, cleaned, or discolored pieces are worth less.

	Mintage	G-4	VG-8	F-12	VF-20	EF-40	AU-50	MS-60	MS-63	PF-63
1865 . . . .(500+)	11,382,000	$7	$9	$10	$12	$15	$25	$50	$90	$650
1866 . . . .(725+)	. .4,801,000	7	9	10	12	15	25	50	90	160
1867 . . . .(625+)	. .3,915,000	7	9	10	12	15	25	50	90	160
1868 . . . .(600+)	. .3,252,000	7	9	10	12	15	25	50	90	160
1869 . . . .(600+)	. .1,604,000	7	9	10	12	15	25	50	90	160
1870 . . . .(1,000+)	. .1,335,000	7	9	10	12	15	25	50	90	160
1871 . . . .(960+)	604,000	7	9	10	12	15	25	50	100	160
1872 . . . .(950+)	862,000	7	9	10	12	15	25	50	100	160
1873 . . . .(1,100+)	390,000	7	9	10	12	15	25	50	90	160
1874 . . . .(700+)	790,000	8	10	11	13	17	27	60	110	160
1875 . . . .(700+)	228,000	9	11	12	14	20	32	80	110	160
1876 . . . .(1,150+)	162,000	9	11	12	15	22	38	110	125	175
1877, Pf only . . .(510+)	. . . .				550	600				900
1878, Pf only . .(2,350)	. . . .				250	375				475
1879 . . . .(3,200)	38,000	20	25	30	40	60	75	130	200	200
1880 . . . .(3,955)	21,000	40	45	50	60	70	85	150	180	200
1881 . . . .(3,575)	1,077,000	7	9	10	12	15	25	50	90	160
1882 . . . .(3,100)	22,200	35	45	50	60	80	100	150	200	225
1883 . . . .(6,609)	4,000	75	85	100	135	160	180	200	375	235
1884 . . . .(3,942)	1,700	155	175	190	250	275	300	400	550	275
1885 . . . .(3,790)	1,000	175	200	225	275	325	325	450	550	275
1886, Pf only . .(4,290)	. . . .				175	200				250
1887 . . . .(2,960)	5,001	120	140	150	160	175	225	250	275	250
1887, 7/6 . . . .*	. . . .				175	200				275
1888 . . . .(4,582)	36,501	20	23	27	35	45	60	140	175	185
1889 . . . .(3,436)	18,125	35	45	60	75	85	100	150	200	185

* Included in number above.

SHIELD (1866–1883)

The Shield type nickel was made possible by the Act of May 16, 1866. Its weight was set at 77-16/100 grains with the same composition as the nickel three-cent piece.

G-4 Good: All letters in motto readable.

VG-8 Very Good: Motto clear and stands out. Rims slightly worn but even. Part of shield lines visible.

F-12 Fine: Half of each olive leaf worn smooth.

EF-40 Extremely Fine: Slight wear to leaf tips and cross over shield.

AU-50 About Uncirculated: Traces of light wear on only the high design points. Half of mint luster present.

MS-60 Uncirculated: No trace of wear. Light blemishes.

MS-63 Choice Uncirculated: Some distracting blemishes in prime focal areas. Impaired luster possible.

PF-63 Choice Proof: Reflective surfaces. Only a few blemishes in secondary focal areas. No major flaws.

With Rays (1866–1867)

Without Rays (1867–1883)

**Typical Example of
1883, 3 Over 2**
Other varieties exist.

Brilliant choice Uncirculated and Proof coins are worth more than prices shown. Spotted, cleaned, or discolored pieces are worth less.

	Mintage	G-4	VG-8	F-12	EF-40	AU-50	MS-60	MS-63	PF-63
1866, Rays	(600+)..14,742,500	$13	$19	$22	$85	$110	$125	$200	$1,250
1867, Rays	(25+)...2,019,000	15	22	27	90	125	225	275	16,000
1867, Without Rays	(600+)..28,890,500	9	10	11	20	25	70	120	220
1868	(600+)..28,817,000	9	10	11	20	25	70	120	220
1869	(600+)..16,395,000	9	10	11	20	25	70	120	220
1870	(1,000+)...4,806,000	9	10	11	20	25	70	120	220
1871	(960+)....561,000	25	30	50	100	135	180	250	250
1872	(950+)...6,036,000	10	11	13	24	50	90	125	220
1873, Close 3	(1,100+)....436,050	10	11	13	30	55	100	175	220
1873, Open 3	4,113,950	9	10	11	25	50	90	125	
1874	(700+)...3,538,000	10	11	13	24	50	90	130	220
1875	(700+)...2,097,000	12	14	20	40	55	100	140	225
1876	(1,150+)...2,530,000	12	14	20	40	55	100	120	220
1877, Proof only	(510+)			400	850				1,300
1878, Proof only	(2,350)			275	450				900
1879	(3,200)....25,900	175	225	275	325	350	400	450	400
1880	(3,955)....16,000	190	240	290	500	800	1,600	2,500	450
1881	(3,575)....68,800	125	150	175	250	275	350	450	300
1882	(3,100)..11,472,900	8	9	10	19	25	60	100	175
1883	(5,419)...1,451,500	8	9	10	19	25	65	100	180
1883, 3 Over 2	*	40	100	150	200	390	475	600	

* Included in number above.

LIBERTY HEAD (1883–1913)

In 1883 the design was changed to the "Liberty head." This type first appeared without the word CENTS on the coin, merely a large letter V. These "CENTS-less" coins were goldplated by fraudsters and passed as $5 pieces. Later in that year the word CENTS was added.

G-4 Good: No details in head. LIBERTY obliterated.
VG-8 Very Good: Some letters in LIBERTY legible.
F-12 Fine: All letters in LIBERTY legible.
VF-20 Very Fine: LIBERTY bold, including letter L.
EF-40 Extremely Fine: LIBERTY sharp. Corn grains at bottom of wreath visible on reverse.
AU-50 About Uncirculated: Traces of light wear on only high points of design. Half of mint luster present.
MS-60 Uncirculated: No trace of wear. Contact marks possible. Surface may be spotted, or luster faded.
MS-63 Choice Uncirculated: No trace of wear. Light blemishes.
PF-63 Choice Proof: Reflective surfaces. Only a few blemishes in secondary focal areas. No major flaws.

Variety 1, Without CENTS (1883 Only)   Variety 2, With CENTS (1883–1913)   Mintmark Location

Brilliant choice Uncirculated and Proof coins are worth more than prices shown; spotted or cleaned coins, less.

	Mintage	G-4	VG-8	F-12	VF-20	EF-40	AU-50	MS-60	MS-63	PF-63
1883, Without CENTS . . . (5,219) . . .5,474,300		$2.25	$2.75	$3.10	$4	$4.75	$6.25	$18	$26	$165
1883, CENTS . .(6,783) . .16,026,200		6.00	7.00	12.00	20	35.00	45.00	75	100	140
1884 . . . .(3,942) . .11,270,000		7.00	12.00	14.00	20	35.00	50.00	100	130	130
1885 . . . .(3,790) . .1,472,700		230.00	275.00	325.00	450	550.00	700.00	850	1,100	700
1886 . . . .(4,290) . .3,326,000		100.00	125.00	200.00	250	310.00	395.00	450	800	375
1887 . . . .(2,960) . .15,260,692		4.00	7.00	11.00	20	40.00	45.00	75	125	150
1888 . . . .(4,582) . .10,167,901		10.00	15.00	25.00	50	65.00	90.00	135	180	150
1889 . . . .(3,336) . .15,878,025		3.00	5.00	11.00	20	35.00	50.00	75	125	140
1890 . . . .(2,740) . .16,256,532		2.50	4.00	10.00	15	25.00	30.00	75	125	140
1891 . . . .(2,350) . .16,832,000		2.50	4.00	10.00	15	25.00	30.00	75	125	140
1892 . . . .(2,745) . .11,696,897		2.50	4.00	10.00	15	25.00	30.00	75	125	140
1893 . . . .(2,195) . .13,368,000		2.50	4.00	10.00	15	30.00	35.00	80	135	140
1894 . . . .(2,632) . .5,410,500		6.00	10.00	40.00	75	115.00	150.00	180	210	140
1895 . . . .(2,062) . .9,977,822		1.50	2.50	7.00	10	25.00	30.00	75	130	140
1896 . . . .(1,862) . .8,841,058		2.00	5.00	15.00	20	35.00	50.00	90	140	140
1897 . . . .(1,938) . .20,426,797		2.00	5.00	9.00	12	22.00	24.00	50	125	140
1898 . . . .(1,795) . .12,530,292		2.00	5.00	9.00	12	22.00	24.00	50	125	140
1899 . . . .(2,031) . .26,027,000		0.75	1.00	3.00	6	14.00	22.00	50	100	140
1900 . . . .(2,262) . .27,253,733		0.75	1.00	3.00	6	14.00	20.00	40	90	135
1901 . . . .(1,985) . .26,478,228		0.75	1.00	3.00	6	14.00	20.00	40	80	135
1902 . . . .(2,018) . .31,487,561		0.75	1.00	3.00	6	14.00	20.00	40	80	135
1903 . . . .(1,790) . .28,004,935		0.75	1.00	2.00	4	12.00	20.00	40	80	135
1904 . . . .(1,817) . .21,403,167		0.75	1.00	2.00	4	12.00	20.00	40	80	135
1905 . . . .(2,152) . .29,825,124		0.75	1.00	2.00	4	12.00	20.00	40	80	135
1906 . . . .(1,725) . .38,612,000		0.75	1.00	2.00	4	12.00	20.00	40	80	135
1907 . . . .(1,475) . .39,213,325		0.75	1.00	2.00	4	12.00	20.00	40	80	135
1908 . . . .(1,620) . .22,684,557		0.75	1.00	2.00	4	12.00	20.00	40	80	135

Chart continued on next page.

	Mintage	G-4	VG-8	F-12	VF-20	EF-40	AU-50	MS-60	MS-63	PF-63
1909 . . . . .(4,763) . .11,585,763		$0.75	$1.00	$2	$4	$12	$22	$45	$95	$135
1910 . . . . .(2,405) . .30,166,948		0.75	1.00	2	4	12	20	40	80	135
1911 . . . . .(1,733) . .39,557,639		0.75	1.00	2	4	12	20	40	80	135
1912 . . . . .(2,145) . .26,234,569		0.75	1.00	2	4	12	20	40	80	135
1912D 8,474,000		1.00	1.50	4	13	35	85	135	160	
1912S 238,000		65.00	100.00	125	225	425	650	750	950	
1913 Liberty Head *(5 known)*									2,000,000	

INDIAN HEAD OR BUFFALO (1913–1938)

The Buffalo nickel was designed by James E. Fraser, whose initial F is below the date. He modeled the bison after Black Diamond in the New York Central Park Zoo.

G-4 Good: Legends and date readable. Buffalo's horn does not show.
VG-8 Very Good: Horn worn nearly flat.
F-12 Fine: Horn and tail smooth but partially visible. Obverse rim intact.
VF-20 Very Fine: Much of horn visible. Indian's cheekbone worn.
EF-40 Extremely Fine: Horn lightly worn. Slight wear on Indian's hair ribbon.
AU-50 About Uncirculated: Traces of light wear on high points of design. Half of mint luster present.
MS-60 Uncirculated: No trace of wear. May have several blemishes.
MS-63 Choice Uncirculated: No trace of wear. Light blemishes.
Matte PF-63 Choice Proof: Crisp surfaces. Only a few blemishes in secondary focal areas. No major flaws.

Variety 1 – FIVE CENTS on Raised Ground (1913)

Brilliant choice Uncirculated coins are worth more than prices shown. Spotted, cleaned, weakly struck, or discolored pieces are worth less.

	Mintage	G-4	VG-8	F-12	VF-20	EF-40	AU-50	MS-60	MS-63	MATTE PF-63
1913, Variety 1 . .(1,520)	30,992,000	$4	$5	$6	$8	$11	$12	$21	$30	$750
1913D, Variety 1	5,337,000	6	8	10	14	18	23	35	45	
1913S, Variety 1	2,105,000	17	22	24	28	40	50	70	90	

Variety 2 – FIVE CENTS in Recess (1913–1938)

Mintmark Below FIVE CENTS	1916, Doubled-Die Obverse	1918-D, 8 Over 7

	Mintage	G-4	VG-8	F-12	VF-20	EF-40	AU-50	MS-60	MS-63	MATTE PF-63
1913, Variety 2 29,857,186		$4.25	$5.50	$6.50	$7.50	$11	$15	$22	$32	
. . . .(1,514)										$600
1913D, Variety 2 4,156,000		50.00	60.00	75.00	90.00	120	135	150	175	
1913S, Variety 2 1,209,000		150.00	165.00	210.00	240.00	325	375	500	625	
1914 20,664,463		10.00	11.00	12.00	14.00	16	22	35	50	
. . . .(1,275)										675

NICKEL FIVE-CENT PIECES

Brilliant choice Uncirculated coins are worth more than prices shown. Spotted, cleaned, weakly struck, or discolored pieces are worth less.

	Mintage	G-4	VG-8	F-12	VF-20	EF-40	AU-50	MS-60	MS-63	MATTE PF-63
1914D	3,912,000	$35.00	$50.00	$65.00	$100.00	$150	$200	$235	$325	
1914S	3,470,000	12.00	14.00	18.00	35.00	50	80	100	240	
1915	20,986,220	2.50	2.50	4.00	5.00	12	30	45	50	
	(1,050)									$700
1915D	7,569,000	8.00	11.00	18.00	35.00	75	85	140	175	
1915S	1,505,000	19.00	25.00	40.00	72.00	150	185	275	425	
1916	63,497,466	2.00	2.50	3.00	3.50	5	10	28	35	
	(600)									900
1916, DblDie Obv	*	1,000.00	1,800.00	3,600.00	5,600.00	8,500	14,000	30,000	70,000	
1916D	13,333,000	6.50	10.00	11.00	22.00	45	60	90	135	
1916S	11,860,000	4.00	6.00	9.00	22.00	45	65	100	165	
1917	51,424,019	2.00	2.50	3.00	4.00	7	16	30	60	
1917D	9,910,000	7.00	10.00	14.00	42.00	75	110	175	375	
1917S	4,193,000	9.00	13.00	20.00	50.00	85	135	225	600	
1918	32,086,314	1.50	2.00	2.50	6.00	16	22	60	135	

	Mintage	G-4	VG-8	F-12	VF-20	EF-40	AU-50	MS-60	MS-63
1918D, 8 Over 7	**	$550.00	$650.00	$1,300.00	$2,500.00	$4,500.00	$6,000	$15,000	$32,000
1918D	8,362,000	8.00	14.00	18.00	70.00	130.00	175	235	600
1918S	4,882,000	5.00	12.00	16.00	45.00	90.00	150	210	1,500
1919	60,868,000	0.50	0.55	0.80	2.00	7.00	15	32	60
1919D (a)	8,006,000	6.00	10.00	30.00	70.00	130.00	160	325	770
1919S (a)	7,521,000	4.00	8.00	17.00	60.00	130.00	160	325	900
1920	63,093,000	0.45	0.60	1.25	2.50	6.00	15	32	70
1920D (a)	9,418,000	3.00	6.00	12.00	65.00	150.00	175	275	800
1920S	9,689,000	1.50	4.00	10.00	50.00	120.00	150	275	900
1921	10,663,000	0.80	2.00	3.00	10.00	25.00	35	70	140
1921S	1,557,000	32.00	55.00	90.00	315.00	465.00	550	865	1,200
1923	35,715,000	0.45	0.60	0.80	4.00	7.50	18	32	80
1923S (a)	6,142,000	3.00	3.50	9.00	60.00	150.00	180	235	550
1924	21,620,000	0.40	0.60	0.80	4.00	9.00	25	40	80
1924D	5,258,000	3.50	4.00	10.00	40.00	120.00	140	190	500
1924S	1,437,000	8.00	18.00	40.00	240.00	650.00	875	1,200	2,200
1925	35,565,100	0.75	1.25	2.00	4.00	8.00	16	25	47
1925D	4,450,000	4.00	5.00	18.00	45.00	85.00	125	210	325
1925S	6,256,000	2.00	5.00	10.00	50.00	90.00	125	230	1,200
1926	44,693,000	0.35	0.45	0.60	3.00	5.00	12	22	32
1926D	5,638,000	3.00	6.00	10.00	50.00	90.00	140	160	235
1926S	970,000	9.00	16.00	40.00	235.00	450.00	1,300	2,000	4,200
1927	37,981,000	0.35	0.45	0.60	1.50	6.00	10	24	36
1927D	5,730,000	0.85	2.00	2.50	15.00	40.00	55	85	160
1927S	3,430,000	0.60	0.90	1.75	18.00	45.00	75	250	1,100
1928	23,411,000	0.40	0.45	0.60	2.00	5.00	10	22	30
1928D	6,436,000	0.45	0.85	1.75	6.00	20.00	23	28	48
1928S	6,936,000	0.60	0.75	1.25	5.00	15.00	50	125	300
1929	36,446,000	0.35	0.40	0.60	2.00	5.00	10	16	35
1929D	8,370,000	0.45	0.60	0.80	3.00	15.00	18	32	65
1929S	7,754,000	0.40	0.60	0.75	0.90	5.50	12	25	45

* Included in number above. ** Included in number below. **a.** Uncirculated pieces with full, sharp details are worth considerably more.

1937-D, "3-Legged" Variety

1938-D, D Over S

Brilliant choice Uncirculated coins are worth more than prices shown. Spotted, cleaned, weakly struck, or discolored pieces are worth less.

	Mintage	G-4	VG-8	F-12	VF-20	EF-40	AU-50	MS-60	MS-63	PF-63
1930	22,849,000	$0.40	$0.50	$0.70	$0.80	$5.00	$11.00	$16	$35	
1930S	5,435,000	0.40	0.50	0.70	0.80	6.00	15.00	25	60	
1931S	1,200,000	7.00	8.00	8.80	9.25	15.00	25.00	28	45	
1934	20,213,003	0.35	0.45	0.55	0.75	3.00	9.00	16	30	
1934D	7,480,000	0.50	0.75	1.25	3.00	9.00	21.00	35	55	
1935	58,264,000	0.35	0.45	0.55	0.75	1.25	4.25	10	22	
1935D	12,092,000	0.35	0.50	1.00	3.00	6.00	19.00	30	40	
1935S	10,300,000	0.35	0.45	0.55	0.75	2.00	7.50	15	36	
1936	(4,420) 118,997,000	0.35	0.45	0.55	0.75	1.25	4.00	10	23	$650
1936D	24,814,000	0.45	0.60	0.75	0.95	1.75	4.50	16	19	
1936S	14,930,000	0.35	0.45	0.55	0.75	1.25	4.50	11	16	
1937	(5,769) 79,480,000	0.35	0.45	0.55	0.75	1.25	2.75	13	16	550
1937D	17,826,000	0.35	0.45	0.55	0.75	1.25	4.00	11	16	
1937D, 3-Legged	*	250.00	350.00	450.00	550.00	650.00	750.00	1,250	2,800	
1937S	5,635,000	0.35	0.45	0.55	0.75	1.25	4.00	11	20	
1938D	7,020,000	1.00	1.10	1.50	1.75	2.00	4.00	11	15	
1938D, D Over S	*	1.00	1.25	4.00	5.00	8.00	12.00	25	36	

* Included in number above.

JEFFERSON (1938 TO DATE)

This nickel was originally designed by Felix Schlag. He won an award of $1,000 in a competition with some 390 artists. It established the definite public approval of portrait and pictorial rather than symbolic devices on our coinage. On October 8, 1942, the wartime five-cent piece composed of copper (56%), silver (35%), and manganese (9%) was introduced to eliminate nickel, a critical war material. A larger mintmark was placed above the dome. The letter P (Philadelphia) was used for the first time, indicating the change of alloy. The designer's initials FS were added below the bust starting in 1966. The mintmark position was moved to the obverse starting in 1968.

VG-8 Very Good: Second porch pillar from right nearly gone, other three still visible but weak.

F-12 Fine: Jefferson's cheekbone worn flat. Hair lines and eyebrow faint. Second pillar weak, especially at bottom.

VF-20 Very Fine: Second pillar plain and complete on both sides.

EF-40 Extremely Fine: Cheekbone, hair lines, eyebrow slightly worn but well defined. Base of triangle above pillars visible but weak.

MS-63 Select Uncirculated: No trace of wear. Slight blemishes.

MS-65 Choice Uncirculated: No trace of wear. Barely noticeable blemishes.

PF-65 Gem Proof: Brilliant surfaces. No noticeable blemishes or flaws. May have a few barely noticeable marks or hairlines.

Mintmark Located at Right of Building

Wartime Silver

Mintmark, Starting 1968

NICKEL FIVE-CENT PIECES

Uncirculated pieces with fully struck steps are valued higher.

	Mintage	VG-8	F-12	VF-20	EF-40	MS-63	MS-65	PF-65
1938 . . . . (19,365) . .	19,496,000	$0.10	$0.12	$0.20	$0.25	$1.10	$5.00	$50
1938D	5,376,000	0.25	0.35	0.75	1.00	2.25	7.00	
1938S	4,105,000	0.40	0.60	0.85	1.50	2.75	8.00	
1939 . . . . (12,535) . .	120,615,000	0.08	0.10	0.12	0.25	1.00	2.00	50
1939D	3,514,000	1.20	1.60	2.50	4.00	35.00	50.00	
1939S	6,630,000	0.25	0.30	0.50	1.35	12.00	20.00	
1940 . . . . (14,158) . .	176,485,000			0.05	0.10	1.00	2.00	45
1940D	43,540,000			0.05	0.10	1.25	3.50	
1940S	39,690,000			0.05	0.10	1.25	3.50	
1941 . . . . (18,720) . .	203,265,000			0.05	0.10	0.50	2.00	45
1941D	53,432,000			0.05	0.10	1.25	3.00	
1941S	43,445,000			0.05	0.10	1.50	3.50	
1942 . . . . (29,600) . .	49,789,000			0.05	0.10	1.25	4.00	45
1942D	13,938,000	0.10	0.15	0.25	1.00	16.00	23.00	

Wartime Silver Alloy (1942–1945)

	Mintage	VG-8	F-12	VF-20	EF-40	MS-63	MS-65	PF-65
1942P . . . . (27,600) . .	57,873,000	$0.75	$0.75	$0.75	$1	$4	$8.00	$100
1942S	32,900,000	0.75	0.75	0.75	1	4	9.00	
1943P, 3 Over 2 . . . . *			15.00	20.00	35	130	320.00	
1943P	271,165,000	0.75	0.75	0.75	1	3	6.00	
1943D	15,294,000	0.75	0.75	0.75	1	5	7.00	
1943S	104,060,000	0.75	0.75	0.75	1	3	6.00	
1944P	119,150,000	0.75	0.75	0.75	1	5	8.50	
1944D	32,309,000	0.75	0.75	0.75	1	5	8.00	
1944S	21,640,000	0.75	0.75	0.75	1	4	8.00	
1945P	119,408,100	0.75	0.75	0.75	1	3	8.00	
1945D	37,158,000	0.75	0.75	0.75	1	3	7.00	
1945S	58,939,000	0.75	0.75	0.75	1	3	7.00	

* Included in number below.

Prewar Composition, Mintmark Style Resumed (1946–1967)

1943, 3 Over 2

1954-S, S Over D

1955-D, D Over S

	Mintage	VF-20	EF-40	MS-63	MS-65	PF-65
1946	161,116,000	$0.05	$0.05	$0.60	$2.50	
1946D	45,292,200	0.05	0.05	0.60	2.50	
1946S	13,560,000	0.05	0.06	0.25	1.75	
1947	95,000,000	0.05	0.05	0.35	1.75	
1947D	37,822,000	0.05	0.05	0.35	1.75	
1947S	24,720,000	0.05	0.06	0.35	1.75	
1948	89,348,000	0.05	0.05	0.35	1.75	
1948D	44,734,000	0.05	0.06	0.50	2.00	
1948S	11,300,000	0.05	0.06	0.50	2.00	
1949	60,652,000	0.05	0.06	2.00	3.00	

Chart continued on next page.

	Mintage	VF-20	EF-40	MS-63	MS-65	PF-65
1949D	...36,498,000	$0.05	$0.05	$0.50	$2.00	
1949D, D Over S	...*	18.00	30.00	100.00	160.00	
1949S	...9,716,000	0.05	0.10	0.40	2.00	
1950	(51,386)...9,796,000	0.05	0.10	0.50	2.50	$30.00
1950D	...2,630,030	3.00	3.50	8.00	11.00	
1951	(57,500)...28,552,000	0.05	0.06	1.25	3.00	25.00
1951D	...20,460,000	0.05	0.06	2.00	3.50	
1951S	...7,776,000	0.05	0.10	0.50	2.50	
1952	(81,980)...63,988,000	0.05	0.05	0.35	1.75	18.00
1952D	...30,638,000	0.05	0.05	2.00	3.00	
1952S	...20,572,000	0.05	0.05	0.55	1.50	
1953	(128,800)...46,644,000	0.05	0.05	0.10	0.35	16.00
1953D	...59,878,600	0.05	0.05	0.10	0.35	
1953S	...19,210,900	0.05	0.05	0.25	0.50	
1954	(233,300)...47,684,050	0.05	0.05	0.50	1.00	8.00
1954D	...117,183,060	0.05	0.05	0.20	0.50	
1954S	...29,384,000	0.05	0.05	0.50	1.00	
1954S, S Over D	...*	2.50	5.00	18.00	35.00	
1955	(378,200)...7,888,000	0.06	0.08	0.40	0.50	6.00
1955D	...74,464,100	0.05	0.05	0.20	40.00	
1955D, D Over S (a)	...*	3.00	5.00	23.00	35.00	
1956	(669,384)...35,216,000	0.05	0.05	0.10	0.40	1.00
1956D	...67,222,940	0.05	0.05	0.10	0.40	
1957	(1,247,952)...38,408,000	0.05	0.05	0.10	0.40	1.00
1957D	...136,828,900	0.05	0.05	0.20	0.60	
1958	(875,652)...17,088,000	0.05	0.05	0.20	0.60	1.50
1958D	...168,249,120	0.05	0.05	0.10	0.40	
1959	(1,149,291)...27,248,000	0.05	0.05	0.10	0.20	0.75
1959D	...160,738,240	0.05	0.05	0.10	0.20	
1960	(1,691,602)...55,416,000	0.05	0.05	0.10	0.20	0.75
1960D	...192,582,180	0.05	0.05	0.10	0.20	
1961	(3,028,144)...73,640,100	0.05	0.05	0.10	0.20	0.75
1961D	...229,342,760	0.05	0.05	0.10	0.20	
1962	(3,218,019)...97,384,000	0.05	0.05	0.10	0.20	0.75
1962D	...280,195,720	0.05	0.05	0.10	0.25	
1963	(3,075,645)...175,776,000	0.05	0.05	0.10	0.20	0.75
1963D	...276,829,460	0.05	0.05	0.10	0.20	
1964	(3,950,762)...1,024,672,000	0.05	0.05	0.10	0.20	0.75
1964D	...1,787,297,160	0.05	0.05	0.10	0.20	
1965	...136,131,380	0.05	0.05	0.10	0.20	

* Included in number above. **a.** Varieties exist. Values are for the variety illustrated.

1966 Through 2003

	Mintage	MS-63	MS-65	PF-65		Mintage	MS-63	MS-65	PF-65
1966	...156,208,283	$0.10	$0.20		1970D	...515,485,380	$0.10	$0.20	
1967	...107,325,800	0.10	0.20		1970S	...238,832,004	0.10	0.20	
1968D	...91,227,880	0.10	0.20			...(2,632,810)			$0.75
1968S	...100,396,004	0.10	0.20		1971	...106,884,000	0.25	0.50	
	...(3,041,506)			$0.75	1971D	...316,144,800	0.10	0.20	
1969D	...202,807,500	0.10	0.20		1971S	...(3,220,733)			1.00
1969S	...120,165,000	0.10	0.20		1972	...202,036,000	0.10	0.20	
	...(2,934,631)			0.75	1972D	...351,694,600	0.10	0.20	

NICKEL FIVE-CENT PIECES

	Mintage	MS-63	MS-65	PF-65
1972S	(3,260,996)			$1.00
1973	384,396,000	$0.10	$0.20	
1973D	261,405,000	0.10	0.20	
1973S	(2,760,339)			1.00

	Mintage	MS-63	MS-65	PF-65
1974	601,752,000	$0.10	$0.20	
1974D	277,373,000	0.10	0.20	
1974S	(2,612,568)			$1.00

	Mintage	MS-65	PF-65
1975	181,772,000	$0.35	
1975D	401,875,300	0.20	
1975S	(2,845,450)		$0.85
1976	367,124,000	0.20	
1976D	563,964,147	0.20	
1976S	(4,149,730)		0.85
1977	585,376,000	0.20	
1977D	297,313,422	0.50	
1977S	(3,251,152)		0.75
1978	391,308,000	0.20	
1978D	313,092,780	0.20	
1978S	(3,127,781)		0.75
1979	463,188,000	0.20	
1979D	325,867,672	0.20	
1979S, Filled S	(3,677,175)		0.75
1979S, Clear S	*		1.00
1980P	593,004,000	0.20	
1980D	502,323,448	0.20	
1980S	(3,554,806)		0.75
1981P	657,504,000	0.20	
1981D	364,801,843	0.20	
1981S	(4,063,083)		0.85
1982P	292,355,000	2.00	
1982D	373,726,544	1.50	
1982S	(3,857,479)		1.00
1983P	561,615,000	1.50	
1983D	536,726,276	1.25	
1983S	(3,279,126)		1.00
1984P	746,769,000	1.25	
1984D	517,675,146	0.20	
1984S	(3,065,110)		1.50
1985P	647,114,962	0.25	
1985D	459,747,446	0.25	
1985S	(3,362,821)		1.25
1986P	536,883,483	0.25	
1986D	361,819,140	0.60	
1986S	(3,010,497)		2.50
1987P	371,499,481	0.20	
1987D	410,590,604	0.20	
1987S	(4,227,728)		1.00
1988P	771,360,000	0.20	
1988D	663,771,652	0.20	
1988S	(3,262,948)		2.00
1989P	898,812,000	0.20	
1989D	570,842,474	0.20	
1989S	(3,220,194)		1.50

* Included in number above.

	Mintage	MS-65	PF-65
1990P	.661,636,000	$0.20	
1990D	.663,938,503	0.20	
1990S	.(3,299,559)		$1.75
1991P	.614,104,000	0.20	
1991D	.436,496,678	0.20	
1991S	.(2,867,787)		2.00
1992P	.399,552,000	1.00	
1992D	.450,565,113	0.20	
1992S	.(4,176,560)		1.50
1993P	.412,076,000	0.20	
1993D	.406,084,135	0.20	
1993S	.(3,394,792)		1.50
1994P	.722,160,000	0.20	
1994D	.715,762,110	0.20	
1994S	.(3,269,923)		1.50
1995P	.774,156,000	0.40	
1995D	.888,112,000	0.20	
1995S	.(2,797,481)		2.00
1996P	.829,332,000	0.20	
1996D	.817,736,000	0.20	
1996S	.(2,525,265)		1.00
1997P	.470,972,000	0.20	
1997D	.466,640,000	0.20	
1997S	.(2,796,678)		1.75
1998P	.688,272,000	0.20	
1998D	.635,360,000	0.20	
1998S	.(2,086,507)		1.75
1999P	.1,212,000,000	0.20	
1999D	.1,066,720,000	0.20	
1999S	.(3,347,966)		2.00
2000P	.846,240,000	0.20	
2000D	.1,509,520,000	0.20	
2000S	.(4,047,993)		1.75
2001P	.675,704,000	0.20	
2001D	.627,680,000	0.20	
2001S	.(3,184,606)		1.75
2002P	.539,280,000	0.20	
2002D	.691,200,000	0.20	
2002S	.(3,211,995)		1.50
2003P	.441,840,000	0.20	
2003D	.383,040,000	0.20	
2003S	.(3,298,439)		1.50

"Westward Journey" Nickels

The Westward Journey Nickel Series™ (2004–2006) commemorates the bicentennial of the Louisiana Purchase and the journey of Meriwether Lewis and William Clark to explore that vast territory. **2004**—*Obverse:* traditional portrait of Jefferson. *Reverses:* Louisiana Purchase / Peace Medal reverse, by Mint sculptor Norman E. Nemeth. Keelboat reverse, by Mint sculptor Al Maletsky. **2005**—*Obverse:* new portrait of Jefferson, designed by Joe Fitzgerald after a 1789 marble bust by Jean-Antoine Houdon, and rendered by Mint sculptor Don Everhart. *Reverses:* American Bison reverse, designed by

Jamie Franki and produced by Norman E. Nemeth. "Ocean in View" reverse, designed by Joe Fitzgerald and produced by Mint sculptor Donna Weaver. **2006**—*Obverse:* facing portrait of Jefferson, designed by Jamie Franki and sculpted by Donna Weaver. *Reverse:* traditional depiction of Monticello.

2004 Obverse

Peace Medal

Keelboat

2005 Obverse

American Bison

Ocean in View

2006 Obverse

Monticello

Design used from 2006 to date.

	Mintage	MS-65	PF-65
2004P, Peace Medal	361,440,000	$0.25	
2004D, Peace Medal	372,000,000	0.25	
2004S, Peace Medal	(2,992,069)		$1.10
2004P, Keelboat	366,720,000	0.25	
2004D, Keelboat	344,880,000	0.25	
2004S, Keelboat	(2,992,069)		1.10
2005P, American Bison	448,320,000	0.25	
2005D, American Bison	487,680,000	0.25	
2005S, American Bison	(3,344,679)		1.10
2005P, Ocean in View	394,080,000	0.25	
2005D, Ocean in View	411,120,000	0.25	
2005S, Ocean in View	(3,344,679)		1.10
2006P, Monticello	693,120,000	0.25	
2006D, Monticello	809,280,000	0.25	
2006S, Monticello	(3,054,436)		1.10
2007P	571,680,000	0.20	
2007D	626,160,000	0.20	
2007S	(2,577,166)		1.10
2008P	279,840,000	0.20	
2008D	345,600,000	0.20	
2008S	(2,180,548)		1.10
2009P	39,840,000	0.20	
2009D	46,800,000	0.20	
2009S	(1,994,998)		1.10
2010P		0.20	
2010D		0.20	
2010S			1.10

The half dime types present the same general characteristics as larger United States silver coins. Authorized by the Act of April 2, 1792, they were not coined until February 1795, although dated 1794. At first the weight was 20.8 grains, and fineness .8924. By the Act of January 18, 1837, the weight was slightly reduced to 20-5/8 grains and the fineness changed to .900. Finally, the weight was reduced to 19.2 grains by the Act of February 21, 1853.

FLOWING HAIR (1794–1795)

AG-3 About Good: Details clear enough to identify.
G-4 Good: Eagle, wreath, bust outlined but lack details.
VG-8 Very Good: Some details on face. All lettering legible.
F-12 Fine: Hair ends visible. Hair at top smooth.
VF-20 Very Fine: Hair lines at top visible. Hair about ear defined.
EF-40 Extremely Fine: Hair above forehead and at neck well defined but shows some wear.
AU-50 About Uncirculated: Slight wear on high waves of hair, near ear and face, and on head and tips of eagle's wings.
MS-60 Uncirculated: No trace of wear. Light blemishes.
MS-63 Choice Uncirculated: Some distracting marks or blemishes in prime focal areas. Some impairment of luster possible.

Weakly struck Uncirculated coins are worth less than values shown.

	Mintage	AG-3	G-4	VG-8	F-12	VF-20	EF-40	AU-50	MS-60	MS-63
1794 86,416		$375	$750	$900	$1,250	$1,800	$3,500	$5,500	$9,500	$17,500
1795 . . . .*		250	600	700	900	1,500	2,500	3,500	6,750	11,000

* Included in number above.

DRAPED BUST (1796–1805)

AG-3 About Good: Details clear enough to identify.
G-4 Good: Date, stars, LIBERTY readable. Bust of Liberty outlined, but no details.
VG-8 Very Good: Some details visible.
F-12 Fine: Hair and drapery lines worn, but visible.
VF-20 Very Fine: Only left side of drapery indistinct.
EF-40 Extremely Fine: Details visible in all hair lines.
AU-50 About Uncirculated: Slight wear on bust, shoulder, and hair; wear on eagle's head and top of wings.
MS-60 Uncirculated: No trace of wear. Light blemishes.
MS-63 Choice Uncirculated: Some distracting marks or blemishes in prime focal areas. Impaired luster possible.

Small Eagle Reverse (1796–1797)

	Mintage	AG-3	G-4	VG-8	F-12	VF-20	EF-40	AU-50	MS-60	MS-63
1796, 6 Over 5 10,230		$250	$500	$625	$1,000	$1,800	$3,000	$5,500	$11,000	$20,000
1796 . . . .*		230	480	600	950	1,500	2,750	4,500	6,250	13,000
1796, LIBERTY . . . .*		230	480	600	950	1,500	2,750	4,500	6,500	15,000
1797, 15 Stars 44,527		230	480	600	950	1,500	2,750	4,000	6,250	12,000
1797, 16 Stars . . . .*		230	480	690	900	1,500	2,750	4,000	6,250	12,000
1797, 13 Stars . . . .*		230	500	700	1,000	1,650	3,400	5,500	13,000	17,000

* Included in number above.

Heraldic Eagle Reverse (1800–1805)

1800 LIBEKTY

	Mintage	AG-3	G-4	VG-8	F-12	VF-20	EF-40	AU-50	MS-60	MS-63
1800 24,000		$150	$300	$450	$700	$1,000	$1,500	$3,000	$4,500	$9,500
1800, LIBEKTY 16,000		150	300	450	700	1,000	1,500	3,000	4,500	9,500
1801 27,760		150	300	500	800	1,100	1,700	3,500	6,000	10,500
1802 3,060		8,000	12,000	16,000	27,000	45,000	80,000	—	—	—
1803 37,850		175	400	500	850	1,150	1,750	3,750	6,200	10,500
1805 15,600		175	400	500	850	1,500	2,600	7,500	—	—

CAPPED BUST (1829–1837)

G-4 Good: Bust of Liberty outlined, no detail. Date and legend legible.
VG-8 Very Good: Complete legend and date plain. At least three letters of LIBERTY on edge of cap show clearly.
F-12 Fine: All letters in LIBERTY visible.
VF-20 Very Fine: Full rims. Ear and shoulder clasp show plainly.
EF-40 Extremely Fine: Ear very distinct; eyebrow and hair well defined.
AU-50 About Uncirculated: Traces of light wear on many of the high points. At least half of mint luster still present.
MS-60 Uncirculated: No trace of wear. Light blemishes.
MS-63 Choice Uncirculated: No trace of wear. Light blemishes. Attractive mint luster.

	Mintage	G-4	VG-8	F-12	VF-20	EF-40	AU-50	MS-60	MS-63
1829 1,230,000		$18	$25	$30	$45	$75	$110	$185	$400
1830 1,240,000		18	25	30	45	75	110	185	400
1831 1,242,700		18	25	30	45	75	110	185	400
1832 965,000		18	25	30	45	75	110	185	400
1833 1,370,000		18	25	30	45	75	110	185	400
1834 1,480,000		18	25	30	45	75	110	185	400
1835 2,760,000		18	25	30	45	75	110	185	400
1836 1,900,000		18	25	30	45	75	110	185	400
1837, Small 5c 871,000		22	30	40	75	115	200	475	1,000
1837, Large 5c . . . .*		18	25	30	45	75	110	185	400

* Included in number above.

LIBERTY SEATED (1837–1873)

G-4 Good: LIBERTY on shield smooth. Date and letters legible.
VG-8 Very Good: At least three letters in LIBERTY visible.
F-12 Fine: Entire LIBERTY visible, weak spots.
VF-20 Very Fine: Entire LIBERTY strong and even.
EF-40 Extremely Fine: LIBERTY and scroll edges distinct.
AU-50 About Uncirculated: Traces of light wear on many of the high points. At least half of mint luster still present.
MS-60 Uncirculated: No trace of wear. Light blemishes.
MS-63 Choice Uncirculated: No trace of wear. Light blemishes. Attractive mint luster.

Variety 1 – No Stars on Obverse (1837–1838)

See next page for chart.

	Mintage	G-4	VG-8	F-12	VF-20	EF-40	AU-50	MS-60	MS-63
1837 1,405,000		$15	$20	$30	$60	$100	$175	$400	$500
18380, No Stars 70,000		35	60	100	200	325	500	850	3,400

Variety 2 – Stars on Obverse (1838–1853)

From 1838 through 1859 the mintmark is located above
the bow on the reverse. Large, medium, or small mintmark varieties occur for several dates.

	Mintage	G-4	VG-8	F-12	VF-20	EF-40	AU-50	MS-60	MS-63
1838 2,255,000		$7	$8	$11	$14	$30	$65	$150	$180
1839 1,069,150		7	8	11	14	30	65	150	180
18390 1,060,000		9	11	13	20	35	65	185	800
1840 1,344,085		7	8	11	14	30	65	150	180
18400 935,000		9	11	13	20	35	85	275	950
1841 1,150,000		7	8	11	14	30	65	100	125
18410 815,000		8	10	15	20	45	115	325	650
1842 815,000		7	8	13	16	32	65	90	125
18420 350,000		13	15	27	75	210	375	525	850
1843 1,165,000		7	8	11	14	30	65	90	130
1844 430,000		7	8	11	14	30	65	90	130
18440 220,000		32	45	85	225	485	1,450	2,400	6,000
1845 1,564,000		7	8	11	14	30	65	90	130
1846 27,000		100	160	300	400	1,100	2,200	6,000	9,500
1847 1,274,000		7	8	11	14	30	65	110	220
1848 668,000		7	8	11	14	30	65	100	130
18480 600,000		9	11	15	23	45	110	190	270
1849, 9 Over 6 . . . .*		10	12	16	23	45	110	200	600
1849, 9 Over 8 . . . .*		10	13	25	40	75	125	275	700
1849, Normal Date . .1,309,000		7	8	11	14	30	65	100	200
18490 140,000		12	17	33	90	200	400	1,000	1,900
1850 955,000		7	8	11	15	35	60	90	145
18500 690,000		8	10	13	21	45	135	325	700
1851 781,000		7	8	11	15	35	60	90	125
18510 860,000		8	10	12	18	45	100	225	350
1852 1,000,500		7	8	11	14	28	60	90	125
18520 260,000		12	17	27	55	110	210	385	775
1853, No Arrows 135,000		14	18	27	55	110	175	325	475
18530, No Arrows 160,000		80	125	160	300	650	1,200	2,600	5,500

* Included in number below.

Variety 3 – Arrows at Date (1853–1855)

As on the dimes, quarters, and halves, arrows were
placed at the sides of the date for a short period starting
in 1853 to denote the reduction of weight.

	Mintage	G-4	VG-8	F-12	VF-20	EF-40	AU-50	MS-60	MS-63	PF-63
1853 13,210,020		$7	$8	$10	$14	$30	$55	$110	$130	
18530 2,200,000		8	9	12	19	32	70	135	400	
1854 5,740,000		7	8	10	14	30	60	110	140	$4,000

	Mintage	G-4	VG-8	F-12	VF-20	EF-40	AU-50	MS-60	MS-63	PF-63
1854O	1,560,000	$8	$9	$11	$18	$30	$70	$135	$350	
1855	1,750,000	7	8	10	14	30	55	110	130	$3,500
1855O	600,000	7	10	11	24	80	110	275	485	

Variety 2 Resumed (1856–1859: Weight Standard of 1853)

 1858 Over Inverted Date

	Mintage	G-4	VG-8	F-12	VF-20	EF-40	AU-50	MS-60	MS-63	PF-63
1856	4,880,000	$7	$8	$9	$12	$25	$50	$80	$120	$2,000
1856O	1,100,000	7	8	10	20	40	100	210	450	
1857	7,280,000	7	8	9	12	25	50	80	120	1,750
1857O	1,380,000	7	8	10	16	30	80	175	210	
1858	3,500,000	7	8	9	12	25	50	80	120	750
1858, Over Inverted Date	*	15	20	30	50	95	150	300	600	
1858O	1,660,000	7	8	10	18	28	60	125	200	
1859	340,000	8	9	12	20	50	90	130	175	650
1859O	560,000	8	9	12	20	50	90	130	150	

* Included in number above.

Variety 4 – Legend on Obverse (1860–1873)

	Mintage	G-4	VG-8	F-12	VF-20	EF-40	AU-50	MS-60	MS-63	PF-63
1860	(1,000)	799,000	$7	$8	$10	$12	$19	$30	$75	$100	$300
1860O	1,060,000	7	8	10	12	19	35	100	135	
1861	(1,000)	3,360,000	7	8	10	12	19	30	75	100	300
1862	(550)	1,492,000	9	12	18	20	25	40	110	125	300
1863	(460)	18,000	60	70	95	125	200	270	300	400	350
1863S	100,000	11	15	18	21	60	160	350	450	
1864	(470)	48,000	110	175	210	275	400	500	550	600	350
1864S	90,000	18	20	35	50	110	180	310	700	
1865	(500)	13,000	100	125	180	210	275	300	400	600	350
1865S	120,000	11	15	18	22	60	200	450	850	
1866	(725)	10,000	100	115	150	200	300	320	375	600	320
1866S	120,000	10	15	18	22	60	180	200	400	
1867	(625)	8,000	175	200	250	300	350	400	475	620	350
1867S	120,000	9	13	18	25	60	140	210	500	
1868	(600)	88,600	20	25	40	70	120	200	300	400	350
1868S	280,000	7	9	11	13	19	40	125	250	
1869	(600)	208,000	7	9	11	13	19	60	120	150	300
1869S	230,000	7	9	11	13	19	50	150	350	
1870	(1,000)	535,000	7	9	10	11	19	30	70	120	300
1870S (unique)								—		
1871	(960)	1,873,000	7	9	10	11	19	30	70	120	300
1871S	161,000	8	11	15	25	40	75	135	210	
1872	(950)	2,947,000	7	9	10	11	19	30	70	120	300
1872S	837,000	7	9	10	11	19	30	70	120	
1873	(600)	7,126,000	7	9	10	11	19	30	70	120	300
1873S	324,000	7	9	10	11	19	30	70	120	

The designs of the dimes, first coined in 1796, followed closely those of the half dimes up through the Liberty Seated type. The dimes in each instance weigh twice as much as the half dimes.

DRAPED BUST (1796–1807)
Small Eagle Reverse (1796–1797)

AG-3 About Good: Details clear enough to identify.
G-4 Good: Date legible. Bust outlined, but no detail.
VG-8 Very Good: All but deepest drapery folds worn smooth. Hair lines nearly gone and curls lacking in detail.
F-12 Fine: All drapery lines visible. Hair partly worn.
VF-20 Very Fine: Only left side of drapery indistinct.
EF-40 Extremely Fine: Hair well outlined with details visible.
AU-50 About Uncirculated: Traces of light wear on many of the high points. At least half of mint luster still present.
MS-60 Uncirculated: No trace of wear. Light blemishes.
MS-63 Choice Uncirculated: Some distracting marks or blemishes in prime focal areas. Impaired luster possible.

1797, 16 Stars   **1797, 13 Stars**

	Mintage	AG-3	G-4	VG-8	F-12	VF-20	EF-40	AU-50	MS-60	MS-63
1796 22,135		$400	$900	$1,200	$1,700	$2,300	$4,000	$6,000	$8,000	$15,000
1797, All kinds 25,261										
1797, 16 Stars		400	900	1,200	1,700	2,500	4,100	6,250	9,000	17,500
1797, 13 Stars		400	900	1,200	1,700	2,500	4,100	6,250	9,000	17,500

Heraldic Eagle Reverse (1798–1807)

	Mintage	AG-3	G-4	VG-8	F-12	VF-20	EF-40	AU-50	MS-60	MS-63
1798, All kinds 27,550										
1798, 98 Over 97, 16 Stars on Reverse		$125	$275	$425	$500	$800	$1,250	$2,100	$3,200	$7,250
1798, 98 Over 97, 13 Stars on Reverse		250	700	1,000	1,500	2,500	3,500	—	—	
1798		125	225	300	425	650	1,100	1,600	2,700	7,000
1800 21,760		125	225	300	425	600	1,100	1,600	2,700	7,000
1801 34,640		125	250	300	500	1,200	2,100	3,750	7,000	14,000
1802 10,975		160	425	550	900	1,400	3,200	4,600	12,500	
1803 33,040		110	225	325	450	700	1,800	3,700	6,500	
1804 8,265		275	550	850	1,450	2,500	5,500	12,500	—	
1805 120,780		100	220	285	400	525	950	1,200	2,800	4,800
1807 165,000		100	220	285	400	525	950	1,200	2,800	4,750

CAPPED BUST (1809–1837)

G-4 Good: Date, letters, and stars discernible. Bust outlined, no details.
VG-8 Very Good: Legends and date plain. Some letters in LIBERTY visible.
F-12 Fine: Clear LIBERTY. Ear and shoulder clasp visible. Part of rim visible on both sides.
VF-20 Very Fine: LIBERTY distinct. Full rim. Ear and clasp plain and distinct.
EF-40 Extremely Fine: LIBERTY sharp. Ear distinct. Hair above eye well defined.
AU-50 About Uncirculated: Traces of light wear on only the high points of the design. Half of mint luster present.
MS-60 Uncirculated: No trace of wear. Light blemishes.
MS-63 Choice Uncirculated: Some distracting marks or blemishes in prime focal areas. Impaired luster possible.

Variety 1 – Wide Border (1809–1828)

| | 1823, 3 Over 2 | 1824, 4 Over 2 | | 1828, Large Date | 1828, Small Date |

	Mintage	G-4	VG-8	F-12	VF-20	EF-40	AU-50	MS-60	MS-63
1809	.51,065	$55	$85	$150	$250	$550	$850	$1,900	$2,900
1811, 11 Over 09	.65,180	40	60	125	225	500	800	1,700	2,750
1814	.421,500	14	17	28	70	200	275	500	1,200
1820	.942,587	14	17	25	60	200	275	500	1,200
1821	.1,186,512	14	17	25	60	200	275	500	1,200
1822	.100,000	175	300	500	750	1,400	2,400	5,000	8,500
1823, 3 Over 2, All kinds	.440,000								
1823, 3 Over 2, Small E's		14	17	25	60	200	275	550	1,100
1823, 3 Over 2, Large E's		14	17	25	60	200	275	550	1,100
1824, 4 Over 2	.510,000	15	20	40	140	300	600	1,000	1,800
1825	.*	14	17	20	50	175	275	500	1,100
1827	.1,215,000	14	17	20	50	175	275	500	1,100
1828, Large Date, Curl Base 2	.125,000	17	30	50	140	300	600	1,000	1,800

* Included in number above.

Variety 2 – Modified Design (1828–1837)

| | 1829, Small 10c | 1829, Large 10c | | 1830, 30 Over 29 |

	Mintage	G-4	VG-8	F-12	VF-20	EF-40	AU-50	MS-60	MS-63
1828, Sm Date, Square Base 2	.*	$14	$18	$30	$65	$200	$325	$625	$1,100
1829, Small 10c	.770,000	13	15	18	35	120	180	400	750
1829, Medium 10c	.*	13	15	18	35	120	180	350	650
1829, Large 10c	.*	13	16	22	50	135	200	400	675
1830, 30 Over 29	.510,000	14	25	45	90	250	275	500	1,100

* Included in number above.

Chart continued on next page.

	Mintage	G-4	VG-8	F-12	VF-20	EF-40	AU-50	MS-60	MS-63
1830, Large 10c . . . .*	$13	$15	$18	$35	$120	$180	$350	$675
1830, Small 10c . . . .*	13	15	18	35	120	180	350	675
1831 771,350	13	15	18	35	120	180	350	675
1832 522,500	13	15	18	35	120	180	350	675
1833 485,000	13	15	18	35	120	180	350	675
1834 635,000	13	15	18	35	120	180	350	675
1835 1,410,000	13	15	18	35	120	180	350	675
1836 1,190,000	13	15	18	35	120	180	350	675
1837 359,500	13	15	18	35	120	180	350	675

* Included in mintage for 1830, 30 Over 29 (previous page).

LIBERTY SEATED (1837–1891)
Variety 1 – No Stars on Obverse (1837–1838)

G-4 Good: LIBERTY on shield smooth. Date and letters legible.
F-12 Fine: LIBERTY visible, weak spots.
VF-20 Very Fine: LIBERTY strong and even.
EF-40 Extremely Fine: LIBERTY and scroll edges distinct.
AU-50 About Uncirculated: Wear on Liberty's shoulder and hair high points.
MS-60 Uncirculated: No trace of wear. Light blemishes.
MS-63 Choice Uncirculated: Some distracting marks or blemishes in focal areas. Impaired luster possible.

No Drapery From Elbow
No Stars on Obverse

Mintmarks on Liberty Seated dimes on reverse, within or below the wreath. Size of mintmark varies on many dates.

	Mintage	G-4	F-12	VF-20	EF-40	AU-50	MS-60	MS-63
1837 682,500	$18	$35	$125	$220	$325	$600	$850
1838O 406,034	21	60	160	300	550	1,300	3,000

Variety 2 – Stars on Obverse (1838–1853)

No Drapery From Elbow, Tilted Shield (1838–1840)

1838, Small Stars   **1838, Large Stars**

Drapery From Elbow, Upright Shield (1840–1891)

	Mintage	G-4	F-12	VF-20	EF-40	AU-50	MS-60	MS-63
1838, All kinds 1,992,500							
1838, Small Stars	$9	$18	$35	$70	$175	$400	$600
1838, Large Stars	8	11	14	40	100	150	350
1838, Partial Drapery	9	18	35	75	210	425	1,000
1839 .1,053,115	8	11	14	40	100	150	350
1839O 1,291,600	9	13	16	45	120	175	500
1840, No Drapery 981,500	8	11	14	40	100	150	350
1840O, No Drapery 1,175,000	9	13	20	50	120	475	950
1840, Drapery 377,500	13	30	55	125	170	425	2,200

	Mintage	G-4	F-12	VF-20	EF-40	AU-50	MS-60	MS-63
1841	1,622,500	$8	$11	$14	$20	$50	$135	$250
1841O	2,007,500	9	13	15	28	90	425	900
1842	1,887,500	8	11	14	20	50	135	250
1842O	2,020,000	9	13	17	100	500	1,300	2,600
1843	1,370,000	8	11	14	20	50	135	300
1843O	150,000	16	45	100	250	800	2,000	—
1844	72,500	100	225	350	600	800	1,400	4,000
1845	1,755,000	8	11	14	20	50	135	300
1845O	230,000	9	20	80	185	475	1,300	—
1846	31,300	30	75	150	400	900	1,800	6,500
1847	245,000	9	16	27	55	120	400	1,000
1848	451,500	8	11	16	35	60	210	400
1849	839,000	8	11	14	20	50	150	425
1849O	300,000	8	17	50	110	300	1,000	2,400
1850	1,931,500	8	11	14	20	50	125	300
1850O	510,000	9	13	33	65	150	425	975
1851	1,026,500	8	11	14	20	50	160	325
1851O	400,000	9	17	35	100	175	1,000	1,400
1852	1,535,500	8	11	14	20	50	150	300
1852O	430,000	10	20	50	100	175	800	1,300
1853, No Arrows	95,000	22	55	90	150	225	375	400

Variety 3 – Arrows at Date (1853–1855)

Arrows at Date (1853–1855)

	Mintage	G-4	F-12	VF-20	EF-40	AU-50	MS-60	MS-63	PF-63
1853, With Arrows	12,078,010	$7	$8	$12	$22	$60	$150	$300	
1853O	1,100,000	7	8	17	45	120	475	1,300	
1854	4,470,000	7	8	12	22	60	150	300	$5,250
1854O	1,770,000	7	8	13	35	75	285	500	
1855	2,075,000	7	8	12	22	60	175	400	5,250

Variety 2 Resumed (1856–1860)

Small Date, Arrows Removed (1856–1860)

	Mintage	G-4	F-12	VF-20	EF-40	AU-50	MS-60	MS-63	PF-63
1856, All kinds	5,780,000								
1856, Large Date		$7	$8	$11	$18	$40	$140	$275	
1856, Small Date		7	8	11	18	40	140	275	$1,800
1856O	1,180,000	7	8	11	24	90	300	650	
1856S	70,000	40	130	225	425	650	1,450	—	

Chart continued on next page.

	Mintage	G-4	F-12	VF-20	EF-40	AU-50	MS-60	MS-63	PF-63
1857	5,580,000	$7	$8	$10	$18	$40	$135	$275	$1,800
1857O	1,540,000	7	8	11	18	70	190	275	
1858 . . . . (300+) . . .	1,540,000	7	8	10	18	40	135	275	900
1858O	290,000	8	15	35	75	125	300	450	
1858S	60,000	35	90	160	350	650	1,450		
1859 . . . . (800+) . . .	429,200	7	8	11	25	50	135	275	700
1859O	480,000	7	9	18	37	100	180	375	
1859S	60,000	35	110	175	450	850	4,000		
1860S	140,000	12	20	50	125	350	950	1,800	

Variety 4 – Legend on Obverse (1860–1873)

	Mintage	G-4	F-12	VF-20	EF-40	AU-50	MS-60	MS-63	PF-63
1860 . . . . (1,000) . . .	606,000	$7	$8	$10	$18	$40	$135	$250	$400
1860O	40,000	155	350	675	1,600	2,500	5,500	—	
1861 . . . . (1,000) . .	1,883,000	7	8	10	18	40	100	180	400
1861S	172,500	13	40	80	160	210	600	1,800	
1862 . . . . (550) . . .	847,000	7	8	10	16	25	100	120	350
1862S	180,750	11	21	50	100	125	600	1,000	
1863 . . . . (460) . . .	14,000	100	200	300	350	400	550	600	400
1863S	157,500	11	20	40	70	125	450	1,200	
1864 . . . . (470) . . .	11,000	80	170	210	350	425	550	600	400
1864S	230,000	8	17	32	60	110	500	550	
1865 . . . . (500) . . .	10,000	75	200	250	310	375	525	600	400
1865S	175,000	8	17	32	100	250	800	1,900	
1866 . . . . (725) . . .	8,000	120	235	375	400	600	700	800	400
1866S	135,000	11	20	40	100	135	550	1,100	
1867 . . . . (625) . . .	6,000	175	275	400	475	550	675	800	450
1867S	140,000	9	20	40	100	220	600	900	
1868 . . . . (600) . . .	464,000	7	8	16	31	60	175	375	300
1868S	260,000	7	13	30	50	75	185	450	
1869 . . . . (600) . . .	256,000	7	13	25	40	70	185	400	300
1869S	450,000	7	11	17	35	65	185	375	
1870 . . . . (1,000) . . .	470,500	7	8	11	18	40	110	200	300
1870S	50,000	100	150	200	280	350	750	1,000	
1871 . . . . (960) . . .	906,750	7	8	11	15	65	140	180	300
1871CC	20,100	450	1,250	2,000	4,000	8,500	—	—	
1871S	320,000	7	8	11	15	65	110	200	
1872 . . . . (950) . .	2,395,500	7	8	11	13	35	75	110	300
1872CC	35,480	200	600	1,400	2,800	7,000	—	—	
1872S	190,000	10	35	50	95	175	500	1,000	
1873, Close 3 (1,100) .	1,506,900	7	8	11	13	30	100	125	300
1873, Open 3	60,000	9	20	30	60	90	195	550	
1873CC (unique)	12,400							—	

Variety 5 – Arrows at Date (1873–1874)

In 1873, the dime was increased in weight from 2.49 grams to 2.50 grams. Arrows at the date in 1873 and 1874 indicate this change.

	Mintage	G-4	F-12	VF-20	EF-40	AU-50	MS-60	MS-63	PF-63
1873 . . . . . . (800) . . .2,377,700		$7	$11	$22	$55	$120	$275	$450	$700
1873CC 18,791		400	1,400	3,200	7,500	14,000	—	—	
1873S 455,000		8	16	28	65	175	450	950	
1874 . . . . . . (700) . . .2,939,300		7	11	22	55	125	285	450	700
1874CC 10,817		1,200	2,750	5,750	9,000	15,000	—		
1874S 240,000		11	27	45	90	220	400	900	

Variety 4 Resumed (1875–1891)

	Mintage	G-4	F-12	VF-20	EF-40	AU-50	MS-60	MS-63	PF-63
1875 . . . . . . (700) . .10,350,000		$6	$7	$9	$13	$30	$75	$110	$250
1875CC 4,645,000		6	7	10	15	32	125	185	
1875S 9,070,000		6	7	9	13	30	75	110	
1876 . . . .(1,150) . .11,450,000		6	7	9	13	30	75	110	250
1876CC 8,270,000		6	7	9	15	32	100	175	
1876S 10,420,000		6	7	9	13	30	75	110	
1877 . . . . . . (510) . .7,310,000		6	7	9	13	30	75	110	275
1877CC 7,700,000		6	7	9	13	30	100	160	
1877S 2,340,000		6	7	9	13	30	75	110	
1878 . . . . . . (800) . . .1,677,200		6	7	9	13	30	80	110	250
1878CC 200,000		20	50	75	150	200	450	700	
1879 . . . .(1,100) 14,000		70	120	180	210	275	325	350	250
1880 . . . .(1,355) 36,000		50	100	125	175	225	275	350	250
1881 . . . . . . (975) 24,000		50	100	125	175	225	300	350	250
1882 . . . .(1,100) . . .3,910,000		6	7	9	13	30	75	110	250
1883 . . . .(1,039) . . .7,674,673		6	7	9	13	30	75	110	250
1884 . . . . . . (875) . . .3,365,505		6	7	9	13	30	75	110	250
1884S 564,969		9	13	20	35	110	325	575	
1885 . . . . . . (930) . . .2,532,497		6	7	9	13	30	75	110	250
1885S 43,690		150	335	600	1,000	2,000	2,600	4,200	
1886 . . . . . . (886) . .6,376,684		6	7	9	13	30	75	110	250
1886S 206,524		10	20	30	50	90	275	500	
1887 . . . . . . (710) . .11,283,229		6	7	9	13	30	75	110	250
1887S 4,454,450		6	7	9	13	30	75	110	
1888 . . . . . . (832) . .5,495,655		6	7	9	13	30	75	110	250
1888S 1,720,000		6	7	9	15	40	120	300	
1889 . . . . . . (711) . .7,380,000		6	7	9	13	30	75	110	250
1889S 972,678		7	10	20	35	60	200	400	
1890 . . . . . . (590) . . .9,910,951		6	7	9	13	30	75	110	250
1890S 1,423,076		7	9	17	30	60	135	275	
1891 . . . . . . (600) . .15,310,000		6	7	9	13	30	75	110	275
18910 4,540,000		6	7	9	15	40	110	150	
1891S 3,196,116		6	7	9	13	35	100	125	

BARBER OR LIBERTY HEAD (1892–1916)

This type was designed by Charles E. Barber, chief engraver of the Mint. His initial B is at the truncation of the neck. He also designed the quarters and half dollars of the same period.

G-4 Good: Date and letters plain. LIBERTY obliterated.
VG-8 Very Good: Some letters visible in LIBERTY.
F-12 Fine: Letters in LIBERTY visible, though some weak.
VF-20 Very Fine: Letters of LIBERTY evenly plain.
EF-40 Extremely Fine: All letters in LIBERTY sharp, distinct. Headband edges distinct.
AU-50 About Uncirculated: Slight traces of wear on hair cheekbone and on leaf tips in wreath.
MS-60 Uncirculated: No trace of wear. Light blemishes.
MS-63 Choice Uncirculated: Some distracting blemishes in prime focal areas. Impaired luster possible.

Mintmark location is on reverse, below wreath.

Mintage	G-4	VG-8	F-12	VF-20	EF-40	AU-50	MS-60	MS-63	PF-63
1892 . . . . .(1,245) . .12,120,000	$2.00	$4.00	$9	$14	$16.00	$35	$80	$120	$300
1892O 3,841,700	5.00	7.00	15	24	35.00	45	100	175	
1892S 990,710	35.00	45.00	85	125	160.00	180	240	400	
1893, 3/2 . . . .*					120.00	160	350	1,000	525
1893 . . . . . .(792) . .3,339,940	4.00	6.00	10	15	24.00	35	100	140	300
1893O 1,760,000	15.00	25.00	65	80	90.00	125	175	350	
1893S 2,491,401	7.00	14.00	18	25	40.00	75	150	375	
1894 . . . . . .(972) . .1,330,000	8.00	20.00	55	75	90.00	100	175	350	300
1894O 720,000	30.00	45.00	100	150	210.00	360	825	1,400	
1894S 24							600,000		
1895 . . . . . .(880) 690,000	35.00	45.00	100	250	290.00	325	400	810	335
1895O 440,000	180.00	210.00	450	720	1,400.00	1,700	3,000	4,250	
1895S 1,120,000	20.00	30.00	75	100	125.00	175	300	625	
1896 . . . . . .(762) . .2,000,000	4.00	10.00	28	36	50.00	60	100	275	300
1896O 610,000	35.00	75.00	160	200	280.00	325	575	1,300	
1896S 575,056	40.00	70.00	150	200	275.00	310	500	825	
1897 . . . . . .(731) . .10,868,533	1.50	1.75	3	5	12.00	22	80	125	300
1897O 666,000	35.00	50.00	140	200	250.00	325	500	950	
1897S 1,342,844	8.00	16.00	50	75	90.00	125	250	650	
1898 . . . . . .(735) . .16,320,000	1.50	1.75	3	6	12.00	30	65	100	300
1898O 2,130,000	3.00	4.00	30	60	80.00	120	275	650	
1898S 1,702,507	2.00	5.00	16	25	40.00	75	180	600	
1899 . . . . . .(846) . .19,580,000	1.50	1.75	3	6	12.50	30	65	100	300
1899O 2,650,000	4.50	6.00	35	45	70.00	100	210	575	
1899S 1,867,493	4.00	4.50	8	16	20.00	55	160	425	
1900 . . . . . .(912) . .17,600,000	1.50	1.75	3	6	12.00	30	65	100	300

* Included in number below.

	Mintage	G-4	VG-8	F-12	VF-20	EF-40	AU-50	MS-60	MS-63	PF-63
19000	2,010,000	$8.00	$20.00	$45	$50.00	$120	$160	$320	$500	
1900S	5,168,270	1.75	2.00	5	7.00	13	35	120	220	
1901 ......(813)	18,859,665	1.50	1.75	3	6.00	12	32	65	100	$300
19010	5,620,000	1.75	2.00	5	9.00	30	50	250	460	
1901S	593,022	45.00	70.00	185	250.00	300	350	635	875	
1902 ......(777)	21,380,000	1.40	1.50	2	4.00	12	30	65	100	300
19020	4,500,000	1.70	2.00	6	12.00	25	50	180	450	
1902S	2,070,000	3.00	6.00	18	30.00	45	70	180	450	
1903 ......(755)	19,500,000	1.40	1.50	2	4.00	12	30	65	100	300
19030	8,180,000	1.75	2.10	7	9.00	18	35	160	295	
1903S	613,300	40.00	60.00	200	250.00	400	500	750	1,000	
1904 ......(670)	14,600,357	1.40	1.50	2	4.00	12	30	65	90	300
1904S	800,000	20.00	35.00	75	100.00	150	250	425	850	
1905 ......(727)	14,551,623	1.40	1.50	2	4.00	12	30	65	90	300
19050	3,400,000	1.75	3.00	13	25.00	50	75	150	250	
1905S	6,855,199	1.50	2.00	4	7.00	18	40	140	200	
1906 ......(675)	19,957,731	1.40	1.50	2	5.00	12	30	65	90	300
1906D	4,060,000	1.50	2.00	4	8.00	13	32	95	200	
19060	2,610,000	2.00	5.00	20	35.00	45	65	120	175	
1906S	3,136,640	1.50	2.00	5	10.00	16	50	125	210	
1907 ......(575)	22,220,000	1.40	1.50	2	4.00	12	30	65	90	300
1907D	4,080,000	1.50	2.50	5	8.00	18	60	150	475	
19070	5,058,000	1.50	3.50	15	18.00	24	45	100	185	
1907S	3,178,470	1.50	2.50	6	12.00	20	45	200	400	
1908 ......(545)	10,600,000	1.40	1.50	2	4.00	12	30	65	90	300
1908D	7,490,000	1.40	1.50	4	6.00	14	35	70	150	
19080	1,789,000	1.75	5.00	22	35.00	50	80	150	275	
1908S	3,220,000	1.50	3.00	6	8.00	16	75	175	350	
1909 ......(650)	10,240,000	1.40	1.50	2	3.50	12	30	65	90	300
1909D	954,000	3.50	10.00	35	50.00	75	100	275	600	
19090	2,287,000	1.75	3.00	6	10.00	20	60	120	275	
1909S	1,000,000	3.00	8.50	40	50.00	90	165	275	650	
1910 ......(551)	11,520,000	1.40	1.50	2	3.50	12	30	65	90	300
1910D	3,490,000	1.75	3.00	5	6.00	18	45	125	225	
1910S	1,240,000	2.00	4.00	21	34.00	60	90	250	370	
1911 ......(543)	18,870,000	1.50	1.75	2	3.50	12	30	65	90	300
1911D	11,209,000	1.40	1.50	2	3.50	12	30	65	90	
1911S	3,520,000	1.50	3.00	8	8.00	16	45	120	220	
1912 ......(700)	19,349,300	1.40	1.50	2	3.50	12	30	65	90	300
1912D	11,760,000	1.40	1.50	2	3.50	12	30	65	100	
1912S	3,420,000	1.75	3.00	5	8.00	16	50	100	165	
1913 ......(622)	19,760,000	1.40	1.50	2	3.50	12	30	65	90	300
1913S	510,000	9.00	18.00	45	80.00	125	175	260	375	
1914 ......(425)	17,360,230	1.40	1.50	2	3.50	12	30	65	90	300
1914D	11,908,000	1.40	1.50	2	3.50	12	30	65	90	
1914S	2,100,000	1.40	2.10	6	8.00	12	30	110	190	
1915 ......(450)	5,620,000	1.40	1.50	2	3.50	12	30	65	90	300
1915S	960,000	2.00	3.00	15	20.00	30	65	140	275	
1916	18,490,000	1.40	1.50	2	3.50	12	30	65	90	
1916S	5,820,000	1.40	1.50	2	3.50	12	30	65	90	

WINGED LIBERTY HEAD
OR "MERCURY" (1916–1945)

Although this coin is commonly called the *Mercury* dime, the main device is in fact a representation of Liberty. The wings crowning her cap are intended to symbolize liberty of thought. The designer's monogram AW is at the right of the neck.

G-4 Good: Letters and date clear. Lines and bands in fasces obliterated.
VG-8 Very Good: Half of sticks discernible in fasces.
F-12 Fine: All sticks in fasces defined. Diagonal bands worn nearly flat.
VF-20 Very Fine: Diagonal bands definitely visible.
EF-40 Extremely Fine: Only slight wear on diagonal bands. Braids and hair before ear clearly visible.
AU-50 About Uncirculated: Slight trace of wear. Most mint luster present.
MS-63 Choice Uncirculated: No trace of wear. Light blemishes. Attractive mint luster.
MS-65 Gem Uncirculated: Only light, scattered marks that are not distracting. Strong luster, good eye appeal.

Mintmark location is on reverse, left of fasces.

Uncirculated values shown are for average pieces with minimum blemishes; those with sharp strikes and split bands on reverse are worth much more.

	Mintage	G-4	VG-8	F-12	VF-20	EF-40	MS_60	MS-63	MS-65
1916	22,180,080	$1.50	$2.10	$3.50	$4.25	$5.50	$18	$24	$50
1916D	264,000	500.00	800.00	1,200.00	1,600.00	2,750.00	8,000	9,000	16,000
1916S	10,450,000	3.00	4.00	5.00	6.00	10.00	20	35	125
1917	55,230,000	1.30	1.40	1.75	3.00	4.00	15	26	85
1917D	9,402,000	2.25	3.25	5.00	8.00	22.00	65	180	700
1917S	27,330,000	1.30	1.40	3.00	3.50	6.00	30	90	250
1918	26,680,000	1.30	1.40	3.00	6.00	13.00	40	90	225
1918D	22,674,800	1.30	1.40	3.00	6.00	12.00	55	120	250
1918S	19,300,000	1.30	1.40	2.00	5.00	8.50	45	150	375
1919	35,740,000	1.30	1.40	1.75	3.00	6.00	22	55	175
1919D	9,939,000	1.30	1.40	4.00	10.00	20.00	110	250	1,000
1919S	8,850,000	1.30	1.40	3.00	8.00	20.00	110	270	650
1920	59,030,000	1.30	1.40	1.50	3.50	5.00	27	35	150
1920D	19,171,000	1.30	1.40	2.00	6.00	11.00	85	220	450
1920S	13,820,000	1.30	1.40	2.00	6.00	10.00	65	175	650
1921	1,230,000	30.00	40.00	80.00	175.00	300.00	650	900	1,700
1921D	1,080,000	35.00	70.00	100.00	200.00	400.00	675	1,000	1,750
1923	50,130,000	1.30	1.40	1.75	3.00	4.00	15	25	65
1923S	6,440,000	1.30	1.40	4.00	8.00	32.00	80	220	600
1924	24,010,000	1.30	1.40	1.75	3.00	7.00	23	60	120
1924D	6,810,000	1.30	1.40	3.50	8.00	26.00	95	280	600
1924S	7,120,000	1.30	1.40	3.00	5.00	24.00	90	290	625
1925	25,610,000	1.30	1.40	1.75	3.00	4.50	28	45	125
1925D	5,117,000	2.50	3.25	6.00	22.00	60.00	180	425	950
1925S	5,850,000	1.30	1.40	3.00	7.00	30.00	90	275	800
1926	32,160,000	1.30	1.40	1.50	3.00	4.50	25	35	130
1926D	6,828,000	1.30	1.40	3.00	6.00	17.00	60	150	350
1926S	1,520,000	3.50	6.25	12.00	32.00	140.00	600	850	1,800
1927	28,080,000	1.30	1.40	1.75	3.00	4.00	13	32	80
1927D	4,812,000	1.30	1.40	3.00	12.00	35.00	110	225	725

	Mintage	G-4	VG-8	F-12	VF-20	EF-40	MS-60	MS-63	MS-65
1927S	4,770,000	$1.30	$1.40	$2.00	$4.00	$15.00	$120	$275	$800
1928	19,480,000	1.30	1.40	1.75	3.00	4.50	25	30	70
1928D	4,161,000	1.30	1.40	4.00	10.00	24.00	85	180	475
1928S	7,400,000	1.30	1.40	1.75	2.50	8.00	35	160	265
1929	25,970,000	1.30	1.40	1.75	2.00	3.00	13	20	40
1929D	5,034,000	1.30	1.40	1.75	4.00	8.00	17	22	40
1929S	4,730,000	1.30	1.40	1.75	2.50	5.00	18	25	60
1930	6,770,000	1.30	1.40	1.75	2.50	4.00	15	25	60
1930S	1,843,000	1.30	1.40	3.00	3.80	8.00	30	65	110
1931	3,150,000	1.30	1.40	1.75	3.00	5.00	20	40	80
1931D	1,260,000	4.00	5.00	7.00	11.00	18.00	48	75	140
1931S	1,800,000	2.00	2.50	3.00	5.00	8.50	38	75	150

	Mintage	VG-8	F-12	VF-20	EF-40	MS-60	MS-63	MS-65	PF-63
1934	24,080,000	$1.30	$1.30	$1.40	$1.40	$10.00	$15	$25	
1934D	6,772,000	1.30	1.30	1.40	1.40	20.00	30	45	
1935	58,830,000	1.30	1.30	1.40	1.40	6.50	9	18	
1935D	10,477,000	1.30	1.30	1.40	1.40	20.00	25	50	
1935S	15,840,000	1.30	1.30	1.40	1.40	12.00	16	25	
1936	(4,130) 87,500,000	1.30	1.30	1.40	1.40	5.00	12	16	$1,200
1936D	16,132,000	1.30	1.30	1.40	1.40	14.00	20	30	
1936S	9,210,000	1.30	1.30	1.40	1.40	12.00	15	22	
1937	(5,756) 56,860,000	1.30	1.30	1.40	1.40	4.00	9	15	425
1937D	14,146,000	1.30	1.30	1.40	1.40	14.00	16	24	
1937S	9,740,000	1.30	1.30	1.40	1.40	12.00	15	22	
1938	(8,728) 22,190,000	1.30	1.30	1.40	1.40	7.00	9	15	250
1938D	5,537,000	1.30	1.30	1.40	1.40	9.00	10	16	
1938S	8,090,000	1.30	1.30	1.40	1.40	8.00	9	15	
1939	(9,321) 67,740,000	1.30	1.30	1.40	1.40	4.50	8	12	225
1939D	24,394,000	1.30	1.30	1.40	1.40	4.50	8	14	
1939S	10,540,000	1.30	1.30	1.40	1.40	12.00	15	25	
1940	(11,827) 65,350,000	1.30	1.30	1.40	1.40	4.50	7	15	210
1940D	21,198,000	1.30	1.30	1.40	1.40	4.50	9	16	
1940S	21,560,000	1.30	1.30	1.40	1.40	4.50	8	16	
1941	(16,557) 175,090,000	1.30	1.30	1.40	1.40	4.50	7	15	200
1941D	45,634,000	1.30	1.30	1.40	1.40	4.50	9	16	
1941S	43,090,000	1.30	1.30	1.40	1.40	4.50	8	16	
1942, 2 Over 1	*	275.00	375.00	400.00	500.00	1,200.00	2,200	8,500	
1942	(22,329) 205,410,000	1.30	1.30	1.40	1.40	4.50	7	15	200
1942D, 2 Over 1	*	275.00	375.00	400.00	500.00	1,200.00	2,400	4,500	
1942D	60,740,000	1.30	1.30	1.40	1.40	5.50	9	16	
1942S	49,300,000	1.30	1.30	1.40	1.40	6.50	9	16	
1943	191,710,000	1.30	1.30	1.40	1.40	4.50	6	15	
1943D	71,949,000	1.30	1.30	1.40	1.40	5.50	7	16	
1943S	60,400,000	1.30	1.30	1.40	1.40	5.50	7	15	
1944	231,410,000	1.30	1.30	1.40	1.40	4.50	6	15	
1944D	62,224,000	1.30	1.30	1.40	1.40	4.50	6	15	
1944S	49,490,000	1.30	1.30	1.40	1.40	4.50	6	15	
1945	159,130,000	1.30	1.30	1.40	1.40	4.50	6	15	
1945D	40,245,000	1.30	1.30	1.40	1.40	4.50	6	16	
1945S	41,920,000	1.30	1.30	1.40	1.40	4.50	7	16	
1945S, Micro S	*	1.30	1.30	1.40	1.50	9.00	15	45	

*Included in regular mintage.

91

ROOSEVELT (1946 TO DATE)

John R. Sinnock (whose initials JS are at the truncation of the neck) designed this dime showing a portrait of Franklin D. Roosevelt. The design has heavier lettering and a more modernistic character than preceding types.

VF-20 Very Fine: Moderate wear on high points of design. All major details are clear.

EF-40 Extremely Fine: All lines of torch, flame, and hair very plain.

MS-63 Choice Uncirculated: Some distracting contact marks or blemishes in prime focal areas. Impaired luster possible.

MS-65 Gem Uncirculated: Only light, non-distracting scattered marks. Strong luster, good eye appeal.

PF-65 Gem Proof: Nearly perfect.

Mintmark on reverse, 1946–1964. *Mintmark on obverse, starting 1968.*

Silver Coinage (1946–1964)

	Mintage	VF-20	EF-40	MS-63	MS-65	PF-65
1946	255,250,000	$1.20	$1.20	$1.50	$6.00	
1946D	61,043,500	1.20	1.20	1.50	7.00	
1946S	27,900,000	1.20	1.20	2.25	10.00	
1947	121,520,000	1.20	1.20	3.00	6.00	
1947D	46,835,000	1.20	1.20	3.25	6.00	
1947S	34,840,000	1.20	1.20	3.00	6.00	
1948	74,950,000	1.20	1.20	2.00	6.00	
1948D	52,841,000	1.20	1.20	3.00	6.00	
1948S	35,520,000	1.20	1.20	2.75	6.00	
1949	30,940,000	1.20	1.20	12.50	16.00	
1949D	26,034,000	1.20	1.20	5.00	9.00	
1949S	13,510,000	1.20	1.20	20.00	25.00	
1950	(51,386) 50,130,114	1.20	1.20	6.00	7.00	$25
1950D	46,803,000	1.20	1.20	3.00	6.00	
1950S	20,440,000	1.20	1.20	18.00	22.00	
1951	(57,500) 103,880,102	1.20	1.20	1.50	5.00	25
1951D	56,529,000	1.20	1.20	1.50	5.00	
1951S	31,630,000	1.20	1.20	6.00	10.00	
1952	(81,980) 99,040,093	1.20	1.20	1.50	5.00	16
1952D	122,100,000	1.20	1.20	1.50	3.00	
1952S	44,419,500	1.20	1.20	4.00	6.00	
1953	(128,800) 53,490,120	1.20	1.20	4.00	6.00	
1953D	136,433,000	1.20	1.20	1.50	4.00	
1953S	39,180,000	1.20	1.20	1.50	4.00	
1954	(233,300) 114,010,203	1.20	1.20	1.50	4.00	10
1954D	106,397,000	1.20	1.20	1.50	4.00	
1954S	22,860,000	1.20	1.20	1.50	4.00	
1955	(378,200) 12,450,181	1.20	1.20	1.50	5.00	8
1955D	13,959,000	1.20	1.20	1.50	4.00	
1955S	18,510,000	1.20	1.20	1.50	4.00	
1956	(669,384) 108,640,000	1.20	1.20	1.50	4.00	2
1956D	108,015,100	1.20	1.20	1.50	3.50	
1957	(1,247,952) 160,160,000	1.20	1.20	1.50	3.50	2

	Mintage	VF-20	EF-40	MS-63	MS-65	PF-65
1957D	.113,354,330	$1.20	$1.20	$1.50	$3.25	
1958	(875,652)....31,910,000	1.20	1.20	1.50	4.00	$2
1958D	.136,564,600	1.20	1.20	1.50	4.00	
1959	(1,149,291)...85,780,000	1.20	1.20	1.50	3.50	2
1959D	.164,919,790	1.20	1.20	1.50	3.50	
1960	(1,691,602)....70,390,000	1.20	1.20	1.50	3.50	2
1960D	.200,160,400	1.20	1.20	1.50	3.00	
1961	(3,028,244)....93,730,000	1.20	1.20	1.50	3.00	2
1961D	.209,146,550	1.20	1.20	1.50	3.00	
1962	(3,218,019)....72,450,000	1.20	1.20	1.50	3.00	2
1962D	.334,948,380	1.20	1.20	1.50	3.00	
1963	(3,075,645)...123,650,000	1.20	1.20	1.50	3.00	2
1963D	.421,476,530	1.20	1.20	1.50	3.00	
1964	(3,950,762)...929,360,000	1.20	1.20	1.50	3.00	2
1964D	.1,357,517,180	1.20	1.20	1.50	3.00	

Clad Coinage and Silver Proofs (1965 to Date)

	Mintage	MS-63	MS-65	PF-65
1965	.1,652,140,570	$0.15	$0.75	
1966	.1,382,734,540	0.15	0.65	
1967	.2,244,007,320	0.15	0.50	
1968	.424,470,400	0.15	0.50	
1968D	.480,748,280	0.15	0.50	
1968S	(3,041,506)			$0.50
1969	.145,790,000	0.25	0.50	
1969D	.563,323,870	0.15	0.20	
1969S	(2,394,631)			0.50
1970	.345,570,000	0.15	0.25	
1970D	.754,942,100	0.15	0.25	
1970S	(2,632,810)			0.50
1971	.162,690,000	0.18	0.30	
1971D	.377,914,240	0.16	0.20	
1971S	(3,220,733)			0.50
1972	.431,540,000	0.15	0.25	
1972D	.330,290,000	0.15	0.25	
1972S	(3,260,996)			0.50
1973	.315,670,000	0.15	0.25	
1973D	.455,032,426	0.15	0.25	
1973S	(2,760,339)			0.50
1974	.470,248,000	0.15	0.25	
1974D	.571,083,000	0.15	0.25	
1974S	(2,612,568)			0.50
1975	.585,673,900	0.15	0.25	
1975D	.313,705,300	0.15	0.25	
1975S	(2,845,450)			0.70
1976	.568,760,000	0.15	0.25	
1976D	.695,222,774		0.15	
1976S	(4,149,730)			0.70
1977	.796,930,000	0.15	0.25	
1977D	.376,607,228	0.15	0.25	

	Mintage	MS-63	MS-65	PF-65
1977S	(3,251,152)			$0.50
1978	.663,980,000		$0.15	
1978D	.282,847,540		0.15	
1978S	(3,127,781)			0.40
1979	.315,440,000	$0.15	0.25	
1979D	.390,921,184	0.15	0.25	
1979S, Filled S	(3,677,175)			0.50
1979S, Clear S	.........*			1.40
1980P	.735,170,000	0.15	0.25	
1980D	.719,354,321	0.15	0.25	
1980S	(3,554,806)			0.40
1981P	.676,650,000	0.15	0.25	
1981D	.712,284,143	0.15	0.25	
1981S	(4,063,083)			0.40
1982, No Mmk	....	85.00	115.00	
1982P	.519,475,000	1.50	2.00	
1982D	.542,713,584	0.60	1.10	
1982S	(3,857,479)			0.60
1983P	.647,025,000	1.25	1.50	
1983D	.730,129,224	0.35	0.60	
1983S	(3,279,126)			0.50
1984P	.856,669,000	0.15	0.25	
1984D	.704,803,976	0.20	0.35	
1984S	(3,065,110)			0.65
1985P	.705,200,962	0.15	0.25	
1985D	.587,979,970	0.15	0.25	
1985S	(3,362,821)			0.50
1986P	.682,649,693	0.25	0.35	
1986D	.473,326,970	0.25	0.35	
1986S	(3,010,497)			1.00
1987P	.762,709,481	0.15	0.35	
1987D	.653,203,402	0.15	0.35	

* Included in number above.

Chart continued on next page.

Mintage	MS-63	MS-65	PF-65
1987S . . . .(4,227,728)			$0.60
1988P 1,030,550,000	$0.12	$0.20	
1988D 962,385,489	0.12	0.20	
1988S . . . .(3,262,948)			1.00
1989P 1,298,400,000	0.10	0.20	
1989D 896,535,597	0.10	0.20	
1989S . . . .(3,220,194)			1.00
1990P 1,034,340,000	0.10	0.20	
1990D 839,995,824	0.10	0.20	
1990S . . . .(3,299,559)			0.75
1991P 927,220,000	0.10	0.20	
1991D 601,241,114	0.12	0.20	
1991S . . . .(2,867,787)			1.20
1992P 593,500,000	0.10	0.15	
1992D 616,273,932	0.10	0.15	
1992S . . . .(2,858,981)			2.00
1992S, Silver . .(1,317,579)			3.00
1993P 766,180,000	0.10	0.15	
1993D 750,110,166	0.10	0.15	
1993S . . . .(2,633,439)			2.00
1993S, Silver . . . .(761,353)			2.50
1994P 1,189,000,000	0.10	0.15	
1994D 1,303,268,110	0.10	0.15	
1994S . . . .(2,484,594)			2.00
1994S, Silver . . . .(785,329)			2.75
1995P 1,125,500,000	0.10	0.20	
1995D 1,274,890,000	0.15	0.25	
1995S . . . .(2,117,496)			4.00
1995S, Silver . . . .(679,985)			6.50
1996P 1,421,163,000	0.10	0.20	
1996D 1,400,300,000	0.10	0.20	
1996W 1,457,000	6.00	10.00	
1996S . . . .(1,750,244)			2.00
1996S, Silver . . . .(775,021)			3.00
1997P 991,640,000	0.10	0.15	
1997D 979,810,000	0.10	0.15	
1997S . . . .(2,055,000)			3.00
1997S, Silver . . . .(741,678)			10.00
1998P 1,163,000,000	0.10	0.15	
1998D 1,172,250,000	0.10	0.15	
1998S . . . .(2,086,507)			2.00
1998S, Silver . . . .(878,792)			3.00
1999P 2,164,000,000	0.10	0.15	
1999D 1,397,750,000	0.10	0.15	
1999S . . . .(2,543,401)			1.00

Mintage	MS-63	MS-65	PF-65
1999S, Silver . . . .(804,565)			$3.50
2000P 1,842,500,000	$0.10	$0.15	
2000D 1,818,700,000	0.10	0.15	
2000S . . . .(3,082,572)			1.00
2000S, Silver . . . .(965,421)			2.00
2001P 1,369,590,000	0.10	0.15	
2001D 1,412,800,000	0.10	0.15	
2001S . . . .(2,294,909)			0.50
2001S, Silver . . . .(889,697)			2.00
2002P 1,187,500,000	0.10	0.15	
2002D 1,379,500,000	0.10	0.15	
2002S . . . .(2,319,766)			0.75
2002S, Silver . . . .(892,229)			2.00
2003P 1,085,500,000	0.10	0.15	
2003D 986,500,000	0.10	0.15	
2003S . . . .(2,172,684)			0.50
2003S, Silver . . .(1,125,755)			2.00
2004P 1,328,000,000	0.10	0.15	
2004D 1,159,500,000	0.10	0.15	
2004S . . . .(1,789,488)			0.60
2004S, Silver . . .(1,175,934)			2.00
2005P 1,412,000,000	0.10	0.15	
2005D 1,423,500,000	0.10	0.15	
2005S . . . .(2,275,000)			0.60
2005S, Silver . . .(1,069,679)			2.00
2006P 1,381,000,000	0.10	0.15	
2006D 1,447,000,000	0.10	0.15	
2006S . . . .(2,000,428)			0.60
2006S, Silver . . .(1,054,008)			1.70
2007P 1,047,500,000	0.10	0.15	
2007D 1,042,000,000	0.10	0.15	
2007S . . . .(1,702,116)			0.50
2007S, Silver . . . .(875,050)			1.50
2008P 391,000,000	0.10	0.15	
2008D 624,500,000	0.10	0.15	
2008S . . . .(1,405,674)			0.50
2008S, Silver . . . .(774,874)			1.50
2009P 96,500,000	0.10	0.15	
2009D 49,500,000	0.10	0.15	
2009S . . . .(1,376,750)			0.50
2009S, Silver . . .(618,248)			1.50
2010P	0.10	0.15	
2010D	0.10	0.15	
2010S			0.50
2010S, Silver			1.50

* Included in number above.

LIBERTY SEATED (1875–1878)

The twenty-cent piece was a short-lived coin authorized by the Act of March 3, 1875. The edge of the coin is plain. Most of the 1876-CC coins were melted at the Mint and never released. The mintmark is on the reverse below the eagle.

G-4 Good: LIBERTY on shield obliterated. Letters and date legible.
VG-8 Very Good: One or two letters in LIBERTY barely visible. Other details bold.
F-12 Fine: Some letters of LIBERTY possibly visible.
VF-20 Very Fine: LIBERTY readable, but partly weak.
EF-40 Extremely Fine: LIBERTY mostly sharp. Only slight wear on high points of coin.
AU-50 About Uncirculated: Slight trace of wear on breast, head, and knees.
MS-60 Uncirculated: No trace of wear. Light blemishes.
MS-63 Choice Uncirculated: Some distracting blemishes in prime focal areas. Some impairment of luster possible.
PF-63 Choice Proof: Reflective surfaces with only a few blemishes in secondary focal places. No major flaws.

	Mintage	G-4	VG-8	F-12	VF-20	EF-40	AU-50	MS-60	MS-63	PF-63
1875 . . . .(2,790) 36,910		$80	$100	$125	$185	$235	$270	$425	$725	$1,300
1875CC 133,290		160	185	250	275	400	475	800	1,650	
1875S 1,155,000		52	57	65	85	125	155	275	600	
1876 . . . .(1,260) 14,640		90	125	150	200	250	300	450	750	1,350
1876CC 10,000								80,000		
1877 . . . .(350)					1,000	1,200				2,200
1878 . . . .(600)					900	1,000				1,800

A NOTE ON COUNTERFEIT COINS

Many United States coins have been extensively counterfeited, including very deceptive issues produced in China in recent years. These include issues from half cents to $20 gold, some rarities, and many issues that are not necessarily rare, but sell for significant premiums. There is no effective policing of offerings on Internet mail bid sales or other sales. It is desirable, indeed mandatory, that a coin thought to be rare or expensive, if not bought from a recognized professional numismatist, be certified by a coin grading service.

Authorized in 1792, this denomination was not issued until four years later. The first type weighed 104 grains, the standard until modified to 103-1/8 grains by the Act of January 18, 1837. As with the dime and half dime, the weight was reduced and arrows placed at the date in 1853. Rays were placed in the field of the reverse during that year only.

DRAPED BUST (1796–1807)

AG-3 About Good: Details clear enough to identify.
G-4 Good: Date readable. Bust outlined, but no detail.
VG-8 Very Good: All but deepest drapery folds worn smooth. Hairlines nearly gone and curls lacking in detail.
F-12 Fine: All drapery lines visible. Hair partly worn.
VF-20 Very Fine: Only left side of drapery indistinct.
EF-40 Extremely Fine: Hair well outlined and detailed.
AU-50 About Uncirculated: Slight trace of wear on shoulder and highest waves of hair.
MS-60 Uncirculated: No trace of wear. Light blemishes.
MS-63 Choice Uncirculated: Some distracting marks or blemishes in focal areas. Impaired luster possible.

Small Eagle Reverse (1796)

	Mintage	AG-3	G-4	VG-8	F-12	VF-20	EF-40	AU-50	MS-60	MS-63
1796 6,146		$2,750	$5,000	$6,750	$14,000	$18,000	$25,000	$30,000	$42,000	$65,000

Heraldic Eagle Reverse (1804–1807)

	Mintage	AG-3	G-4	VG-8	F-12	VF-20	EF-40	AU-50	MS-60	MS-63
1804 6,738		$800	$1,600	$2,100	$3,250	$5,200	$10,500	$20,000	$28,000	$65,000
1805 121,394		60	150	200	300	550	1,300	2,000	3,750	6,500
1806, 6 Over 5 . . . .*		75	200	225	350	600	1,400	2,200	4,000	9,000
1806 206,124		70	160	210	325	575	1,200	2,100	3,750	6,000
1807 220,643		70	160	210	325	575	1,200	2,100	3,750	6,000

* Included in number below.

CAPPED BUST (1815–1838)
Variety 1 – Large Diameter (1815–1828)

AG-3 About Good: Details clear enough to identify.
G-4 Good: Date, letters, stars legible. Hair under Liberty's headband smooth. Cap lines worn smooth.
VG-8 Very Good: Rim well defined. Main details visible. Full LIBERTY on cap. Hair above eye nearly smooth.
F-12 Fine: All hair lines visible, but only partial detail visible in drapery. Shoulder clasp distinct.
VF-20 Very Fine: All details visible, but some wear evident. Clasp and ear sharp.
EF-40 Extremely Fine: All details distinct. Hair well outlined.
AU-50 About Uncirculated: Slight trace of wear on tips of curls and above the eye, and on the wing and claw tips.
MS-60 Uncirculated: No trace of wear. Light blemishes.
MS-63 Choice Uncirculated: Some distracting marks or blemishes in focal areas. Impaired luster possible.

	Mintage	AG-3	G-4	VG-8	F-12	VF-20	EF-40	AU-50	MS-60	MS-63
1815	.89,235	$20	$45	$55	$75	$200	$550	$775	$1,300	$2,300
1818, 8 Over 5	.*	18	42	50	70	180	500	750	1,500	2,500
1818, Normal Date	.361,174	18	42	50	70	180	500	750	1,200	2,300
1819	.144,000	18	42	50	70	180	500	750	1,200	2,300
1820	.127,444	18	42	50	70	180	500	750	1,200	2,300
1821	.216,851	18	42	50	70	180	500	750	1,200	2,300
1822	.64,080	18	42	50	80	200	550	775	1,400	2,800
1822, 25 Over 50c	.*	300	700	1,400	2,400	3,250	5,500	10,000	17,500	
1823, 3 Over 2	.17,800	7,000	15,000	18,000	22,000	25,000	35,000	65,000	—	
1824, 4 Over 2	.**	25	45	65	160	300	800	2,000	4,750	
1825	.168,000	18	42	50	70	180	500	750	1,300	2,300
1827, Original (Curl Base 2 in 25c)	.4,000								100,000	
1827, Restrike (Square Base 2 in 25c)	.*								40,000	
1828	.102,000	18	42	50	65	175	450	700	1,300	2,600
1828, 25 Over 50c	.*	35	65	115	250	500	950	1,750	4,500	

* Included in regular mintage. ** Included in 1825 mintage.

Variety 2 – Reduced Diameter, Motto Removed (1831–1838)

G-4 Good: Bust of Liberty well defined. Hair under headband smooth. Date, letters, stars legible. Scant rims.
VG-8 Very Good: Details apparent but worn on high spots. Rims strong. Full LIBERTY.
F-12 Fine: All hair lines visible. Drapery partly worn. Shoulder clasp distinct.
VF-20 Very Fine: Only top spots worn. Clasp sharp. Ear distinct.
EF-40 Extremely Fine: Hair details and clasp bold and clear.

AU-50 About Uncirculated: Slight trace of wear on hair around forehead, on cheek, and at top and bottom tips of eagle's wings and left claw.
MS-60 Uncirculated: No trace of wear. Light blemishes.
MS-63 Choice Uncirculated: Some distracting contact marks or blemishes in prime focal areas. Impaired luster possible.

	Mintage	G-4	VG-8	F-12	VF-20	EF-40	AU-50	MS-60	MS-63
1831	.398,000	$32	$40	$45	$65	$170	$290	$500	$1,700
1832	.320,000	32	40	45	65	170	290	500	1,700
1833	.156,000	32	40	50	70	200	320	650	2,100
1834	.286,000	32	40	45	65	170	290	500	1,700
1835	.1,952,000	32	40	45	65	170	290	500	1,700
1836	.472,000	32	40	45	65	170	290	500	1,700
1837	.252,400	32	40	45	65	170	290	500	1,700
1838	.366,000	32	40	45	65	170	290	500	1,700

LIBERTY SEATED (1838–1891)

G-4 Good: Scant rim. LIBERTY on shield worn off. Date and letters legible.
VG-8 Very Good: Rim fairly defined, at least three letters in LIBERTY evident.
F-12 Fine: LIBERTY complete, but partly weak.
VF-20 Very Fine: LIBERTY strong.
EF-40 Extremely Fine: Complete LIBERTY and edges of scroll. Clasp clear.
AU-50 About Uncirculated: Slight wear on Liberty's knees and breast and on eagle's neck, wing tips, and claws.
MS-60 Uncirculated: No trace of wear. Light blemishes.
MS-63 Choice Uncirculated: Some distracting marks or blemishes in focal areas. Impaired luster possible.

Variety 1 – No Motto Above Eagle (1838–1853)

Small Date

Mintmark location is on reverse, below eagle.

Large Date

	Mintage	G-4	VG-8	F-12	VF-20	EF-40	AU-50	MS-60	MS-63
1838 466,000		$10	$13	$20	$36	$110	$220	$625	$1,750
1839 491,146		10	13	20	35	110	220	625	1,750
1840 188,127		9	12	21	32	70	110	400	1,100
18400 425,200		11	15	27	45	125	225	650	2,000
1841 120,000		18	30	45	65	110	125	425	850
18410 452,000		10	12	19	32	80	120	350	700
1842, Small Date (Proof only)									28,000
1842, Large Date 88,000		30	40	75	130	175	250	750	1,500
18420, Small Date . . . .*		150	250	475	775	1,500	3,500	7,500	
18420, Large Date 769,000		10	11	17	31	70	125	650	1,800
1843 645,600		9	10	16	22	40	60	225	600
18430 968,000		10	13	20	45	100	275	900	2,200
1844 421,200		9	10	16	22	40	60	225	600
18440 740,000		10	11	18	32	80	120	550	1,400
1845 922,000		9	10	16	22	40	60	225	625
1846 510,000		9	10	16	22	40	60	225	600
1847 734,000		9	10	16	22	40	60	225	600
18470 368,000		12	17	27	50	110	275	900	2,500
1848 146,000		11	17	28	50	80	125	450	1,100
1849 340,000		10	12	20	27	70	100	400	700
18490 . . . .(a)		175	260	450	950	1,600	2,500	6,000	—
1850 190,800		13	17	25	35	65	100	400	750
18500 412,000		13	17	25	35	65	180	550	1,100
1851 160,000		15	20	28	50	85	100	400	725
18510 88,000		65	100	200	300	650	1,100	2,900	
1852 177,060		16	21	30	55	90	110	375	650
18520 96,000		80	120	175	300	600	1,500	3,500	9,000
1853, Recut Date, No Arrows or Rays . .44,200		110	140	175	275	500	750	1,300	2,000

* Included in number below. **a.** Mintage for 1849-O included with 1850-O.

Variety 2 – Arrows at Date, Rays Around Eagle (1853)

1853, 3 Over 4

QUARTER DOLLARS

	Mintage	G-4	VG-8	F-12	VF-20	EF-40	AU-50	MS-60	MS-63
1853 15,210,020	$9	$12	$15	$20	$65	$125	$450	$975
1853, 3 Over 4 . . . .*	20	35	55	110	160	250	900	2,250
1853O 1,332,000	9	12	17	30	115	450	1,300	4,000

* Included in number above.

Variety 3 – Arrows at Date, No Rays (1854–1855)

	Mintage	G-4	VG-8	F-12	VF-20	EF-40	AU-50	MS-60	MS-63
1854 12,380,000	$9	$11	$14	$18	$35	$100	$250	$600
1854O 1,484,000	9	11	16	20	40	110	325	850
1855 2,857,000	9	11	14	18	35	100	275	650
1855O 176,000	17	25	45	115	160	500	1,800	5,750
1855S 396,400	17	25	35	60	125	325	900	2,500

Variety 1 Resumed (1856–1865; Weight Standard of 1853)

	Mintage	G-4	VG-8	F-12	VF-20	EF-40	AU-50	MS-60	MS-63	PF-63
1856 7,264,000	$9	$11	$14	$19	$27	$60	$170	$300	$2,600
1856O 968,000	9	11	14	21	40	100	500	825	
1856S 286,000	15	20	35	80	175	325	1,250	4,500	
1857 9,644,000	9	11	14	19	26	60	150	300	1,800
1857O 1,180,000	9	11	14	19	37	110	500	1,200	
1857S 82,000	25	40	70	150	250	400	1,200	3,250	
1858 . . . .(300+) . .7,368,000	9	11	14	19	26	60	150	300	1,000
1858O 520,000	9	11	14	25	50	150	650	1,750	
1858S 121,000	19	32	50	100	225	800	4,000	—	
1859 . . . .(800) . . .1,343,200	9	11	14	19	26	60	150	425	650
1859O 260,000	9	14	20	26	50	150	500	1,600	
1859S 80,000	35	55	90	160	700	4,500	—	—	
1860 . . . . . .(1,000) 804,400	9	11	14	19	26	60	175	300	600
1860O 388,000	9	11	14	20	32	150	450	850	
1860S 56,000	90	150	250	1,000	3,750	7,500	—	—	
1861 . . . . . .(1,000) . . .4,853,600	9	11	14	19	26	60	175	350	600
1861S 96,000	27	50	100	190	500	2,500	—	—	
1862 . . . .(550) 932,000	9	11	14	19	26	60	175	350	600
1862S 67,000	20	32	80	110	250	475	1,400	3,500	
1863 . . . .(460) 191,600	14	18	30	45	70	120	300	450	600
1864 . . . .(470) 93,600	30	35	45	70	110	180	300	600	600
1864S 20,000	110	160	300	425	950	1,850	—	—	
1865 . . . .(500) 58,800	25	30	45	70	110	180	300	600	600
1865S 41,000	30	40	60	140	225	450	1,250	2,000	

Variety 4 – Motto Above Eagle (1866–1873)

	Mintage	G-4	VG-8	F-12	VF-20	EF-40	AU-50	MS-60	MS-63	PF-63
1866 . . . .(725) 16,800	$150	$200	$225	$350	$550	$700	$850	$1,200	$450
1866S 28,000	75	110	200	350	500	900	1,600	2,500	

Chart continued on next page.

99

	Mintage	G-4	VG-8	F-12	VF-20	EF-40	AU-50	MS-60	MS-63	PF-63
1867 . . . .(625) 20,000		$80	$100	$175	$210	$260	$450	$750	$1,100	$450
1867S 48,000		85	120	170	275	700	2,000	5,500	—	
1868 . . . .(600) 29,400		40	60	80	100	125	210	400	700	450
1868S 96,000		30	40	50	90	200	350	1,100	2,800	
1869 . . . .(600) 16,000		90	110	170	200	275	400	600	1,100	450
1869S 76,000		30	45	80	125	235	450	1,000	2,100	
1870 . . . .(1,000) 86,400		20	25	40	60	90	175	400	500	450
1870CC 8,340		2,500	4,000	5,000	7,500	13,000	22,000	—		
1871 . . . .(960) 118,200		11	16	22	40	60	125	225	425	450
1871CC 10,890		750	1,500	2,400	6,500	10,000	17,500	—		
1871S 30,900		100	150	200	320	450	900	1,300	2,000	
1872 . . . .(950) 182,000		11	16	22	40	60	100	300	700	450
1872CC 22,850		200	350	600	1,300	2,750	4,500	17,000		
1872S 83,000		235	450	600	800	1,300	2,100	3,750		
1873 . . . .(650) 212,600		11	16	22	35	50	90	200	425	450
1873CC 4,000					—	40,000	—	—		

Variety 5 – Arrows at Date (1873–1874)

	Mintage	G-4	VG-8	F-12	VF-20	EF-40	AU-50	MS-60	MS-63	PF-63
1873 . . . .(540) . .1,271,160		$10	$11	$16	$35	$90	$175	$425	$700	$800
1873CC 12,462		850	1,300	3,600	6,000	8,500	12,000	25,000	40,000	
1873S 156,000		11	14	23	45	110	200	600	1,000	
1874 . . . .(700) 471,200		10	11	16	35	90	175	450	750	800
1874S 392,000		11	13	20	45	110	175	450	750	

Variety 4 Resumed (1875–1891)

1877-S, S Over Horizontal S

	Mintage	G-4	VG-8	F-12	VF-20	EF-40	AU-50	MS-60	MS-63	PF-63
1875 . . . .(700) . . .4,292,800		$9	$11	$14	$18	$25	$60	$125	$200	$400
1875CC 140,000		25	35	65	125	200	300	700	1,100	
1875S 680,000		10	16	23	35	70	125	275	500	
1876 . . . . . .(1,150) . .17,816,000		9	11	14	19	25	60	125	200	400
1876CC 4,944,000		11	16	18	23	35	75	200	400	
1876S 8,596,000		9	11	14	18	25	60	125	200	
1877 . . . .(510) . .10,911,200		9	11	14	18	25	60	125	200	400
1877CC 4,192,000		10	16	18	23	35	75	200	350	
1877S 8,996,000		9	11	14	19	25	60	125	200	

	Mintage	G-4	VG-8	F-12	VF-20	EF-40	AU-50	MS-60	MS-63	PF-63
1877S, S Over Horizontal S .....*		$11	$16	$35	$50	$90	$125	$300	$500	
1878 ....(800) ...2,260,000		9	11	14	19	25	60	125	200	$400
1878CC 996,000		11	16	20	30	55	95	250	400	
1878S 140,000		45	80	100	125	200	425	700	1,250	
1879 ...(1,100) 13,600		40	50	75	80	100	135	200	375	400
1880 .....(1,355) 13,600		40	50	75	80	100	135	200	375	400
1881 ....(975) 12,000		50	65	85	100	120	190	225	400	450
1882 .....(1,100) 15,200		45	50	80	100	110	150	275	375	400
1883 .....(1,039) 14,400		45	50	80	100	110	150	275	375	400
1884 ....(875) 8,000		90	100	120	125	150	200	350	450	400
1885 ....(930) 13,600		40	50	75	100	110	200	300	400	400
1886 ....(886) 5,000		95	110	150	175	275	375	475	500	450
1887 ....(710) 10,000		80	90	100	125	175	200	300	400	400
1888 ....(832) 10,001		70	80	90	135	200	225	300	375	400
1888S 1,216,000		9	11	14	18	25	65	150	275	
1889 ....(711) 12,000		50	60	90	110	120	200	300	400	400
1890 ....(590) 80,000		20	25	35	50	80	125	275	375	400
1891 ....(600) ...3,920,000		8	9	11	15	22	65	150	250	400
1891O 68,000		50	65	110	325	475	525	1,600	2,200	
1891S 2,216,000		9	11	14	18	25	65	150	250	

* Included in 1877S regular mintage (previous page).

BARBER OR LIBERTY HEAD (1892–1916)

Like other silver coins of this type, the quarter dollars minted from 1892 to 1916 were designed by Charles E. Barber. His initial B is found at the truncation of the neck of Miss Liberty.

G-4 Good: Date and legends legible. LIBERTY worn off headband.
VG-8 Very Good: Some letters in LIBERTY legible.
F-12 Fine: LIBERTY completely legible but not sharp.
VF-20 Very Fine: All letters in LIBERTY evenly plain.
EF-40 Extremely Fine: LIBERTY bold, its ribbon distinct.
AU-50 About Uncirculated: Slight trace of wear above forehead, on cheek, and on eagle's head, wings, and tail.
MS-60 Uncirculated: No trace of wear. Light blemishes.
MS-63 Choice Uncirculated: Some distracting marks or blemishes in focal areas. Impaired luster possible.

PF-63 Choice Proof: Reflective surfaces with only a few blemishes in secondary focal places. No major flaws.

	Mintage	G-4	VG-8	F-12	VF-20	EF-40	AU-50	MS-60	MS-63	PF-63
1892 ......(1,245) ...8,236,000		$3.60	$3.75	$9	$13	$27	$50	$115	$125	$325
1892O 2,460,000		4.00	5.00	11	18	35	60	150	200	
1892S 964,079		10.00	18.00	30	40	70	130	200	425	
1893 ....(792) ...5,444,023		3.60	3.75	9	13	30	50	115	165	325
1893O 3,396,000		3.60	4.00	10	14	35	60	160	220	
1893S 1,454,535		6.00	10.00	20	40	70	130	200	500	
1894 ....(972) ...3,432,000		3.60	3.75	10	15	30	60	110	200	325
1894O 2,852,000		3.60	3.75	10	20	35	90	160	300	
1894S 2,648,821		3.60	3.75	11	20	35	90	160	300	
1895 ....(880) ...4,440,000		3.60	3.75	10	14	30	60	110	200	325
1895O 2,816,000		3.75	5.00	15	27	45	90	185	400	
1895S 1,764,681		5.00	8.50	25	50	65	120	225	450	
1896 ....(762) ...3,874,000		3.60	3.75	9	14	32	60	125	200	325
1896O 1,484,000		10.00	18.00	50	110	150	275	450	750	

Chart continued on next page.

	Mintage	G-4	VG-8	F-12	VF-20	EF-40	AU-50	MS-60	MS-63	PF-63
1896S	188,039	$300.00	$500.00	$825.00	$1,350	$2,000	$2,700	$3,350	$7,500	
1897	(731) . .8,140,000	3.60	3.75	9.00	13	28	50	90	125	$325
1897O	1,414,800	5.00	12.00	40.00	100	130	275	425	750	
1897S	542,229	15.00	22.00	90.00	120	130	275	425	750	
1898	(735) . .1,868,000	3.60	3.75	9.00	13	30	50	90	125	325
1898O	1,868,000	5.00	9.00	22.00	55	110	150	300	650	
1898S	1,020,592	4.00	7.00	15.00	20	35	90	200	600	
1899	(846) . .12,624,000	3.60	3.75	9.00	13	26	50	90	125	325
1899O	2,644,000	4.00	5.00	9.00	16	32	100	200	400	
1899S	708,000	5.00	12.00	18.00	35	45	125	225	550	
1900	(912) . .10,016,000	3.60	3.75	9.00	13	25	60	90	125	325
1900O	3,416,000	4.00	9.00	20.00	30	50	150	250	400	
1900S	1,858,585	3.60	4.00	11.00	16	30	50	175	450	
1901	(813) . .8,892,000	3.60	4.00	8.00	14	30	60	100	120	325
1901O	1,612,000	18.00	25.00	55.00	100	175	250	400	900	
1901S	72,664	2,800.00	4,250.00	6,500.00	8,500	12,000	14,000	18,500	25,000	
1902	(777) . .12,196,967	3.60	3.75	8.00	14	30	50	90	125	325
1902O	4,748,000	3.60	4.00	12.00	25	50	90	200	600	
1902S	1,524,612	4.50	7.00	18.00	30	60	100	220	475	
1903	(755) . .9,759,309	3.60	3.75	8.00	14	30	50	90	175	325
1903O	3,500,000	3.60	4.00	11.00	20	32	100	150	600	
1903S	1,036,000	4.00	6.00	14.00	25	45	100	210	400	
1904	(670) . .9,588,143	3.60	3.75	8.00	14	25	50	90	125	325
1904O	2,456,000	3.60	4.00	16.00	30	90	175	350	600	
1905	(727) . .4,967,523	3.60	3.75	8.50	14	30	50	90	150	325
1905O	1,230,000	4.00	10.00	35.00	60	110	160	200	550	
1905S	1,884,000	3.60	4.25	16.00	22	42	90	175	500	
1906	(675) . .3,655,760	3.60	3.75	8.00	14	25	50	90	125	325
1906D	3,280,000	3.60	3.75	9.00	15	26	60	110	200	
1906O	2,056,000	3.60	3.75	12.00	17	30	90	135	250	
1907	(575) . .7,132,000	3.60	3.75	8.00	14	25	50	90	125	325
1907D	2,484,000	3.60	3.75	9.00	15	26	60	125	350	
1907O	4,560,000	3.60	3.75	8.00	14	25	55	100	250	
1907S	1,360,000	4.00	5.00	16.00	22	50	100	200	400	
1908	(545) . .4,232,000	3.60	3.75	8.00	14	25	50	90	125	325
1908D	5,788,000	3.60	3.75	8.00	14	25	50	110	200	
1908O	6,244,000	3.60	3.75	8.00	14	25	50	100	125	
1908S	784,000	6.00	13.00	35.00	60	150	200	350	550	
1909	(650) . .9,268,000	3.60	3.75	8.00	14	25	50	90	125	325
1909D	5,114,000	3.60	3.75	8.00	14	25	60	110	160	
1909O	712,000	6.00	13.00	30.00	70	125	225	400	850	
1909S	1,348,000	3.60	3.75	10.00	16	30	90	150	350	
1910	(551) . .2,244,000	3.60	3.75	8.00	14	25	60	90	150	325
1910D	1,500,000	3.60	3.75	15.00	18	35	110	175	400	
1911	(543) . .3,720,000	3.60	3.75	8.00	14	25	50	90	125	325
1911D	933,600	3.60	3.75	30.00	90	130	225	325	600	
1911S	988,000	3.60	3.75	18.00	30	60	120	175	350	
1912	(700) . .4,400,000	3.60	3.75	8.00	14	25	50	90	125	325
1912S	708,000	3.60	4.50	15.00	18	35	100	175	400	
1913	(613) . .484,000	6.00	9.00	25.00	67	185	210	550	600	400
1913D	1,450,800	3.60	4.00	11.00	17	35	75	140	185	
1913S	40,000	650.00	900.00	2,000.00	2,750	3,250	4,000	5,000	6,750	

	Mintage	G-4	VG-8	F-12	VF-20	EF-40	AU-50	MS-60	MS-63	PF-63
1914 . . . .(380) . . .6,244,230		$3.60	$3.75	$8.00	$14	$25	$50	$90	$125	$375
1914D 3,046,000		3.60	3.75	8.00	14	25	50	90	125	
1914S 264,000		30.00	40.00	85.00	125	200	300	450	675	
1915 . . . .(450) . . .3,480,000		3.60	3.75	8.00	14	25	50	90	125	375
1915D 3,694,000		3.60	3.75	8.00	14	25	50	90	125	
1915S 704,000		3.60	3.75	9.00	15	32	90	125	200	
1916 1,788,000		3.60	3.75	8.00	14	25	50	90	125	
1916D 6,540,800		3.60	3.75	8.00	14	25	50	90	125	

STANDING LIBERTY (1916–1930)

This design is by Hermon A. MacNeil, whose initial M is above and to the right of the date. Liberty bears a shield of protection in her left arm, while the right hand holds the olive branch of peace. There was a modification in 1917. The reverse had a new arrangement of stars and the eagle was higher. After 1924 the date was "recessed," thereby giving it greater protection from the effects of circulation.

G-4 Good: Date and lettering legible. Top of date worn. Liberty's right leg and toes worn off. Much wear evident on left leg and drapery lines.

VG-8 Very Good: Distinct date. Toes faintly visible. Drapery lines visible above Liberty's left leg.

F-12 Fine: High curve of right leg flat from thigh to ankle. Only slight wear evident on left leg. Drapery lines over right thigh seen only at sides of leg.

VF-20 Very Fine: Garment line across right leg worn, but visible at sides.

EF-40 Extremely Fine: Flattened only at high spots. Liberty's toes are sharp. Drapery lines across right leg evident.

AU-50 About Uncirculated: Slight trace of wear on head, kneecap, shield's center, and highest point on eagle's body.

MS-60 Uncirculated: No trace of wear, but contact marks, surface spots, or faded luster possible.

MS-63 Choice Uncirculated: No trace of wear. Light blemishes. Attractive mint luster.

Variety 1 – No Stars Below Eagle (1916–1917)

Mintmark location is on obverse, to left of date.

	Mintage	G-4	VG-8	F-12	VF-20	EF-40	AU-50	MS-60	MS-63
1916 52,000		$1,600	$2,000	$3,600	$4,750	$5,750	$6,500	$7,250	$11,000
1917, Variety 1 8,740,000		13	18	26	32	50	100	140	180
1917D, Variety 1 1,509,200		15	19	27	35	60	110	150	200
1917S, Variety 1 1,952,000		16	22	28	40	75	125	170	250

Variety 2 – Stars Below Eagle (1917–1930)
Pedestal Date (1917–1924)

See next page for chart.

1918-S, 8 Over 7

	Mintage	G-4	VG-8	F-12	VF-20	EF-40	AU-50	MS-60	MS-63
1917, Variety 2 13,880,000		$11	$13	$16	$18	$27	$55	$100	$140
1917D, Variety 2 6,224,400		18	22	32	40	60	85	125	175
1917S, Variety 2 5,552,000		18	22	32	40	65	90	125	175
1918 14,240,000		8	9	15	17	25	50	100	145
1918D 7,380,000		13	16	26	34	50	85	125	200
1918S, Normal Date 11,072,000		9	11	17	20	30	50	120	175
1918S, 8 Over 7 . . . .*		825	1,000	1,650	2,500	3,500	7,000	10,000	21,000
1919 11,324,000		18	22	27	35	40	60	100	125
1919D 1,944,000		50	70	100	150	225	300	375	800
1919S 1,836,000		50	70	100	150	275	325	400	900
1920 27,860,000		8	10	15	20	25	40	100	125
1920D 3,586,400		25	30	40	45	65	100	125	450
1920S 6,380,000		9	12	16	20	30	50	110	400
1921 1,916,000		85	110	160	200	275	425	600	850
1923 9,716,000		8	10	15	17	20	40	100	150
1923S 1,360,000		150	200	240	400	500	700	975	1,700
1924 10,920,000		8	10	12	15	20	50	100	150
1924D 3,112,000		25	35	50	65	100	125	150	175
1924S 2,860,000		12	15	20	25	60	125	150	500

* Included in number above.

Recessed Date (1925–1930)

	Mintage	G-4	VG-8	F-12	VF-20	EF-40	AU-50	MS-60	MS-63
1925 12,280,000		$3.40	$3.60	$4	$6	$16	$35	$70	$140
1926 11,316,000		3.40	3.60	4	6	16	35	70	140
1926D 1,716,000		3.50	4.00	8	16	26	50	100	170
1926S 2,700,000		3.40	3.60	6	11	50	125	200	400
1927 11,912,000		3.40	3.60	4	6	16	35	70	140
1927D 976,000		6.00	8.00	13	30	65	90	160	200
1927S 396,000		15.00	21.00	45	175	640	1,600	2,500	4,200
1928 6,336,000		3.40	3.60	4	6	16	35	70	135
1928D 1,627,600		3.40	3.60	4	6	16	35	70	135
1928S 2,644,000		3.40	3.60	4	6	16	35	70	140
1929 11,140,000		3.40	3.60	4	6	16	35	70	140
1929D 1,358,000		3.40	3.60	4	6	16	35	70	140
1929S 1,764,000		3.40	3.60	4	6	16	35	70	140
1930 5,632,000		3.40	3.60	4	6	16	35	70	135
1930S 1,556,000		3.40	3.60	4	6	16	35	70	135

WASHINGTON (1932 TO DATE)

This type was intended to be a commemorative issue marking the 200th anniversary of Washington's birth. John Flanagan, a New York sculptor, was the designer. The initials JF are found at the base of the neck. The mintmark is on the reverse below the wreath for coins from 1932 to 1964. Starting in 1968, the mintmark was moved to the obverse at the right of the ribbon.

F-12 Fine: Hair lines about Washington's ear visible. Tiny feathers on eagle's breast faintly visible.
VF-20 Very Fine: Most hair details visible. Wing feathers clear.
EF-40 Extremely Fine: Hair lines sharp. Wear spots confined to top of eagle's legs and center of breast.
MS-60 Uncirculated: No trace of wear, but many contact marks, surface spotting, or faded luster possible.
MS-63 Choice Uncirculated: No trace of wear. Light blemishes. Attractive mint luster.
MS-64 Uncirculated: A few scattered contact marks. Good eye appeal and attractive luster.
MS-65 Gem Uncirculated: Only light, scattered, non-distracting marks. Strong luster, good eye appeal.
PF-65 Gem Proof: Hardly any blemishes, and no flaws.

Silver Coinage (1932–1964)

	Mintage	VG-8	F-12	VF-20	EF-40	MS-60	MS-63	MS-65	PF-65
1932	5,404,000	$3.50	$3.50	$3.50	$4.00	$13	$23	$200	
1932D	436,800	75.00	90.00	120.00	175.00	525	1,500	9,500	
1932S	408,000	75.00	90.00	100.00	130.00	275	575	2,800	
1934	31,912,052	3.00	3.00	3.00	3.50	9	17	45	
1934D	3,527,200	3.00	3.00	3.50	10.00	100	175	650	
1935	32,484,000	3.00	3.00	3.00	3.50	9	15	45	
1935D	5,780,000	3.00	3.00	3.25	8.00	100	140	400	
1935S	5,660,000	3.00	3.00	3.00	5.00	40	60	140	
1936	(3,837) 41,300,000	3.00	3.00	3.00	3.50	8	16	40	$850
1936D	5,374,000	3.00	3.00	3.00	18.00	180	350	725	
1936S	3,828,000	3.00	3.00	3.00	4.00	40	75	200	
1937	(5,542) 19,696,000	3.00	3.00	3.00	3.50	8	15	48	325
1937D	7,189,600	3.00	3.00	3.00	4.00	25	45	70	
1937S	1,652,000	3.00	3.00	3.50	10.00	70	100	150	
1938	(8,045) 9,472,000	3.00	3.00	3.00	4.00	30	50	120	200
1938S	2,832,000	3.00	3.00	3.00	4.50	35	60	125	
1939	(8,795) 33,540,000	3.00	3.00	3.00	3.50	5	12	25	175
1939D	7,092,000	3.00	3.00	3.00	3.50	14	20	50	
1939S	2,628,000	3.00	3.00	3.00	5.00	45	65	150	

	Mintage	F-12	VF-20	EF-40	MS-60	MS-63	MS-65	PF-65
1940	(11,246) 35,704,000	$3	$3.00	$3.00	$5.00	$12	$30	$150
1940D	2,797,600	3	3.25	7.50	50.00	80	140	
1940S	8,244,000	3	3.00	3.00	7.00	13	25	
1941	(15,287) 79,032,000	3	3.00	3.00	3.50	6	20	100
1941D	16,714,800	3	3.00	3.50	12.00	22	25	
1941S	16,080,000	3	3.00	3.00	7.50	18	25	
1942	(21,123) 102,096,000	3	3.00	3.00	3.50	4	10	100
1942D	17,487,200	3	3.00	3.00	6.00	12	20	
1942S	19,384,000	3	3.00	4.00	27.00	45	90	
1943	99,700,000	3	3.00	3.00	3.50	4	20	
1943D	16,095,600	3	3.00	3.00	8.00	16	20	
1943S	21,700,000	3	3.00	3.00	8.00	19	25	
1944	104,956,000	3	3.00	3.00	3.50	4	18	
1944D	14,600,800	3	3.00	3.00	4.00	10	18	
1944S	12,560,000	3	3.00	3.00	5.00	12	18	
1945	74,372,000	3	3.00	3.00	3.50	4	18	
1945D	12,341,600	3	3.00	3.00	6.00	12	20	
1945S	17,004,001	3	3.00	3.00	3.75	5	15	
1946	53,436,000	3	3.00	3.00	3.50	4	16	
1946D	9,072,800	3	3.00	3.00	3.50	4	15	
1946S	4,204,000	3	3.00	3.00	3.50	4	16	
1947	22,556,000	3	3.00	3.00	3.50	5	15	

Chart continued on next page.

	Mintage	F-12	VF-20	EF-40	MS-60	MS-63	MS-65	PF-65
1947D	15,338,400	$3	$3	$3.00	$3.50	$4.00	$15.00	
1947S	5,532,000	3	3	3.00	3.50	4.00	15.00	
1948	35,196,000	3	3	3.00	3.50	4.00	15.00	
1948D	16,766,800	3	3	3.00	3.50	5.00	30.00	
1948S	15,960,000	3	3	3.00	3.50	5.00	18.00	
1949	9,312,000	3	3	3.75	10.00	18.00	30.00	
1949D	10,068,400	3	3	3.25	6.00	11.00	22.00	
1950	(51,386) 24,920,126	3	3	3.00	3.50	5.00	13.00	$30.00
1950D	21,075,600	3	3	3.00	3.50	5.00	13.00	
1950D, D Over S	*		25	75.00	125.00	175.00	500.00	
1950S	10,284,004	3	3	3.25	5.00	6.00	25.00	
1950S, S Over D	*		25	80.00	140.00	200.00	400.00	
1951	(57,500) 43,448,102	3	3	3.00	3.50	4.00	14.00	27.50
1951D	35,354,800	3	3	3.00	3.50	4.00	14.00	
1951S	9,048,000	3	3	3.25	5.00	12.00	18.00	
1952	(81,980) 38,780,093	3	3	3.00	3.50	4.00	11.00	25.00
1952D	49,795,200	3	3	3.00	3.50	4.00	16.00	
1952S	13,707,800	3	3	3.25	5.00	10.00	16.00	
1953	(128,800) 18,536,120	3	3	3.00	3.50	4.00	16.00	22.00
1953D	56,112,400	3	3	3.00	3.50	4.00	15.00	
1953S	14,016,000	3	3	3.00	3.50	4.00	12.00	
1954	(233,300) 54,412,203	3	3	3.00	3.50	4.00	13.00	12.00
1954D	42,305,500	3	3	3.00	3.50	3.75	17.00	
1954S	11,834,722	3	3	3.00	3.50	3.75	15.00	
1955	(378,200) 18,180,181	3	3	3.00	3.50	3.75	12.00	12.00
1955D	3,182,400	3	3	3.00	3.50	3.85	20.00	
1956	(669,384) 44,144,000	3	3	3.00	3.50	3.75	8.00	4.00
1956D	32,334,500	3	3	3.00	3.50	3.75	10.00	
1957	(1,247,952) 46,532,000	3	3	3.00	3.50	3.75	10.00	4.00
1957D	77,924,160	3	3	3.00	3.50	3.75	10.00	
1958	(875,652) 6,360,000	3	3	3.00	3.50	3.75	9.00	4.00
1958D	78,124,900	3	3	3.00	3.50	3.75	9.00	
1959	(1,149,291) 24,384,000	3	3	3.00	3.50	3.75	9.00	4.00
1959D	62,054,232	3	3	3.00	3.50	3.75	12.00	
1960	(1,691,602) 29,164,000	3	3	3.00	3.50	3.75	6.50	4.00
1960D	63,000,324	3	3	3.00	3.50	3.75	6.50	
1961	(3,028,244) 37,036,000	3	3	3.00	3.50	3.75	6.50	4.00
1961D	83,656,928	3	3	3.00	3.50	3.75	6.50	
1962	(3,218,019) 36,156,000	3	3	3.00	3.50	3.75	6.50	4.00
1962D	127,554,756	3	3	3.00	3.50	3.75	6.50	
1963	(3,075,645) 74,316,000	3	3	3.00	3.50	3.75	6.50	4.00
1963D	135,288,184	3	3	3.00	3.50	3.75	6.50	
1964	(3,950,762) 560,390,585	3	3	3.00	3.50	3.75	6.50	4.00
1964D	704,135,528	3	3	3.00	3.50	3.75	6.50	

* Included in number above.

Clad Coinage and Silver Proofs (1965 to Date)

	Mintage	MS-63	MS-65	PF-65		Mintage	MS-63	MS-65	PF-65
1965	1,819,717,540	$0.30	$2.00		1968D	101,534,000	$0.30	$1.00	
1966	821,101,500	0.30	1.00		1968S	(3,041,506)			$1
1967	1,524,031,848	0.30	1.00		1969	176,212,000	0.75	1.50	
1968	220,731,500	0.50	1.50		1969D	114,372,000	0.50	1.50	

QUARTER DOLLARS

Mintage	MS-63	MS-65	PF-65
1969S . . . .(2,934,631)			$1
1970 136,420,000	$0.25	$1.75	
1970D 417,341,364	0.25	1.00	
1970S . . . .(2,632,810)			1
1971 109,284,000	0.30	1.00	
1971D 258,634,428	0.30	0.50	
1971S . . . .(3,220,733)			1
1972 215,048,000	0.30	1.00	

Mintage	MS-63	MS-65	PF-65
1972D 311,067,732	$0.30	$1.50	
1972S . . . .(3,260,996)			$1
1973 346,924,000	0.30	1.50	
1973D 232,977,400	0.30	2.00	
1973S . . . .(2,760,339)			1
1974 801,456,000	0.30	1.00	
1974D 353,160,300	0.30	1.50	
1974S . . . .(2,612,568)			1

Bicentennial (1776–1976)

	Mintage	MS-63	MS-65	PF-65
1776–1976, Copper-Nickel Clad 809,784,016		$0.30	$1	
1776–1976D, Copper-Nickel Clad 860,118,839		0.30	1	
1776–1976S, Copper-Nickel Clad . . . .(7,059,099)				$1
1776–1976S, Silver Clad 11,000,000		1.40	2	
1776–1976S, Silver Clad . . . .(4,000,000)				2

Note: Mintage figures for 1976-S coins are approximate; many were melted in 1982.

Eagle Reverse Resumed (1977–1998)
(Dies Slightly Modified to Lower Relief)

Mintage	MS-63	MS-65	PF-65
1977 468,556,000	$0.27		
1977D 256,524,978	0.27	$1.00	
1977S . . . .(3,251,152)			$1
1978 521,452,000	0.27	1.50	
1978D 287,373,152	0.27	1.50	
1978S . . . .(3,127,781)			1
1979 515,708,000	0.28	1.50	
1979D 489,789,780	0.27	1.25	
1979S . . . .(3,677,175)			
Filled S			1
Clear S			1
1980P 635,832,000	0.27	1.50	
1980D 518,327,487	0.27	1.25	
1980S . . . .(3,554,806)			1
1981P 601,716,000	0.27	1.50	
1981D 575,722,833	0.27	1.00	
1981S . . . .(4,063,083)			1
1982P 500,931,000	1.00	8.00	
1982D 480,042,788	0.70	6.00	
1982S . . . .(3,857,479)			1
1983P 673,535,000	4.00	20.00	
1983D 617,806,446	3.00	14.00	
1983S . . . .(3,279,126)			1

Mintage	MS-63	MS-65	PF-65
1984P 676,545,000	$0.30	$2.00	
1984D 546,483,064	0.30	2.00	
1984S . . . .(3,065,110)			$1.00
1985P 775,818,962	0.50	6.00	
1985D 519,962,888	0.35	2.50	
1985S . . . .(3,362,821)			1.00
1986P 551,199,333	1.00	4.00	
1986D 504,298,660	3.00	9.00	
1986S . . . .(3,010,497)			1.00
1987P 582,499,481	0.27	2.50	
1987D 655,594,696	0.27	1.00	
1987S . . . .(4,227,728)			1.00
1988P 562,052,000	0.50	5.00	
1988D 596,810,688	0.50	4.00	
1988S . . . .(3,262,948)			1.00
1989P 512,868,000	0.30	4.25	
1989D 896,535,597	0.27	1.00	
1989S . . . .(3,220,194)			1.00
1990P 613,792,000	0.27	4.00	
1990D 927,638,181	0.28	4.00	
1990S . . . .(3,299,559)			1.75
1991P 570,968,000	0.30	4.00	
1991D 630,966,693	0.30	1.50	

Chart continued on next page.

	Mintage	MS-63	MS-65	PF-65
1991S . . . .(2,867,787)				$1.25
1992P 384,764,000	$0.35	$4.25	
1992D 389,777,107	0.35	4.25	
1992S . . . .(2,858,981)				1.25
1992S, Silver . . .(1,317,579)				3.50
1993P 639,276,000	0.30	1.75	
1993D 645,476,128	0.30	1.75	
1993S . . . .(2,633,439)				1.25
1993S, Silver . . .(761,353)				3.50
1994P 825,600,000	0.30	4.00	
1994D 880,034,110	0.30	4.00	
1994S . . . .(2,484,594)				1.00
1994S, Silver . . . .(785,329)				4.00
1995P 1,004,336,000	0.30	4.00	
1995D 1,103,216,000	0.30	2.50	

	Mintage	MS-63	MS-65	PF-65
1995S . . . .(2,117,496)				$4.00
1995S, Silver . . .(679,985)				4.00
1996P 925,040,000	$0.25	$2.00	
1996D 906,868,000	0.25	2.00	
1996S . . . .(1,750,244)				1.75
1996S, Silver . . . .(775,021)				4.00
1997P 595,740,000	0.25	1.25	
1997D 599,680,000	0.25	1.25	
1997S . . . .(2,055,000)				3.00
1997S, Silver . . . .(741,678)				3.50
1998P 896,268,000	0.25	1.00	
1998D 821,000,000	0.25	1.00	
1998S . . . .(2,086,507)				2.50
1998S, Silver . . . .(878,792)				3.50

State Quarters (1999–2008)

The United States Mint 50 State Quarters® Program, which began in 1999, produced a series of 50 quarter dollar coins with special designs honoring each state. Five different designs were issued each year during the period 1999 to 2008. States were commemorated in the order of their entrance into statehood.

These are all legal tender coins of standard weight and composition. The obverse side depicting President George Washington was modified to include some of the wording previously used on the reverse. The modification was authorized by special legislation, and carried out by Mint Sculptor-Engraver William Cousins, whose initials were added to the truncation of Washington's neck adjacent to those of the original designer, John Flanagan.

Each state theme was proposed and approved by the governor of the state. Final designs were created by Mint personnel.

Circulation coins are made at the Philadelphia and Denver mints. Proof coins are made in San Francisco. Both copper-nickel and silver Proof coins were made each year.

	Mintage	AU-50	MS-63	PF-65
Delaware				
1999P 373,400,000	$0.25	$0.50	
1999D 401,424,000	0.25	0.50	
1999S . . . . . .(3,713,359)				$1.75
1999S, Silver . .(804,565)				7.00
Pennsylvania				
1999P 349,000,000	0.25	0.50	
1999D 358,332,000	0.25	0.50	
1999S . . . . . .(3,713,359)				1.75
1999S, Silver . .(804,565)				6.00

	Mintage	AU-50	MS-63	PF-65
New Jersey				
1999P 363,200,000	$0.25	$0.30	
1999D 299,028,000	0.25	0.35	
1999S . . . . . .(3,713,359)				$1.75
1999S, Silver . .(804,565)				6.00
Georgia				
1999P 451,188,000	0.25	0.30	
1999D 488,744,000	0.25	0.30	
1999S . . . . . .(3,713,359)				1.75
1999S, Silver . .(804,565)				6.00

QUARTER DOLLARS

	Mintage	AU-50	MS-63	PF-65
Connecticut				
1999P	688,744,000	$0.25	$0.30	
1999D	657,880,000	0.25	0.30	

	Mintage	AU-50	MS-63	PF-65
Connecticut				
1999S	(3,713,359)			$1.75
1999S, Silver . .	(804,565)			7.00

	Mintage	AU-50	MS-63	PF-65
Massachusetts				
2000P	628,600,000	$0.25	$0.30	
2000D	535,184,000	0.25	0.30	
2000S	(4,020,172)			$1.50
2000S, Silver . .	(965,421)			3.50
Maryland				
2000P	678,200,000	0.25	0.30	
2000D	556,532,000	0.25	0.30	
2000S	(4,020,172)			1.50
2000S, Silver . .	(965,421)			3.50
South Carolina				
2000P	742,576,000	0.25	0.32	
2000D	566,208,000	0.25	0.32	

	Mintage	AU-50	MS-63	PF-65
South Carolina				
2000S	(4,020,172)			$1.50
2000S, Silver . .	(965,421)			3.50
New Hampshire				
2000P	673,040,000	$0.25	$0.30	
2000D	495,976,000	0.25	0.30	
2000S	(4,020,172)			1.50
2000S, Silver . .	(965,421)			3.50
Virginia				
2000P	943,000,000	0.25	0.30	
2000D	651,616,000	0.25	0.30	
2000S	(4,020,172)			1.50
2000S, Silver . .	(965,421)			3.50

	Mintage	AU-50	MS-63	PF-65
New York				
2001P	655,400,000	$0.25	$0.30	
2001D	619,640,000	0.25	0.30	
2001S	(3,094,140)			$1.50
2001S, Silver . .	(889,697)			3.50
North Carolina				
2001P	627,600,000	0.25	0.30	
2001D	427,876,000	0.25	0.30	
2001S	(3,094,140)			1.50
2001S, Silver . .	(889,697)			3.50
Rhode Island				
2001P	423,000,000	0.25	0.30	
2001D	447,100,000	0.25	0.30	

	Mintage	AU-50	MS-63	PF-65
Rhode Island				
2001S	(3,094,140)			$1.50
2001S, Silver . .	(889,697)			3.50
Vermont				
2001P	423,400,000	$0.25	$0.30	
2001D	459,404,000	0.25	0.30	
2001S	(3,094,140)			1.50
2001S, Silver . .	(889,697)			3.50
Kentucky				
2001P	353,000,000	0.25	0.30	
2001D	370,564,000	0.25	0.30	
2001S	(3,094,140)			1.50
2001S, Silver . .	(889,697)			3.50

	Mintage	AU-50	MS-63	PF-65
Tennessee				
2002P 361,600,000	$0.30	$0.40	
2002D 286,468,000	0.30	0.40	
2002S . . . . . .(3,084,245)			$1.50
2002S, Silver . .(892,229)			3.50
Ohio				
2002P 217,200,000	0.25	0.30	
2002D 414,832,000	0.25	0.30	
2002S . . . . . .(3,084,245)			1.50
2002S, Silver . .(892,229)			3.50
Louisiana				
2002P 362,000,000	0.25	0.30	
2002D 402,204,000	0.25	0.30	

	Mintage	AU-50	MS-63	PF-65
Louisiana				
2002S . . . . . .(3,084,245)			$1.50
2002S, Silver . .(892,229)			3.50
Indiana				
2002P 362,600,000	$0.25	$0.30	
2002D 327,200,000	0.25	0.30	
2002S . . . . . .(3,084,245)			1.50
2002S, Silver . .(892,229)			3.50
Mississippi				
2002P 290,000,000	0.25	0.30	
2002D 289,600,000	0.25	0.30	
2002S . . . . . .(3,084,245)			1.50
2002S, Silver . .(892,229)			3.50

	Mintage	AU-50	MS-63	PF-65
Illinois				
2003P 225,800,000	$0.25	$0.30	
2003D 237,400,000	0.25	0.30	
2003S . . . .(3,408,516)			$1.50
2003S, Silver . .(1,125,755)			3.50
Alabama				
2003P 225,000,000	0.25	0.30	
2003D 232,400,000	0.25	0.30	
2003S . . . .(3,408,516)			1.50
2003S, Silver . .(1,125,755)			3.50
Maine				
2003P 217,400,000	0.25	0.30	
2003D 231,400,000	0.25	0.30	

	Mintage	AU-50	MS-63	PF-65
Maine				
2003S . . . .(3,408,516)			$1.50
2003S, Silver . .(1,125,755)			3.50
Missouri				
2003P 225,000,000	$0.25	$0.30	
2003D 228,200,000	0.25	0.30	
2003S . . . .(3,408,516)			1.50
2003S, Silver . .(1,125,755)			3.50
Arkansas				
2003P 228,000,000	0.25	0.30	
2003D 229,800,000	0.25	0.30	
2003S . . . .(3,408,516)			1.50
2003S, Silver . .(1,125,755)			3.50

	Mintage	AU-50	MS-63	PF-65
Michigan				
2004P 233,800,000		$0.25	$0.30	
2004D 225,800,000		0.25	0.30	
2004S . . . .(2,740,684)				$1.50
2004S, Silver . .(1,769,786)				3.50
Florida				
2004P 240,200,000		0.25	0.30	
2004D 241,600,000		0.25	0.30	
2004S . . . .(2,740,684)				1.50
2004S, Silver . .(1,769,786)				3.50
Texas				
2004P 278,800,000		0.25	0.30	
2004D 263,000,000		0.25	0.30	

	Mintage	AU-50	MS-63	PF-65
Texas				
2004S . . . .(2,740,684)				$1.50
2004S, Silver . .(1,769,786)				3.50
Iowa				
2004P 213,800,000		$0.25	$0.30	
2004D 251,400,000		0.25	0.30	
2004S . . . .(2,740,684)				1.50
2004S, Silver . .(1,769,786)				3.50
Wisconsin				
2004P 226,400,000		0.25	0.30	
2004D 226,800,000		0.25	0.30	
2004S . . . .(2,740,684)				1.50
2004S, Silver . .(1,769,786)				3.50

	Mintage	AU-50	MS-63	PF-65
California				
2005P 257,200,000		$0.25	$0.30	
2005D 263,200,000		0.25	0.30	
2005S . . . .(3,262,960)				$1.50
2005S, Silver . .(1,678,649)				3.50
Minnesota				
2005P 239,600,000		0.25	0.30	
2005D 248,400,000		0.25	0.30	
2005S . . . .(3,262,960)				1.50
2005S, Silver . .(1,678,649)				3.50
Oregon				
2005P 316,200,000		0.25	0.30	
2005D 404,000,000		0.25	0.30	

	Mintage	AU-50	MS-63	PF-65
Oregon				
2005S . . . .(3,262,960)				$1.50
2005S, Silver . .(1,678,649)				3.50
Kansas				
2005P 263,400,000		$0.25	$0.30	
2005D 300,000,000		0.25	0.30	
2005S . . . .(3,262,960)				1.50
2005S, Silver . .(1,678,649)				3.50
West Virginia				
2005P 365,400,000		0.25	0.30	
2005D 356,200,000		0.25	0.30	
2005S . . . .(3,262,960)				1.50
2005S, Silver . .(1,678,649)				3.50

	Mintage	AU-50	MS-63	PF-65
Nevada				
2006P	277,000,000	$0.25	$0.30	
2006D	312,800,000	0.25	0.30	
2006S	(2,882,428)			$1.50
2006S, Silver	(1,585,008)			3.50
Nebraska				
2006P	318,000,000	0.25	0.30	
2006D	273,000,000	0.25	0.30	
2006S	(2,882,428)			1.50
2006S, Silver	(1,585,008)			3.50
Colorado				
2006P	274,800,000	0.25	0.30	
2006D	294,200,000	0.25	0.30	

	Mintage	AU-50	MS-63	PF-65
Colorado				
2006S	(2,882,428)			$1.50
2006S, Silver	(1,585,008)			3.50
North Dakota				
2006P	305,800,000	$0.25	$0.30	
2006D	359,000,000	0.25	0.30	
2006S	(2,882,428)			1.50
2006S, Silver	(1,585,008)			3.50
South Dakota				
2006P	245,000,000	0.25	0.30	
2006D	265,800,000	0.25	0.30	
2006S	(2,882,428)			1.50
2006S, Silver	(1,585,008)			3.50

	Mintage	AU-50	MS-63	PF-65
Montana				
2007P	257,000,000	$0.25	$0.30	
2007D	256,240,000	0.25	0.30	
2007S	(2,374,778)			$1.50
2007S, Silver	(1,313,481)			3.50
Washington				
2007P	265,200,000	0.25	0.30	
2007D	280,000,000	0.25	0.30	
2007S	(2,374,778)			1.50
2007S, Silver	(1,313,481)			3.50
Idaho				
2007P	294,600,000	0.25	0.30	
2007D	286,800,000	0.25	0.30	

	Mintage	AU-50	MS-63	PF-65
Idaho				
2007S	(2,374,778)			$1.50
2007S, Silver	(1,313,481)			3.50
Wyoming				
2007P	243,600,000	$0.25	$0.30	
2007D	320,800,000	0.25	0.30	
2007S	(2,374,778)			1.50
2007S, Silver	(1,313,481)			3.50
Utah				
2007P	255,000,000	0.25	0.30	
2007D	253,200,000	0.25	0.30	
2007S	(2,374,778)			1.50
2007S, Silver	(1,313,481)			3.50

	Mintage	AU-50	MS-63	PF-65
Oklahoma				
2008P 222,000,000		$0.25	$0.30	
2008D 194,600,000		0.25	0.30	
2008S . . . .(2,047,284)				$1.50
2008S, Silver . .(1,020,768)				3.50
New Mexico				
2008P 244,200,000		0.25	0.30	
2008D 244,400,000		0.25	0.30	
2008S . . . .(2,047,284)				1.50
2008S, Silver . .(1,020,768)				3.50
Arizona				
2008P 244,600,000		0.25	0.30	
2008D 265,000,000		0.25	0.30	

	Mintage	AU-50	MS-63	PF-65
Arizona				
2008S . . . .(2,047,284)				$1.50
2008S, Silver . .(1,020,768)				3.50
Alaska				
2008P 251,800,000		$0.25	$0.30	
2008D 254,000,000		0.25	0.30	
2008S . . . .(2,047,284)				1.50
2008S, Silver . .(1,020,768)				3.50
Hawaii				
2008P 254,000,000		0.25	0.30	
2008D 263,600,000		0.25	0.30	
2008S . . . .(2,047,284)				1.50
2008S, Silver . .(1,020,768)				3.50

Some statehood quarters were accidentally made with "dis-oriented" dies and are valued higher than ordinary pieces. Normal United States coins have dies oriented in "coin alignment," such that the reverse appears upside down when the coin is rotated from right to left. Values for the rotated-die quarters vary according to the amount of shifting. The most valuable are those that are shifted 180 degrees, so that both sides appear upright when the coin is turned over (called *medal alignment*).

Manufacturing varieties showing die doubling or other minor, unintentional characteristics are of interest to collectors and are often worth premium prices.

District of Columbia and U.S. Territories Quarters (2009)

At the ending of the U.S. Mint 50 State Quarters® Program a new series of quarter-dollar reverse designs was authorized to recognize the District of Columbia and the five U.S. territories: the Commonwealth of Puerto Rico, Guam, American Samoa, the U.S. Virgin Islands, and the Commonwealth of the Northern Mariana Islands. Each of these coins, issued sequentially during 2009, has the portrait of George Washington, as in the past, and is made of the same weight and composition. Each coin commemorates the history, geography, or traditions of the place it represents.

See next page for chart.

	Mintage	AU-50	MS-63	PF-65
District of Columbia				
2009P	*83,600,000*	$0.25	$0.30	
2009D	*88,800,000*	0.25	0.30	
2009S	*(1,964,624)*			$1.50
2009S, Silver	*(880,631)*			3.50
Puerto Rico				
2009P	*53,200,000*	0.25	0.30	
2009D	*86,000,000*	0.25	0.30	
2009S	*(1,964,624)*			1.50
2009S, Silver	*(880,631)*			3.50
Guam				
2009P	*45,000,000*	0.25	0.30	
2009D	*42,600,000*	0.25	0.30	
2009S	*(1,964,624)*			1.50
2009S, Silver	*(880,631)*			3.50

	Mintage	AU-50	MS-63	PF-65
American Samoa				
2009P	*42,600,000*	$0.25	$0.30	
2009D	*39,600,000*	0.25	0.30	
2009S	*(1,964,624)*			$1.50
2009S, Silver	*(880,631)*			3.50
U.S. Virgin Islands				
2009P	*41,000,000*	0.25	0.30	
2009D	*41,000,000*	0.25	0.30	
2009S	*(1,964,624)*			1.50
2009S, Silver	*(880,631)*			3.50
Northern Mariana Islands				
2009P	*35,200,000*	0.25	0.30	
2009D	*37,600,000*	0.25	0.30	
2009S	*(1,964,624)*			1.50
2009S, Silver	*(880,631)*			3.50

America the Beautiful™ Quarters Program (2010–2021)

Following up on the popularity of the 50 State Quarters® Program, Congress has authorized the production of new circulating commemorative quarters from 2010 to 2021. The coins will honor a site of "natural or historic significance" from each of the 50 states, five U.S. territories, and the District of Columbia. They will continue to bear George Washington's portrait on the obverse.

Five designs will be released each year, in the order the coins' featured locations were designated national parks or national sites. At the discretion of the secretary of the Treasury, this series could be extended an additional 11 years by featuring a second national park or site from each state, district, and territory.

QUARTER DOLLARS

	Mintage	AU-50	MS-63	PF-65
Hot Springs National Park				
2010P		$0.25	$0.30	
2010D		0.25	0.30	
2010S				$1.50
2010S, Silver				3.50
Yellowstone National Park				
2010P		0.25	0.30	
2010D		0.25	0.30	
2010S				1.50
2010S, Silver				3.50
Yosemite National Park				
2010P		0.25	0.30	
2010D		0.25	0.30	
2010S				1.50
2010S, Silver				3.50
Grand Canyon National Park				
2010P		0.25	0.30	
2010D		0.25	0.30	
2010S				1.50
2010S, Silver				3.50
Mt. Hood National Forest				
2010P		0.25	0.30	
2010D		0.25	0.30	
2010S				1.50
2010S, Silver				3.50

	Mintage	AU-50	MS-63	PF-65
Gettysburg National Military Park				
2011P		$0.25	$0.30	
2011D		0.25	0.30	
2011S				$1.50
2011S, Silver				3.50
Glacier National Park				
2011P		0.25	0.30	
2011D		0.25	0.30	
2011S				1.50
2011S, Silver				3.50
Olympic National Park				
2011P		0.25	0.30	
2011D		0.25	0.30	
2011S				1.50
2011S, Silver				3.50
Vicksburg National Military Park				
2011P		0.25	0.30	
2011D		0.25	0.30	
2011S				1.50
2011S, Silver				3.50
Chickasaw National Recreation Area				
2011P		0.25	0.30	
2011D		0.25	0.30	
2011S				1.50
2011S, Silver				3.50

The half dollar, authorized by the Act of April 2, 1792, was not minted until December, 1794. The weight of the half dollar was 208 grains and its fineness .8924 when first issued. This standard was not changed until 1837 when the Act of January 18, 1837 specified 206-1/4 grains, .900 fine. This fineness continued in use until 1965.

Arrows at the date in 1853 indicate the reduction of weight to 192 grains. During that year only, rays were added to the reverse. Arrows remained in 1854 and 1855. In 1873 the weight was raised by .9 grains and arrows were again placed at the date.

FLOWING HAIR (1794–1795)

AG-3 About Good: Clear enough to identify.
G-4 Good: Date and letters sufficient to be legible. Main devices outlined, but lacking in detail.
VG-8 Very Good: Major details discernible. Letters well formed but worn.
F-12 Fine: Hair ends distinguishable. Top hair lines visible, but otherwise worn smooth.
VF-20 Very Fine: Some detail visible in hair in center; other details more bold.
EF-40 Extremely Fine: Hair above head and down neck detailed, with slight wear.
AU-50 About Uncirculated: All hair visible; slight wear on bust of Liberty and on top edges of eagle's wings, head, and breast.

2 Leaves Under Wings · 3 Leaves Under Wings

	Mintage	AG-3	G-4	VG-8	F-12	VF-20	EF-40	AU-50
1794 23,464		$900	$1,300	$2,200	$4,250	$8,000	$17,250	$37,500
1795 .299,680		160	335	475	900	2,000	5,000	8,500
1795, Recut Date . . . .*		160	335	475	900	2,000	5,000	8,500
1795, 3 Leaves Under Each Wing . . . .*		500	800	1,000	2,000	3,000	6,500	12,000

* Included in number above.

DRAPED BUST (1796–1807)

AG-3 About Good: Clear enough to identify.
G-4 Good: Date and letters sufficiently clear to be legible. Main devices outlined, but lacking in detail.
VG-8 Very Good: Major details discernible. Letters well formed but worn.
F-12 Fine: Hair ends distinguishable. Top hair lines visible, but otherwise worn smooth.
VF-20 Very Fine: Right side of drapery slightly worn. Left side to curls smooth.
EF-40 Extremely Fine: All lines in drapery on bust distinctly visible around to hair curls.
AU-50 About Uncirculated: Slight trace of wear on cheek, hair, and shoulder.

Small Eagle Reverse (1796–1797)

1796, 16 Stars · 1797, 15 Stars

HALF DOLLARS

	Mintage	AG-3	G-4	VG-8	F-12	VF-20	EF-40	AU-50
1796, All kinds 3,918								
1796, 15 Stars		$7,500	$15,000	$17,000	$24,000	$34,000	$50,000	$75,000
1796, 16 Stars		8,000	16,000	18,000	26,000	36,000	52,500	80,000
1797, 15 Stars		7,500	15,000	17,000	24,000	34,000	50,000	75,000

Heraldic Eagle Reverse (1801–1807)

1805, 5 Over 4

1806, 6 Over 5

	Mintage	G-4	VG-8	F-12	VF-20	EF-40	AU-50	MS-60
1801 30,289		$300	$500	$1,000	$1,500	$4,000	$6,000	$16,000
1802 29,890		300	500	1,000	1,500	4,000	6,000	15,000
1803 188,234		75	90	150	250	600	1,900	4,200
1805, All kinds 211,722								
1805, 5 Over 4		100	150	275	375	1,100	2,600	10,000
1805, Normal Date		80	100	120	225	600	1,600	4,000
1806, All kinds 839,576								
1806, Normal Date		80	100	120	200	450	1,200	2,800
1806, 6 Over 5		80	100	120	200	450	1,200	2,800
1806, 6 Over Inverted 6		90	120	200	450	900	2,200	4,750
1807 301,076		80	100	120	200	450	1,200	2,800

CAPPED BUST, LETTERED EDGE (1807–1836)

John Reich designed this capped head concept of Liberty. Reich's design of Liberty facing left was used on all U.S. silver denominations for the next 30 years.

G-4 Good: Date and letters legible. Bust worn smooth with outline distinct.

VG-8 Very Good: LIBERTY faint. Legends distinguishable. Clasp at shoulder visible; curl above it nearly smooth.

F-12 Fine: Clasp and adjacent curl clearly outlined with slight details.

VF-20 Very Fine: Clasp at shoulder clear. Wear visible on highest point of curl. Hair over brow distinguishable.

EF-40 Extremely Fine: Clasp and adjacent curl fairly sharp. Brow and hair above distinct. Curls well defined.

AU-50 About Uncirculated: Trace of wear on hair over eye and over ear.

MS-60 Uncirculated: No trace of wear. Light blemishes. Possible slide marks from storage handling.

MS-63 Choice Uncirculated: Some distracting contact marks or blemishes in prime focal areas. Impaired luster possible.

First Style (1807–1808)

See next page for chart.

	Mintage	G-4	VG-8	F-12	VF-20	EF-40	AU-50	MS-60	MS-63
1807 750,500	$40	$60	$100	$200	$550	$1,200	$2,200	$4,000
1808, 8 Over 7 . . . .*	30	40	60	90	200	600	1,200	3,000
1808 1,368,600	25	32	40	55	125	255	825	1,600

* Included in number below.

Remodeled Portrait and Eagle (1809–1836)

	Mintage	G-4	VG-8	F-12	VF-20	EF-40	AU-50	MS-60	MS-63
1809 1,405,810	$24	$28	$37	$50	$100	$250	$700	$1,600
1810 1,276,276	24	28	37	50	100	225	675	1,500
1811 1,203,644	24	28	35	42	85	185	600	1,100

1812, 2 Over 1	1813, 50 C. Over UNI	1814, 4 Over 3

	Mintage	G-4	VG-8	F-12	VF-20	EF-40	AU-50	MS-60	MS-63
1812, All kinds 1,628,059								
1812, 2 Over 1	$24	$30	$40	$65	$150	$250	$1,000	$2,200
1812	22	29	37	55	100	200	500	1,000
1813 1,241,903	24	29	37	55	100	185	500	1,000
1813, 50 C. Over UNI . . . .*	24	29	42	70	140	300	700	2,100
1814, All kinds 1,039,075								
1814, 4 Over 3	24	30	45	80	150	350	800	2,100
1814	24	29	40	55	100	185	500	1,100

* Included in number above.

1817, 7 Over 3	1817, 7 Over 4	1817, "Punctuated" Date

	Mintage	G-4	VG-8	F-12	VF-20	EF-40	AU-50	MS-60	MS-63
1815, 5 Over 2 47,150	$500	$750	$900	$1,200	$2,200	$3,000	$5,500	$15,000
1817, All kinds 1,215,567								
1817, 7 Over 3	30	45	100	200	350	650	1,500	4,500
1817, 7 Over 4 *(8 known)* . . .			80,000	110,000	150,000			
1817, Dated 181.7	24	29	39	50	85	175	475	1,000
1817	24	29	39	45	65	150	450	1,000

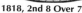

1818, 2nd 8 Over 7

1819, 9 Over 8

1820, 20 Over 19

Mintage	G-4	VG-8	F-12	VF-20	EF-40	AU-50	MS-60	MS-63
1818, 2nd 8 Over 7 . . . .*	$24	$29	$35	$42	$65	$175	$500	$1,000
1818 1,960,322	24	29	35	42	65	150	450	925
1819, 9 Over 8 . . . .*	24	29	35	42	65	150	450	925
1819 2,208,000	22	29	35	42	65	150	450	925
1820, 20 Over 19 . . . .*	24	34	40	55	120	300	600	1,000
1820 751,122	22	29	35	42	60	150	475	950
1821 1,305,797	22	29	35	42	60	150	450	950
1822 1,559,573	22	29	35	42	60	150	475	1,000
1823 1,694,200	22	29	35	42	60	150	400	900

* Included in number below.

"Various Dates"
*Probably 4 Over
2 Over 0.*

1824, 4 Over 1

**1828, Curl Base,
Knob 2**

**1828, Square
Base 2**

Mintage	G-4	VG-8	F-12	VF-20	EF-40	AU-50	MS-60	MS-63
1824, All kinds 3,504,954								
1824, 4 Over Various Dates	$22	$27	$34	$42	$60	$150	$450	$850
1824, 4 Over 1	22	29	34	42	60	150	475	850
1824	22	27	34	42	60	150	500	875
1825 2,943,166	22	27	34	42	60	150	425	825
1826 4,004,180	22	27	34	42	60	150	425	825
1827, All kinds 5,493,400								
1827, 7 Over 6	24	34	40	49	75	150	525	900
1827	22	27	34	42	60	150	425	825
1828, All kinds 3,075,200								
1828, Curl Base No Knob 2	22	27	34	42	60	150	425	825
1828, Curl Base Knob 2	27	37	47	60	75	170	575	850
1828, Square Base 2	22	27	34	42	60	150	425	825
1829, 9 Over 7 . . . .*	22	29	37	49	75	190	450	1,000
1829 3,712,156	22	27	34	42	60	150	400	850
1830 4,764,800	22	27	34	42	60	150	400	850
1831 5,873,660	22	27	34	42	60	150	400	850
1832 4,797,000	22	27	34	42	60	150	400	850
1833 5,206,000	22	27	34	42	60	150	400	850
1834 6,412,004	22	27	34	42	60	150	400	850
1835 5,352,006	22	27	34	42	60	150	400	850
1836 6,545,000	22	27	34	42	60	150	400	850
1836, 50 Over 00 . . . .*	27	40	50	70	100	225	675	1,700

* Included in regular mintage.

CAPPED BUST, REEDED EDGE (1836–1839)

G-4 Good: LIBERTY barely discernible on headband.
VG-8 Very Good: Some letters in LIBERTY clear.
F-12 Fine: LIBERTY complete but faint.
VF-20 Very Fine: LIBERTY sharp. Shoulder clasp clear.
EF-40 Extremely Fine: LIBERTY sharp and strong. Hair details visible.
AU-50 About Uncirculated: Slight trace of wear on cap, cheek, and hair above forehead, and on eagle's claws, wing tops, and head.
MS-60 Uncirculated: No trace of wear. Light blemishes.
MS-63 Choice Uncirculated: Some distracting marks or blemishes in focal areas. Impaired luster possible.

Reverse 50 CENTS (1836–1837)

	Mintage	G-4	VG-8	F-12	VF-20	EF-40	AU-50	MS-60	MS-63
1836 . . . .*1,200+*	$400	$500	$700	$900	$1,200	$2,000	$4,500	$8,000
1837 3,629,820	23	25	35	50	90	175	475	1,000

Reverse HALF DOL. (1838–1839)

On half dollars of 1838 and 1839, the mintmark appears on the obverse; on those thereafter, it is on the reverse below the eagle.

	Mintage	G-4	VG-8	F-12	VF-20	EF-40	AU-50	MS-60	MS-63
1838 3,546,000	$23	$25	$35	$50	$80	$150	$425	$1,000
1838O 20						100,000	150,000	
1839 1,392,976	20	25	35	50	75	150	525	1,000
1839O 116,000	65	100	135	185	325	600	1,500	2,750

LIBERTY SEATED (1839–1891)

G-4 Good: Scant rim. LIBERTY on shield worn off. Date and letters legible.
VG-8 Very Good: Rim fairly defined. Some letters in LIBERTY evident.
F-12 Fine: LIBERTY complete, but weak.
VF-20 Very Fine: LIBERTY mostly sharp.
EF-40 Extremely Fine: LIBERTY entirely sharp. Scroll edges and clasp distinct.
AU-50 About Uncirculated: Slight wear on Liberty's breast and knees; eagle's head, claws, and wing tops.
MS-60 Uncirculated: No trace of wear. Light blemishes.
MS-63 Choice Uncirculated: Some distracting blemishes in prime focal areas. Impaired luster possible.
PF-63 Choice Proof: Reflective surfaces with only a few blemishes in secondary focal places. No major flaws.

Variety 1 – No Motto Above Eagle (1839–1853)

No Drapery From Elbow

Drapery From Elbow (Starting 1839)

1842, Small Date

	Mintage	G-4	VG-8	F-12	VF-20	EF-40	AU-50	MS-60	MS-63
1839, No Drapery From Elbow ....*		$18	$30	$50	$140	$325	$500	$2,600	$8,500
1839, Drapery 1,972,400		11	13	19	30	50	65	275	950
1840 1,435,008		11	14	21	35	60	70	275	650
1840O 855,100		11	13	18	30	48	60	300	800
1841 310,000		13	15	22	65	110	140	500	800
1841O 401,000		10	14	19	30	50	65	375	750
1842, Small Date 2,012,764		10	13	20	35	55	70	450	950
1842, Medium Date ....**		10	13	19	30	50	65	300	850
1842O, Small Date 754,000		200	375	600	1,100	1,900	2,750	5,500	—
1842O, Medium Date ....**		10	12	18	28	45	65	300	1,600
1843 3,844,000		10	12	18	28	45	65	300	425
1843O 2,268,000		10	12	18	28	45	65	300	450
1844 1,766,000		10	12	18	28	45	65	300	425
1844O 2,005,000		10	12	18	28	45	65	300	900
1845 589,000		11	13	20	32	50	90	380	1,200
1845O 2,094,000		10	12	17	24	45	65	360	450
1846 2,210,000		10	12	17	24	45	65	300	500
1846, 6 Over Horizontal 6 ....**		45	80	125	175	300	500	1,100	4,000
1846O 2,304,000		11	13	17	24	45	75	450	900
1847 1,156,000		10	12	17	24	45	65	300	425
1847O 2,584,000		10	12	17	24	45	65	300	1,000
1848 580,000		14	18	28	40	75	180	420	600
1848O 3,180,000		10	12	17	24	45	65	360	700
1849 1,252,000		10	12	17	24	45	65	340	700
1849O 2,310,000		10	12	17	24	45	65	300	800
1850 227,000		75	100	175	190	300	350	725	1,600
1850O 2,456,000		10	12	17	24	45	65	300	575
1851 200,750		75	125	190	250	275	400	850	1,400
1851O 402,000		10	12	18	23	45	65	300	500
1852 77,130		125	180	280	360	400	550	800	1,100
1852O 144,000		20	30	45	70	180	225	1,000	3,200
1853O (3 known)			100,000	150,000	250,000				

* Included in number below. **Included in number above.

Variety 2 – Arrows at Date, Rays Around Eagle (1853)

	Mintage	G-4	VG-8	F-12	VF-20	EF-40	AU-50	MS-60	MS-63
1853	3,532,708	$11	$14	$20	$60	$120	$300	$950	$1,500
1853O	1,328,000	12	16	22	65	130	340	1,400	2,000

Variety 3 – Arrows at Date, No Rays (1854–1855)

	Mintage	G-4	VG-8	F-12	VF-20	EF-40	AU-50	MS-60	MS-63
1854	2,982,000	$10	$12	$18	$30	$55	$85	$360	$650
1854O	5,240,000	10	12	18	30	55	85	360	650
1855, Over 1854	*	15	35	70	120	220	275	800	1,400
1855	759,500	10	12	18	30	55	85	360	650
1855O	3,688,000	10	12	18	30	55	85	360	650
1855S	129,950	150	185	300	600	1,400	2,750	7,000	—

* Included in number below.

Variety 1 Resumed (1856–1866; Weight Standard of 1853)

	Mintage	G-4	VG-8	F-12	VF-20	EF-40	AU-50	MS-60	MS-63	PF-63
1856	938,000	$10	$12	$18	$23	$40	$80	$220	$400	
1856O	2,658,000	10	12	20	24	40	80	220	400	
1856S	211,000	15	20	37	90	200	425	1,700	—	
1857	1,988,000	10	12	18	23	40	80	220	400	
1857O	818,000	10	12	20	24	40	80	240	650	
1857S	158,000	18	30	45	85	180	425	1,800	—	
1858	(300+) 4,225,700	10	11	18	28	40	80	220	400	$1,400
1858O	7,294,000	10	11	18	23	40	80	220	400	
1858S	476,000	12	14	22	30	55	120	525	1,500	
1859	(800) 747,200	10	11	18	23	45	85	225	450	900
1859O	2,834,000	10	11	18	23	45	85	225	450	
1859S	566,000	12	14	22	30	80	85	250	1,000	
1860	(1,000) 302,700	12	14	20	28	50	85	225	450	700
1860O	1,290,000	10	11	18	23	45	80	225	450	
1860S	472,000	12	14	22	25	45	80	350	1,000	
1861	(1,000) 2,887,400	10	11	18	23	45	80	225	400	700
1861O	2,532,633	10	11	18	23	45	80	225	400	
1861S	939,500	10	11	18	23	45	80	275	425	
1862	(550) 253,000	14	20	25	50	80	100	450	650	700
1862S	1,352,000	10	11	18	23	45	80	275	450	
1863	(460) 503,200	12	16	22	28	55	85	275	675	700
1863S	916,000	10	11	18	23	45	85	275	450	
1864	(470) 379,100	14	18	24	32	55	100	275	450	700
1864S	658,000	10	11	18	23	45	85	275	1,000	
1865	(500) 511,400	12	14	22	28	50	90	300	450	700
1865S	675,000	10	11	18	23	45	85	275	400	
1866S, No Motto	60,000	100	200	300	400	900	1,200	2,300	5,000	

Variety 4 – Motto Above Eagle (1866–1873, 1875–1891)

	Mintage	G-4	VG-8	F-12	VF-20	EF-40	AU-50	MS-60	MS-63	PF-63
1866 . . . .(725) 744,900		$9	$11	$17	$23	$45	$80	$220	$450	$550
1866S 994,000		9	11	17	23	45	90	320	800	
1867 . . . .(625) 449,300		11	15	25	35	65	95	275	500	550
1867S 1,196,000		9	10	17	22	45	80	300	650	
1868 . . . .(600) 417,600		13	15	23	30	70	120	325	475	550
1868S 1,160,000		9	11	17	23	40	90	325	600	
1869 . . . .(600) 795,300		9	11	17	23	40	90	275	450	550
1869S 656,000		9	11	17	23	42	90	350	850	
1870 . . . .(1,000) 633,900		9	11	17	23	40	80	300	450	550
1870CC 54,617		325	650	1,200	2,500	7,000	14,000	—	—	
1870S 1,004,000		9	11	17	23	45	95	300	1,000	
1871 . . . .(960) . .1,203,600		9	11	17	23	45	95	275	450	550
1871CC 153,950		65	100	170	300	900	1,500	6,500	22,000	
1871S 2,178,000		9	11	17	23	42	90	300	500	
1872 . . . .(950) 880,600		9	11	17	23	40	90	275	550	550
1872CC 257,000		30	45	100	200	650	1,600	5,000	35,000	
1872S 580,000		10	15	22	35	75	140	425	1,000	
1873 . . . .(600) 801,200		9	11	17	23	40	95	250	450	550
1873CC 122,500		60	100	150	275	650	1,900	4,500	27,000	

Variety 5 – Arrows at Date (1873–1874)

	Mintage	G-4	VG-8	F-12	VF-20	EF-40	AU-50	MS-60	MS-63	PF-63
1873 . . . .(550) . .1,815,150		$13	$19	$25	$48	$130	$160	$500	$900	$1,200
1873CC 214,560		60	95	150	400	800	1,100	2,750	8,500	
1873S 228,000		20	30	45	95	180	300	950	2,750	
1874 . . . .(700) . .2,359,600		13	19	22	48	130	160	500	900	1,200
1874CC 59,000		125	210	425	800	1,600	3,750	6,750	10,000	
1874S 394,000		16	25	40	90	150	250	875	1,600	

Variety 4 Resumed (1875–1891)

	Mintage	G-4	VG-8	F-12	VF-20	EF-40	AU-50	MS-60	MS-63	PF-63
1875 . . . .(700) . .6,026,800		$9	$10	$16	$22	$35	$75	$220	$300	$550
1875CC 1,008,000		9	12	25	35	60	100	275	500	
1875S 3,200,000		9	10	16	22	35	75	220	300	
1876 . . . .(1,150) . .8,418,000		9	10	16	22	35	75	220	300	550
1876CC 1,956,000		9	10	16	22	40	80	275	575	
1876S 4,528,000		9	10	16	22	35	75	220	300	
1877 . . . .(510) . .8,304,000		9	10	16	22	35	75	220	300	550
1877CC 1,420,000		9	10	16	22	40	85	260	500	
1877S 5,356,000		9	10	16	22	35	75	220	300	
1878 . . . .(800) . .1,377,600		9	10	16	22	35	75	220	300	550
1878CC 62,000		125	200	350	600	1,200	2,000	3,500	10,500	
1878S 12,000		7,500	15,000	18,000	20,000	22,500	26,000	30,000	50,000	
1879 . . . .(1,100) 4,800		90	110	130	170	190	250	350	400	550
1880 . . . .(1,355) 8,400		90	110	130	170	190	250	350	400	550
1881 . . . .(975) 10,000		90	110	130	170	190	250	350	400	550
1882 . . . .(1,100) 4,400		100	120	180	200	210	280	425	400	550
1883 . . . .(1,039) 8,000		90	110	130	170	190	245	350	400	550
1884 . . . .(875) 4,400		100	120	180	200	210	280	450	525	550
1885 . . . .(930) 5,200		100	120	180	200	210	260	475	550	550
1886 . . . .(886) 5,000		100	120	180	200	210	260	475	550	550
1887 . . . .(710) 5,000		125	150	180	200	220	270	485	575	550
1888 . . . .(832) 12,001		90	120	130	170	190	250	425	500	550
1889 . . . .(711) 12,000		90	110	130	170	190	250	425	500	550
1890 . . . .(590) 12,000		90	110	130	170	190	250	425	500	550
1891 . . . .(600) . . .200,000		20	25	40	50	65	95	275	370	550

BARBER OR LIBERTY HEAD (1892–1915)

Like the dime and quarter dollar, this type was designed by Charles E. Barber, whose initial B is on the truncation of the neck.

G-4 Good: Date and legends legible. LIBERTY worn off headband.

VG-8 Very Good: Some letters legible in LIBERTY.

F-12 Fine: LIBERTY nearly completely legible, but worn.

VF-20 Very Fine: All letters in LIBERTY evenly plain.

EF-40 Extremely Fine: LIBERTY bold, and its ribbon distinct.

AU-50 About Uncirculated: Slight trace of wear above forehead, leaf tips, and cheek, and on eagle's head, tail, and wing tips.

MS-60 Uncirculated: No trace of wear. Light blemishes.

MS-63 Choice Uncirculated: Some distracting contact marks or blemishes in prime focal areas. Impaired luster possible.

PF-63 Choice Proof: Reflective surfaces with only a few blemishes in secondary focal places. No major flaws.

Mintmark location on reverse, below eagle.

HALF DOLLARS

	Mintage	G-4	VG-8	F-12	VF-20	EF-40	AU-50	MS-60	MS-63	PF-63
1892 . . . . (1,245)	934,000	$11.00	$14	$30	$40	$125	$160	$220	$400	$475
1892O	390,000	115.00	150	190	210	250	275	460	850	
1892S	1,029,028	100.00	120	175	200	240	300	475	1,200	
1893 . . . . (792) .	1,826,000	8.00	12	28	40	100	150	300	700	475
1893O	1,389,000	10.00	20	32	65	160	200	310	750	
1893S	740,000	60.00	80	100	160	240	325	620	1,750	
1894 . . . . (972) .	1,148,000	10.00	20	32	60	130	170	270	500	475
1894O	2,138,000	7.50	10	30	50	130	160	260	500	
1894S	4,048,690	8.00	12	28	45	120	150	255	675	
1895 . . . . (880) .	1,834,338	7.50	12	28	40	110	150	260	500	475
1895O	1,766,000	8.00	12	28	50	110	165	275	675	
1895S	1,108,086	10.00	14	40	70	125	175	275	650	
1896 . . . . (762) . . .	950,000	8.00	10	28	50	110	150	275	425	500
1896O	924,000	14.00	17	60	85	175	300	650	2,600	
1896S	1,140,948	35.00	45	70	110	185	240	600	1,600	
1897 . . . . (731) .	2,480,000	7.50	8	15	35	65	140	220	400	500
1897O	632,000	50.00	100	200	325	400	550	800	1,600	
1897S	933,900	50.00	75	125	210	350	450	675	1,600	
1898 . . . . (735) .	2,956,000	7.50	8	13	30	75	150	200	400	500
1898O	874,000	10.00	25	100	125	185	250	475	1,600	
1898S	2,358,550	8.00	12	22	50	100	150	400	1,700	
1899 . . . . (846) .	5,538,000	7.50	8	14	30	65	140	200	400	500
1899O	1,724,000	8.00	10	22	50	100	160	325	700	
1899S	1,686,411	8.00	10	22	45	100	150	300	1,000	
1900 . . . . (912) .	4,762,000	7.50	8	14	35	65	140	200	400	475
1900O	2,744,000	7.50	9	20	40	125	160	325	1,450	
1900S	2,560,322	7.50	9	18	40	100	140	275	1,100	
1901 . . . . (813) .	4,268,000	7.50	8	14	30	60	150	200	400	475
1901O	1,124,000	7.50	10	25	60	140	200	700	2,600	
1901S	847,044	13.50	23	70	150	285	450	900	3,100	
1902 . . . . (777) .	4,922,000	7.50	8	14	30	60	150	200	450	475
1902O	2,526,000	7.50	8	18	35	90	150	350	1,750	
1902S	1,460,670	7.50	9	20	45	110	165	350	1,000	
1903 . . . . (755) .	2,278,000	7.50	8	14	35	70	150	210	750	475
1903O	2,100,000	7.50	8	16	40	90	160	300	1,000	
1903S	1,920,772	7.50	8	16	40	95	170	300	950	
1904 . . . . (670) .	2,992,000	7.50	8	14	30	65	140	200	550	475
1904O	1,117,600	9.00	12	28	90	150	225	550	1,500	
1904S	553,038	15.00	27	110	225	450	700	3,000	8,000	
1905 . . . . (727) . .	662,000	9.00	12	30	50	110	140	230	700	475
1905O	505,000	10.00	15	40	80	140	175	350	850	
1905S	2,494,000	7.50	8	18	40	90	150	300	900	
1906 . . . . (675) .	2,638,000	7.50	8	14	36	75	120	200	375	475
1906D	4,028,000	7.50	8	15	36	75	120	200	375	
1906O	2,446,000	7.50	8	16	38	80	120	275	700	
1906S	1,740,154	7.50	8	18	40	90	120	275	525	
1907 . . . . (575) .	2,598,000	7.50	8	14	32	70	120	200	400	475
1907D	3,856,000	7.50	8	14	32	70	120	200	400	
1907O	3,946,600	7.50	8	14	32	70	140	220	400	
1907S	1,250,000	7.50	8	23	60	120	275	525	2,750	
1908 . . . . (545) .	1,354,000	7.50	8	14	30	70	120	200	400	475
1908D	3,280,000	7.50	8	14	30	65	120	200	400	
1908O	5,360,000	7.50	8	14	30	70	120	210	425	
1908S	1,644,828	7.50	8	20	50	110	170	350	1,200	
1909 . . . . (650) .	2,368,000	7.50	8	14	30	65	120	200	400	475

Chart continued on next page.

	Mintage	G-4	VG-8	F-12	VF-20	EF-40	AU-50	MS-60	MS-63	PF-63
19090	925,400	$7.50	$8	$18	$45	$120	$200	$350	$850	
1909S	1,764,000	7.50	8	14	32	90	140	260	550	
1910 ......(551)	418,000	8.00	11	28	55	130	150	290	500	$475
1910S	1,948,000	7.50	8	14	35	85	130	250	850	
1911 ......(543)	1,406,000	7.50	8	14	28	65	120	180	400	475
1911D	695,080	7.50	8	15	30	75	125	240	425	
1911S	1,272,000	7.50	8	14	30	75	130	250	600	
1912 ......(700)	1,550,000	7.50	8	14	28	70	120	200	400	475
1912D	2,300,800	7.50	8	14	28	70	120	200	400	
1912S	1,370,000	7.50	8	14	30	75	130	240	475	
1913 ......(627)	188,000	25.00	30	85	150	220	350	500	800	550
1913D	534,000	7.50	8	16	35	90	120	225	425	
1913S	604,000	7.50	10	20	40	100	140	275	550	
1914 ......(380)	124,230	60.00	70	135	220	290	425	600	900	750
1914S	992,000	7.50	8	14	30	80	140	275	500	
1915 ......(450)	138,000	40.00	65	110	150	250	380	600	1,100	650
1915D	1,170,400	7.50	8	12	28	60	130	200	400	
1915S	1,604,000	7.50	8	12	28	60	130	200	400	

LIBERTY WALKING (1916–1947)

This type was designed by Adolph A. Weinman, whose monogram, AW, appears under the tip of the tail feathers. On the 1916 coins and some of the 1917 coins, the mintmark is located on the obverse below the motto.

G-4 Good: Rims defined. Motto IN GOD WE TRUST legible.

VG-8 Very Good: Motto distinct. About half of skirt lines at left clear.

F-12 Fine: All skirt lines evident, but worn in spots. Clear details in sandal below motto.

VF-20 Very Fine: Skirt lines sharp, including leg area. Little wear on breast and right arm.

EF-40 Extremely Fine: All skirt lines bold.

AU-50 About Uncirculated: Slight trace of wear on Liberty's head, knee, and breast tips and on eagle's claws and head.

MS-60 Uncirculated: No trace of wear. Light blemishes.

MS-63 Choice Uncirculated: Some distracting contact marks or blemishes in prime focal areas. Impaired luster possible.

PF-63 Choice Proof: Reflective surfaces with only a few blemishes in secondary focal places. No major flaws.

PF-65 Gem Proof: Brilliant surfaces with no noticeable blemishes or flaws. A few scattered, barely noticeable marks or hairlines possible.

1916–1917

1917–1947

Mintmark Locations

Choice Uncirculated well-struck specimens are worth more than values listed.

	Mintage	G-4	VG-8	F-12	VF-20	EF-40	AU-50	MS-60	MS-63
1916	608,000	$19	$25	$40	$90	$125	$150	$200	$250
1916D, Obverse Mintmark	1,014,400	20	26	35	70	115	145	200	300
1916S, Obverse Mintmark	508,000	50	65	100	225	325	400	650	1,200
1917	12,292,000	6	6	7	12	20	35	75	120

	Mintage	G-4	VG-8	F-12	VF-20	EF-40	AU-50	MS-60	MS-63
1917D, Obverse Mintmark	765,400	$10.00	$15	$32	$70	$110	$150	$275	$650
1917D, Reverse Mintmark	1,940,000	6.50	9	25	60	140	250	450	950
1917S, Obverse Mintmark	952,000	15.00	21	60	165	375	700	1,300	2,500
1917S, Reverse Mintmark	5,554,000	6.00	7	8	20	38	85	175	900
1918	6,634,000	6.00	7	8	35	90	150	300	650
1918D	3,853,040	6.00	7	8	45	120	250	650	1,400
1918S	10,282,000	6.00	7	8	20	40	100	250	1,300
1919	962,000	10.00	15	35	150	275	400	650	1,800
1919D	1,165,000	9.00	15	40	160	350	850	2,500	8,500
1919S	1,552,000	9.00	14	35	140	400	900	1,600	5,200
1920	6,372,000	6.00	7	8	22	45	85	150	350
1920D	1,551,000	6.00	8	30	120	240	450	750	2,200
1920S	4,624,000	6.00	7	10	40	110	220	400	1,500
1921	246,000	95.00	120	175	500	900	1,500	2,500	5,000
1921D	208,000	175.00	200	300	600	1,000	1,900	2,750	7,000
1921S	548,000	25.00	35	110	450	2,500	4,400	7,000	16,000
1923S	2,178,000	6.00	6	12	55	185	400	1,000	1,800
1927S	2,392,000	6.00	6	8	25	70	200	600	1,200
1928S	1,940,000	6.00	6	9	35	75	220	600	1,300
1929D	1,001,200	6.00	6	8	15	45	140	225	400
1929S	1,902,000	6.00	6	8	15	50	140	225	500
1933S	1,786,000	6.00	6	8	9	30	140	320	650
1934	6,964,000	6.00	6	6	6	6	14	40	50
1934D	2,361,000	6.00	6	6	6	18	45	75	125
1934S	3,652,000	6.00	6	6	6	15	60	175	450
1935	9,162,000	6.00	6	6	6	6	12	25	40
1935D	3,003,800	6.00	6	6	6	18	30	75	125
1935S	3,854,000	6.00	6	6	6	18	60	125	235

	Mintage	G-4	VG-8	F-12	VF-20	EF-40	AU-50	MS-60	MS-63	PF-63	PF-65
1936 ...(3,901)	12,614,000	$6	$6	$6	$6	$6	$12	$27	$40	$950	$3,500
1936D	4,252,400	6	6	6	6	12	20	45	60		
1936S	3,884,000	6	6	6	6	12	22	75	90		
1937 ...(5,728)	9,522,000	6	6	6	6	6	12	22	35	300	800
1937D	1,676,000	6	6	6	6	18	50	120	150		
1937S	2,090,000	6	6	6	6	12	32	85	120		
1938 ...(8,152)	4,110,000	6	6	6	6	7	25	35	65	275	650
1938D	491,600	50	60	70	80	95	140	275	350		
1939 ...(8,808)	6,812,000	6	6	6	6	6	12	22	35	250	575
1939D	4,267,800	6	6	6	6	6	12	22	40		
1939S	2,552,000	6	6	6	6	10	35	70	90		

	Mintage	VG-8	F-12	VF-20	EF-40	AU-50	MS-60	MS-63	PF-63	PF-65
1940 .....(11,279)	9,156,000	$6	$6	$6	$6	$7	$15	$22	$225	$550
1940S	4,550,000	6	6	6	6	7	30	40		
1941 .....(15,412)	24,192,000	6	6	6	6	7	15	30	235	500
1941D	11,248,400	6	6	6	6	7	18	35		
1941S	8,098,000	6	6	6	6	20	32	55		
1942 .....(21,120)	47,818,000	6	6	6	6	7	15	25	235	500
1942D	10,973,800	6	6	6	6	7	18	35		
1942S	12,708,000	6	6	6	6	7	20	28		
1943	53,190,000	6	6	6	6	7	15	21		
1943D	11,346,000	6	6	6	6	7	22	32		
1943S	13,450,000	6	6	6	6	7	20	25		
1944	28,206,000	6	6	6	6	7	15	21		
1944D	9,769,000	6	6	6	6	7	18	25		

Chart continued on next page.

	Mintage	VG-8	F-12	VF-20	EF-40	AU-50	MS-60	MS-63
1944S	8,904,000	$6	$6	$6	$6	$7	$22	$28
1945	31,502,000	6	6	6	6	7	15	21
1945D	9,966,800	6	6	6	6	7	15	22
1945S	10,156,000	6	6	6	6	7	15	25
1946	12,118,000	6	6	6	6	7	15	21
1946D	2,151,000	6	6	6	6	7	15	21
1946S	3,724,000	6	6	6	6	7	15	21
1947	4,094,000	6	6	6	6	7	15	21
1947D	3,900,600	6	6	6	6	7	15	21

FRANKLIN (1948–1963)

The Benjamin Franklin half dollar and the Roosevelt dime were both designed by John R. Sinnock. His initials appear below the shoulder.

VF-20 Very Fine: At least half of the lower and upper incused lines on rim of Liberty Bell on reverse visible.
EF-40 Extremely Fine: Wear spots at top of end of Franklin's curls and hair at back of ears. Wear evident at top and on lettering of Liberty Bell.
MS-60 Uncirculated: No trace of wear. Light blemishes.
MS-63 Choice Uncirculated: Some distracting contact marks or blemishes in prime focal areas. Impaired luster possible.
MS-65 Gem Uncirculated: Only light, scattered contact marks that are not distracting. Strong luster, good eye appeal.
PF-63 Choice Proof: Reflective surfaces with only a few blemishes in secondary focal places. No major flaws.
PF-65 Gem Proof: Brilliant surfaces with no noticeable blemishes or flaws. A few scattered, barely noticeable marks or hairlines possible.

Mintmark Location

Choice, well-struck Uncirculated halves with full bell lines command higher prices.

	Mintage	VF-20	EF-40	MS-60	MS-63	MS-65	PF-63	PF-65
1948	3,006,814	$6	$6	$7	$10	$40		
1948D	4,028,600	6	6	7	8	65		
1949	5,614,000	6	6	15	20	70		
1949D	4,120,600	6	8	15	23	385		
1949S	3,744,000	6	9	25	35	60		
1950	(51,386) 7,742,123	6	6	12	16	50	$115	$200
1950D	8,031,600	6	6	9	15	225		
1951	(57,500) 16,802,102	6	6	7	8	30	65	150
1951D	9,475,200	6	6	11	17	120		
1951S	13,696,000	6	6	9	15	50		
1952	(81,980) 21,192,093	6	6	7	8	27	35	100
1952D	25,395,600	6	6	7	8	100		
1952S	5,526,000	6	6	15	20	55		
1953	(128,800) 2,668,120	6	6	7	12	100	26	60
1953D	20,900,400	6	6	7	8	50		
1953S	4,148,000	6	6	9	15	30		

HALF DOLLARS

	Mintage	VF-20	EF-40	MS-60	MS-63	MS-65	PF-63	PF-65
1954 ....(233,300) ..13,188,202		$6	$6	$7	$7.00	$27	$18	$45
1954D 25,445,580		6	6	7	8.00	65		
1954S 4,993,400		6	6	7	8.50	25		
1955 ....(378,200) ...2,498,181		6	6	9	16.00	30	14	40
1956 ....(669,384) ...4,032,000		6	6	7	8.00	20	7	20
1957 ....(1,247,952) ...5,114,000		6	6	7	7.00	20	7	12
1957D 19,966,850		6	6	7	7.00	20		
1958 ....(875,652) ...4,042,000		6	6	7	7.00	25	7	15
1958D 23,962,412		6	6	7	7.00	20		
1959 ....(1,149,291) ...6,200,000		6	6	7	7.00	50	5	7
1959D 13,053,750		6	6	7	7.00	65		
1960 ....(1,691,602) ...6,024,000		6	6	7	7.00	65	5	7
1960D 18,215,812		6	6	7	7.00	100		
1961 ....(3,028,244) ...8,290,000		6	6	7	7.00	40	5	7
1961D 20,276,442		6	6	7	7.00	65		
1962 ....(3,218,019) ...9,714,000		6	6	7	7.00	65	5	7
1962D 35,473,281		6	6	7	7.00	65		
1963 ....(3,075,645) ..22,164,000		6	6	7	7.00	25	5	7
1963D 67,069,292		6	6	7	7.00	25		

KENNEDY (1964 TO DATE)

Gilroy Roberts, then chief engraver of the Mint, designed the obverse of this coin. His stylized initials are on the truncation of the forceful bust of President John F. Kennedy. The reverse, which uses the eagle from the Great Seal for the motif, is the work of assistant engraver Frank Gasparro.

Mintmark Location (1964)

Mintmark Location (1968 to Date)

Silver Coinage (1964)

	Mintage	MS-63	PF-63	PF-65
1964 ....(3,950,762) ...273,304,004		$7	$7.50	$8
1964D 156,205,446		7		

Silver Clad Coinage (1965–1970)

	Mintage	MS-63	PF-63	PF-65
1965 65,879,366		$3		
1966 108,984,932		3		
1967 295,046,978		3		
1968D 246,951,930		3		
1968S ....(3,041,506)			$3.50	$4

	Mintage	MS-63	PF-63	PF-65
1969D 129,881,800		$3		
1969S ....(2,934,631)			$3.50	$4
1970D 2,150,000		10		
1970S ....(2,632,810)			4.00	8

Clad Coinage and Silver Proofs (1971 to Date)

	Mintage	MS-63	PF-63	PF-65
1971	155,164,000	$0.55		
1971D	302,097,424	0.55		
1971S	(3,220,733)		$1.50	$3
1972	153,180,000	0.60		
1972D	141,890,000	0.60		
1972S	(3,260,996)		1.50	3

	Mintage	MS-63	PF-63	PF-65
1973	64,964,000	$0.55		
1973D	83,171,400	0.55		
1973S	(2,760,339)		$1.50	$2.50
1974	201,596,000	0.55		
1974D	79,066,300	0.55		
1974S	(2,612,568)		1.50	3.00

Bicentennial (1776–1976)

	Mintage	MS-63	PF-63	PF-65
1776–1976, Clad	234,308,000	$0.55		
1776–1976D, Clad	287,565,248	0.55		
1776–1976S, Clad	(7,059,099)		$0.75	$1.25
1776–1976S, Silver	11,000,000	2.50		
1776–1976S, Silver	(4,000,000)		3.00	3.50

Note: Mintage figures for 1976-S silver coins are approximate; many were melted in 1982.

Eagle Reverse Resumed (1977 to Date)

	Mintage	MS-63	PF-63	PF-65
1977	43,598,000	$0.60		
1977D	31,449,106	0.60		
1977S	(3,251,152)		$1	$1.25
1978	14,350,000	0.60		
1978D	13,765,799	1.00		
1978S	(3,127,781)		1	1.50
1979	68,312,000	0.55		
1979D	15,815,422	0.55		
1979S	(3,677,175)			
Filled S			1	1.25
Clear S			6	9.00
1980P	44,134,000	0.55		
1980D	33,456,449	0.55		
1980S	(3,554,806)		1	1.50
1981P	29,544,000	0.75		
1981D	27,839,533	0.55		
1981S	(4,063,083)		1	1.50
1982P	10,819,000	1.50		
1982D	13,140,102	1.50		
1982S	(3,857,479)		1	1.50
1983P	34,139,000	2.00		

	Mintage	MS-63	PF-63	PF-65
1983D	32,472,244	$2.00		
1983S	(3,279,126)		$1.00	$1.75
1984P	26,029,000	0.75		
1984D	26,262,158	0.75		
1984S	(3,065,110)		1.00	2.00
1985P	18,706,962	1.50		
1985D	19,814,034	1.25		
1985S	(3,362,821)		1.00	1.75
1986P	13,107,633	2.50		
1986D	15,336,145	2.00		
1986S	(3,010,497)		3.00	4.50
1987P **(a)**	2,890,758	2.00		
1987D **(a)**	2,890,758	2.00		
1987S	(4,227,728)		1.00	1.75
1988P	13,626,000	1.50		
1988D	12,000,096	1.00		
1988S	(3,262,948)		2.00	2.50
1989P	24,542,000	1.00		
1989D	23,000,216	0.90		
1989S	(3,220,194)		1.50	3.00
1990P	22,278,000	1.00		

a. Not issued for circulation.

HALF DOLLARS

	Mintage	MS-63	PF-63	PF-65
1990D	20,096,242	$1.10		
1990S	(3,299,559)		$1.50	$2.00
1991P	14,874,000	0.75		
1991D	15,054,678	1.25		
1991S	(2,867,787)		4.00	5.00
1992P	17,628,000	0.50		
1992D	17,000,106	1.00		
1992S	(2,858,981)		3.00	3.50
1992S, Silver	(1,317,579)		7.00	7.50
1993P	15,510,000	0.50		
1993D	15,000,006	0.50		
1993S	(2,633,439)		5.00	6.00
1993S, Silver	(761,353)		10.00	16.00
1994P	23,718,000	0.50		
1994D	23,828,110	0.50		
1994S	(2,484,594)		3.00	4.00
1994S, Silver	(785,329)		12.00	17.00
1995P	26,496,000	0.50		
1995D	26,288,000	0.50		
1995S	(2,117,496)		10.00	14.00
1995S, Silver	(679,985)		35.00	45.00
1996P	24,442,000	0.50		
1996D	24,744,000	0.50		
1996S	(1,750,244)		3.00	5.00
1996S, Silver	(775,021)		15.00	20.00
1997P	20,882,000	0.50		
1997D	19,876,000	0.50		
1997S	(2,055,000)		9.00	14.00
1997S, Silver	(741,678)		20.00	30.00
1998P	15,646,000	0.50		
1998D	15,064,000	0.50		
1998S	(2,086,507)		5.00	7.00
1998S, Silver	(878,792)		9.00	12.00
1998S, Silver, Matte Finish	(b)		100.00	125.00
1999P	8,900,000	0.55		
1999D	10,682,000	0.55		
1999S	(2,543,401)		3.00	5.00
1999S, Silver	(804,565)		9.00	15.00
2000P	22,600,000	0.60		
2000D	19,466,000	0.60		
2000S	(3,082,483)		2.00	3.00

	Mintage	MS-63	PF-63	PF-65
2000S, Silver	(965,421)		$7.00	$8
2001P (a)	21,200,000	$4.00		
2001D	19,504,000	0.55		
2001S	(2,294,909)		3.25	4
2001S, Silver	(889,697)		8.00	9
2002P (a)	3,100,000	0.65		
2002D (a)	2,500,000	0.65		
2002S	(2,319,766)		2.00	3
2002S, Silver	(892,229)		8.00	9
2003P (a)	2,500,000	0.65		
2003D (a)	2,500,000	0.65		
2003S	(2,172,684)		2.00	3
2003S, Silver	(1,125,755)		8.00	9
2004P (a)	2,900,000	0.65		
2004D (a)	2,900,000	0.65		
2004S	(1,789,488)		3.00	5
2004S, Silver	(1,175,934)		8.00	9
2005P (a)	3,800,000	0.65		
2005D (a)	3,500,000	0.65		
2005S	(2,275,000)		2.00	3
2005S, Silver	(1,069,679)		7.00	8
2006P (a)	2,400,000	0.65		
2006D (a)	2,000,000	0.65		
2006S	(2,000,428)		2.00	3
2006S, Silver	(1,054,008)		7.00	8
2007P (a)	2,400,000	0.65		
2007D (a)	2,400,000	0.65		
2007S	(1,702,116)		2.00	3
2007S, Silver	(875,050)		7.00	8
2008P (a)	1,700,000	0.65		
2008D (a)	1,700,000	0.65		
2008S	(1,405,674)		2.00	3
2008S, Silver	(774,874)		7.00	8
2009P (a)	1,900,000	0.65		
2009D (a)	1,900,000	0.65		
2009S	(1,376,750)		2.00	3
2009S, Silver	(618,248)		7.00	8
2010P (a)		0.65		
2010D (a)		0.65		
2010S			2.00	3
2010S, Silver			7.00	8

a. Not issued for circulation. **b.** Included in commemorative set (see page 219).

131

The silver dollar was authorized by Congress April 2, 1792. Its weight was specified at 416 grains and its fineness at .8924. The first issues appeared in 1794, and until 1804 all silver dollars had the value stamped on the edge: HUNDRED CENTS, ONE DOLLAR OR UNIT. After a lapse in coinage of the silver dollar during the period 1804 to 1835, coins were made with either plain (1836 only) or reeded edges and the value was placed on the reverse side.

The weight was changed by the law of January 18, 1837, to 412-1/2 grains, fineness .900. The coinage was discontinued by the Act of February 12, 1873, and reauthorized by the Act of February 28, 1878. The dollar was again discontinued after 1935, and since then copper-nickel and other base-metal pieces have been coined for circulation.

FLOWING HAIR (1794–1795)

AG-3 About Good: Clear enough to identify.
G-4 Good: Date and letters legible. Main devices outlined, but lacking in detail.
VG-8 Very Good: Major details discernible. Letters well formed but worn.
F-12 Fine: Hair ends distinguishable. Top hair lines visible, but otherwise worn smooth.
VF-20 Very Fine: Some detail visible in hair in center. Other details more bold.
EF-40 Extremely Fine: Hair well defined but with some wear.
AU-50 About Uncirculated: Slight trace of wear on tips of highest curls; breast feathers usually weak.
MS-60 Uncirculated: No trace of wear. Light blemishes.

	Mintage	AG-3	G-4	VG-8	F-12	VF-20	EF-40	AU-50	MS-60
1794	1,758	$15,000	$27,000	$40,000	$50,000	$90,000	$140,000	$200,000	—
1795	160,295	425	800	1,000	2,000	3,000	8,000	12,000	$28,000

DRAPED BUST (1795–1804)
Small Eagle Reverse (1795–1798)

AG-3 About Good: Clear enough to identify.
G-4 Good: Bust outlined, no detail. Date legible, some leaves evident.
VG-8 Very Good: Drapery worn except deepest folds. Hair lines smooth.
F-12 Fine: All drapery lines distinguishable. Some detail visible in hair lines near cheek and neck.
VF-20 Very Fine: Left side of drapery worn smooth.
EF-40 Extremely Fine: Drapery distinctly visible. Hair well outlined and detailed.
AU-50 About Uncirculated: Slight trace of wear on the bust shoulder and hair to left of forehead, as well as on eagle's breast and top edges of wings.
MS-60 Uncirculated: No trace of wear. Light blemishes.

SILVER AND RELATED DOLLARS

	Mintage	AG-3	G-4	VG-8	F-12	VF-20	EF-40	AU-50	MS-60
1795, Bust Type	42,738	$375	$650	$900	$1,500	$2,600	$5,500	$8,500	$22,000
1796	79,920	375	650	900	1,500	2,600	5,500	8,500	22,000
1797	7,776	375	650	900	1,500	2,600	5,500	8,500	22,000
1798	327,536	375	650	900	1,500	2,600	5,500	9,000	22,000

Heraldic Eagle Reverse (1798–1804)

G-4 Good: Letters and date legible. E PLURIBUS UNUM illegible.
VG-8 Very Good: Motto partially legible. Only deepest drapery details visible. All other lines smooth.
F-12 Fine: All drapery lines distinguishable. Some detail visible in hair lines near cheek and neck.
VF-20 Very Fine: Left side of drapery worn smooth.
EF-40 Extremely Fine: Drapery distinct. Hair well detailed.
AU-50 About Uncirculated: Slight trace of wear on the bust shoulder and hair to left of forehead, as well as on eagle's breast and top edges of wings.
MS-60 Uncirculated: No trace of wear. Light blemishes.

	Mintage	G-4	VG-8	F-12	VF-20	EF-40	AU-50	MS-60
1798, Heraldic Eagle	*	$450	$550	$750	$1,300	$2,500	$5,000	$11,000
1799	423,515	450	550	750	1,300	2,500	5,000	11,000
1800	220,920	450	550	750	1,300	2,500	5,000	11,000
1801	54,454	450	550	750	1,300	2,500	5,000	11,000
1802	41,650	450	550	750	1,300	2,500	5,000	11,000
1803	85,634	450	550	750	1,300	2,500	5,000	12,000
1804, Variety 1, O Above Cloud					*Proof: $3,500,000*			
1804, Variety 2, O Above Space Between Clouds					*Proof: $2,500,000*			

* Included in number above.

GOBRECHT DOLLARS (1836–1839)

Silver dollars of 1836, 1838, and 1839 were mostly made as patterns and restrikes, but some were made in quantities for general circulation.

	VF-20	EF-40	AU-50	PF-60
1836, C. GOBRECHT F. on base. Reverse eagle flying upward amid stars. Plain edge. Although scarce, this is the most common variety and was issued for circulation as regular coinage.	$5,250	$8,000	$11,000	$13,500
1838, Similar obverse, designer's name omitted, stars added around border. Reverse eagle flying left in plain field. Reeded edge.	8,750	13,500	16,000	19,000
1839, Obverse as above. Reverse eagle in plain field. Reeded edge. Issued for circulation as regular coinage.	8,000	11,000	14,000	16,000

LIBERTY SEATED (1840–1873)

In 1840, silver dollars were again issued for general circulation. The seated figure of Liberty device was adopted for the obverse, and a heraldic eagle for the reverse.

VG-8 Very Good: Any three letters of LIBERTY at least two-thirds complete.
F-12 Fine: All seven letters of LIBERTY visible, though weak.
VF-20 Very Fine: LIBERTY strong, but slight wear visible on its ribbon.
EF-40 Extremely Fine: Horizontal lines of shield complete. Eagle's eye plain.
AU-50 About Uncirculated: Traces of light wear on only the high points of the design. Half of mint luster present.
MS-60 Uncirculated: No trace of wear. Light marks or blemishes.
PF-60 Proof: Several contact marks, hairlines, or light rubs possible on surface. Luster possibly dull and eye appeal lacking.
PF-63 Choice Proof: Reflective surfaces with only a few blemishes in secondary focal places. No major flaws.

No Motto (1840–1865)

Location of mintmark, when present, is on reverse, below eagle.

SILVER AND RELATED DOLLARS

	Mintage	VG-8	F-12	VF-20	EF-40	AU-50	MS-60	PF-60	PF-63
1840	61,005	$150	$175	$200	$350	$500	$1,800	$8,250	$20,000
1841	173,000	120	140	175	285	420	1,150	8,500	22,000
1842	184,618	120	140	175	285	420	1,000	8,500	20,000
1843	165,100	120	140	175	285	420	1,000	8,500	20,000
1844	20,000	125	175	200	325	600	1,600	7,000	19,000
1845	24,500	135	185	225	350	675	4,750	8,000	19,000
1846	110,600	120	140	175	285	420	1,000	6,500	16,500
18460	59,000	150	200	225	325	600	2,800		
1847	140,750	120	140	175	285	420	1,000	8,250	16,500
1848	15,000	225	285	375	525	900	2,100	8,250	19,000
1849	62,600	120	140	175	285	375	1,100	9,500	25,000
1850	7,500	325	350	550	875	1,300	3,000	8,750	17,500
18500	40,000	150	235	400	825	1,750	7,100		
1851	1,300	3,000	4,750	6,500	9,000	14,000	18,000	16,000	21,500
1852	1,100	2,750	4,750	6,500	8,750	14,000	17,000	17,500	23,000
1853	46,110	135	185	235	370	780	1,500	13,000	23,000
1854	33,140	825	1,300	1,600	2,500	4,000	5,200	7,500	12,000
1855	26,000	600	800	1,250	2,000	3,100	5,200	7,500	13,000
1856	63,500	225	300	375	800	1,400	2,800	3,750	10,000
1857	94,000	225	300	375	800	1,200	1,900	3,100	5,000
1858 ...(300+)		1,900	2,250	2,800	3,500	4,500		5,500	8,000
1859 ...(800)	255,700	150	225	275	350	500	1,400	1,300	2,800
18590	360,000	120	140	175	285	420	750		
1859S	20,000	185	280	370	1,100	2,500	8,500		
1860 ...(1,330)	217,600	125	175	230	325	450	775	1,100	2,300
18600	515,000	120	140	175	285	420	700		
1861 ...(1,000)	77,500	325	450	575	700	1,350	1,850	1,100	2,300
1862 ...(550)	11,540	290	385	490	675	1,250	1,850	1,100	2,400
1863 ...(460)	27,200	215	250	270	375	800	1,700	1,100	2,400
1864 ...(470)	30,700	135	185	300	400	800	2,000	1,100	2,400
1865 ...(500)	46,500	135	185	300	400	800	1,800	1,100	2,400

With Motto IN GOD WE TRUST (1866–1873)

Motto IN GOD WE TRUST on Reverse (1866–1873)

	Mintage	VG-8	F-12	VF-20	EF-40	AU-50	MS-60	PF-60	PF-63
1866 ...(725)	48,900	$135	$185	$235	$350	$675	$1,200	$850	$2,000
1867 ...(625)	46,900	135	175	235	325	575	1,200	850	2,000
1868 ...(600)	162,100	120	150	220	260	525	1,000	850	2,000
1869 ...(600)	423,700	120	150	200	260	475	975	850	2,000

Chart continued on next page.

	Mintage	VG-8	F-12	VF-20	EF-40	AU-50	MS-60	PF-60	PF-63
1870 ....(1,000) 415,000		$125	$155	$185	$250	$375	$875	$850	$2,000
1870CC 11,758		300	400	600	950	2,300	7,500		
1870S			100,000	200,000	300,000	500,000	700,000		
1871 .....(960) ...1,073,800		125	155	185	250	400	800	850	2,000
1871CC 1,376		1,400	2,200	3,000	6,000	14,000	37,000		
1872 .....(950) ...1,105,500		125	155	185	250	400	800	850	2,000
1872CC 3,150		775	1,200	1,800	3,000	7,000	15,000		
1872S 9,000		200	275	375	900	1,700	5,500		
1873 .....(600) 293,000		150	180	200	300	475	975	850	2,000
1873CC 2,300		2,750	4,000	6,500	10,000	17,500	50,000		

TRADE DOLLARS (1873–1885)

This trade dollar was issued for circulation in the Orient to compete with dollar-size coins of other countries. It weighed 420 grains compared to 412-1/2 grains, the weight of the regular silver dollar.

VG-8 Very Good: About half of mottoes IN GOD WE TRUST (on Liberty's pedestal) and E PLURIBUS UNUM (on obverse ribbon) visible. Rim on both sides well defined.

F-12 Fine: Mottoes and LIBERTY legible but worn.

EF-40 Extremely Fine: Mottoes and LIBERTY sharp. Only slight wear on rims.

AU-50 About Uncirculated: Slight trace of wear on Liberty's left breast and left knee and on hair above ear, as well as on eagle's head, knee, and wing tips.

MS-60 Uncirculated: No trace of wear. Light blemishes.

MS-63 Choice Uncirculated: Some distracting contact marks or blemishes in prime focal areas. Impaired luster possible.

PF-63 Choice Proof: Reflective surfaces with only a few blemishes in secondary focal places. No major flaws.

1875-S, S Over CC

	Mintage	VG-8	F-12	EF-40	AU-50	MS-60	MS-63	PF-63
1873 ....(865) 396,635		$60	$70	$90	$150	$425	$1,850	$1,900
1873CC 124,500		100	175	320	800	3,500	10,000	
1873S 703,000		60	70	90	175	500	1,100	
1874 ....(700) 987,100		60	70	90	150	275	850	1,900
1874CC 1,373,200		100	150	250	300	700	3,800	
1874S 2,549,000		60	70	90	150	275	850	
1875 ....(700) 218,200		80	180	295	500	1,000	1,700	1,900
1875CC 1,573,700		80	180	285	450	900	1,500	
1875S 4,487,000		60	70	90	150	275	850	
1875S, S Over CC ....*		125	200	450	700	1,500	6,000	
1876 ....(1,150) 455,000		60	70	90	150	275	850	1,900
1876CC 509,000		80	125	225	600	1,750	14,000	

* Included in number above.

	Mintage	VG-8	F-12	EF-40	AU-50	MS-60	MS-63	PF-63
1876S	5,227,000	$60	$70	$90	$150	$275	$850	
1877	(510) . . . 3,039,200	60	70	90	150	275	850	$1,900
1877CC	534,000	100	150	300	375	700	3,500	
1877S	9,519,000	60	70	90	150	275	850	
1878	(900)			600				1,900
1878CC **(a)**	97,000	250	375	1,100	2,000	6,500	13,000	
1878S	4,162,000	60	70	90	150	275	850	
1879	(1,541)			600				1,900
1880	(1,987)			600				1,900
1881	(960)			600				1,900
1882	(1,097)			600				1,900
1883	(979)			600				1,900
1884 **(b)**	(10)							300,000
1885 **(b)**	(5)							950,000

a. 44,148 trade dollars were melted on July 19, 1878. Many of these may have been 1878-CC. **b.** The trade dollars of 1884 and 1885 were unknown to collectors until 1908. None are listed in the Mint director's report, and numismatists believe that they are not a part of the regular Mint issue.

MORGAN (1878–1921)

George T. Morgan, formerly a pupil of William Wyon's at the Royal Mint in London, designed the new dollar. His initial M is found at the truncation of the neck, at the last tress. It also appears on the reverse on the left-hand loop of the ribbon.

Sharply struck prooflike coins have a highly reflective surface and usually command substantial premiums.

VF-20 Very Fine: Two thirds of hair lines from top of forehead to ear visible. Ear well defined. Feathers on eagle's breast worn.

EF-40 Extremely Fine: All hair lines strong and ear bold. Eagle's feathers all plain but with slight wear on breast and wing tips.

AU-50 About Uncirculated: Slight trace of wear on the bust shoulder and hair left of forehead, and on eagle's breast and top edges of wings.

MS-60 Uncirculated: No trace of wear. Full mint luster present, but may be noticeably marred by scuff marks or bag abrasions.

MS-63 Choice Uncirculated: No trace of wear; full mint luster; few noticeable surface marks.

MS-64 Uncirculated: A few scattered contact marks. Good eye appeal and attractive luster.

MS-65 Gem Uncirculated: Only light, scattered contact marks that are not distracting. Strong luster, good eye appeal.

8 Tail Feathers, 1878, Philadelphia Only

Mintmark location on reverse, below wreath.

Most Proof Morgan dollars, where indicated in mintage records (quantity shown in parentheses), are valued approximately as follows:

Proof-60 – $600; Proof-63 – $1,200; Proof-65 – $3,000.

Most Uncirculated silver dollars have scratches or nicks because of handling of mint bags. Choice sharply struck coins with full brilliance and without blemishes are worth more than listed values.

	Mintage	VF-20	EF-40	AU-50	MS-60	MS-63	MS-65
1878, 8 Feathers ....(500) 749,500		$16	$18	$21	$70	$95	$750
1878, 7 Feathers ....(250) ...9,759,300		13	15	16	35	55	725
1878, 7/8 Clear Doubled Feathers ....*		16	20	26	75	140	1,400
1878CC 2,212,000		52	65	70	120	200	975
1878S 9,774,000		13	15	17	27	42	165
1879 ....(1,100) ..14,806,000		13	15	16	18	32	500
1879CC, CC Over CC 756,000		75	250	600	1,800	3,300	13,500
1879O 2,887,000		13	15	16	36	100	1,600
1879S 9,110,000		13	15	16	24	27	90
1880 ....(1,355) ..12,600,000		13	15	16	24	27	380
1880CC 591,000		100	130	170	300	350	750
1880O 5,305,000		13	15	16	32	185	9,500
1880S 8,900,000		13	15	16	22	27	95
1881 ....(984) ...9,163,000		13	15	16	22	30	430
1881CC 296,000		145	185	200	220	280	475
1881O 5,708,000		13	14	16	22	27	730
1881S 12,760,000		13	14	16	22	26	95
1882 ....(1,100) ..11,100,000		13	14	16	22	28	170
1882CC 1,133,000		55	65	70	100	130	250
1882O 6,090,000		13	14	16	22	26	425
1882S 9,250,000		13	14	16	22	26	95
1883 ....(1,039) ..12,290,000		13	14	16	22	26	95
1883CC 1,204,000		60	70	80	100	130	235
1883O 8,725,000		13	14	16	22	26	95
1883S 6,250,000		15	16	70	300	1,350	12,000
1884 ....(875) ..14,070,000		13	14	16	22	26	135
1884CC 1,136,000		70	80	90	115	135	230
1884O 9,730,000		13	14	15	22	26	95
1884S 3,200,000		16	22	240	2,500	14,000	97,500
1885 ....(930) ..17,787,000		13	14	16	22	26	95
1885CC 228,000		250	275	290	310	350	775
1885O 9,185,000		13	14	16	22	26	95
1885S 1,497,000		15	20	50	90	135	800
1886 ....(886) ..19,963,000		13	14	16	22	26	95
1886O 10,710,000		15	16	50	325	1,900	95,000
1886S 750,000		30	40	60	140	235	1,500
1887 ....(710) ..20,290,000		13	14	16	22	26	95
1887O 11,550,000		13	14	16	23	65	1,200
1887S 1,771,000		13	15	20	60	125	1,500
1888 ....(833) ..19,183,000		13	14	16	22	26	100
1888O 12,150,000		13	14	16	22	26	210
1888S 657,000		80	95	110	150	210	1,600
1889 ....(811) ..21,726,000		13	14	16	22	26	95
1889CC 350,000		775	1,850	3,750	11,000	17,000	155,000
1889O 11,875,000		13	15	22	75	200	2,200

* Included in number above.

SILVER AND RELATED DOLLARS

	Mintage	VF-20	EF-40	AU-50	MS-60	MS-63	MS-65
1889S	700,000	$28	$37	$55	$125	$225	$900
1890 (590)	16,802,000	13	14	16	22	26	950
1890CC	2,309,041	60	80	95	180	450	3,000
1890O	10,701,000	13	14	16	30	55	750
1890S	8,230,373	13	14	16	30	55	450
1891 (650)	8,693,556	13	14	16	30	90	2,750
1891CC	1,618,000	60	75	100	200	450	2,300
1891O	7,954,529	13	15	25	75	180	3,350
1891S	5,296,000	13	14	16	23	70	600
1892 (1,245)	1,036,000	13	15	40	85	210	1,750
1892CC	1,352,000	125	220	300	750	1,200	4,600
1892O	2,744,000	13	15	35	85	165	2,300
1892S	1,200,000	50	140	1,000	16,500	33,000	100,000
1893 (792)	378,000	100	130	175	325	700	3,400
1893CC	677,000	225	800	975	1,800	3,600	27,000
1893O	300,000	150	275	460	1,100	3,750	110,000
1893S	100,000	3,500	4,800	12,000	42,000	80,000	275,000
1894 (972)	110,000	800	1,000	1,300	2,500	3,500	17,000
1894O	1,723,000	27	50	130	325	2,100	23,000
1894S	1,260,000	40	67	185	310	600	3,000
1895 (880)		15,000 (a)	18,000 (a)	23,000 (a)	30,000 (a)	42,000 (a)
1895O	450,000	220	350	800	8,500	24,000	120,000
1895S	400,000	175	325	775	1,900	3,000	11,000
1896 (762)	9,976,000	13	14	16	22	26	95
1896O	4,900,000	13	15	90	550	4,000	90,000
1896S	5,000,000	30	95	375	675	1,500	8,600
1897 (731)	2,822,000	13	14	16	22	28	125
1897O	4,004,000	13	15	60	360	2,750	28,000
1897S	5,825,000	13	14	16	30	55	300
1898 (735)	5,884,000	13	14	16	22	26	126
1898O	4,440,000	13	14	16	22	26	95
1898S	4,102,000	15	20	45	135	225	1,000
1899 (846)	330,000	90	120	150	200	225	500
1899O	12,290,000	13	14	16	22	26	95
1899S	2,562,000	15	23	60	170	260	900
1900 (912)	8,830,000	13	14	16	22	26	95
1900O	12,590,000	13	14	16	22	26	100
1900S	3,540,000	15	25	45	150	225	750
1901 (813)	6,962,000	26	55	250	1,100	8,500	115,000
1901O	13,320,000	13	14	16	22	26	100
1901S	2,284,000	16	25	75	250	370	1,900
1902 (777)	7,994,000	13	14	16	25	55	225
1902O	8,636,000	13	14	16	23	26	95
1902S	1,530,000	70	100	135	200	325	1,400
1903 (755)	4,652,000	25	32	36	45	50	130
1903O	4,450,000	200	210	225	240	260	425
1903S	1,241,000	90	185	900	2,000	3,250	5,250
1904 (650)	2,788,000	13	14	20	45	150	1,900

a. Values are for Proofs.

Chart continued on next page.

	Mintage	VF-20	EF-40	AU-50	MS-60	MS-63	MS-65
19040	3,720,000	$13	$14	$16	$22	$26	$95
1904S	2,304,000	35	120	320	675	1,600	4,000
1921	44,690,000	13	13	14	15	16	90
1921D	20,345,000	13	14	15	17	32	175
1921S	21,695,000	13	14	15	16	32	610

PEACE (1921–1935)

Anthony De Francisci, a medalist, designed this dollar. His monogram is located in the field of the coin under the neck of Liberty.

VF-20 Very Fine: Hair over eye well worn. Some strands over ear well defined. Some eagle feathers on top and outside edge of right wing visible.

EF-40 Extremely Fine: Hair lines over brow and ear are strong, though slightly worn. Outside wing feathers at right and those at top visible but faint.

AU-50 About Uncirculated: Slight trace of wear. Most luster present, although marred by contact marks.

MS-60 Uncirculated: No trace of wear. Full mint luster, but possibly noticeably marred by stains, surface marks, or bag abrasions.

MS-63 Choice Uncirculated: Some distracting contact marks or blemishes in prime focal areas. Impaired luster possible.

MS-64 Uncirculated: A few scattered contact marks. Good eye appeal and attractive luster.

MS-65 Gem Uncirculated: Only light, scattered, non-distracting contact marks. Strong luster, good eye appeal.

PF-65 Choice Proof: Satin surfaces, no noticeable blemishes or flaws.

Mintmark location on reverse, below ONE.

Most Uncirculated silver dollars have scratches or nicks because of handling of mint bags. Choice sharply struck coins with full brilliance and without blemishes are worth more than listed values.

	Mintage	VF-20	EF-40	AU-50	MS-60	MS-63	MS-65	PF-65
1921	1,006,473	$50	$60	$75	$125	$240	$1,400	$22,000
1922	51,737,000	13	13	14	15	20	80	30,000
1922D	15,063,000	13	14	14	15	25	200	
1922S	17,475,000	13	14	14	15	33	1,250	
1923	30,800,000	13	13	14	15	19	82	
1923D	6,811,000	13	14	15	18	65	550	
1923S	19,020,000	13	14	14	16	40	3,250	
1924	11,811,000	13	13	14	15	19	85	
1924S	1,728,000	13	14	30	100	235	4,800	
1925	10,198,000	13	13	14	15	19	85	
1925S	1,610,000	13	14	16	33	90	12,000	
1926	1,939,000	13	14	14	18	40	175	

	Mintage	VF-20	EF-40	AU-50	MS-60	MS-63	MS-65
1926D	2,348,700	$13	$14	$16	$31	$85	$275
1926S	6,980,000	13	14	14	20	47	425
1927	848,000	13	16	24	37	85	1,400
1927D	1,268,900	13	15	45	80	200	2,800
1927S	866,000	13	15	40	75	200	5,750
1928	360,649	215	245	275	300	390	2,300
1928S	1,632,000	13	15	26	85	325	12,000
1934	954,057	13	14	20	60	100	500
1934D	1,569,500	13	14	20	70	185	925
1934S	1,011,000	33	80	295	1,000	2,200	5,000
1935	1,576,000	13	14	15	45	65	335
1935S	1,964,000	13	14	50	125	235	700

EISENHOWER (1971–1978)
Eagle Reverse (1971–1974)

Honoring both President Dwight D. Eisenhower and the first landing of man on the moon, this design is the work of Chief Engraver Frank Gasparro, whose initials are on the truncation and below the eagle. The reverse is an adaptation of the official Apollo 11 insignia.

Mintmark location is above date.

	Mintage	EF-40	MS-63	PF-63	PF-65
1971, Copper-Nickel Clad	47,799,000	$1.05	$1.75		
1971D, Copper-Nickel Clad	68,587,424	1.05	1.30		
1971S, Silver Clad	(4,265,234) . . 6,868,530		6.00	$6.50	$7.25
1972, Copper-Nickel Clad	75,890,000	1.05	1.30		
1972D, Copper-Nickel Clad	92,548,511	1.05	1.30		
1972S, Silver Clad	(1,811,631) . . 2,193,056		5.75	6.00	6.50
1973, Copper-Nickel Clad **(a)**	2,000,056	1.50	5.50		
1973D, Copper-Nickel Clad **(a)**	2,000,000	1.50	5.50		
1973S, Copper-Nickel Clad	(2,760,339)			3.00	7.00
1973S, Silver Clad	(1,013,646) . . 1,883,140		6.00	10.00	18.50
1974, Copper-Nickel Clad	27,366,000	1.05	2.00		
1974D, Copper-Nickel Clad	45,517,000	1.05	2.00		
1974S, Copper-Nickel Clad	(2,612,568)			2.50	3.50
1974S, Silver Clad	(1,306,579) . . 1,900,156		6.00	6.50	7.00

a. 1,769,258 of each sold only in sets and not released for circulation. Unissued coins destroyed at mint.

Bicentennial (1776–1976)

Obverse

Reverse Variety 2   Reverse Variety 1

Variety 1: Design in low relief, bold lettering on reverse.
Variety 2: Sharp design, delicate lettering on reverse.

	Mintage	EF-40	MS-63	PF-63	PF-65
1776–1976, Copper-Nickel Clad, Variety 1	4,019,000	$1.10	$3.00		
1776–1976, Copper-Nickel Clad, Variety 2	113,318,000	1.10	1.50		
1776–1976D, Copper-Nickel Clad, Variety 1	21,048,710	1.10	1.50		
1776–1976D, Copper-Nickel Clad, Variety 2	82,179,564	1.10	1.50		
1776–1976S, Copper-Nickel Clad, Variety 1	(2,845,450)			$2.50	$5.50
1776–1976S, Copper-Nickel Clad, Variety 2	(4,149,730)			2.50	3.50
1776–1976S, Silver Clad, Variety 1	11,000,000	6.00			
1776–1976S, Silver Clad, Variety 1	(4,000,000)			6.00	10.00

Eagle Reverse Resumed (1977–1978)

	Mintage	EF-40	MS-63	PF-63	PF-65
1977, Copper-Nickel Clad	12,596,000	$1.05	$2.00		
1977D, Copper-Nickel Clad	32,983,006	1.05	1.50		
1977S, Copper-Nickel Clad	(3,251,152)			$2.50	$4.00
1978, Copper-Nickel Clad	25,702,000	1.05	1.25		
1978D, Copper-Nickel Clad	33,012,890	1.05	1.50		
1978S, Copper-Nickel Clad	(3,127,781)			2.50	4.75

SUSAN B. ANTHONY (1979–1999)

Clear S   Filled S

	Mintage	MS-63
1979P, Narrow Rim	360,222,000	$1.00
1979P, Wide Rim	*	8.50
1979D	288,015,744	1.00

* Included in number above.

	Mintage	MS-63	PF-63	PF-65
1979S	109,576,000	$1.00		
1979S, Proof, Filled S	(3,677,175)		$2.50	$5
1979S, Proof, Clear S	*		35.00	60
1980P	27,610,000	1.05		
1980D	41,628,708	1.05		
1980S	20,422,000	1.05		
1980S, Proof	(3,554,806)		2.50	5
1981P	3,000,000	2.00		
1981D	3,250,000	2.00		
1981S	3,492,000	2.00		
1981S, Proof, First S	(4,063,083)		2.50	4
1981S, Proof, Clear S	*		90.00	125
1999P	29,592,000	1.25		
1999P, Proof	(75,000)		10.00	15
1999D	11,776,000	1.25		

* Included in number above.

SACAGAWEA (2000–2008)

The design of this coin was selected in national competition from among 120 submissions that were considered by a panel appointed by Treasury Secretary Robert Rubin. The adopted motif depicts Sacagawea, a young Native American Shoshone, as rendered by artist Glenna Goodacre. On her back she carries Jean Baptiste, her infant son. The reverse shows an eagle in flight, designed by Mint engraver Thomas D. Rogers Sr.

The composition exemplifies the spirit of Liberty, Peace, and Freedom shown by Sacagawea in her conduct as interpreter and guide to explorers Meriwether Lewis and William Clark during their famed journey westward from the great northern plains to the Pacific.

These coins have a distinctive golden color and a plain edge to distinguish them from other denominations or coins of a similar size. The change in composition and appearance was mandated under the United States Dollar Coin Act of 1997.

Several distinctive finishes can be identified on the Sacagawea dollars as a result of the mint attempting to adjust the dies, blanks, strikes, or finishing to produce coins with minimal spotting and a better surface color. One group of 5,000 pieces dated 2000 with a special finish were presented to sculptor Glenna Goodacre in payment for the obverse design. Unexplained error coins made from mismatched dies (a state quarter obverse combined with a Sacagawea dollar reverse) are extremely rare.

	Mintage	MS-63	PF-63	PF-65
2000P	767,140,000	$1		
2000D	518,916,000	1		
2000S	(4,047,904)		$3	$6

Chart continued on next page.

	Mintage	MS-63	PF-63	PF-65
2001P 62,468,000	$1.00			
2001D 70,939,500	1.00			
2001S . . . .(3,183,740)			$20	$40
2002P **(a)** 3,865,610	1.10			
2002D **(a)** 3,732,000	1.10			
2002S . . . .(3,211,995)			8	15
2003P 3,080,000	1.20			
2003D 3,080,000	1.20			
2003S . . . .(3,298,439)			4	8
2004P 2,660,000	1.10			
2004D 2,660,000	1.10			
2004S . . . .(2,965,422)			4	8

	Mintage	MS-63	PF-63	PF-65
2005P 2,520,000	$1.10			
2005D 2,520,000	1.10			
2005S . . . .(3,344,679)			$3	$5
2006P 4,900,000	1.10			
2006D 2,800,000	1.10			
2006S . . . .(3,054,436)			3	5
2007P **(a)** 3,640,000	1.10			
2007D **(a)** 3,920,000	1.10			
2007S . . . .(2,577,166)			3	5
2008P **(a)** 9,800,000	1.10			
2008D **(a)** 14,840,000	1.10			
2008S . . . .(2,180,548)			3	5

a. Not issued for circulation.

NATIVE AMERICAN (2009 TO DATE)

Agriculture (2009)　　　　　　　　　　　**Great Law of Peace (2010)**

	Mintage	MS-65	PF-65
2009P, Agriculture 37,380,000	$1.10	
2009D, Agriculture 33,880,000	1.10	
2009S, Agriculture		$3

	Mintage	MS-65	PF-65
2010P, Great Law	$1.10	
2010D, Great Law	1.10	
2010S, Great Law		$3

PRESIDENTIAL (2007–2016)

Four different coins, each bearing the image of a former U.S. president, are issued each year in the order that the presidents served. The size and composition of these coins is the same as that of the Sacagawea dollars that are also made each year. A companion series of $10 gold bullion coins (listed in the Bullion section) honors the spouse of each president.

Presidential Dollars Reverse　　　　**Date, Mintmark, and Motto Incused on Edge**

	Mintage	MS-65	PF-65
2007P, Washington	176,680,000	$1	$3
2007D, Washington	163,680,000	1	3
2007S, Washington	. . . . .(3,965,989)	1	3
2007P, J. Adams	112,420,000	1	3
2007D, J. Adams	112,140,000	1	3
2007S, J. Adams	. . . . . .(3,965,989)	1	3

	Mintage	MS-65	PF-65
2007P, Jefferson	100,800,000	$1	$3
2007D, Jefferson	102,810,000	1	3
2007S, Jefferson	. . . . . .(3,965,989)	1	3
2007P, Madison	84,560,000	1	3
2007D, Madison	87,780,000	1	3
2007S, Madison	. . . .(3,965,989)	1	3

	Mintage	MS-65	PF-65
2008P, Monroe	64,260,000	$1	$3
2008D, Monroe	60,230,000	1	3
2008S, Monroe	. . . .(3,094,927)	1	3
2008P, J.Q. Adams	57,540,000	1	3
2008D, J.Q. Adams	57,720,000	1	3
2008S, J.Q. Adams	. . . . .(3,094,927)	1	3

	Mintage	MS-65	PF-65
2008P, Jackson	61,180,000	$1	$3
2008D, Jackson	61,070,000	1	3
2008S, Jackson	. . . .(3,094,927)	1	3
2008P, Van Buren	51,520,000	1	3
2008D, Van Buren	50,960,000	1	3
2008S, Van Buren	. . . . . .(3,094,927)	1	3

Note: Errors have been reported in the Presidential dollar series, including coins minted without edge lettering. Depending on their rarity, dealers may pay a premium for such errors.

	Mintage	MS-65	PF-65
2009P, Harrison	43,260,000	$1	$3
2009D, Harrison	55,160,000	1	3
2009S, Harrison	(2,604,824)	1	3
2009P, Tyler	43,540,000	1	3
2009D, Tyler	43,540,000	1	3
2009S, Tyler	(2,604,824)	1	3

	Mintage	MS-65	PF-65
2009P, Polk	46,620,000	$1	$3
2009D, Polk	41,720,000	1	3
2009S, Polk	(2,604,824)	1	3
2009P, Taylor	41,580,000	1	3
2009D, Taylor	36,680,000	1	3
2009S, Taylor	(2,604,824)	1	3

	Mintage	MS-65	PF-65
2010P, Fillmore		$1	$3
2010D, Fillmore		1	3
2010S, Fillmore		1	3
2010P, Pierce		1	3
2010D, Pierce		1	3
2010S, Pierce		1	3

	Mintage	MS-65	PF-65
2010P, Buchanan		$1	$3
2010D, Buchanan		1	3
2010S, Buchanan		1	3
2010P, Lincoln		1	3
2010D, Lincoln		1	3
2010S, Lincoln		1	3

Coinage of the gold dollar was authorized by the Act of March 3, 1849. The weight was 25.8 grains, fineness .900. The first type, struck until 1854, is known as the Liberty Head type.

In 1854, the piece was made larger in diameter and thinner. The design was changed to a feather headdress on a female, generally referred to as the Indian Princess Head type. In 1856 the type was changed slightly by enlarging the size of the head.

LIBERTY HEAD (1849–1854)

VF-20 Very Fine: LIBERTY on headband complete and legible. Knobs on coronet defined.
EF-40 Extremely Fine: Slight wear on Liberty's hair. Knobs on coronet sharp.
AU-50 About Uncirculated: Trace of wear on headband. Nearly full luster.
AU-55 Choice About Uncirculated: Evidence of friction on design high points.
MS-60 Uncirculated: No trace of wear. Light marks and blemishes.
MS-63 Choice Uncirculated: Some distracting contact marks or blemishes in prime focal areas. Impaired luster possible.

	Mintage	VF-20	EF-40	AU-50	AU-55	MS-60	MS-63
1849, Open Wreath, No L on Truncation	688,567	$140	$185	$225	$235	$475	$1,200
1849, Close Wreath . . . .*		140	175	200	215	450	850
1849C	11,634	750	1,100	1,700	2,000	5,250	12,000
1849D	21,588	900	1,350	1,850	2,250	3,750	8,500
1849O	215,000	150	200	250	375	525	2,250
1850	481,953	140	175	195	205	275	800
1850C	6,966	750	1,000	1,850	3,000	5,250	20,000
1850D	8,382	900	1,250	2,100	3,500	8,000	16,500
1850O	14,000	200	325	550	1,050	2,250	4,500
1851	3,317,671	140	160	175	190	225	800
1851C	41,267	800	1,100	1,300	1,700	2,500	4,500
1851D	9,882	900	1,250	1,600	1,850	3,750	11,500
1851O	290,000	150	175	195	225	575	1,750
1852	2,045,351	140	160	175	190	225	800
1852C	9,434	750	1,000	1,350	1,500	3,400	7,500
1852D	6,360	800	1,250	1,650	1,750	6,250	19,000
1852O	140,000	150	200	250	450	850	2,500
1853	4,076,051	140	160	175	190	225	800
1853C	11,515	750	1,000	1,550	1,950	3,750	8,500
1853D	6,583	900	1,200	1,850	3,000	6,250	18,500
1853O	290,000	150	175	200	225	450	1,500
1854	855,502	140	160	175	190	225	800
1854D	2,935	900	2,400	3,750	4,250	7,500	22,000
1854S	14,632	250	500	550	825	1,800	3,750

* Included in number above.

INDIAN PRINCESS HEAD,
SMALL HEAD (1854–1856)

VF-20 Very Fine: Feather-curl tips on headdress outlined but details worn.

EF-40 Extremely Fine: Slight wear on tips of feather curls on headdress.

AU-50 About Uncirculated: Trace of wear on feathers, nearly full luster.

AU-55 Choice About Uncirculated: Evidence of friction on design high points. Most of original mint luster present.

MS-60 Uncirculated: No trace of wear. Light marks and blemishes.

MS-63 Choice Uncirculated: Some distracting contact marks or blemishes in prime focal areas. Impaired luster possible.

PF-63 Choice Proof: Reflective surfaces with only a few blemishes in secondary focal areas. No major flaws.

	Mintage	VF-20	EF-40	AU-50	AU-55	MS-60	MS-63	PF-63
1854	783,943	$225	$325	$400	$700	$1,350	$7,000	$100,000
1855	758,269	225	325	400	700	1,350	7,000	125,000
1855C	9,803	1,000	2,500	6,500	8,500	15,000		
1855D	1,811	3,500	7,500	17,000	23,000	37,500	65,000	
1855O	55,000	325	450	1,100	1,750	4,500	17,500	
1856S	24,600	575	900	1,800	2,000	4,750	20,000	

INDIAN PRINCESS HEAD,
LARGE HEAD (1856–1889)

VF-20 Very Fine: Slight detail in curled feathers in headdress. Details worn smooth at eyebrow, hair below headdress, and behind ear and bottom curl.

EF-40 Extremely Fine: Slight wear above and to right of eye and on top of curled feathers.

AU-50 About Uncirculated: Trace of wear on feathers, nearly full luster.

AU-55 Choice About Uncirculated: Evidence of friction on design high points. Most of original mint luster present.

MS-60 Uncirculated: No trace of wear. Light marks and blemishes.

MS-63 Choice Uncirculated: Some distracting contact marks or blemishes in prime focal areas. Impaired luster possible.

PF-63 Choice Proof: Reflective surfaces with only a few blemishes in secondary focal places. No major flaws.

	Mintage	VF-20	EF-40	AU-50	AU-55	MS-60	MS-63	PF-63
1856	1,762,936	$140	$160	$190	$210	$235	$700	$17,500
1856D	1,460	2,750	4,250	5,000	6,500	19,000	45,000	
1857	774,789	140	175	200	225	250	700	8,500
1857C	13,280	775	1,100	2,100	2,750	7,500	22,000	
1857D	3,533	900	1,350	2,750	3,500	7,000	25,000	
1857S	10,000	375	450	850	1,100	4,250	14,000	
1858	117,995	140	175	200	225	250	700	5,000
1858D	3,477	900	1,150	2,250	2,750	6,500	17,000	

GOLD DOLLARS

	Mintage	VF-20	EF-40	AU-50	AU-55	MS-60	MS-63	PF-63
1858S 10,000		$250	$350	$1,000	$1,250	$4,000	$12,000	
1859 ....(80) 168,244		140	175	200	225	265	700	$4,500
1859C 5,235		775	1,150	2,250	2,750	7,000	23,500	
1859D 4,952		900	1,200	2,100	2,400	6,500	15,000	
1859S 15,000		200	350	850	1,100	4,000	10,000	
1860 ....(154) 36,514		140	175	200	225	250	700	4,000
1860D 1,566		1,750	2,750	5,000	6,500	12,500	40,000	
1860S 13,000		250	350	550	750	2,000	4,500	
1861 ....(349) ...527,150		140	175	200	215	250	700	4,000
1861D *1,250*		6,000	12,000	22,500	27,500	40,000	65,000	
1862 ....(35) ...1,361,355		140	175	200	215	250	700	4,250
1863 ....(50) 6,200		400	800	2,000	2,500	4,200	7,000	4,250
1864 ....(50) 5,900		275	350	600	750	900	2,000	6,000
1865 ....(25) 3,725		275	425	550	650	1,100	2,200	4,500
1866 ....(30) 7,100		275	325	500	650	700	1,500	4,500
1867 ....(50) 5,200		275	350	475	600	750	1,500	4,500
1868 ....(25) ...10,500		200	300	350	500	700	1,500	5,000
1869 ....(25) 5,900		250	350	450	550	750	1,500	5,000
1870 ....(35) 6,300		210	300	350	450	600	1,250	5,000
1870S 3,000		350	500	900	1,100	1,750	4,500	
1871 ....(30) 3,900		200	300	350	450	550	1,100	4,000
1872 ....(30) 3,500		200	275	350	450	650	1,500	6,000
1873, Close 3 ....(25) 1,800		300	600	650	750	1,100	2,500	10,000
1873, Open 3 123,300		140	175	200	215	250	700	
1874 ....(20) ...198,800		140	175	200	215	250	700	6,000
1875 ....(20) 400		1,500	2,850	3,750	4,250	6,500	9,000	12,000
1876 ....(45) 3,200		200	250	350	400	485	700	4,000
1877 ....(20) 3,900		150	250	350	400	485	700	5,000
1878 ....(20) 3,000		175	250	350	400	485	700	4,000
1879 ....(30) 3,000		150	200	225	250	325	700	4,000
1880 ....(36) 1,600		150	190	200	215	325	700	4,000
1881 ....(87) 7,620		150	190	200	215	325	700	4,000
1882 ....(125) 5,000		150	190	200	215	325	700	4,000
1883 ....(207) ...10,800		150	190	200	215	325	700	4,000
1884 ....(1,006) 5,230		150	190	200	215	325	700	4,000
1885 ....(1,105) ...11,156		150	190	200	215	325	700	3,750
1886 ....(1,016) 5,000		150	185	200	215	325	700	3,750
1887 ....(1,043) 7,500		150	185	200	215	325	700	3,750
1888 ....(1,079) ...15,501		145	185	200	215	300	700	3,750
1889 ....(1,779) ...28,950		140	175	190	200	300	700	3,750

Although authorized by the Act of April 2, 1792, coinage of quarter eagles ($2.50 gold coins) was not begun until 1796.

CAPPED BUST TO RIGHT (1796–1807)

F-12 Fine: Hair worn smooth on high spots. E PLURIBUS UNUM on ribbon weak but legible.
VF-20 Very Fine: Some wear on high spots.
EF-40 Extremely Fine: Only slight wear on Liberty's hair and cheek.
AU-50 About Uncirculated: Trace of wear on cap, hair, cheek, and drapery.
AU-55 Choice About Uncirculated: Evidence of friction on design high points. Some original mint luster.
MS-60 Uncirculated: No trace of wear. Light blemishes.

No Stars on Obverse (1796)

Stars on Obverse (1796–1807)

	Mintage	F-12	VF-20	EF-40	AU-50	AU-55	MS-60
1796, No Stars on Obverse	.963	$35,000	$50,000	$65,000	$85,000	$100,000	$165,000
1796, Stars on Obverse	.432	25,000	35,000	50,000	75,000	95,000	135,000
1797	.427	10,000	15,000	25,000	35,000	45,000	100,000
1798	.1,094	3,250	5,000	8,500	14,000	20,000	50,000
1802, 2 Over 1	.3,035	3,250	5,000	8,500	12,500	15,000	21,500
1804, 13-Star Reverse	*	20,000	30,000	60,000	100,000	125,000	200,000
1804, 14-Star Reverse	.3,327	3,250	5,000	8,500	12,500	15,000	20,000
1805	.1,781	3,250	5,000	8,500	12,500	15,000	20,000
1806, 6/4, 8 Stars Left, 5 Right	.1,136	3,500	5,500	8,500	12,500	15,000	20,000
1806, 6/5, 7 Stars Left, 6 Right	.480	4,500	6,500	10,000	15,000	25,000	50,000
1807	.6,812	3,250	5,000	8,500	12,500	15,000	20,000

* Included in number below.

CAPPED BUST TO LEFT, LARGE SIZE (1808)

F-12 Fine: E PLURIBUS UNUM on reverse, and LIBERTY on headband, legible but weak.
VF-20 Very Fine: Motto and LIBERTY clear.
EF-40 Extremely Fine: All details of hair plain.
AU-50 About Uncirculated: Trace of wear above eye, on top of cap, and on cheek and hair.
AU-55 Choice About Uncirculated: Evidence of friction on design high points. Some original mint luster present.
MS-60 Uncirculated: No trace of wear. Light blemishes.

	Mintage	F-12	VF-20	EF-40	AU-50	AU-55	MS-60
1808	.2,710	$17,550	$25,000	$35,000	$65,000	$75,000	$115,000

CAPPED HEAD TO LEFT (1821–1834)

Those dated 1829 to 1834 are smaller in diameter than the 1821 to 1827 pieces.

	Mintage	F-12	VF-20	EF-40	AU-50	AU-55	MS-60
1821	6,448	$4,000	$5,500	$7,500	$10,000	$14,000	$21,000
1824, 4 Over 1	2,600	4,000	5,500	7,500	9,500	13,000	21,000
1825	4,434	4,500	6,000	7,500	9,500	13,000	20,000
1826, 6 Over 6	760	4,500	6,000	8,000	10,000	14,000	27,500
1827	2,800	4,000	6,000	8,500	10,000	15,000	22,000
1829	3,403	3,500	4,500	5,500	8,000	10,000	13,500
1830	4,540	3,500	4,500	5,500	8,000	10,000	13,500
1831	4,520	3,500	4,500	5,500	8,000	10,000	13,500
1832	4,400	3,500	4,500	5,500	8,000	10,000	13,500
1833	4,160	3,500	4,500	5,500	8,000	10,000	13,500
1834, With Motto	4,000	5,500	7,500	10,000	15,000	20,000	30,000

CLASSIC HEAD, NO MOTTO ON REVERSE (1834–1839)

In 1834, the quarter eagle was redesigned. A ribbon binding the hair, bearing the word LIBERTY, replaces the Liberty cap. The motto was omitted from the reverse.

F-12 Fine: LIBERTY on headband legible and complete. Curl under ear outlined but no detail.
VF-20 Very Fine: LIBERTY plain; detail in hair curl.
EF-40 Extremely Fine: Small amount of wear on top of hair and below L in LIBERTY. Wear evident on wing.
AU-50 About Uncirculated: Trace of wear on coronet and hair above ear.
AU-55 Choice About Uncirculated: Evidence of friction on design high points. Some of original mint luster present.
MS-60 Uncirculated: No trace of wear. Light blemishes.
MS-63 Choice Uncirculated: Some distracting contact marks or blemishes in prime focal areas. Impaired luster possible.

Mintmark location.

	Mintage	F-12	VF-20	EF-40	AU-50	AU-55	MS-60	MS-63
1834, No Motto	112,234	$225	$350	$550	$800	$1,000	$2,500	$7,000
1835	131,402	225	350	550	800	1,000	2,500	7,000
1836	547,986	225	350	550	800	1,000	2,500	7,000
1837	45,080	250	500	750	800	1,000	3,000	10,000
1838	47,030	225	400	600	800	1,000	2,750	7,000
1838C	7,880	850	1,250	2,250	5,500	7,500	15,000	30,000
1839	27,021	350	500	750	1,100	1,350	3,250	13,000
1839C	18,140	900	1,400	3,000	4,000	6,000	17,500	30,000
1839D	13,674	1,000	1,500	3,500	5,000	7,500	20,000	40,000
1839O	17,781	350	650	1,000	1,200	1,500	5,000	15,000

LIBERTY HEAD (1840–1907)

Mintmark location.

4 Plain 4

4 Crosslet 4

	Mintage	VF-20	EF-40	AU-50	AU-55	MS-60	MS-63
1840	18,859	$250	$500	$1,500	$2,000	$4,000	$8,000
1840C	12,822	1,000	1,500	2,250	2,750	7,500	20,000
1840D	3,532	1,800	4,500	6,500	8,000	20,000	
1840O	33,580	250	500	1,250	1,500	6,500	15,000

Chart continued on next page.

	Mintage	VF-20	EF-40	AU-50	AU-55	MS-60	MS-63
1841 ....(unknown)		$40,000	$75,000	$95,000	$120,000		
1841C 10,281		1,000	1,350	2,250	2,750	$10,000	$30,000
1841D 4,164		1,500	3,000	6,000	7,500	15,000	35,000
1842 2,823		850	2,000	4,000	5,500	12,500	30,000
1842C 6,729		1,500	2,200	4,250	6,000	15,000	30,000
1842D 4,643		1,500	3,000	6,500	8,000	25,000	55,000
1842O 19,800		250	600	1,500	2,000	6,500	20,000
1843 100,546		225	300	500	750	1,500	4,500
1843C 26,064		1,000	1,250	2,000	3,000	5,000	13,000
1843D 36,209		1,000	1,500	1,800	2,500	4,500	20,000
1843O 364,002		225	250	300	350	1,000	4,500
1844 6,784		250	500	1,350	1,850	5,000	13,500
1844C 11,622		1,000	1,500	3,500	4,500	12,000	32,500
1844D 17,332		1,200	1,350	2,000	2,500	4,500	18,000
1845 91,051		225	250	300	450	750	3,500
1845D 19,460		1,100	1,300	2,000	3,000	6,500	25,000
1845O 4,000		600	1,500	5,000	7,500	13,500	32,500
1846 21,598		225	300	500	750	3,500	15,000
1846C 4,808		1,200	2,000	3,500	5,000	12,500	23,000
1846D 19,303		1,200	1,800	2,500	3,500	6,500	20,000
1846O 62,000		250	300	750	900	3,000	12,500
1847 29,814		225	250	500	650	2,200	5,000
1847C 23,226		1,000	1,350	2,000	3,000	4,500	10,000
1847D 15,784		1,100	1,500	2,000	3,000	5,500	15,000
1847O 124,000		225	275	750	1,250	3,000	13,500
1848 6,500		350	550	1,200	1,450	3,500	9,500

CAL. Gold Quarter Eagle (1848)

In 1848, about 230 ounces of gold were sent to Secretary of War William L. Marcy by Colonel R.B. Mason, military governor of California. The gold was turned over to the Mint and made into quarter eagles. The distinguishing mark "CAL." was punched above the eagle on the reverse side, while the coins were in the die.

CAL. Above Eagle on Reverse (1848)

	Mintage	VF-20	EF-40	AU-50	AU-55	MS-60	MS-63
1848, CAL. Above Eagle 1,389		$20,000	$25,000	$35,000	$45,000	$60,000	$85,000
1848C 16,788		900	1,450	2,200	3,000	8,500	25,000
1848D 13,771		1,000	1,500	2,350	2,750	6,500	22,000
1849 23,294		225	300	500	650	1,500	4,500
1849C 10,220		950	1,450	3,250	4,250	12,500	35,000
1849D 10,945		1,000	1,500	2,250	2,850	9,500	25,000
1850 252,923		225	275	300	325	650	2,500
1850C 9,148		950	1,350	2,250	2,750	7,000	25,000
1850D 12,148		1,000	1,500	2,350	2,850	10,000	30,000

	Mintage	VF-20	EF-40	AU-50	AU-55	MS-60	MS-63	PF-63
1850O	84,000	$250	$300	$700	$850	$2,750	$10,000	
1851	1,372,748	225	250	275	285	300	800	
1851C	14,923	1,000	1,400	2,200	2,500	6,000	21,000	
1851D	11,264	1,100	1,600	2,400	2,750	6,500	25,000	
1851O	148,000	235	275	500	600	2,500	9,500	
1852	1,159,681	225	250	275	300	325	950	
1852C	9,772	950	1,500	2,750	3,250	9,500	23,500	
1852D	4,078	1,000	2,000	4,500	5,500	10,000	32,000	
1852O	140,000	250	275	550	750	3,000	7,500	
1853	1,404,668	225	245	265	285	300	900	
1853D	3,178	1,350	2,200	3,250	4,000	8,500	35,000	
1854	596,258	225	245	265	285	300	950	
1854C	7,295	950	1,500	3,000	4,500	7,500	25,000	
1854D	1,760	2,250	4,750	7,500	9,500	16,000	50,000	
1854O	153,000	225	245	300	400	1,000	6,000	
1854S	246	100,000	150,000	250,000				
1855	235,480	225	245	265	285	300	1,000	
1855C	3,677	1,100	2,000	3,000	3,500	14,500	30,000	
1855D	1,123	2,250	5,000	8,500	11,000	35,000	60,000	
1856	384,240	225	250	275	285	300	850	$40,000
1856C	7,913	950	1,800	2,500	3,000	8,500	22,000	
1856D	874	4,500	8,500	22,500	27,500	50,000	95,000	
1856O	21,100	250	450	850	1,100	4,500	20,000	
1856S	72,120	250	300	600	750	2,750	7,500	
1857	214,130	225	250	275	285	300	1,000	35,000
1857D	2,364	1,000	1,800	2,500	3,000	8,000	22,000	
1857O	34,000	250	300	650	850	2,800	9,500	
1857S	69,200	250	300	600	750	3,000	9,500	
1858	47,377	225	250	275	285	800	2,400	25,000
1858C	9,056	950	1,500	2,250	2,750	6,500	22,000	
1859	(80)	39,364	225	250	325	350	850	2,250	15,000
1859D	2,244	1,250	2,000	2,500	4,000	12,000	45,000	
1859S	15,200	275	650	1,500	1,850	3,000	12,500	
1860	(112)	22,563	225	250	300	325	750	2,000	15,000
1860C	7,469	1,000	1,500	2,500	5,000	13,500	25,000	
1860S	35,600	275	450	750	900	2,500	10,000	
1861	(90)	1,283,788	225	250	275	300	550	1,200	15,000
1861S	24,000	300	600	2,000	3,000	5,000	10,000	
1862, 2 Over 1	*	650	1,350	2,750	3,250	6,500	10,000	
1862	(35)	98,508	250	400	1,250	1,500	5,000	20,000	13,500
1862S	8,000	500	1,350	3,000	4,000	12,500	25,000	
1863, Proof only	(30)							35,000
1863S	10,800	350	1,000	2,250	3,500	9,000	20,000	
1864	(50)	2,824	4,000	8,500	15,000	20,000	35,000		10,000
1865	(25)	1,520	3,000	5,000	12,000	15,000	27,500		12,000
1865S	23,376	250	450	950	1,350	3,000	7,000	
1866	(30)	3,080	750	2,500	4,000	5,250	8,000	18,000	9,000
1866S	38,960	275	450	900	1,500	4,500	14,000	
1867	(50)	3,200	275	500	750	1,250	3,500	6,000	9,000
1867S	28,000	250	425	1,000	1,350	3,000	8,000	
1868	(25)	3,600	250	300	450	650	1,250	5,000	9,000

* Included in number below.

Chart continued on next page.

	Mintage	VF-20	EF-40	AU-50	AU-55	MS-60	MS-63	PF-63
1868S	34,000	$225	$275	$750	$950	$2,500	$8,000	
1869	(25) 4,320	250	325	450	850	2,000	7,500	$7,000
1869S	29,500	275	350	550	1,000	2,750	6,000	
1870	(35) 4,520	250	300	500	900	2,750	6,500	7,000
1870S	16,000	250	300	500	1,150	3,000	10,000	
1871	(30) 5,320	250	275	425	600	1,500	3,000	7,000
1871S	22,000	250	275	400	550	1,500	3,000	
1872	(30) 3,000	300	500	750	1,600	3,000	10,000	6,000
1872S	18,000	225	300	600	1,100	3,000	8,000	
1873	(25) 178,000	225	250	275	285	350	900	6,000
1873S	27,000	225	250	500	750	1,800	5,000	
1874	(20) 3,920	250	275	450	700	1,500	4,500	8,000
1875	(20) 400	2,500	4,000	7,500	9,000	18,000	30,000	20,000
1875S	11,600	225	275	500	850	2,500	6,000	
1876	(45) 4,176	250	450	600	1,100	2,250	4,500	6,000
1876S	5,000	250	400	600	1,300	2,000	6,500	
1877	(20) 1,632	250	500	700	1,100	2,000	6,500	6,000
1877S	35,400	250	275	285	295	425	1,800	
1878	(20) 286,240	225	250	275	285	300	900	9,000
1878S	178,000	225	250	275	285	300	1,250	
1879	(30) 88,960	225	250	275	285	300	900	6,500
1879S	43,500	225	250	275	285	300	3,500	
1880	(36) 2,960	250	300	500	600	1,000	2,500	6,500
1881	(51) 640	1,250	2,000	4,500	5,000	7,500	15,000	6,500
1882	(67) 4,000	250	275	300	375	500	2,000	5,000
1883	(82) 1,920	250	275	650	900	1,850	5,000	5,000
1884	(73) 1,950	250	275	425	550	1,000	2,500	5,000
1885	(87) 800	550	1,250	1,800	2,000	3,000	5,000	5,000
1886	(88) 4,000	250	275	300	350	750	2,000	5,000
1887	(122) 6,160	250	275	285	300	500	2,000	4,750
1888	(97) 16,001	250	275	285	300	325	900	4,750
1889	(48) 17,600	225	250	275	285	300	900	4,750
1890	(93) 8,720	225	250	275	285	300	1,000	4,750
1891	(80) 10,960	225	250	275	285	300	850	4,750
1892	(105) 2,440	225	250	275	285	300	1,500	4,750
1893	(106) 30,000	225	250	275	285	300	900	4,750
1894	(122) 4,000	250	275	285	295	300	1,250	4,750
1895	(119) 6,000	225	250	275	285	300	950	4,750
1896	(132) 19,070	225	250	275	285	300	800	4,750
1897	(136) 29,768	225	250	275	285	300	800	4,750
1898	(165) 24,000	225	250	275	285	300	800	4,750
1899	(150) 27,200	225	250	275	285	300	800	4,750
1900	(205) 67,000	225	250	275	285	300	800	4,750
1901	(223) 91,100	225	250	275	285	300	800	4,750
1902	(193) 133,540	225	250	275	285	300	800	4,750
1903	(197) 201,060	225	250	275	285	300	800	4,750
1904	(170) 160,790	225	250	275	285	300	800	4,750
1905	(144) 217,800	225	250	275	285	300	800	4,750
1906	(160) 176,330	225	250	275	285	300	800	4,750
1907	(154) 336,294	225	250	275	285	300	800	4,750

INDIAN HEAD (1908–1929)

Bela Lyon Pratt designed this coin and the similar $5 gold piece. The design is incuse.

VF-20 Very Fine: Hair-cord knot distinct. Feathers at top of head clear. Cheekbone worn.
EF-40 Extremely Fine: Cheekbone, war bonnet, and headband feathers slightly worn.
AU-50 About Uncirculated: Trace of wear on cheekbone and headdress.
MS-60 Uncirculated: No trace of wear. Light blemishes.
MS-63 Choice Uncirculated: Some distracting contact marks or blemishes in prime focal areas. Impaired luster possible.
MS-64 Uncirculated: A few scattered contact marks visible. Good eye appeal and attractive luster.
Matte PF-63 Choice Proof: Few blemishes in secondary focal areas. No major flaws. Matte surfaces.

Mintmark location is on reverse, to left of arrows.

	Mintage	VF-20	EF-40	AU-50	MS-60	MS-63	MS-64	MATTE PF-63
1908 . . . .(236) 564,821		$160	$185	$205	$275	$900	$1,350	$6,000
1909 . . . .(139) 441,760		160	185	205	275	1,200	2,250	6,000
1910 . . . .(682) 492,000		160	185	205	275	1,100	2,250	6,000
1911 . . . .(191) 704,000		160	185	205	275	900	1,300	6,000
1911D .55,680		2,000	3,250	3,500	6,500	15,000	20,000	
1912 . . . .(197) 616,000		160	185	205	275	1,250	2,500	6,000
1913 . . . .(165) 722,000		160	185	205	275	850	1,500	6,000
1914 . . . .(117) 240,000		160	195	225	425	3,500	8,000	6,000
1914D 448,000		160	185	205	275	1,100	2,850	
1915 . . . .(100) 606,000		160	185	205	275	850	1,350	7,500
1925D 578,000		160	185	205	275	700	1,200	
1926 .446,000		160	185	205	275	700	1,200	
1927 .388,000		160	185	205	275	700	1,200	
1928 .416,000		160	185	205	275	700	1,200	
1929 .532,000		160	185	205	275	700	1,200	

The three-dollar gold piece was authorized by the Act of February 21, 1853. Coinage was struck beginning in 1854. It was never popular and saw very little circulation.

VF-20 Very Fine: Eyebrow, hair about forehead and ear, and bottom curl all worn smooth. Faint details visible on curled feather-ends of headdress.

EF-40 Extremely Fine: Light wear above and to right of eye, and on top of curled feathers.

AU-50 About Uncirculated: Trace of wear on top of curled feathers and in hair above and to right of eye.

AU-55 Choice About Uncirculated: Evidence of friction on design high points. Much of original mint luster present.

MS-60 Uncirculated: No trace of wear. Light blemishes.

MS-63 Choice Uncirculated: Some distracting contact marks or blemishes in prime focal areas. Impaired luster possible.

Mintmark location is on reverse, below wreath.

PF-63 Choice Proof: Reflective surfaces with only a few blemishes in secondary focal places. No major flaws.

	Mintage	VF-20	EF-40	AU-50	AU-55	MS-60	MS-63	PF-63
1854	138,618	$650	$900	$1,200	$1,350	$2,000	$5,000	$50,000
1854D	1,120	7,500	15,000	25,000	35,000	65,000		
1854O	24,000	875	1,750	3,000	3,500	15,000	25,000	
1855	50,555	600	875	1,200	1,500	2,000	6,000	30,000
1855S	6,600	950	1,800	5,000	7,500	17,500	65,000	
1856	26,010	675	1,000	1,250	1,750	2,100	6,000	20,000
1856S	34,500	700	1,100	2,250	4,500	8,500	17,000	
1857	20,891	675	975	1,250	2,000	2,100	7,000	18,500
1857S	14,000	750	1,750	4,500	6,000	15,000		
1858	2,133	800	1,300	2,000	3,500	6,000	13,500	18,500
1859	(80) 15,558	675	900	1,250	1,500	2,000	6,000	18,000
1860	(119) 7,036	675	900	1,250	1,650	2,100	6,000	9,000
1860S	7,000	750	1,500	5,000	7,500	14,000	35,000	
1861	(113) 5,959	700	900	1,500	1,750	3,000	7,000	12,000
1862	(35) 5,750	700	900	1,500	1,750	3,000	7,000	10,000
1863	(39) 5,000	700	900	1,500	1,750	3,000	7,000	10,000
1864	(50) 2,630	700	1,000	1,500	1,750	3,000	7,000	10,000
1865	(25) 1,140	1,000	2,000	4,000	5,000	7,000	13,000	15,000
1866	(30) 4,000	700	900	1,350	1,750	3,000	7,500	10,000
1867	(50) 2,600	700	900	1,350	1,750	3,000	7,500	10,000
1868	(25) 4,850	700	900	1,350	1,750	2,750	7,500	10,000
1869	(25) 2,500	700	900	1,350	1,750	3,000	8,000	10,000
1870	(35) 3,500	700	900	1,500	1,850	3,000	8,000	10,000
1870S *(unique)*			—					
1871	(30) 1,300	725	1,000	1,350	1,750	3,200	7,000	10,000
1872	(30) 2,000	725	1,000	1,350	1,750	3,200	7,000	10,000
1873, Open 3 (Original)	(25)	3,500	5,500	15,000	20,000			
1873, Close 3		2,750	4,500	7,500	12,500	24,000	35,000	20,000
1874	(20) 41,800	650	850	1,200	1,700	2,000	5,000	22,000
1875, Proof only	(20)			37,500	55,000			85,000
1876, Proof only	(45)			12,500	17,500			27,500
1877	(20) 1,468	1,250	3,000	6,000	8,000	15,000	30,000	15,000
1878	(20) 82,304	650	850	1,250	1,750	2,000	5,000	14,000
1879	(30) 3,000	675	900	1,250	1,800	2,100	5,250	12,000
1880	(36) 1,000	675	1,500	1,750	1,800	2,400	5,250	12,000
1881	(54) 500	1,200	2,100	3,750	4,500	5,000	11,000	12,000
1882	(76) 1,500	700	900	1,350	1,750	2,500	5,250	9,000
1883	(89) 900	725	1,250	1,700	2,250	2,700	5,250	9,000
1884	(106) 1,000	725	1,350	1,700	2,250	2,700	5,250	9,000
1885	(109) 801	725	1,350	1,850	2,250	3,500	9,000	10,000
1886	(142) 1,000	725	1,200	1,800	2,200	3,250	6,000	9,000
1887	(160) 6,000	650	900	1,350	1,750	2,500	5,000	9,000
1888	(291) 5,000	650	900	1,250	1,750	2,200	5,000	9,000
1889	(129) 2,300	650	850	1,200	1,700	2,000	5,000	9,000

STELLA (1879–1880)

These pattern coins were first suggested by the Hon. John A. Kasson, then U.S. envoy extraordinary and minister plenipotentiary to Austria-Hungary. It was through the efforts of Dr. W.W. Hubbell, who patented the alloy goloid (used in making another pattern piece, the goloid metric dollar) that we have these beautiful and interesting coins.

The $4 Stella—so called because of the five-pointed star on the reverse—was envisioned by Kasson as America's answer to various foreign gold coins popular in the international market. The British sovereign, Italy's 20 lire, and the 20 pesetas of Spain were three such coins: each smaller than a U.S. $5 gold piece, they were used widely in international trade.

The Stella was one of many proposals made to Congress for an international trade coin, and one of only several that made it to pattern coin form (others include the 1868 $5 and 1874 Bickford $10).

Odds were stacked against the Stella from the start. The denomination of four U.S. dollars didn't match any of the coin's European counterparts, and at any rate the U.S. double eagle ($20 coin)—already used in international commerce—was a more convenient medium of exchange. The Stella was never minted in quantities for circulation.

There are two distinct types in both years of issue. Charles E. Barber designed the Flowing Hair type, and George T. Morgan the Coiled Hair. They were struck as patterns in gold, aluminum, copper, and white metal. Only those struck in gold are listed.

Flowing Hair   **Coiled Hair**

	Mintage	EF-40	AU-50	PF-60	PF-63	PF-65
1879, Flowing Hair	(425+)	$60,000	$75,000	$85,000	$100,000	$150,000
1879, Coiled Hair *(12 known)*		100,000	125,000	150,000	225,000	450,000
1880, Flowing Hair *(17 known)*		75,000	85,000	115,000	135,000	275,000
1880, Coiled Hair *(18 known)*		175,000	200,000	250,000	400,000	700,000

The half eagle ($5 gold coin) was the first gold coin struck for the United States. It was authorized to be coined by the Act of April 2, 1792. The first type weighed 135 grains, of .91667 fineness. The weight was changed by the Act of June 28, 1834, to 129 grains, of .899225 fineness. Fineness became .900 by the Act of January 18, 1837.

CAPPED BUST TO RIGHT (1795–1807)

F-12 Fine: Liberty's hair worn smooth but with distinct outline. For heraldic type, E PLURIBUS UNUM faint but legible.

VF-20 Very Fine: Slight to noticeable wear on high spots such as hair, turban, and eagle's head and wings.

EF-40 Extremely Fine: Slight wear on hair and highest part of cheek.

AU-50 About Uncirculated: Trace of wear on cap, hair, cheek, and drapery.

MS-60 Uncirculated: No trace of wear. Light blemishes.

MS-63 Choice Uncirculated: Some distracting marks or blemishes in focal areas. Impaired luster possible.

Small Eagle Reverse (1795–1798)

1795 Obverse

1795 Reverse

1796, 6 Over 5

1797, 15 Stars

1797, 16 Stars

	Mintage	F-12	VF-20	EF-40	AU-50	AU-55	MS-60	MS-63
1795, Small Eagle	.8,707	$13,000	$18,000	$23,000	$32,000	$40,000	$55,000	$125,000
1796, 6 Over 5	.6,196	15,000	19,000	30,000	50,000	65,000	90,000	175,000
1797, 15 Stars	.3,609	16,500	21,000	37,500	75,000	100,000	150,000	
1797, 16 Stars	.*	16,000	20,000	34,000	70,000	90,000	145,000	
1798, Small Eagle *(7 known)*		75,000	150,000	200,000	250,000	450,000	—	

* Included in number above.

Heraldic Eagle Reverse (1795–1807)

	Mintage	F-12	VF-20	EF-40	AU-50	AU-55	MS-60	MS-63
1795, Heraldic Eagle	.*	$10,000	$15,000	$20,000	$35,000	$40,000	$65,000	$115,000
1797, 7 Over 5	.*	8,000	12,000	22,000	45,000	50,000	100,000	
1798, Large 8, 13-Star Reverse	...24,867	3,000	4,000	6,000	8,500	11,000	20,000	
1798, Large 8, 14-Star Reverse	.**	3,000	4,250	8,000	15,000	20,000	50,000	
1799	.7,451	2,500	3,500	5,500	9,000	12,000	18,000	45,000
1800	.37,628	2,500	3,500	5,500	7,500	8,500	11,000	23,000

* Included in number below. ** Included in number above.

	Mintage	F-12	VF-20	EF-40	AU-50	AU-55	MS-60	MS-63
1802, 2 Over 1 53,176		$2,500	$3,500	$5,500	$7,500	$8,500	$11,000	$20,000
1803, 3 Over 2 33,506		2,500	3,500	5,500	7,500	8,500	11,000	22,000
1804 30,475		2,500	3,500	5,500	7,500	8,500	11,000	22,000
1805 33,183		2,500	3,500	5,500	7,500	8,500	11,000	22,000
1806 64,093		2,500	3,500	5,500	7,500	8,500	11,000	22,000
1807 32,488		2,500	3,500	5,500	7,500	8,500	11,000	22,000

CAPPED BUST TO LEFT (1807–1812)

F-12 Fine: LIBERTY on cap legible but partly weak.
VF-20 Very Fine: Headband edges slightly worn. LIBERTY bold.
EF-40 Extremely Fine: Slight wear on highest portions of hair; 80% of major curls plain.
AU-50 About Uncirculated: Trace of wear above eye and on top of cap, cheek, and hair.
AU-55 Choice About Uncirculated: Evidence of friction on design high points. Some mint luster present.
MS-60 Uncirculated: No trace of wear. Light blemishes.

MS-63 Choice Uncirculated: Some distracting contact marks or blemishes in prime focal areas. Impaired luster possible.

	Mintage	F-12	VF-20	EF-40	AU-50	AU-55	MS-60	MS-63
1807 51,605		$2,000	$3,000	$4,000	$6,000	$7,000	$9,000	$20,000
1808, All kinds 55,578								
1808, 8 Over 7		2,250	3,500	4,500	7,000	9,000	12,000	25,000
1808		2,000	3,000	4,000	6,000	7,000	9,000	18,000
1809, 9 Over 8 33,875		2,000	3,000	4,000	6,000	7,000	9,000	18,000
1810 100,287		2,000	3,000	4,000	6,000	7,000	9,000	18,000
1811 99,581		2,000	3,000	4,000	6,000	7,000	9,000	18,000
1812 58,087		2,000	3,000	4,000	6,000	7,000	9,000	18,000

CAPPED HEAD TO LEFT (1813–1834)
Large Diameter (1813–1829)

	Mintage	F-12	VF-20	EF-40	AU-50	AU-55	MS-60	MS-63
1813 95,428		$2,500	$3,000	$4,500	$6,500	$7,500	$8,500	$15,000
1814, 4 Over 3 15,454		3,500	5,000	6,000	8,500	10,000	14,000	24,000
1815 635		25,000	40,000	100,000	150,000	175,000	225,000	275,000
1818 48,588		3,500	5,000	8,500	11,000	13,000	16,000	30,000
1819 51,723		6,500	12,000	25,000	35,000	40,000	50,000	65,000
1820 263,806		4,000	5,500	9,500	11,500	14,000	16,000	28,000
1821 34,641		10,000	15,000	30,000	50,000	65,000	90,000	125,000
1822 *(3 known)* 17,796				3,000,000				
1823 14,485		3,500	5,000	10,000	12,000	15,000	17,500	30,000
1824 17,340		4,000	6,000	24,000	30,000	35,000	45,000	65,000
1825, 5 Over Partial 4 29,060		4,000	6,000	20,000	25,000	30,000	40,000	60,000
1825, 5 Over 4 *(2 known)* ....*				250,000				
1826 18,069		4,000	6,000	15,000	20,000	22,500	30,000	50,000
1827 24,913		4,500	7,500	18,000	20,000	25,000	40,000	60,000
1828, 8 Over 7 *(5 known)* ....**		15,000	25,000	50,000	65,000	75,000	100,000	300,000
1828 28,029		4,500	7,000	20,000	30,000	35,000	50,000	75,000
1829, Large Date 57,442		12,500	25,000	50,000	65,000	75,000	85,000	125,000

* Included in number above. ** Included in number below.

Reduced Diameter (1829–1834)

	Mintage	F-12	VF-20	EF-40	AU-50	AU-55	MS-60	MS-63
1829, Small Date ....*		$25,000	$45,000	$60,000	$85,000	$100,000	$150,000	$200,000
1830 126,351		10,000	20,000	30,000	35,000	40,000	50,000	70,000
1831 140,594		10,000	20,000	30,000	35,000	40,000	50,000	70,000
1832, Curved-Base 2, 12 Stars *(5 known)* 157,487		30,000	45,000	65,000	85,000			
1832, Square-Base 2, 13 Stars ....**		10,000	20,000	30,000	35,000	40,000	50,000	70,000
1833 193,630		10,000	20,000	30,000	35,000	40,000	50,000	70,000
1834 50,141		10,000	20,000	30,000	35,000	40,000	50,000	70,000

* Included in mintage for 1829, Large Date (previous page). ** Included in number above.

CLASSIC HEAD (1834–1838)

	Mintage	F-12	VF-20	EF-40	AU-50	AU-55	MS-60	MS-63
1834 657,460		$350	$425	$600	$850	$1,100	$3,000	$7,500
1835 371,534		350	425	600	1,000	1,200	3,200	7,500
1836 553,147		350	425	600	1,000	1,200	3,200	9,500
1837 207,121		350	425	600	1,300	1,500	3,500	12,000
1838 286,588		350	425	600	1,300	1,500	3,500	9,000
1838C 17,179		1,000	1,800	3,500	7,500	9,500	25,000	50,000
1838D 20,583		1,100	1,750	3,250	6,500	9,000	20,000	40,000

LIBERTY HEAD (1839–1908)
Variety 1 – No Motto Above Eagle (1839–1866)

VF-20 Very Fine: LIBERTY on coronet bold. Major lines show in curls on neck.

EF-40 Extremely Fine: Details clear in curls on neck. Slight wear on top and lower part of coronet and on hair.

AU-50 About Uncirculated: Trace of wear on coronet and hair above eye.

AU-55 Choice About Uncirculated: Evidence of friction on design high points. Some original mint luster.

MS-60 Uncirculated: No trace of wear. Light blemishes.

MS-63 Choice Uncirculated: Some distracting contact marks or blemishes in prime focal areas. Impaired luster possible.

Mintmark: 1839, above date; 1840–1908, below eagle.

PF-63 Choice Proof: Attractive reflective surfaces with only a few blemishes in secondary focal places. No major flaws.

HALF EAGLES

1842, Large Date

Small Letters

Large Letters

	Mintage	VF-20	EF-40	AU-50	AU-55	MS-60	MS-63	PF-63
1839	118,143	$325	$350	$650	$850	$2,500	$15,000	
1839C	17,205	1,250	2,000	3,500	5,000	12,500	35,000	
1839D	18,939	1,500	3,000	4,500	6,500	15,000		
1840	137,382	325	350	750	950	2,200	6,000	
1840C	18,992	1,200	2,000	3,500	5,000	12,500	35,000	
1840D	22,896	1,200	2,000	4,000	5,500	10,000	25,000	
1840O	40,120	325	350	1,100	1,500	6,000	20,000	
1841	15,833	325	350	900	1,100	3,000	7,000	$48,500
1841C	21,467	1,200	1,700	2,200	2,600	8,500	25,000	
1841D	29,392	1,200	1,700	2,200	2,600	8,000	18,000	
1842, Small Letters	27,578	500	1,350	1,500	1,500	7,500	12,000	58,000
1842, Large Letters	*	500	1,100	1,800	2,250	8,000	13,000	
1842C, Small Date	27,432	5,000	12,000	20,000	25,000	50,000		
1842C, Large Date	*	1,200	1,500	2,200	2,600	8,500	23,000	
1842D, Small Date	59,608	1,200	1,600	2,200	2,600	8,500	23,000	
1842D, Large Date	*	1,750	4,000	8,500	12,000	30,000		
1842O	16,400	700	1,500	5,000	8,000	13,000	30,000	
1843	611,205	325	350	375	450	1,300	7,000	
1843C	44,277	1,100	1,600	2,500	3,500	7,000	22,000	
1843D	98,452	1,300	1,650	2,000	2,500	7,000	15,000	
1843O, Small Letters	19,075	400	1,000	1,500	2,000	11,000	32,000	
1843O, Large Letters	82,000	375	850	1,250	1,750	7,500	18,000	
1844	340,330	325	350	375	425	1,500	6,000	
1844C	23,631	1,300	2,000	3,500	4,500	13,500	25,000	
1844D	88,982	1,100	1,600	2,000	2,500	6,500	18,000	
1844O	364,600	350	375	425	550	3,000	10,000	
1845	417,099	325	350	375	425	1,500	7,000	
1845D	90,629	1,250	1,650	2,250	2,750	6,750	16,000	
1845O	41,000	350	500	1,800	2,500	6,000	15,500	
1846, Large Date	395,942	325	350	375	500	1,650	8,500	
1846, Small Date	*	325	350	375	425	1,250	7,500	
1846C	12,995	1,200	2,000	3,500	4,750	13,000	37,500	
1846D	80,294	1,250	1,650	2,500	3,500	7,500	15,000	
1846O	58,000	350	650	2,000	2,500	7,000	18,500	
1847	915,981	325	350	375	425	1,350	4,750	
1847C	84,151	1,200	1,600	2,250	2,750	7,500	20,000	
1847D	64,405	1,250	1,600	2,200	2,700	6,000	12,500	
1847O	12,000	1,250	3,000	5,500	7,000	16,000	25,000	
1848	260,775	325	350	375	425	1,450	8,000	
1848C	64,472	1,200	1,650	2,100	2,600	12,500	30,000	
1848D	47,465	1,250	1,700	2,100	2,600	8,500	18,500	
1849	133,070	325	350	450	550	1,800	9,000	
1849C	64,823	1,250	1,600	2,200	2,650	6,500	15,000	
1849D	39,036	1,250	1,650	2,250	2,650	7,500	20,000	
1850	64,491	325	450	650	800	2,400	14,000	

* Included in number above.

Chart continued on next page.

	Mintage	VF-20	EF-40	AU-50	AU-55	MS-60	MS-63	PF-63
1850C	63,591	$1,250	$1,500	$2,250	$2,650	$7,000	$13,000	
1850D	43,984	1,300	1,700	2,750	3,250	16,500		
1851	377,505	325	350	375	425	1,800	7,000	
1851C	49,176	1,250	1,600	2,300	2,800	8,000	30,000	
1851D	62,710	1,200	1,700	2,250	2,750	8,250	16,000	
1851O	41,000	450	1,000	2,600	3,250	8,000	15,000	
1852	573,901	325	350	375	425	1,200	5,500	
1852C	72,574	1,200	1,500	2,200	2,750	4,500	16,500	
1852D	91,584	1,250	1,600	2,100	2,650	6,500	18,000	
1853	305,770	325	350	375	425	1,250	6,000	
1853C	65,571	1,250	1,600	2,200	2,650	5,000	18,000	
1853D	89,678	1,300	1,750	2,100	2,600	5,250	15,000	
1854	160,675	325	350	375	425	1,500	6,000	
1854C	39,283	1,200	1,650	2,650	3,250	9,000	25,000	
1854D	56,413	1,250	1,500	2,100	2,500	6,000	20,000	
1854O	46,000	350	400	1,000	1,450	5,000	16,000	
1854S *(3 known)*	268			—	750,000	—		
1855	117,098	325	350	375	425	1,500	5,500	
1855C	39,788	1,200	1,600	2,250	2,650	9,000	30,000	
1855D	22,432	1,250	1,750	2,250	2,650	9,500	27,500	
1855O	11,100	500	1,500	3,000	3,500	13,500		
1855S	61,000	350	650	1,500	2,000	8,750		
1856	197,990	325	350	375	425	1,600	6,500	—
1856C	28,457	1,200	1,600	2,250	2,650	13,000	25,000	
1856D	19,786	1,250	1,750	2,500	3,000	7,500	25,000	
1856O	10,000	500	850	3,000	3,500	9,500		
1856S	105,100	350	450	700	950	4,500	18,500	
1857	98,188	325	350	375	425	1,500	5,500	—
1857C	31,360	1,200	1,650	2,250	2,650	5,250	18,500	
1857D	17,046	1,250	1,700	2,400	2,750	8,000	24,000	
1857O	13,000	500	1,000	2,750	3,500	10,000	32,500	
1857S	87,000	350	400	650	900	6,000	12,000	
1858	15,136	325	400	450	550	2,400	6,000	—
1858C	38,856	1,200	1,650	2,250	2,650	6,000	22,500	
1858D	15,362	1,250	1,750	2,450	2,850	8,000	23,000	
1858S	18,600	500	1,700	3,500	4,250	20,000		
1859	(80) 16,734	325	450	550	650	4,500	12,500	$30,000
1859C	31,847	1,200	1,650	2,500	3,250	8,500	27,000	
1859D	10,366	1,250	1,750	2,250	3,000	7,000	30,000	
1859S	13,220	800	2,000	3,250	4,500	16,000		
1860	(62) 19,763	325	425	750	900	2,500	10,000	25,000
1860C	14,813	1,300	1,750	2,600	3,250	8,000	15,000	
1860D	14,635	1,350	1,800	2,600	3,250	8,500	32,000	
1860S	21,200	650	1,400	3,000	3,850	16,000		
1861	(66) 688,084	300	325	350	375	1,300	5,000	25,000
1861C	6,879	1,500	2,500	4,500	6,000	16,000	55,000	
1861D	1,597	6,000	12,000	20,000	25,000	50,000	100,000	
1861S	18,000	650	2,500	3,500	5,000	24,000		
1862	(35) 4,430	450	1,400	2,400	2,800	12,000	28,000	25,000
1862S	9,500	2,000	3,500	5,500	6,750	27,500		
1863	(30) 2,442	800	2,500	3,500	4,500	16,000		25,000
1863S	17,000	950	2,500	5,000	7,000	22,000		
1864	(50) 4,170	450	1,200	2,750	3,450	8,000		25,000
1864S	3,888	2,750	10,000	16,000	20,000	32,500		
1865	(25) 1,270	850	3,000	6,500	7,500	13,500		25,000
1865S	27,612	750	1,500	3,000	3,850	10,000	20,000	
1866S	9,000	1,200	2,500	7,500	9,000	25,000		

Variety 2 – Motto Above Eagle (1866–1908)

VF-20 Very Fine: Half of hair lines above coronet missing. Hair curls under ear evident, but worn. Motto and its ribbon sharp.
EF-40 Extremely Fine: Small amount of wear on top of hair and below L in LIBERTY. Wear evident on wing tips and neck of eagle.
AU-50 About Uncirculated: Trace of wear on tip of coronet and hair above eye.
AU-55 Choice About Uncirculated: Evidence of friction on design high points. Some original mint luster present.
MS-60 Uncirculated: No trace of wear. Light blemishes.
MS-63 Choice Uncirculated: Some distracting contact marks or blemishes in prime focal areas. Impaired luster possible.
PF-63 Choice Proof: Reflective surfaces with only a few blemishes in secondary focal places. No major flaws.

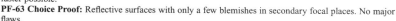

	Mintage	VF-20	EF-40	AU-50	AU-55	MS-60	MS-63	PF-63
1866 . . . .(30) 6,700		$500	$950	$2,100	$2,500	$10,000		$15,000
1866S .34,920		750	1,800	4,500	6,500	15,000		
1867 . . . .(50) 6,870		350	1,000	2,200	2,600	7,500		15,000
1867S .29,000		750	1,500	4,000	5,500	20,000		
1868 . . . .(25) 5,700		450	650	1,800	2,250	6,500		15,000
1868S .52,000		325	950	2,200	2,600	12,000		
1869 . . . .(25) 1,760		600	1,400	2,750	3,500	10,000		15,000
1869S .31,000		350	1,050	2,400	3,250	14,000		
1870 . . . .(35) 4,000		500	1,200	1,500	1,850	11,000		15,000
1870CC .7,675		7,500	15,000	27,500	37,500	75,000		
1870S .17,000		500	1,500	4,000	5,250	16,000		
1871 . . . .(30) 3,200		600	1,100	2,000	2,400	6,500		15,000
1871CC 20,770		1,500	3,000	8,500	13,000	45,000	$75,000	
1871S .25,000		350	600	2,000	2,400	8,000		
1872 . . . .(30) 1,660		525	1,200	2,000	2,400	7,500	12,500	15,000
1872CC 16,980		2,000	4,000	13,000	16,500	40,000		
1872S .36,400		350	500	2,400	2,600	8,000		
1873 . . . .(25) 112,505		275	300	325	350	600	2,750	15,000
1873CC .7,416		2,500	8,000	20,000	25,000	45,000		
1873S .31,000		350	900	2,000	2,400	13,000		
1874 . . . .(20) 3,488		400	1,100	1,400	1,600	7,500	13,500	20,000
1874CC 21,198		750	1,500	6,500	8,500	27,500		
1874S .16,000		400	1,400	2,250	2,600	13,500		
1875 . . . .(20) 200		35,000	45,000	75,000	85,000			50,000
1875CC 11,828		1,250	3,500	8,500	10,000	35,000		
1875S 9,000		425	1,300	3,000	3,500	10,000		
1876 . . . .(45) 1,432		700	1,600	2,750	3,250	8,000	14,000	13,000
1876CC .6,887		850	3,500	9,000	11,000	35,000		
1876S 4,000		1,200	2,000	5,500	6,500	18,000		
1877 . . . .(20) 1,132		550	1,800	2,700	3,250	8,000	15,000	13,000
1877CC .8,680		900	2,500	7,500	10,000	35,000		
1877S .26,700		300	425	900	1,100	5,500	13,000	
1878 . . . .(20) 131,720		275	285	300	315	400	1,500	20,000
1878CC .9,054		2,750	5,500	12,500	15,000	55,000		
1878S 144,700		275	285	300	315	450	2,800	
1879 . . . .(30) 301,920		275	285	300	315	385	1,400	13,000
1879CC 17,281		500	1,000	2,750	3,500	17,500		
1879S 426,200		275	285	300	315	500	2,000	
1880 . . . .(36) . . .3,166,400		275	285	300	315	385	925	12,000
1880CC 51,017		450	650	1,000	2,750	8,500	30,000	
1880S 1,348,900		275	285	300	315	385	925	

Chart continued on next page.

	Mintage	VF-20	EF-40	AU-50	AU-55	MS-60	MS-63	PF-63
1881 . . . .(42) . . .5,708,802		$275	$285	$300	$315	$385	$925	$12,000
1881CC 13,886		550	1,200	5,000	7,500	16,000	50,000	
1881S 969,000		275	285	300	315	385	925	
1882 . . . .(48) . . .2,514,520		275	285	300	315	385	925	11,000
1882CC 82,817		450	525	750	1,000	7,000	30,000	
1882S 969,000		275	285	300	315	385	925	
1883 . . . .(61) 233,400		275	285	300	315	400	1,000	11,000
1883CC 12,598		450	850	2,500	3,500	15,000		
1883S 83,200		275	285	300	315	600	1,800	
1884 . . . .(48) 191,030		275	285	300	315	425	1,200	11,000
1884CC 16,402		500	800	2,500	3,500	16,000		
1884S 177,000		275	285	300	315	400	1,100	
1885 . . . .(66) 601,440		275	285	300	315	385	925	10,000
1885S 1,211,500		275	285	300	315	385	925	
1886 . . . .(72) 388,360		275	285	300	315	385	925	10,000
1886S 3,268,000		275	285	300	315	385	925	
1887, Proof Only . . . . .(87)								42,500
1887S 1,912,000		275	285	300	315	385	925	
1888 . . . .(95) 18,201		275	285	300	315	450	1,100	10,000
1888S 293,900		275	285	300	315	725	2,000	
1889 . . . .(45) 7,520		275	285	300	315	650	1,800	10,000
1890 . . . .(88) 4,240		280	325	375	400	1,250	3,500	10,000
1890CC 53,800		425	500	650	800	1,250	6,000	
1891 . . . .(53) 61,360		275	285	300	315	400	1,200	9,500
1891CC 208,000		425	500	650	800	1,200	2,500	
1892 . . . .(92) 753,480		275	285	300	315	385	925	9,500
1892CC 82,968		425	500	675	800	1,250	5,000	
1892O 10,000		350	600	850	1,100	2,300		
1892S 298,400		275	285	300	315	385	1,500	
1893 . . . .(77) . . .1,528,120		275	285	300	315	385	925	9,500
1893CC 60,000		425	500	600	800	1,150	5,000	
1893O 110,000		300	350	375	450	650	4,000	
1893S 224,000		275	285	300	315	385	925	
1894 . . . .(75) 957,880		275	285	300	315	385	925	9,500
1894O 16,600		300	375	425	475	850	4,500	
1894S 55,900		275	285	400	425	1,800	6,000	
1895 . . . .(81) . . .1,345,855		275	285	300	315	385	925	9,500
1895S 112,000		275	285	325	350	1,850	3,500	
1896 . . . .(103) 58,960		275	285	300	315	385	925	8,500
1896S 155,400		275	285	300	315	750	3,500	
1897 . . . .(83) 867,800		275	285	300	315	385	925	8,500
1897S 354,000		275	285	300	315	550	3,250	
1898 . . . .(75) 633,420		275	285	300	315	385	925	8,500
1898S 1,397,400		275	285	300	315	385	925	
1899 . . . .(99) . . .1,710,630		275	285	300	315	385	925	8,500
1899S 1,545,000		275	285	300	315	385	925	
1900 . . . .(230) . . .1,405,500		275	285	300	315	385	925	8,500
1900S 329,000		275	285	300	315	385	925	
1901 . . . .(140) 615,900		275	285	300	315	385	925	8,500
1901S, 1 Over 0 3,648,000		300	325	375	400	425	1,100	
1901S . . . .*		275	285	300	315	385	925	
1902 . . . .(162) 172,400		275	285	300	315	385	925	8,500
1902S 939,000		275	285	300	315	385	925	
1903 . . . .(154) 226,870		275	285	300	315	385	925	8,500
1903S 1,855,000		275	285	300	315	385	925	

* Included in number above.

	Mintage	VF-20	EF-40	AU-50	AU-55	MS-60	MS-63	PF-63
1904 . . . .(136) 392,000		$275	$285	$300	$315	$385	$925	$8,500
1904S 97,000		275	285	300	315	550	2,200	
1905 . . . .(108) 302,200		275	285	300	315	385	925	8,500
1905S .880,700		275	285	300	315	385	1,300	
1906 . . . .(85) 348,735		275	285	300	315	385	925	8,500
1906D .320,000		275	285	300	315	385	925	
1906S .598,000		275	285	300	315	385	925	
1907 . . . .(92) 626,100		275	285	300	315	385	925	8,500
1907D .888,000		275	285	300	315	385	925	
1908 .421,874		275	285	300	315	385	925	8,500

INDIAN HEAD (1908–1929)

This type conforms in design to the quarter eagle of the same date. The incuse designs and lettering make the Indian Head a unique series, along with the quarter eagle, in United States coinage.

VF-20 Very Fine: Noticeable wear on large middle feathers and tip of eagle's wing.

EF-40 Extremely Fine: Cheekbone, war bonnet, and headband feathers slightly worn. Feathers on eagle's upper wing show considerable wear.

AU-50 About Uncirculated: Trace of wear on cheekbone and headdress.

AU-55 Choice About Uncirculated: Evidence of friction on design high points. Much of original mint luster present.

MS-60 Uncirculated: No trace of wear. Light blemishes.

MS-63 Choice Uncirculated: Some distracting contact marks or blemishes in prime focal areas. Impaired luster possible.

Mintmark Location

Matte PF-63 Choice Proof: Matte surfaces with few blemishes in secondary focal places. No major flaws.

Scarcer coins with well-struck mintmarks command higher prices.

	Mintage	VF-20	EF-40	AU-50	AU-55	MS-60	MS-63	MATTE PF-63
1908 . . . .(167) . . .577,845		$275	$300	$315	$325	$400	$1,600	$9,000
1908D .148,000		275	300	315	325	400	1,600	
1908S 82,000		300	325	350	400	900	5,000	
1909 . . . .(78) . . .627,060		275	300	315	325	400	1,600	9,000
1909D 3,423,560		275	300	315	325	400	1,600	
1909O 34,200		2,250	3,500	6,000	8,500	20,000	60,000	
1909S .297,200		275	300	315	325	900	8,000	
1910 . . . .(250) . . .604,000		275	300	315	325	400	1,600	9,000
1910D .193,600		275	300	315	325	400	2,500	
1910S .770,200		275	300	315	325	650	5,000	
1911 . . . .(139) . . .915,000		275	300	315	325	400	1,600	9,000
1911D 72,500		350	600	900	1,250	5,000	35,000	
1911S 1,416,000		275	300	315	325	600	3,500	
1912 . . . .(144) . . .790,000		275	300	315	325	400	1,600	9,000
1912S .392,000		275	300	320	350	1,100	10,000	
1913 . . . .(99) . . .915,901		275	300	315	325	400	1,600	9,000
1913S .408,000		275	300	325	375	1,100	10,000	
1914 . . . .(125) . . .247,000		275	300	315	325	400	1,600	9,000
1914D .247,000		275	300	315	325	400	1,850	
1914S .263,000		275	300	315	350	1,000	10,000	
1915 . . . .(75) . . .588,000		275	300	315	325	400	1,600	10,000
1915S .164,000		275	300	325	375	1,500	12,500	
1916S .240,000		275	300	315	325	500	5,000	
1929 .662,000		6,000	9,000	10,000	12,000	13,500	25,500	

Coinage authority including specified weights and fineness of the eagle conforms to that of the half eagle. The small eagle reverse was used until 1797, when the large, heraldic eagle replaced it.

CAPPED BUST TO RIGHT (1795–1804)

F-12 Fine: Details on turban and head obliterated.

VF-20 Very Fine: Hair lines in curls on neck and details under turban and over forehead worn but distinguishable.

EF-40 Extremely Fine: Definite wear on hair to left of eye and strand of hair across and around turban, as well as on eagle's wing tips.

AU-50 About Uncirculated: Trace of wear on cap, hair, cheek, and drapery.

AU-55 Choice About Uncirculated: Evidence of friction on design high points. Most of original mint luster present.

MS-60 Uncirculated: No trace of wear. Light blemishes.

MS-63 Choice Uncirculated: Some distracting contact marks or blemishes in prime focal areas. Impaired luster possible.

Small Eagle Reverse (1795–1797)

	Mintage	F-12	VF-20	EF-40	AU-50	AU-55	MS-60	MS-63
1795	5,583	$20,000	$25,000	$35,000	$45,000	$52,500	$80,000	$175,000
1796	4,146	23,000	27,000	40,000	50,000	57,500	87,500	200,000
1797, Small Eagle	3,615	25,000	32,500	50,000	75,000	90,000	115,000	

Heraldic Eagle Reverse (1797–1804)

	Mintage	F-12	VF-20	EF-40	AU-50	AU-55	MS-60	MS-63
1797, Large Eagle	10,940	$7,000	$9,500	$15,000	$16,500	$18,500	$32,500	$80,000
1798, 8 Over 7, 9 Stars Left, 4 Rt	900	10,000	13,000	25,000	35,000	40,000	75,000	175,000
1798, 8 Over 7, 7 Stars Left, 6 Rt	842	23,000	27,500	45,000	85,000	120,000	200,000	
1799	37,449	6,500	7,750	12,000	16,000	17,500	20,000	50,000
1800	5,999	6,500	7,750	12,000	16,000	17,500	20,000	50,000
1801	44,344	6,500	7,750	12,000	16,000	17,500	20,000	50,000
1803	15,017	6,500	7,750	12,000	16,000	17,500	20,000	50,000
1804	3,757	12,000	15,000	23,000	35,000	42,500	55,000	150,000

LIBERTY HEAD, NO MOTTO ABOVE EAGLE (1838–1866)

In 1838 the weight and diameter of the eagle were reduced and the obverse and reverse were redesigned. Liberty now faced left and the word LIBERTY was placed on the coronet.

VF-20 Very Fine: Hair lines above coronet partly worn. Curls under ear worn but defined.

EF-40 Extremely Fine: Small amount of wear on top of hair and below L in LIBERTY. Wear evident on wing tips and neck of eagle.

AU-50 About Uncirculated: Trace of wear on tip of coronet and hair above eye.

AU-55 Choice About Uncirculated: Evidence of friction on design high points. Some of original mint luster present.

MS-60 Uncirculated: No trace of wear. Light blemishes.

Mintmark is on reverse, below eagle.

MS-63 Choice Uncirculated: Some distracting contact marks or blemishes in prime focal areas. Impaired luster possible.

PF-63 Choice Proof: Attractive reflective surfaces with only a few blemishes in secondary focal places. No major flaws.

	Mintage	VF-20	EF-40	AU-50	AU-55	MS-60	MS-63	PF-63
1838 7,200		$1,750	$4,500	$10,000	$12,500	$30,000	$75,000	
1839, Large Letters 25,801		800	1,500	4,000	4,500	20,000	40,000	
1839, Small Letters 12,447		1,100	2,300	4,500	6,000	22,000	70,000	
1840 47,338		625	650	900	1,150	7,000		
1841 63,131		625	650	800	1,000	5,500	22,000	
1841O 2,500		2,000	4,500	12,500	15,000	30,000		
1842 81,507		625	650	850	1,050	10,000	22,000	
1842O 27,400		675	750	2,000	2,500	13,500		
1843 75,462		625	675	1,000	1,200	12,000		
1843O .175,162		650	700	900	1,100	8,500	32,000	
1844 6,361		800	2,000	3,500	4,000	10,000		
1844O .118,700		650	700	1,250	1,500	8,500		
1845 26,153		625	700	1,250	1,500	10,000		
1845O 47,500		650	700	1,800	2,200	10,000	30,000	
1846 20,095		625	850	3,500	4,000	14,000		
1846O 81,780		650	800	2,500	3,000	10,000	25,000	
1847 862,258		625	675	700	750	2,500	15,000	
1847O .571,500		650	700	725	800	4,000	13,000	
1848 145,484		625	650	700	750	3,500	15,000	—
1848O 35,850		700	950	2,350	2,650	11,000	20,000	
1849 653,618		625	675	700	750	2,500	10,000	
1849O 23,900		650	1,600	4,000	5,000	18,000		
1850 291,451		625	650	700	750	2,750	13,000	
1850O 57,500		650	800	1,200	1,450	12,000		
1851 176,328		625	650	700	750	3,000	15,000	
1851O .263,000		650	750	850	1,000	4,500	17,000	
1852 263,106		625	650	700	750	3,500	16,000	
1852O 18,000		650	900	2,500	3,250	18,000		
1853, 3 Over 2 201,253		700	800	1,250	1,500	10,000		
1853 . . . .*		625	650	700	750	2,500	13,000	
1853O 51,000		650	700	875	1,000	8,500		
1854 54,250		625	650	700	750	3,500		
1854O 52,500		650	700	1,200	1,450	6,500	23,000	
1854S .123,826		625	700	950	1,100	6,500	25,000	
1855 121,701		625	650	700	750	3,000	12,000	—
1855O 18,000		750	1,200	4,500	6,000	18,000		

* Included in number above.

Chart continued on next page.

	Mintage	VF-20	EF-40	AU-50	AU-55	MS-60	MS-63	PF-63
1855S	9,000	$1,500	$2,300	$4,250	$6,000	$19,000		
1856	60,490	625	650	700	750	2,500	$12,000	—
1856O	14,500	750	1,100	2,750	3,500	12,000		
1856S	68,000	650	700	850	1,100	6,000		
1857	16,606	650	800	1,250	1,450	7,000		—
1857O	5,500	800	1,250	3,000	3,750	20,000		
1857S	26,000	650	800	1,500	1,800	7,000	13,000	
1858	2,521	3,500	6,000	8,500	10,500	25,000		—
1858O	20,000	650	850	1,200	1,450	6,000	23,000	
1858S	11,800	1,100	2,000	3,000	3,750	22,000		
1859	(80) 16,013	675	700	850	900	6,000	12,000	$45,000
1859O	2,300	3,000	7,000	15,000	20,000	40,000		
1859S	7,000	1,500	3,000	8,500	11,000	30,000		
1860	(50) 15,055	625	650	900	1,000	5,000	12,000	31,000
1860O	11,100	750	1,100	2,200	2,750	8,000		
1860S	5,000	1,850	3,250	8,000	10,000	28,000		
1861	(69) 113,164	625	650	675	685	4,000	12,000	30,000
1861S	15,500	1,000	1,800	4,000	5,000	22,000		
1862	(35) 10,960	650	850	1,500	1,750	8,000	18,000	30,000
1862S	12,500	1,200	2,200	3,250	4,000	24,000		
1863	(30) 1,218	2,750	5,500	8,500	9,500	30,000	50,000	30,000
1863S	10,000	1,200	2,400	6,000	8,000	15,000		
1864	(50) 3,530	1,200	2,400	5,000	7,000	10,000		30,000
1864S	2,500	3,000	7,000	14,000	16,000	36,000		
1865	(25) 3,980	1,300	2,500	4,000	6,000	23,000	37,500	30,000
1865S	16,700	2,350	4,000	10,000	12,500	30,000	50,000	
1866S	8,500	1,600	2,200	7,000	8,500	30,000		

LIBERTY HEAD, MOTTO ABOVE EAGLE (1866–1907)

VF-20 Very Fine: Half of hair lines over coronet visible. Curls under ear worn but defined. IN GOD WE TRUST and its ribbon sharp.

EF-40 Extremely Fine: Small amount of wear on top of hair and below L in LIBERTY. Wear evident on wing tips and neck of eagle.

AU-50 About Uncirculated: Trace of wear on hair above eye and on coronet.

AU-55 Choice About Uncirculated: Evidence of friction on design high points. Some of original mint luster present.

Mintmark is on reverse, below eagle.

MS-60 Uncirculated: No trace of wear. Light blemishes.

MS-63 Choice Uncirculated: Some distracting marks or blemishes in focal areas. Impaired luster possible.

PF-63 Choice Proof: Reflective surfaces with only a few blemishes in secondary focal areas. No major flaws.

	Mintage	VF-20	EF-40	AU-50	AU-55	MS-60	MS-63	PF-63
1866	(30) 3,750	$700	$1,300	$3,000	$3,500	$15,000		$25,000
1866S	11,500	1,100	2,500	4,500	5,500	16,000		
1867	(50) 3,090	1,050	1,650	2,500	3,500	15,000		25,000
1867S	9,000	1,500	3,500	5,000	6,500	25,000		
1868	(25) 10,630	650	700	1,000	1,100	10,000		25,000
1868S	13,500	1,000	1,300	2,250	2,500	13,000		
1869	(25) 1,830	1,050	1,500	2,500	3,000	18,000		25,000
1869S	6,430	1,050	1,500	2,750	3,250	13,000		
1870	(35) 3,990	700	900	1,400	1,600	12,500		22,500
1870CC	5,908	12,500	25,000	50,000	75,000			
1870S	8,000	750	1,400	3,000	4,500	20,000		
1871	(30) 1,790	1,000	1,500	2,500	3,000	11,000		22,500
1871CC	8,085	2,000	4,000	12,000	15,000	40,000		

	Mintage	VF-20	EF-40	AU-50	AU-55	MS-60	MS-63	PF-63
1871S 16,500		$850	$1,300	$3,000	$4,500	$15,000		
1872 . . . .(30) 1,620		1,350	2,000	5,000	6,000	10,000	$23,000	$22,500
1872CC 4,600		2,250	6,000	15,000	20,000	45,000		
1872S 17,300		600	750	1,100	1,500	11,000		
1873 . . . .(25) 800		3,000	7,000	12,000	15,000	30,000		25,000
1873CC 4,543		3,500	7,200	25,000	32,000	50,000		
1873S 12,000		850	1,300	2,500	3,000	15,000		
1874 . . . .(20) 53,140		550	575	585	590	1,200	4,500	25,000
1874CC 16,767		1,000	2,000	6,000	7,500	32,000		
1874S 10,000		850	1,500	3,000	3,500	25,000		
1875 . . . .(20) 100		45,000	65,000	85,000				95,000
1875CC 7,715		3,000	6,000	13,000	25,000	65,000		
1876 . . . .(45) 687		1,800	3,500	10,000	11,500	30,000		20,000
1876CC 4,696		2,750	5,000	12,000	14,000	40,000		
1876S 5,000		850	1,300	3,000	3,500	22,000		
1877 . . . .(20) . . : . .797		2,000	3,500	7,000	8,000	22,000		20,000
1877CC 3,332		2,000	5,000	10,000	12,000	35,000		
1877S 17,000		550	600	1,100	1,250	18,000		
1878 . . . .(20) 73,780		550	575	585	595	600	5,000	20,000
1878CC 3,244		2,500	6,500	13,500	15,000	45,000		
1878S 26,100		550	600	900	1,000	7,500	20,000	
1879 . . . .(30) 384,740		550	575	585	595	600	2,500	17,500
1879CC 1,762		4,000	8,500	17,000	20,000	45,000		
18790 1,500		1,500	3,000	8,000	9,500	25,000		
1879S 224,000		550	575	585	595	600	4,500	
1880 . . . .(36) . . .1,644,840		550	575	585	595	600	2,500	17,500
1880CC 11,190		750	900	1,250	1,500	10,000		
18800 9,200		700	800	1,100	1,350	5,500		
1880S 506,250		550	575	585	595	600	2,500	
1881 . . . .(40) . . .3,877,220		550	575	585	595	600	1,250	17,500
1881CC 24,015		700	775	1,000	1,200	4,000	15,000	
18810 8,350		675	750	950	1,100	5,000		
1881S 970,000		550	575	585	595	600	2,500	
1882 . . . .(40) . . .2,324,440		550	575	585	595	600	1,250	15,000
1882CC 6,764		750	1,000	2,400	2,600	15,000	30,000	
18820 10,820		700	725	950	1,100	4,000	12,500	
1882S 132,000		550	575	585	595	600	3,500	
1883 . . . .(40) 208,700		550	575	585	595	600	2,500	15,000
1883CC 12,000		700	800	2,000	2,500	10,000		
18830 .800		3,000	8,000	12,000	15,000	35,000		
1883S 38,000		550	575	585	595	675	6,000	
1884 . . . .(45) 76,860		550	575	585	595	600	3,000	15,000
1884CC 9,925		750	1,000	2,000	2,400	7,000		
1884S 124,250		550	575	585	595	600	3,500	
1885 . . . .(65) 253,462		550	575	585	595	600	2,200	12,500
1885S 228,000		550	575	585	595	600	1,800	
1886 . . . .(60) 236,100		550	575	585	595	600	3,000	12,500
1886S 826,000		550	575	585	595	600	1,250	
1887 . . . .(80) 53,600		550	575	585	595	650	4,000	12,000
1887S 817,000		550	575	585	595	600	2,000	
1888 . . . .(75) 132,921		550	575	585	595	650	4,000	12,000
18880 21,335		550	575	585	595	650	4,000	
1888S 648,700		550	575	585	595	600	1,350	
1889 . . . .(45) 4,440		550	575	600	650	1,500	4,500	12,000
1889S 425,400		550	575	585	595	600	1,250	
1890 . . . .(63) 57,980		550	575	585	595	600	3,500	10,000
1890CC 17,500		650	700	750	800	1,600	2,000	
1891 . . . .(48) 91,820		550	575	585	595	600	2,500	10,000

	Mintage	VF-20	EF-40	AU-50	AU-55	MS-60	MS-63	PF-63
1891CC 103,732		$700	$750	$800	$850	$1,250	$5,000	
1892 . . . .(72) . .797,480		550	575	585	595	600	1,250	$10,000
1892CC 40,000		700	750	800	850	2,500	7,000	
1892O 28,688		550	575	585	595	600	5,000	
1892S 115,500		550	575	585	595	600	2,500	
1893 . . . .(55) . .1,840,840		550	575	585	595	600	1,250	10,000
1893CC 14,000		700	750	850	1,250	5,000	15,000	
1893O 17,000		550	575	585	595	750	4,500	
1893S 141,350		550	575	585	595	600	2,500	
1894 . . . .(43) . .2,470,735		550	575	585	595	600	1,250	10,000
1894O 107,500		550	575	585	595	750	4,000	
1894S 25,000		550	575	600	650	2,200	8,500	
1895 . . . .(56) . .567,770		550	575	585	595	600	1,250	10,000
1895O 98,000		550	575	585	595	675	4,500	
1895S 49,000		550	575	585	600	1,500	5,000	
1896 . . . .(78) 76,270		550	575	585	595	600	1,800	10,000
1896S 123,750		550	575	585	595	1,500	7,000	
1897 . . . .(69) . .1,000,090		550	575	585	595	600	1,250	10,000
1897O 42,500		550	575	585	595	750	3,500	
1897S 234,750		550	575	585	595	600	3,500	
1898 . . . .(67) . .812,130		550	575	585	595	600	1,250	10,000
1898S 473,600		550	575	585	595	600	3,000	
1899 . . . .(86) . .1,262,219		550	575	585	595	600	1,250	10,000
1899O 37,047		550	575	585	595	600	3,500	
1899S 841,000		550	575	585	595	600	2,250	
1900 . . . .(120) 293,840		550	575	585	595	600	1,250	10,000
1900S 81,000		550	575	585	595	700	4,300	
1901 . . . .(85) . .1,718,740		550	575	585	595	600	1,250	10,000
1901O 72,041		550	575	585	595	600	2,500	
1901S 2,812,750		550	575	585	595	600	1,250	
1902 . . . .(113) 82,400		550	575	585	595	600	2,000	10,000
1902S 469,500		550	575	585	595	600	1,250	
1903 . . . .(96) . .125,830		550	575	585	595	600	1,800	10,000
1903O 112,771		550	575	585	595	600	2,250	
1903S 538,000		550	575	585	595	600	1,250	
1904 . . . .(108) 161,930		550	575	585	595	600	1,500	10,000
1904O 108,950		550	575	585	595	600	2,500	
1905 . . . .(86) 200,992		550	575	585	595	600	1,250	10,000
1905S 369,250		550	575	585	595	650	4,000	
1906 . . . .(77) . .165,420		550	575	585	595	600	1,250	10,000
1906D 981,000		550	575	585	595	600	1,250	
1906O 86,895		550	575	585	595	600	3,000	
1906S 457,000		550	575	585	595	625	3,000	
1907 . . . .(74) . .1,203,899		550	575	585	595	600	1,250	10,000
1907D 1,030,000		550	575	585	595	600	1,300	
1907S 210,500		550	575	585	595	600	3,500	

INDIAN HEAD (1907–1933)

VF-20 Very Fine: Bonnet feathers worn near band. Wear visible on high points of hair.

EF-40 Extremely Fine: Slight wear on cheekbone and headdress feathers. Slight wear visible on eagle's eye and left wing.

AU-50 About Uncirculated: Trace of wear on hair above eye and on forehead.

AU-55 Choice About Uncirculated: Evidence of friction on design high points. Much of original mint luster present.

MS-60 Uncirculated: No trace of wear. Light blemishes.

MS-63 Choice Uncirculated: Some distracting contact marks or blemishes in prime focal areas. Impaired luster possible.

Matte PF-63 Choice Proof: Matte surfaces with few blemishes in secondary focal places. No major flaws.

No Motto
Mintmark is above left tip of branch on 1908-D No Motto.

With Motto IN GOD WE TRUST
Mintmark is at left of arrow points.

Gem Uncirculated (MS-65) coins are rare and worth substantial premiums.

	Mintage	VF-20	EF-40	AU-50	AU-55	MS-60	MS-63
1907, Wire Rim, Periods 500		$10,000	$13,500	$17,500	$19,000	$23,000	$32,500
1907, Rounded Rim, Periods Before and After *E*PLURIBUS*UNUM* 50		25,000	35,000	45,000	50,000	65,000	85,000
1907, No Periods 239,406		575	585	595	600	650	2,500
1908, No Motto 33,500		575	595	600	625	675	3,000
1908D, No Motto 210,000		575	585	595	600	650	4,500

Variety 2 – Motto on Reverse (1908–1933)

	Mintage	VF-20	EF-40	AU-50	AU-55	MS-60	MS-63	MATTE PF-63
1908 ....(116) 341,370		$575	$585	$595	$600	$650	$1,800	$12,000
1908D 836,500		575	585	595	600	650	4,500	
1908S 59,850		575	600	650	700	2,200	7,500	
1909 ....(74) 184,789		575	585	595	600	650	2,500	12,000
1909D 121,540		575	585	595	600	650	4,000	
1909S 292,350		575	585	595	600	675	4,000	
1910 ....(204) 318,500		575	585	595	600	650	1,250	12,000
1910D 2,356,640		575	585	595	600	650	1,250	
1910S 811,000		575	585	595	600	675	5,500	
1911 ....(95) 505,500		575	585	595	600	650	1,250	12,000
1911D 30,100		600	900	1,100	2,000	5,000	20,000	
1911S 51,000		575	585	595	600	675	6,500	
1912 ....(83) 405,000		575	585	595	600	650	1,250	12,000
1912S 300,000		575	585	595	600	850	5,000	
1913 ....(71) 442,000		575	585	595	600	650	1,250	12,000
1913S 66,000		575	600	700	1,000	3,000	20,000	
1914 ....(50) 151,000		575	585	595	600	650	1,500	12,000
1914D 343,500		575	585	595	600	650	1,500	
1914S 208,000		575	585	595	600	800	5,000	
1915 ....(75) 351,000		575	585	595	600	650	1,500	13,500
1915S 59,000		575	600	650	750	2,200	11,000	
1916S 138,500		575	585	595	600	750	4,000	
1920S 126,500		7,500	10,000	12,000	12,500	25,000	65,000	
1926 1,014,000		575	585	595	600	650	1,250	
1930S 96,000		5,000	6,500	8,500	9,500	15,000	27,500	
1932 4,463,000		575	585	595	600	650	1,250	
1933 312,500		40,000	50,000	60,000	100,000	150,000	175,000	

This largest denomination of all regular United States issues was authorized to be coined by the Act of March 3, 1849. The coin's weight was set at 516 grains, and its fineness at .900. A single $20 gold pattern of 1849 resides in the Smithsonian.

LIBERTY HEAD (1849–1907)

VF-20 Very Fine: LIBERTY on crown bold; prongs on crown defined; lower half worn flat. Hair worn about ear.

EF-40 Extremely Fine: Trace of wear on rounded prongs of crown and down hair curls. Minor bagmarks.

AU-50 About Uncirculated: Trace of wear on hair over eye and on coronet.

AU-55 Choice About Uncirculated: Evidence of friction on design high points. Some of original mint luster present.

MS-60 Uncirculated: No trace of wear. Light blemishes.

MS-63 Choice Uncirculated: Some distracting marks or blemishes in focal areas. Impaired luster possible.

PF-63 Choice Proof: Reflective surfaces with only a few blemishes in secondary focal areas. No major flaws.

Without Motto on Reverse (1849–1866)

Mintmark is below eagle.

	Mintage	VF-20	EF-40	AU-50	AU-55	MS-60	MS-63	PF-63
1850	1,170,261	$1,300	$1,500	$2,200	$2,750	$6,000	$30,000	
1850O	141,000	1,450	3,000	5,500	8,500	32,500		
1851	2,087,155	1,150	1,175	1,300	1,325	2,500	15,000	
1851O	315,000	1,300	2,200	3,500	4,500	13,500	45,000	
1852	2,053,026	1,150	1,175	1,300	1,325	2,500	12,000	
1852O	190,000	1,350	2,300	3,000	4,500	15,000	35,000	
1853	1,261,326	1,150	1,175	1,300	1,325	2,800	15,000	
1853O	71,000	1,450	1,600	3,000	4,500	20,000		
1854	757,899	1,150	1,175	1,300	1,325	6,000	17,000	
1854O	3,250	75,000	125,000	220,000	280,000	475,000		
1854S	141,468	1,200	1,400	2,500	3,000	4,000	10,000	
1855	364,666	1,150	1,175	1,300	1,325	6,000	30,000	
1855O	8,000	2,500	10,000	23,000	28,000	60,000		
1855S	879,675	1,150	1,175	1,300	1,350	5,000	10,000	
1856	329,878	1,150	1,175	1,300	1,325	5,500	18,000	
1856O	2,250	75,000	125,000	225,000	300,000	425,000		
1856S	1,189,750	1,150	1,175	1,300	1,450	4,000	10,000	
1857	439,375	1,150	1,175	1,300	1,500	2,500	15,000	
1857O	30,000	1,500	2,000	4,500	6,000	25,000	65,000	
1857S	970,500	1,150	1,300	1,500	1,750	2,750	5,000	
1858	211,714	1,150	1,175	1,500	2,000	3,000	22,500	
1858O	35,250	1,650	2,500	4,500	6,500	25,000		
1858S	846,710	1,150	1,175	1,300	1,500	6,000		
1859	(80) 43,597	1,500	1,850	3,000	5,000	20,000		$65,000
1859O	9,100	3,500	12,000	20,000	25,000	75,000		
1859S	636,445	1,150	1,175	1,300	1,450	3,500	25,000	
1860	(59) 577,670	1,150	1,175	1,300	1,350	2,500	10,000	50,000
1860O	6,600	3,500	10,000	20,000	25,000	75,000		
1860S	544,950	1,150	1,175	1,300	1,450	5,000	10,000	

DOUBLE EAGLES

	Mintage	VF-20	EF-40	AU-50	AU-55	MS-60	MS-63	PF-63
1861 . . . . (66) . . .2,976,453	$1,150	$1,175	$1,200	$1,225	$2,500	$7,500	$50,000
1861O .17,741	3,000	10,000	27,500	35,000	60,000		
1861S 768,000	1,200	1,250	1,500	1,750	6,000	22,000	
1862 . . . . (35) 92,133	1,300	1,800	3,500	4,500	10,000	25,000	40,000
1862S 854,173	1,150	1,175	1,500	1,750	6,500	22,000	
1863 . . . . (30) 142,790	1,200	1,500	2,500	3,000	12,000	23,000	40,000
1863S 966,570	1,150	1,300	1,500	1,700	5,000	20,000	
1864 . . . . (50) 204,235	1,300	1,350	1,600	1,750	7,500		40,000
1864S 793,660	1,150	1,175	1,300	1,450	5,500	20,000	
1865 . . . . (25) 351,175	1,150	1,175	1,300	1,450	4,000	13,000	40,000
1865S 1,042,500	1,150	1,175	1,300	1,450	3,000	6,500	
1866S 120,000	2,000	5,000	20,000	30,000	80,000		

Motto Above Eagle (1866–1907)
Value TWENTY D. (1866–1876)

	Mintage	VF-20	EF-40	AU-50	AU-55	MS-60	MS-63	PF-63
1866 . . . . (30) 698,745	$1,150	$1,175	$1,200	$1,225	$5,000	$15,000	$40,000
1866S 842,250	1,150	1,175	1,200	3,000	10,000		
1867 . . . . (50) 251,015	1,150	1,175	1,200	1,225	2,000	12,000	40,000
1867S 920,750	1,150	1,175	1,200	1,500	7,500		
1868 . . . . (25) 98,575	1,150	1,175	1,500	1,600	7,000	35,000	40,000
1868S 837,500	1,150	1,175	1,200	1,225	6,500	25,000	
1869 . . . . (25) 175,130	1,150	1,175	1,200	1,225	5,000	15,000	40,000
1869S 686,750	1,150	1,175	1,200	1,225	5,000	30,000	
1870 . . . . (35) 155,150	1,150	1,175	1,200	1,225	6,000	30,000	40,000
1870CC 3,789	135,000	200,000	300,000	400,000			
1870S 982,000	1,150	1,175	1,200	1,225	3,500	22,000	
1871 . . . . (30) 80,120	1,150	1,175	1,200	1,225	2,750	15,000	40,000
1871CC 17,387	6,000	12,000	30,000	35,000	65,000		
1871S 928,000	1,150	1,175	1,200	1,225	3,000	15,000	
1872 . . . . (30) 251,850	1,150	1,175	1,200	1,225	2,500	15,000	40,000
1872CC 26,900	1,600	3,500	7,000	8,500	25,000		
1872S 780,000	1,150	1,175	1,200	1,225	2,000	15,000	
1873 . . . . (25) . .1,709,800	1,150	1,175	1,200	1,225	2,000	8,000	40,000
1873CC 22,410	2,500	3,500	7,500	9,500	25,000		
1873S 1,040,600	1,150	1,175	1,200	1,225	1,500	12,000	
1874 . . . . (20) 366,780	1,150	1,175	1,200	1,225	1,500	12,000	40,000
1874CC 115,085	1,400	1,850	2,500	2,750	8,500	35,000	
1874S 1,214,000	1,150	1,175	1,200	1,225	1,500	15,000	
1875 . . . . (20) 295,720	1,150	1,175	1,200	1,225	1,500	8,000	65,000
1875CC 111,151	1,400	1,500	1,800	2,200	3,500	15,000	
1875S 1,230,000	1,150	1,175	1,200	1,225	1,500	8,500	
1876 . . . . (45) 583,860	1,150	1,175	1,200	1,225	1,500	8,000	40,000
1876CC 138,441	1,400	1,500	1,800	2,200	6,000	25,000	
1876S 1,597,000	1,150	1,175	1,200	1,225	1,500	8,000	

Value TWENTY DOLLARS (1877–1907)

	Mintage	VF-20	EF-40	AU-50	AU-55	MS-60	MS-63	PF-63
1877 . . . .(20) 397,650		$1,150	$1,175	$1,185	$1,200	$1,225	$8,000	$25,000
1877CC 42,565		1,400	1,800	3,000	4,500	13,000		
1877S 1,735,000		1,150	1,175	1,185	1,200	1,225	10,000	
1878 . . . .(20) . . .543,625		1,150	1,175	1,185	1,200	1,250	8,500	25,000
1878CC 13,180		2,000	3,000	5,500	7,500	20,000		
1878S 1,739,000		1,150	1,175	1,185	1,200	1,225	12,000	
1879 . . . .(30) 207,600		1,150	1,175	1,185	1,200	1,225	10,000	25,000
1879CC 10,708		2,500	3,500	7,000	10,000	25,000		
1879O 2,325		7,500	12,000	25,000	35,000	60,000	90,000	
1879S 1,223,800		1,150	1,175	1,185	1,200	1,225	24,000	
1880 . . . .(36) . . .51,420		1,150	1,175	1,185	1,200	1,600	15,000	25,000
1880S 836,000		1,150	1,175	1,185	1,200	1,225	11,000	
1881 . . . .(61) 2,199		4,000	7,500	18,000	22,500	45,000		25,000
1881S 727,000		1,150	1,175	1,185	1,200	1,225	13,000	
1882 . . . .(59) 571		10,000	30,000	55,000	65,000	100,000	150,000	25,000
1882CC 39,140		1,300	1,600	1,750	2,500	7,000	35,000	
1882S 1,125,000		1,150	1,175	1,185	1,200	1,225	10,000	
1883, Proof only . . . . . .(92)								50,000
1883CC 59,962		1,300	1,500	1,750	1,850	6,000	18,000	
1883S 1,189,000		1,150	1,175	1,185	1,200	1,225	5,000	
1884, Proof only . . . . . .(71)								50,000
1884CC 81,139		1,300	1,500	1,700	2,000	4,000	13,000	
1884S 916,000		1,150	1,175	1,185	1,200	1,225	4,500	
1885 . . . .(77) 751		6,000	9,000	13,000	16,000	40,000	65,000	25,000
1885CC 9,450		2,000	3,000	5,000	6,500	12,500	30,000	
1885S 683,500		1,150	1,175	1,185	1,200	1,225	3,500	
1886 . . . .(106) 1,000		7,500	12,000	25,000	30,000	55,000	75,000	25,000
1887, Proof Only . . . . .(121)								50,000
1887S 283,000		1,150	1,175	1,185	1,200	1,225	10,000	
1888 . . . .(105) . . .226,161		1,150	1,175	1,185	1,200	1,225	6,000	25,000
1888S 859,600		1,150	1,175	1,185	1,200	1,225	3,000	
1889 . . . .(41) 44,070		1,150	1,175	1,185	1,200	1,225	8,000	25,000
1889CC 30,945		1,500	1,750	2,200	2,450	5,000	13,000	
1889S 774,700		1,150	1,175	1,185	1,200	1,225	4,000	
1890 . . . .(55) 75,940		1,150	1,175	1,185	1,200	1,225	6,000	25,000
1890CC 91,209		1,400	1,700	1,800	2,200	4,000	20,000	
1890S 802,750		1,150	1,175	1,185	1,200	1,225	4,500	
1891 . . . .(52) 1,390		3,500	9,000	12,000	15,000	40,000	75,000	25,000
1891CC 5,000		4,000	7,500	9,000	12,000	17,500	35,000	
1891S 1,288,125		1,150	1,175	1,185	1,200	1,225	2,500	
1892 . . . .(93) 4,430		1,150	2,000	2,500	3,000	7,500	25,000	25,000

	Mintage	VF-20	EF-40	AU-50	AU-55	MS-60	MS-63	PF-63
1892CC 27,265		$1,500	$1,700	$2,000	$2,500	$5,000	$25,000	
1892S 930,150		1,150	1,175	1,185	1,200	1,225	2,500	
1893 ....(59)....344,280		1,150	1,175	1,185	1,200	1,225	1,800	$25,000
1893CC 18,402		1,600	1,800	2,200	2,500	5,000	23,000	
1893S 996,175		1,150	1,175	1,185	1,200	1,225	2,200	
1894 ....(50)...1,368,940		1,150	1,175	1,185	1,200	1,225	2,200	25,000
1894S 1,048,550		1,150	1,175	1,185	1,200	1,225	2,200	
1895 ....(51)...1,114,605		1,150	1,175	1,185	1,200	1,225	1,800	25,000
1895S 1,143,500		1,150	1,175	1,185	1,200	1,225	1,800	
1896 ....(128)....792,535		1,150	1,175	1,185	1,200	1,225	1,800	25,000
1896S 1,403,925		1,150	1,175	1,185	1,200	1,225	1,800	
1897 ....(86)...1,383,175		1,150	1,175	1,185	1,200	1,225	1,800	25,000
1897S 1,470,250		1,150	1,175	1,185	1,200	1,225	1,800	
1898 ....(75)....170,395		1,150	1,175	1,185	1,200	1,225	3,000	25,000
1898S 2,575,175		1,150	1,175	1,185	1,200	1,225	1,800	
1899 ....(84)...1,669,300		1,150	1,175	1,185	1,200	1,225	1,800	25,000
1899S 2,010,300		1,150	1,175	1,185	1,200	1,225	1,800	
1900 ....(124)...1,874,460		1,150	1,175	1,185	1,200	1,225	1,800	25,000
1900S 2,459,500		1,150	1,175	1,185	1,200	1,225	1,800	
1901 ....(96)....111,430		1,150	1,175	1,185	1,200	1,225	1,800	25,000
1901S 1,596,000		1,150	1,175	1,185	1,200	1,225	1,800	
1902 ....(114)....31,140		1,150	1,175	1,185	1,200	1,225	8,000	25,000
1902S 1,753,625		1,150	1,175	1,185	1,200	1,225	2,500	
1903 ....(158)....287,270		1,150	1,175	1,185	1,200	1,225	1,800	25,000
1903S 954,000		1,150	1,175	1,185	1,200	1,225	1,800	
1904 ....(98)...6,256,699		1,150	1,175	1,185	1,200	1,225	1,800	25,000
1904S 5,134,175		1,150	1,175	1,185	1,200	1,225	1,800	
1905 ....(92)....58,919		1,150	1,175	1,185	1,200	1,225	10,000	25,000
1905S 1,813,000		1,150	1,175	1,185	1,200	1,225	1,800	
1906 ....(94)....69,596		1,150	1,175	1,185	1,200	1,225	5,000	25,000
1906D 620,250		1,150	1,175	1,185	1,200	1,225	1,800	
1906S 2,065,750		1,150	1,175	1,185	1,200	1,225	1,800	
1907 ....(78)...1,451,786		1,150	1,175	1,185	1,200	1,225	1,800	25,000
1907D 842,250		1,150	1,175	1,185	1,200	1,225	1,800	
1907S 2,165,800		1,150	1,175	1,185	1,200	1,225	1,800	

SAINT-GAUDENS (1907–1933)

The $20 gold piece designed by Augustus Saint-Gaudens is considered by many to be the most beautiful United States coin. The first coins issued were 11,250 high-relief pieces struck for general circulation. The relief is much higher than that of later issues and the date 1907 is in Roman numerals. A few of the Proof coins were made using the lettered-edge collar from the Ultra High Relief version. These can be distinguished by a pronounced bottom left serif on the N in UNUM, and other minor differences. Flat-relief double eagles were issued later in 1907 with Arabic numerals, and continued through 1933.

The field of the rare, Ultra High Relief experimental pieces is extremely concave and connects directly with the edge without any border, giving it a sharp knifelike appearance. Liberty's skirt shows two folds on the side of her right leg; the Capitol building in the background at left is very small; the sun, on the reverse side, has 14 rays, as opposed to the regular high-relief coins, which have only 13 rays extending from the sun. High-relief Proofs are trial or experimental pieces.

VF-20 Very Fine: Minor wear on Liberty's legs and toes. Eagle's left wing and breast feathers worn.

EF-40 Extremely Fine: Drapery lines on chest visible. Wear on left breast, knee, and below. Eagle's feathers on breast and right wing bold.

AU-50 About Uncirculated: Trace of wear on nose, breast, and knee. Wear visible on eagle's wings.

AU-55 Choice About Uncirculated: Evidence of friction on design high points. Most of mint luster remains.

MS-60 Uncirculated: No trace of wear. Light marks or blemishes.

MS-63 Select Uncirculated: Some distracting contact marks or blemishes in prime focal areas. Impaired luster possible.

Matte PF-63 Choice Proof: Matte surfaces with only a few blemishes in secondary focal places. No major flaws.

Ultra High Relief Pattern, MCMVII (1907)

	PF-67
1907, Ultra High Relief, Plain Edge *(unique)*	—
1907, Ultra High Relief, Lettered Edge	—

Without Motto IN GOD WE TRUST (1907–1908)
High Relief, MCMVII (1907)

	Mintage	VF-20	EF-40	AU-50	AU-55	MS-60	MS-63	PF
1907, High Relief, Roman Numerals (MCMVII), Wire Rim	12,367	$6,000	$7,000	$8,500	$9,000	$11,000	$20,000	—

Arabic Numerals, No Motto (1907–1908)

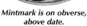

Mintmark is on obverse, above date.

No Motto

Motto IN GOD WE TRUST (1908–1933)

	Mintage	VF-20	EF-40	AU-50	AU-55	MS-60	MS-63	MATTE PF-63
1907	361,667	$1,150	$1,175	$1,185	$1,200	$1,250	$1,500	
1908	4,271,551	1,150	1,175	1,185	1,200	1,250	1,350	
1908D	663,750	1,150	1,175	1,185	1,200	1,250	1,350	
1908, With Motto (101)	156,258	1,150	1,175	1,185	1,200	1,250	1,350	$17,500
1908D, With Motto	349,500	1,150	1,175	1,185	1,200	1,250	1,350	
1908S, With Motto	22,000	1,500	2,500	5,000	5,500	8,500	16,000	

1909, 9 Over 8

	Mintage	VF-20	EF-40	AU-50	AU-55	MS-60	MS-63	MATTE PF-63
1909, 9 Over 8 ....*		$1,150	$1,175	$1,185	$1,200	$1,250	$3,500	
1909 ....(67) 161,282		1,150	1,175	1,185	1,200	1,250	2,200	$17,500
1909D 52,500		1,150	1,175	1,185	1,200	1,250	6,000	
1909S 2,774,925		1,150	1,175	1,185	1,200	1,250	1,350	
1910 ....(167) 482,000		1,150	1,175	1,185	1,200	1,250	1,350	17,500
1910D 429,000		1,150	1,175	1,185	1,200	1,250	1,350	
1910S 2,128,250		1,150	1,175	1,185	1,200	1,250	1,350	
1911 ....(100) 197,250		1,150	1,175	1,185	1,200	1,250	1,800	17,500
1911D 846,500		1,150	1,175	1,185	1,200	1,250	1,350	
1911S 775,750		1,150	1,175	1,185	1,200	1,250	1,350	
1912 ....(74) 149,750		1,150	1,175	1,185	1,200	1,250	2,300	17,500
1913 ....(58) 168,780		1,150	1,175	1,185	1,200	1,250	2,400	17,500
1913D 393,500		1,150	1,175	1,185	1,200	1,250	1,350	
1913S 34,000		1,200	1,250	1,350	1,400	1,600	3,500	
1914 ....(70) 95,250		1,150	1,175	1,185	1,200	1,250	2,600	17,500
1914D 453,000		1,150	1,175	1,185	1,200	1,250	1,350	
1914S 1,498,000		1,150	1,175	1,185	1,200	1,250	1,350	
1915 ....(50) 152,000		1,150	1,175	1,185	1,200	1,250	1,850	20,000
1915S 567,500		1,150	1,175	1,185	1,200	1,250	1,350	
1916S 796,500		1,150	1,175	1,185	1,200	1,250	1,350	
1920 228,250		1,150	1,175	1,185	1,200	1,250	1,500	
1920S 558,000		10,000	15,000	22,000	26,000	42,000	75,000	
1921 528,500		22,000	35,000	45,000	50,000	80,000	175,000	
1922 1,375,500		1,150	1,175	1,185	1,200	1,250	1,350	
1922S 2,658,000		1,200	1,300	1,400	1,500	2,000	4,250	
1923 566,000		1,150	1,175	1,185	1,200	1,250	1,350	
1923D 1,702,250		1,150	1,175	1,185	1,200	1,250	1,350	
1924 4,323,500		1,150	1,175	1,185	1,200	1,250	1,350	
1924D 3,049,500		1,200	1,350	1,400	1,500	3,000	7,500	
1924S 2,927,500		1,250	1,400	1,450	1,600	3,000	8,500	
1925 2,831,750		1,150	1,175	1,185	1,200	1,250	1,350	
1925D 2,938,500		1,500	1,800	2,250	2,650	3,500	8,000	
1925S 3,776,500		1,650	1,900	2,500	3,000	7,500	14,000	
1926 816,750		1,150	1,175	1,185	1,200	1,250	1,350	
1926D 481,000		6,000	11,000	14,000	17,500	21,000	26,000	
1926S 2,041,500		1,600	1,800	2,000	2,200	2,600	4,500	
1927 2,946,750		1,150	1,175	1,185	1,200	1,250	1,350	
1927D 180,000			250,000	300,000	350,000	500,000	850,000	
1927S 3,107,000		4,000	7,000	9,000	11,000	16,000	35,000	
1928 8,816,000		1,150	1,175	1,185	1,200	1,250	1,350	
1929 1,779,750		7,500	10,000	12,000	13,000	15,000	26,000	
1930S 74,000		20,000	30,000	35,000	40,000	50,000	75,000	
1931 2,938,250		7,500	10,000	15,000	20,000	30,000	50,000	
1931D 106,500		7,500	10,000	14,000	18,000	27,500	60,000	
1932 1,101,750		7,500	10,000	14,000	18,000	22,000	50,000	
1933 445,500		*None placed in circulation.*						

* Included in number below.

Collecting United States commemorative coins is like gathering snapshots for an album of important events, places, and people in the nation's history. Because they represent so many different aspects of America—from wars and Olympic games to presidents, state parks, and historical landmarks, every collector can assemble a set with its own special significance.

All U.S. commemorative coins are issued as legal tender, though in most cases the precious metal of the coins surpasses their face values. The weight and fineness for commemoratives follow those of standard-issue gold, silver, and clad coins.

CLASSIC COMMEMORATIVE SILVER AND GOLD

(1892–1893) World's Columbian Exposition Half Dollar

	Distribution	AU-50	MS-60	MS-63	MS-65
1892, World's Columbian Exposition half dollar	950,000	$10	$16	$40	$335
1893, Same type	1,550,405	10	16	38	300

(1893) World's Columbian Exposition, Isabella Quarter Dollar

	Distribution	AU-50	MS-60	MS-63	MS-65
1893, World's Columbian Exposition, Chicago, quarter dollar	24,214	$350	$400	$500	$1,800

(1900) Lafayette Dollar

	Distribution	AU-50	MS-60	MS-63	MS-65
1900, Lafayette silver dollar	36,026	$325	$600	$1,200	$5,750

COMMEMORATIVES

(1903) Louisiana Purchase Exposition

	Distribution	AU-50	MS-60	MS-63	MS-65
1903, Louisiana Purchase / Thomas Jefferson gold dollar 17,500		$360	$425	$600	$1,250
1903, Louisiana Purchase / William McKinley gold dollar 17,500		360	425	600	1,250

(1904–1905) Lewis and Clark Exposition

	Distribution	AU-50	MS-60	MS-63	MS-65
1904, Lewis and Clark Exposition gold dollar 10,025		$550	$750	$1,100	$5,500
1905, Lewis and Clark Exposition gold dollar 10,041		650	850	1,500	11,000

(1915) Panama-Pacific Exposition

	Distribution	AU-50	MS-60	MS-63	MS-65
1915S, Panama-Pacific Exposition half dollar 27,134		$280	$335	$475	$1,500
1915S, Panama-Pacific Exposition gold dollar 15,000		350	400	500	950
1915S, Panama-Pacific Exposition gold $2.50 6,749		950	1,200	2,100	4,250
1915S, Panama-Pacific Exposition gold $50 Round 483		33,000	40,000	50,000	95,000

179

(1915) Panama-Pacific Exposition

	Distribution	AU-50	MS-60	MS-63	MS-65
1915S, Panama-Pacific Exposition gold $50 Octagonal 645	$34,000	$36,000	$46,000	$90,000

(1916–1917) McKinley Memorial

	Distribution	AU-50	MS-60	MS-63	MS-65
1916, McKinley Memorial gold dollar *15,000*	$350	$400	$450	$1,100
1917, McKinley Memorial gold dollar 5,000	400	475	575	1,625

(1918) Illinois Centennial

	Distribution	AU-50	MS-60	MS-63	MS-65
1918, Illinois Centennial half dollar 100,058	$75	$85	$100	$280

(1920) Maine Centennial

	Distribution	AU-50	MS-60	MS-63	MS-65
1920, Maine Centennial half dollar 50,028	$70	$90	$110	$300

(1920–1921) Pilgrim Tercentenary

With 1921 in Field
on Obverse

	Distribution	AU-50	MS-60	MS-63	MS-65
1920, Pilgrim Tercentenary half dollar 152,112		$45	$60	$70	$225
1921, Same, With Date Added in Field 20,053		90	110	120	300

(1921) Missouri Centennial

With 2★4 in Field

	Distribution	AU-50	MS-60	MS-63	MS-65
1921, Missouri Centennial half dollar, "2★4" in Field 9,400		$350	$450	$600	$2,200
1921, Missouri Centennial half dollar, Plain 11,400		210	360	475	2,000

(1921) Alabama Centennial

Without 2X2 in Field

	Distribution	AU-50	MS-60	MS-63	MS-65
1921, Alabama Centennial half dollar, Plain 35,000		$100	$125	$150	$850
1921, Alabama Centennial half dollar, With "2X2" in Field of Obverse . . .30,000		160	185	300	900

(1922) Grant Memorial

	Distribution	AU-50	MS-60	MS-63	MS-65
1922, Grant Memorial, With Star* half dollar 4,256		$525	$725	$1,000	$4,100
1922, Same type, No Star in Obv Field 67,405		65	75	90	450
1922, Grant Memorial, With Star* gold dollar 5,016		900	1,000	1,200	1,800
1922, Same type, No Star in Obv Field 5,016		900	1,000	1,200	1,800

* Fake stars usually have a flattened spot on the reverse.

(1923) Monroe Doctrine Centennial

	Distribution	AU-50	MS-60	MS-63	MS-65
1923S, Monroe Doctrine Centennial half dollar 274,077		$30	$40	$82	$1,200

(1924) Huguenot-Walloon Tercentenary

	Distribution	AU-50	MS-60	MS-63	MS-65
1924, Huguenot-Walloon Tercentenary half dollar 142,080		$75	$80	$100	$250

(1925) Lexington-Concord Sesquicentennial

	Distribution	AU-50	MS-60	MS-63	MS-65
1925, Lexington-Concord Sesquicentennial half dollar 162,013	$50	$67	$85	$375

(1925) Stone Mountain Memorial

	Distribution	AU-50	MS-60	MS-63	MS-65
1925, Stone Mountain Memorial half dollar 1,314,709	$30	$42	$50	$135

(1925) California Diamond Jubilee

	Distribution	AU-50	MS-60	MS-63	MS-65
1925S, California Diamond Jubilee half dollar 86,594	$100	$125	$190	$575

(1925) Fort Vancouver Centennial

	Distribution	AU-50	MS-60	MS-63	MS-65
1925, Fort Vancouver Centennial half dollar 14,994	$180	$225	$250	$750

(1926) Sesquicentennial of American Independence

	Distribution	AU-50	MS-60	MS-63	MS-65
1926, Sesquicentennial of American Independence half dollar	141,120	$50	$65	$75	$1,950
1926, Sesquicentennial of American Independence gold $2.50	46,019	235	280	400	1,800

(1926–1939) Oregon Trail Memorial

	Distribution	AU-50	MS-60	MS-63	MS-65
1926, Oregon Trail Memorial half dollar	47,955	$75	$95	$100	$180
1926S, Same type, S mint	83,055	75	95	100	180
1928, Oregon Trail Memorial half dollar (same as 1926)	6,028	95	110	120	200
1933D, Oregon Trail Memorial half dollar	5,008	195	210	250	330
1934D, Oregon Trail Memorial half dollar	7,006	95	110	120	210
1936, Oregon Trail Memorial half dollar	10,006	85	100	130	180
1936S, Same type, S mint	5,006	85	100	130	200
1937D, Oregon Trail Memorial half dollar	12,008	85	100	130	180
1938, Oregon Trail Memorial half dollar (same as 1926)	6,006				
1938D, Same type, D mint	6,005	*Set:*	250	300	500
1938S, Same type, S mint	6,006				
1939, Oregon Trail Memorial half dollar (same as 1926)	3,004				
1939D, Same type, D mint	3,004	*Set:*	850	925	1,100
1939S, Same type, S mint	3,005				
Oregon Trail Memorial half dollar, single type coin		75	95	100	180

(1927) Vermont Sesquicentennial

	Distribution	AU-50	MS-60	MS-63	MS-65
1927, Vermont Sesquicentennial (Battle of Bennington) half dollar	28,142	$140	$160	$175	$530

(1928) Hawaiian Sesquicentennial

	Distribution	AU-50	MS-60	MS-63	MS-65
1928, Hawaiian Sesquicentennial half dollar 10,008		$1,200	$1,450	$1,800	$3,750
1928, Hawaiian Sesquicentennial, Sandblast Proof Presentation Piece . . . . .(50)				6,500	14,500

(1934) Maryland Tercentenary

	Distribution	AU-50	MS-60	MS-63	MS-65
1934, Maryland Tercentenary half dollar .25,015		$85	$95	$100	$200

(1934–1938) Texas Independence Centennial

	Distribution	AU-50	MS-60	MS-63	MS-65
1934, Texas Independence Centennial half dollar 61,463		$75	$80	$90	$135
1935, Texas Independence Centennial half dollar (same as 1934) . . .9,996					
1935D, Same type, D mint 10,007		Set:	200	225	425
1935S, Same type, S mint 10,008					
1936, Texas Independence Centennial half dollar (same as 1934) . . .8,911					
1936D, Same type, D mint 9,039		Set:	200	225	425
1936S, Same type, S mint 9,055					
1937, Texas Independence Centennial half dollar (same as 1934) . . .6,571					
1937D, Same type, D mint 6,605		Set:	200	225	425
1937S, Same type, S mint 6,637					

Chart continued on next page.

	Distribution	AU-50	MS-60	MS-63	MS-65
1938, Texas Independence Centennial half dollar (same as 1934) . . .3,780					
1938D, Same type, D mint 3,775		*Set:*	$375	$400	$750
1938S, Same type, S mint 3,814					
Texas Independence Centennial half dollar, single type coin		$75	80	90	135

(1934–1938) Daniel Boone Bicentennial   **1934 Added on Reverse**

	Distribution	AU-50	MS-60	MS-63	MS-65
1934, Daniel Boone Bicentennial half dollar 10,007		$75	$85	$90	$140
1935, Same type 10,010					
1935D, Same type, D mint 5,005		*Set:*	200	250	400
1935S, Same type, S mint 5,005					
1935, Same as 1934, Small 1934 on Reverse 10,008					
1935D, Same type, D mint 2,003		*Set:*	400	475	1,100
1935S, Same type, S mint 2,004					
1936, Daniel Boone half dollar (same as preceding) 12,012					
1936D, Same type, D mint 5,005		*Set:*	200	250	400
1936S, Same type, S mint 5,006					
1937, Daniel Boone half dollar (same as preceding) 9,810					
1937D, Same type, D mint 2,506		*Set:*	380	450	750
1937S, Same type, S mint 2,506					
1938, Daniel Boone half dollar (same as preceding) 2,100					
1938D, Same type, D mint 2,100		*Set:*	550	675	900
1938S, Same type, S mint 2,100					
Daniel Boone Bicentennial half dollar, single type coin		75	85	90	140

(1935) Connecticut Tercentenary

	Distribution	AU-50	MS-60	MS-63	MS-65
1935, Connecticut Tercentenary half dollar 25,018		$135	$165	$180	$300

(1935–1939)
Arkansas Centennial

	Distribution	AU-50	MS-60	MS-63	MS-65
1935, Arkansas Centennial half dollar	13,012				
1935D, Same type, D mint	5,505	Set:	$165	$220	$400
1935S, Same type, S mint	5,506				
1936, Arkansas Centennial half dollar (same as 1935 but 1936 on rev)	9,660				
1936D, Same type, D mint	9,660	Set:	165	220	425
1936S, Same type, S mint	9,662				
1937, Arkansas Centennial half dollar (same as 1935)	5,505				
1937D, Same type, D mint	5,505	Set:	180	225	500
1937S, Same type S mint	5,506				
1938, Arkansas Centennial half dollar (same as 1935)	3,156				
1938D, Same type, D mint	3,155	Set:	250	265	900
1938S, Same type, S mint	3,156				
1939, Arkansas Centennial half dollar (same as 1935)	2,104				
1939D, Same type, D mint	2,104	Set:	525	625	1,650
1939S, Same type, S mint	2,105				
Arkansas Centennial half dollar, single type coin		$45	60	70	100

(1936) Arkansas
Centennial – Robinson

	Distribution	AU-50	MS-60	MS-63	MS-65
1936, Arkansas Centennial (Robinson) half dollar	25,265	$75	$85	$100	$215

(1935) Hudson, New
York, Sesquicentennial

	Distribution	AU-50	MS-60	MS-63	MS-65
1935, Hudson, New York, Sesquicentennial half dollar	10,008	$375	$485	$665	$1,200

(1935–1936) California-Pacific International Exposition

	Distribution	AU-50	MS-60	MS-63	MS-65
1935S, California-Pacific International Exposition half dollar 70,132		$50	$65	$80	$95
1936D, California-Pacific International Exposition half dollar 30,092		50	75	85	100

(1935) Old Spanish Trail

	Distribution	AU-50	MS-60	MS-63	MS-65
1935, Old Spanish Trail half dollar 10,008		$575	$725	$800	$1,200

(1936) Providence, Rhode Island, Tercentenary

	Distribution	AU-50	MS-60	MS-63	MS-65
1936, Providence, Rhode Island, Tercentenary half dollar 20,013					
1936D, Same type, D mint 15,010		Set:	$170	$190	$410
1936S, Same type, S mint 15,011					
Providence, Rhode Island, Tercentenary half dollar, single type coin		$55	60	70	140

(1936) Cleveland Centennial / Great Lakes Exposition

	Distribution	AU-50	MS-60	MS-63	MS-65
1936, Cleveland Centennial / Great Lakes Exposition half dollar 50,030		$65	$70	$75	$100

(1936) Wisconsin Territorial Centennial

	Distribution	AU-50	MS-60	MS-63	MS-65
1936, Wisconsin Territorial Centennial half dollar 25,015		$120	$140	$150	$200

(1936) Cincinnati Music Center

	Distribution	AU-50	MS-60	MS-63	MS-65
1936, Cincinnati Music Center half dollar 5,005					
1936D, Same type, D mint 5,005	*Set:*	$450	$500	$1,200
1936S, Same type, S mint 5,006					
Cincinnati Music Center half dollar, single type coin		$140	150	160	390

(1936) Long Island Tercentenary

	Distribution	AU-50	MS-60	MS-63	MS-65
1936, Long Island Tercentenary half dollar 81,826	$50	$60	$65	$225

(1936) York County, Maine, Tercentenary

	Distribution	AU-50	MS-60	MS-63	MS-65
1936, York County, Maine, Tercentenary half dollar 25,015	$120	$130	$140	$175

(1936) Bridgeport, Connecticut, Centennial

	Distribution	AU-50	MS-60	MS-63	MS-65
1936, Bridgeport, Connecticut, Centennial half dollar 25,015	$75	$85	$110	$160

(1936) Lynchburg, Virginia, Sesquicentennial

	Distribution	AU-50	MS-60	MS-63	MS-65
1936, Lynchburg, Virginia, Sesquicentennial half dollar 20,013	$125	$140	$160	$210

(1936) Elgin, Illinois, Centennial

	Distribution	AU-50	MS-60	MS-63	MS-65
1936, Elgin, Illinois, Centennial half dollar .20,015		$125	$140	$160	$190

(1936) Albany, New York, Charter

	Distribution	AU-50	MS-60	MS-63	MS-65
1936, Albany, New York, Charter half dollar 17,671		$170	$180	$190	$225

(1936) San Francisco – Oakland Bay Bridge Opening

	Distribution	AU-50	MS-60	MS-63	MS-65
1936S, San Francisco–Oakland Bay Bridge Opening half dollar 71,424		$90	$100	$110	$210

(1936) Delaware Tercentenary

	Distribution	AU-50	MS-60	MS-63	MS-65
1936, Delaware Tercentenary half dollar .20,993		$160	$175	$190	$250

(1936) Columbia, South Carolina, Sesquicentennial

	Distribution	AU-50	MS-60	MS-63	MS-65
1936, Columbia, South Carolina, Sesquicentennial half dollar 9,007					
1936D, Same type, D mint 8,009	*Set:*	$425	$475	$600
1936S, Same type, S mint 8,007					
Columbia, South Carolina, Sesquicentennial half dollar, single type coin	$145	150	175	200

(1936) Battle of Gettysburg Anniversary

	Distribution	AU-50	MS-60	MS-63	MS-65
1936, Battle of Gettysburg Anniversary half dollar 26,928	$235	$275	$300	$450

(1936) Norfolk, Virginia, Bicentennial

	Distribution	AU-50	MS-60	MS-63	MS-65
1936, Norfolk, Virginia, Bicentennial half dollar 16,936	$255	$265	$285	$325

(1937) Roanoke Island, North Carolina, 350th Anniversary

	Distribution	AU-50	MS-60	MS-63	MS-65
1937, Roanoke Island, North Carolina, 350th Anniversary half dollar	29,030	$130	$140	$150	$175

(1937) Battle of Antietam Anniversary

	Distribution	AU-50	MS-60	MS-63	MS-65
1937, Battle of Antietam Anniversary half dollar	18,028	$365	$400	$450	$510

(1938) New Rochelle, New York, 250th Anniversary

	Distribution	AU-50	MS-60	MS-63	MS-65
1938, New Rochelle, New York, 250th Anniversary half dollar	15,266	$215	$225	$250	$315

(1946) Iowa Centennial

	Distribution	AU-50	MS-60	MS-63	MS-65
1946, Iowa Centennial half dollar	100,057	$65	$70	$75	$90

(1946–1951) Booker T. Washington Memorial

	Distribution	AU-50	MS-60	MS-63	MS-65
1946, Booker T. Washington Memorial half dollar **(a)**	700,546				
1946D, Same type, D mint	50,000	Set:	$32	$42	$90
1946S, Same type, S mint	500,279				
1947, Same type as 1946	6,000				
1947D, Same type, D mint	6,000	Set:	50	75	150
1947S, Same type, S mint	6,000				
1948, Same type as 1946	8,005				
1948D, Same type, D mint	8,005	Set:	95	110	160
1948S, Same type, S mint	8,005				
1949, Same type as 1946	6,004				
1949D, Same type, D mint	6,004	Set:	135	145	190
1949S, Same type, S mint	6,004				
1950, Same type as 1946	6,004				
1950D, Same type, D mint	6,004	Set:	80	90	130
1950S, Same type, S mint	62,091				
1951, Same type as 1946	210,082				
1951D, Same type, D mint	7,004	Set:	80	90	120
1951S, Same type, S mint	7,004				
Booker T. Washington Memorial half dollar, single type coin		$8	10	15	25

a. Minted; quantity melted unknown.

(1951–1954) Carver/Washington Commemorative

	Distribution	AU-50	MS-60	MS-63	MS-65
1951, Carver/Washington half dollar	20,018				
1951D, Same type, D mint	10,004	Set:	$65	$80	$310
1951S, Same type, S mint	10,004				
1952, Same type as 1951	1,106,292				
1952D, Same type, D mint	8,006	Set:	65	80	225
1952S, Same type, S mint	8,006				

	Distribution	AU-50	MS-60	MS-63	MS-65
1953, Same type as 1951 8,003					
1953D, Same type, D mint 8,003		*Set:*	$65	$80	$300
1953S, Same type, S mint 88,020					
1954, Same type as 1951 12,006					
1954D, Same type, D mint 12,006		*Set:*	65	80	225
1954S, Same type, S mint 42,024					
Carver/Washington half dollar, single type coin		$8	10	15	25

MODERN COMMEMORATIVES

(1982) George Washington 250th Anniversary of Birth

	Distribution	MS-67	PF-67
1982D, George Washington, 250th Anniversary half dollar 2,210,458		$7	
1982S, Same type, S mint, Proof . . . .(4,894,044)			$7

(1983–1984) Los Angeles Olympiad

	Distribution	MS-67	PF-67
1983P, Discus Thrower silver dollar 294,543		$16	
1983D, Same type, D mint 174,014		16	
1983S, Same type, S mint . . . .(1,577,025) 174,014		16	$16

Entry continued on next page.

195

(1983–1984) Los Angeles Olympiad

	Distribution	MS-67	PF-67
1984P, Olympic Coliseum silver dollar	217,954	$16	
1984D, Same type, D mint	116,675	16	
1984S, Same type, S mint	(1,801,210) 116,675	16	$16
1984P, Olympic gold $10	(33,309)		535
1984D, Same type, D mint	(34,533)		535
1984S, Same type, S mint	(48,551)		535
1984W, Same type, W mint	(381,085) 75,886	535	535

(1986) Statue of Liberty Centennial

	Distribution	MS-67	PF-67
1986D, Statue of Liberty Centennial half dollar	928,008	$4.50	
1986S, Same type, S mint, Proof	(6,925,627)		$4.50
1986P, Statue of Liberty Centennial silver dollar	723,635	16.00	
1986S, Same type, S mint, Proof	(6,414,638)		16.00
1986W, Statue of Liberty Centennial gold $5	(404,013) 95,248	265.00	265.00

(1987) U.S. Constitution Bicentennial

	Distribution	MS-67	PF-67
1987P, U.S. Constitution Bicentennial silver dollar 451,629		$16	
1987S, Same type, S mint, Proof . . . .(2,747,116)			$16
1987W, U.S. Constitution Bicentennial gold $5 . . . .(651,659) 214,225		265	265

(1988) Seoul Olympiad

	Distribution	MS-67	PF-67
1988D, Seoul Olympiad silver dollar 191,368		$16	
1988S, Same type, S mint, Proof . . . .(1,359,366)			$16
1988W, Seoul Olympiad gold $5 . . . .(281,465) 62,913		265	265

(1989) Congress Bicentennial

	Distribution	MS-67	PF-67
1989D, Congress Bicentennial half dollar	163,753	$6	
1989S, Same type, S mint, Proof	(767,897)		$6
1989D, Congress Bicentennial silver dollar	135,203	17	
1989S, Same type, S mint, Proof	(762,198)		18
1989W, Congress Bicentennial gold $5	(164,690) 46,899	265	265

(1990) Eisenhower Centennial

	Distribution	MS-67	PF-67
1990W, Eisenhower Centennial silver dollar	241,669	$15	
1990P, Same type, P mint, Proof	(1,144,461)		$16

(1991) Mount Rushmore Golden Anniversary

	Distribution	MS-67	PF-67
1991D, Mount Rushmore Golden Anniversary half dollar 172,754		$14	
1991S, Same type, S mint, Proof . . . .(753,257)			$13
1991P, Mount Rushmore Golden Anniversary silver dollar 133,139		20	
1991S, Same type, S mint, Proof . . . .(738,419)			18
1991W, Mount Rushmore Golden Anniversary gold $5 . . . .(111,991) 31,959		270	265

(1991) Korean War Memorial

	Distribution	MS-67	PF-67
1991D, Korean War Memorial silver dollar 213,049		$16	
1991P, Same type, P mint, Proof . . . .(618,488)			$17

(1991) United Service Organizations

	Distribution	MS-67	PF-67
1991D USO silver dollar 124,958		$16	
1991S, Same type, S mint, Proof ....(321,275)...........			$16

(1992) XXV Olympiad

	Distribution	MS-67	PF-67
1992P, XXV Olympiad clad half dollar 161,607		$7	
1992S, Same type, S mint, Proof ....(519,645)...........			$7.50
1992D, XXV Olympiad silver dollar 187,552		18	
1992S, Same type, S mint, Proof ....(504,505)...........			18.00
1992W, XXV Olympiad gold $5 ....(77,313).....27,732		265	265.00

COMMEMORATIVES

(1992) White House 200th Anniversary

	Distribution	MS-67	PF-67
1992D, White House 200th Anniversary silver dollar	123,803	$20	
1992W, Same type, W mint, Proof	(375,851)		$18

(1992) Christopher Columbus Quincentenary

	Distribution	MS-67	PF-67
1992D, Christopher Columbus Quincentenary half dollar	135,702	$9	
1992S, Same type, S mint, Proof	(390,154)		$8
1992D, Christopher Columbus Quincentenary silver dollar	106,949	20	
1992P, Same type, P mint, Proof	(385,241)		22
1992W, Christopher Columbus Quincentenary gold $5	(79,730) 24,329	275	265

(1993) Bill of Rights

	Distribution	MS-67	PF-67
1993W, Bill of Rights silver half dollar 193,346		$14	
1993S, Same type, S mint, Proof . . . .(586,315)			$12
1993D, Bill of Rights silver dollar 98,383		16	
1993S, Same type, S mint, Proof . . . .(534,001)			17
1993W, Bill of Rights gold $5 . . . .(78,651) 23,266		285	265

(1991–1995) 50th Anniversary of World War II

	Distribution	MS-67	PF-67
(1993P) 1991–1995 World War II clad half dollar . . . .(317,396) 197,072		$20	$18

(1991–1995) 50th Anniversary of World War II

	Distribution	MS-67	PF-67
(1993D) 1991–1995 World War II silver dollar 107,240		$24	
(1993W) Same type, W mint, Proof ....(342,041)			$30
(1993W) 1991–1995 World War II gold $5 ....(67,026) 23,672		300	275

(1994) World Cup Tournament

	Distribution	MS-67	PF-67
1994D, World Cup Tournament clad half dollar 168,208		$7	
1994P, Same type, P mint, Proof ....(609,354)			$6
1994D, World Cup Tournament silver dollar 81,524		17	
1994S, Same type, S mint, Proof ....(577,090)			18
1994W, World Cup Tournament gold $5 ....(89,614) 22,447		265	265

(1993 [1994]) Thomas Jefferson

	Distribution	MS-67	PF-67
1993 (1994) Thomas Jefferson silver dollar, P mint	266,927	$16	
1993 (1994) Same type, S mint, Proof	(332,891)		$17

(1994) Vietnam Veterans Memorial

	Distribution	MS-67	PF-67
1994W, Vietnam Veterans Memorial silver dollar	57,290	$65	
1994P, Same type, P mint, Proof	(227,671)		$52

(1994) U.S. Prisoner of War Museum

	Distribution	MS-67	PF-67
1994W, U.S. Prisoner of War Museum silver dollar	54,893	$70	
1994P, Same type, P mint, Proof	(224,449)		$32

(1994) Women in Military Service Memorial

	Distribution	MS-67	PF-67
1994W, Women in Military Service Memorial silver dollar	69,860	$30	
1994P, Same type, P mint, Proof	(241,278)		$30

(1994) U.S. Capitol Bicentennial

	Distribution	MS-67	PF-67
1994D, U.S. Capitol Bicentennial silver dollar	68,332	$16	
1994S, Same type, S mint, Proof	(279,579)		$18

(1995) Civil War Battlefield Preservation

	Distribution	MS-67	PF-67
1995S, Civil War Battlefield Preservation clad half dollar	119,520	$30	
1995S, Same type, S mint, Proof	(330,002)		$28

Entry continued on next page.

(1995) Civil War Battlefield Preservation

	Distribution	MS-67	PF-67
1995P, Civil War Battlefield Preservation silver dollar	45,866	$55	
1995S, Same type, S mint, Proof	(437,114)		$55
1995W, Civil War Battlefield Preservation gold $5	12,735	700	
1995W, Same type, W mint, Proof	(55,246)		300

(1995) XXVI Olympiad

	Distribution	MS-67	PF-67
1995S, XXVI Olympiad, Basketball clad half dollar	171,001	$15	
1995S, Same type, S mint, Proof	(169,655)		$13
1995S, XXVI Olympiad, Baseball clad half dollar	164,605	15	
1995S, Same type, S mint, Proof	(118,087)		13
1996S, XXVI Olympiad, Swimming clad half dollar	49,533	110	
1996S, Same type, S mint, Proof	(114,315)		25
1996S, XXVI Olympiad, Soccer clad half dollar	52,836	105	
1996S, Same type, S mint, Proof	(112,412)		65
1995D, XXVI Olympiad, Gymnastics silver dollar	42,497	45	
1995P, Same type, P mint, Proof	(182,676)		30

(1995) XXVI Olympiad

	Distribution	MS-67	PF-67
1995D, XXVI Olympiad, Paralympics silver dollar	28,649	$60	
1995P, Same type, P mint, Proof	(138,337)		$40
1995D, XXVI Olympiad, Track and Field silver dollar	24,976	70	
1995P, Same type, P mint, Proof	(136,935)		38
1995D, XXVI Olympiad, Cycling silver dollar	19,662	110	
1995P, Same type, P mint, Proof	(118,795)		35
1996D, XXVI Olympiad, Tennis silver dollar	15,983	225	
1996P, Same type, P mint, Proof	(92,016)		65
1996D, XXVI Olympiad, Paralympics silver dollar	14,497	265	
1996P, Same type, P mint, Proof	(84,280)		60
1996D, XXVI Olympiad, Rowing silver dollar	16,258	260	
1996P, Same type, P mint, Proof	(151,890)		50
1996D, XXVI Olympiad, High Jump silver dollar	15,697	290	
1996P, Same type, P mint, Proof	(124,502)		45
1995W, XXVI Olympiad, Torch Runner gold $5	14,675	680	
1995W, Same type, W mint, Proof	(57,442)		280
1995W, XXVI Olympiad, Stadium gold $5	10,579	1,500	
1995W, Same type, W mint, Proof	(43,124)		450
1996W, XXVI Olympiad, Flag Bearer gold $5	9,174	1,500	
1996W, Same type, W mint, Proof	(32,886)		520
1996W, XXVI Olympiad, Cauldron gold $5	9,210	1,500	
1996W, Same type, W mint, Proof	(38,555)		450

(1995) Special Olympics World Games

	Distribution	MS-67	PF-67
1995W, Special Olympics World Games silver dollar	89,301	$23	
1995P, Same type, P mint, Proof	(351,764)		$20

(1996) National Community Service

	Distribution	MS-67	PF-67
1996S, National Community Service silver dollar	23,500	$160	
1996S, Same type, S mint, Proof	(101,543)		$55

(1996) Smithsonian Institution 150th Anniversary

	Distribution	MS-67	PF-67
1996D, Smithsonian Institution 150th Anniversary silver dollar	31,320	$100	
1996P, Same type, P mint, Proof	(129,152)		$40
1996W, Smithsonian Institution 150th Anniversary gold $5	9,068	800	
1996W, Same type, W mint, Proof	(21,772)		385

(1997) U.S. Botanic Garden

	Distribution	MS-67	PF-67
1997P, U.S. Botanic Garden silver dollar	58,505	$30	
1997P, Same type, P mint, Proof	(189,671)		$28

(1997) Jackie Robinson

	Distribution	MS-67	PF-67
1997S, Jackie Robinson silver dollar	30,180	$75	
1997S, Same type, S mint, Proof	(110,002)		$75
1997W, Jackie Robinson gold $5	5,174	3,500	
1997W, Same type, W mint, Proof	(24,072)		500

(1997) Franklin D. Roosevelt

	Distribution	MS-67	PF-67
1997W, Franklin D. Roosevelt gold $5	11,894	$1,000	
1997W, Same type, W mint, Proof	(29,474)		$325

(1997) National Law Enforcement Officers Memorial

	Distribution	MS-67	PF-67
1997P, National Law Enforcement Officers Memorial silver dollar	28,575	$125	
1997P, Same type, P mint, Proof	(110,428)		$80

(1998) Robert F. Kennedy

	Distribution	MS-67	PF-67
1998S, Robert F. Kennedy silver dollar 106,422		$25	
1998S, Same type, S mint, Proof ....(99,020)...........			$34

(1998) Black Revolutionary War Patriots

	Distribution	MS-67	PF-67
1998S, Black Revolutionary War Patriots silver dollar 37,210		$120	
1998S, Same type, S mint, Proof ....(75,070)...........			$75

(1999) Dolley Madison

	Distribution	MS-67	PF-67
1999P, Dolley Madison silver dollar 89,104		$30	
1999P, Same type, P mint, Proof ....(224,403)...........			$20

(1999) George Washington Death Bicentennial

	Distribution	MS-67	PF-67
1999W, George Washington Death Bicentennial gold $5	22,511	$315	
1999W, Same type, W mint, Proof	(41,693)		$275

(1999) Yellowstone National Park

	Distribution	MS-67	PF-67
1999P, Yellowstone National Park silver dollar	82,563	$40	
1999S, Same type, S mint, Proof	(187,595)		$35

(2000) Library of Congress Bicentennial

	Distribution	MS-67	PF-67
2000P, Library of Congress Bicentennial silver dollar	53,264	$37	
2000P, Same type, P mint, Proof	(198,503)		$37
2000W, Library of Congress Bicentennial bimetallic (gold/platinum) $10	7,261	4,000	
2000W, Same type, W mint, Proof	(27,445)		850

(2000) Leif Ericson Millennium

	Distribution	MS-67	PF-67
2000P, Leif Ericson Millennium silver dollar	28,150	$70	
2000P, Same type, P mint, Proof	(144,748)		$55
2001D, American Buffalo silver dollar	227,131	150	
2001P, Same type, P mint, Proof	(272,869)		150
2001P, Capitol Visitor Center clad half dollar	99,157	10	
2001P, Same type, P mint, Proof	(77,962)		12
2001P, Capitol Visitor Center silver dollar	35,380	24	
2001P, Same type, P mint, Proof	(143,793)		30
2001W, Capitol Visitor Center gold $5	6,761	1,100	
2001W, Same type, W mint, Proof	(27,652)		300
2002D, Salt Lake Olympic Games silver dollar	40,257	25	
2002P, Same type, P mint, Proof	(166,864)		30
2002W, Salt Lake Olympic Games gold $5	10,585	375	
2002W, Same type, W mint, Proof	(32,877)		300
2002W, West Point Bicentennial silver dollar	103,201	16	
2002W, Same type, W mint, Proof	(288,293)		16
2003P, First Flight Centennial clad half dollar	57,122	11	
2003P, Same type, P mint, Proof	(109,710)		12
2003P, First Flight Centennial silver dollar	53,533	26	
2003P, Same type, P mint, Proof	(190,240)		23
2003W, First Flight Centennial gold $10	10,009	575	
2003W, Same type, W mint, Proof	(21,676)		550
2004P, Thomas Alva Edison silver dollar	92,510	22	
2004P, Same type, P mint, Proof	(211,055)		25
2004P, Lewis and Clark Bicentennial silver dollar	142,015	20	
2004P, Same type, P mint, Proof	(351,989)		18
2005P, Chief Justice John Marshall silver dollar	67,096	23	
2005P, Same type, P mint, Proof	(196,753)		25
2005P, Marine Corps 230th Anniversary silver dollar	49,671	30	
2005P, Same type, P mint, Proof	(548,810)		32
2006P, Benjamin Franklin "Scientist" silver dollar	58,000	25	
2006P, Same type, P mint, Proof	(142,000)		35

	Distribution	MS-67	PF-67
2006P, Benjamin Franklin "Founding Father" silver dollar	58,000	$25	
2006P, Same type, P mint, Proof	(142,000)		$35
2006S, San Francisco Old Mint Centennial silver dollar	67,100	30	
2006S, Same type, S mint, Proof	(160,870)		30
2006S, San Francisco Old Mint Centennial gold $5	17,500	275	
2006S, Same type, S mint, Proof	(44,174)		275
2007P, Jamestown 400th Anniversary silver dollar		25	
2007P, Same type, P mint, Proof			28
2007W, Jamestown 400th Anniversary gold $5		275	
2007W, Same type, W mint, Proof			275
2007P, Little Rock Central High School Desegregation silver dollar		25	
2007S, Same type, S mint, Proof			28
2008S, Bald Eagle clad half dollar		7	
2008S, Same type, S mint, Proof			8
2008P, Bald Eagle silver dollar		28	
2008P, Same type, P mint, Proof			32
2008W, Bald Eagle gold $5		275	
2008W, Same type, W mint, Proof			275
2009P, Louis Braille Bicentennial silver dollar		24	
2009P, Same type, P mint, Proof			25
2009P, Abraham Lincoln Bicentennial silver dollar		30	
2009P, Same type, P mint, Proof			32
2010W, American Veterans Disabled for Life silver dollar		24	
2010W, Same type, W mint, Proof			25
2010P, Boy Scouts of America Centennial silver dollar		24	
2010W, Same type, S mint, Proof			25

GOVERNMENT COMMEMORATIVE SETS

Values are for commemorative coins and sets in all of their original packaging.

	Value
(1983–1984) Los Angeles Olympiad	
1983 and 1984 Proof dollars	$32
1983 and 1984 6-coin set. One each of 1983 and 1984 dollars, both Proof and Uncirculated gold $10 **(a)**	1,135
1983 3-piece collector set. 1983 P, D, and S Uncirculated dollars	50
1984 3-piece collector set. 1984 P, D, and S Uncirculated dollars	50
1983 and 1984 gold and silver Uncirculated set. One each of 1983 and 1984 Uncirculated dollar and one 1984 Uncirculated gold $10	570
1983 and 1984 gold and silver Proof set. One each of 1983 and 1984 Proof dollars and one 1984 Proof gold $10	570
(1986) Statue of Liberty	
2-coin set. Proof silver dollar and clad half dollar	21
3-coin set. Proof silver dollar, clad half dollar, and gold $5	290
2-coin set. Uncirculated silver dollar and clad half dollar	21
2-coin set. Uncirculated and Proof gold $5	530
3-coin set. Uncirculated silver dollar, clad half dollar, and gold $5	290
6-coin set. One each of Proof and Uncirculated half dollar, silver dollar, and gold $5 **(a)**	575

a. Packaged in cherrywood box.

	Value
(1987) Constitution	
2-coin set. Uncirculated silver dollar and gold $5	$280
2-coin set. Proof silver dollar and gold $5	280
4-coin set. One each of Proof and Uncirculated silver dollar and gold $5 **(a)**	560
(1988) Seoul Olympiad	
2-coin set. Uncirculated silver dollar and gold $5	280
2-coin set. Proof silver dollar and gold $5	280
4-coin set. One each of Proof and Uncirculated silver dollar and gold $5 **(a)**	560
(1989) Congress	
2-coin set. Proof clad half dollar and silver dollar	24
3-coin set. Proof clad half dollar, silver dollar, and gold $5	290
2-coin set. Uncirculated clad half dollar and silver dollar	23
3-coin set. Uncirculated clad half dollar, silver dollar, and gold $5	290
6-coin set. One each of Proof and Uncirculated clad half dollar, silver dollar, and gold $5 **(a)**	580
(1991) Mount Rushmore	
2-coin set. Uncirculated clad half dollar and silver dollar	34
2-coin set. Proof clad half dollar and silver dollar	31
3-coin set. Uncirculated clad half dollar, silver dollar, and gold $5	300
3-coin set. Proof half dollar, silver dollar, and gold $5	295
6-coin set. One each of Proof and Uncirculated clad half dollar, silver dollar, and gold $5 **(a)**	600
(1992) XXV Olympiad	
2-coin set. Uncirculated clad half dollar and silver dollar	25
2-coin set. Proof clad half dollar and silver dollar	26
3-coin set. Uncirculated clad half dollar, silver dollar, and gold $5	290
3-coin set. Proof half dollar, silver dollar, and gold $5	290
6-coin set. One each of Proof and Uncirculated clad half dollar, silver dollar, and gold $5 **(a)**	580
(1992) Christopher Columbus	
2-coin set. Uncirculated clad half dollar and silver dollar	30
2-coin set. Proof clad half dollar and silver dollar	32
3-coin set. Uncirculated clad half dollar, silver dollar, and gold $5	305
3-coin set. Proof half dollar, silver dollar, and gold $5	295
6-coin set. One each of Proof and Uncirculated clad half dollar, silver dollar, and gold $5 **(a)**	600
(1993) Bill of Rights	
2-coin set. Uncirculated silver half dollar and silver dollar	30
2-coin set. Proof silver half dollar and silver dollar	30
3-coin set. Uncirculated silver half dollar, silver dollar, and gold $5	315
3-coin set. Proof half dollar, silver dollar, and gold $5	295
6-coin set. One each of Proof and Uncirculated silver half dollar, silver dollar, and gold $5 **(a)**	610
"Young Collector" set. Silver half dollar	15
Educational set. Silver half dollar and James Madison medal	16
Proof silver half dollar and 25-cent stamp	15
(1993) World War II	
2-coin set. Uncirculated clad half dollar and silver dollar	45
2-coin set. Proof clad half dollar and silver dollar	50
3-coin set. Uncirculated clad half dollar, silver dollar, and gold $5	345
3-coin set. Proof clad half dollar, silver dollar, and gold $5	325
6-coin set. One each of Proof and Uncirculated clad half dollar, silver dollar, and gold $5 **(a)**	670
"Young Collector" set. Clad half dollar	23
"Victory" set. Silver dollar and French franc	24
Victory Medal set. Uncirculated clad half dollar and reproduction medal	25

a. Packaged in cherrywood box.

	Value
(1993) Thomas Jefferson	
3-piece set (issued in 1994). Silver dollar, Jefferson nickel, and $2 note	$65
(1994) World Cup Soccer	
2-coin set. Uncirculated clad half dollar and silver dollar	23
2-coin set. Proof clad half dollar and silver dollar	24
3-coin set. Uncirculated clad half dollar, silver dollar, and gold $5	290
3-coin set. Proof clad half dollar, silver dollar, and gold $5	290
6-coin set. One each of Proof and Uncirculated clad half dollar, silver dollar, and gold $5 **(a)**	580
"Young Collector" set. Uncirculated clad half dollar	9
"Special Edition" set. Proof clad half dollar and silver dollar	26
(1993) U.S. Veterans	
3-coin set. Uncirculated POW, Vietnam, and Women in Military Service silver dollars	165
3-coin set. Proof POW, Vietnam, and Women in Military Service silver dollars	115
(1995) Special Olympics	
2-coin set. Proof Special Olympics silver dollar, 1995S Kennedy half dollar	70
(1995) Civil War Battlefield Preservation	
2-coin set. Uncirculated clad half dollar and silver dollar	85
2-coin set. Proof clad half dollar and silver dollar	85
3-coin set. Uncirculated clad half dollar, silver dollar, and gold $5	785
3-coin set. Proof clad half dollar, silver dollar, and gold $5	385
6-coin set. One each of Proof and Uncirculated clad half dollar, silver dollar, and gold $5 **(a)**	1,200
"Young Collector" set. Uncirculated clad half dollar	35
2-coin "Union" set. Clad half dollar and silver dollar	85
3-coin "Union" set. Clad half dollar, silver dollar, and gold $5	525
(1995–1996) Centennial Olympic Games	
4-coin set #1. Uncirculated half dollar (Basketball), dollars (Gymnastics, Paralympics),	
gold $5 (Torch Bearer)	800
4-coin set #2. Proof half dollar (Basketball), dollars (Gymnastics, Paralympics), gold $5 (Torch Bearer) . .	365
2-coin set #1: Proof silver dollars (Gymnastics, Paralympics)	70
"Young Collector" set. Uncirculated Basketball, Baseball, Swimming, or Soccer half dollar	—
1995–1996 16-coin Uncirculated set. One each of all Uncirculated coins **(a)**	6,750
1995–1996 16-coin Proof set. One each of all Proof coins **(a)**	2,180
1995–1996 8-coin Proof silver dollars set **(a)**	375
1995–1996 32-coin set. One each of all Uncirculated and Proof coins **(a)**	8,930
(1996) National Community Service	
Proof silver dollar and Saint-Gaudens stamp	70
(1996) Smithsonian Institution 150th Anniversary	
2-coin set. Proof silver dollar and gold $5	425
4-coin set. One each of Proof and Uncirculated silver dollar and gold $5 **(a)**	1,325
"Young Collector" set. Proof silver dollar	55
(1997) U.S. Botanic Garden	
"Coinage and Currency" set. Uncirculated silver dollar, Jefferson nickel, and $1 note	150
(1997) Jackie Robinson	
2-coin set. Proof silver dollar and gold $5	575
4-coin set. One each of Proof and Uncirculated silver dollar and gold $5 **(a)**	4,150
3-piece "Legacy" set. Baseball card, pin, and gold $5	700
(1997) National Law Enforcement Officers Memorial	
Insignia set. Silver dollar, lapel pin, and patch	150

a. Packaged in cherrywood box.

	Value
(1998) Robert F. Kennedy	
2-coin set. RFK silver dollar and JFK silver half dollar	$225
2-coin set. Proof and Uncirculated RFK silver dollars	60
(1998) Black Revolutionary War Patriots	
2-coin set. Uncirculated and Proof silver dollars	210
"Young Collector" set. Uncirculated silver dollar	130
Black Revolutionary War Patriots set. Silver dollar and four stamps	100
(1999) Dolley Madison Commemorative	
2-coin set. Proof and Uncirculated silver dollars	50
(1999) George Washington Death	
2-coin set. One each of Proof and Uncirculated gold $5	600
(1999) Yellowstone National Park	
2-coin set. One each of Proof and Uncirculated silver dollars	80
(2000) Leif Ericson Millennium	
2-coin set. Proof silver dollar and Icelandic 1,000 kronur	90
(2000) Millennium Coin and Currency Set	
3-piece set. Uncirculated 2000 Sacagawea dollar; Uncirculated 2000 Silver Eagle; George	
Washington $1 note, series 1999	65
(2001) American Buffalo	
2-coin set. One each of Proof and Uncirculated silver dollar	300
"Coinage and Currency" set. Uncirculated American Buffalo silver dollar, face reprint of 1899 $5 Indian	
Chief Silver Certificate, 1987 Chief Red Cloud 10¢ stamp, 2001 Bison 21¢ stamp	190
(2001) Capitol Visitor Center	
3-coin set. Proof clad half dollar, silver dollar, and gold $5	345
(2002) Salt Lake Olympic Games	
2-coin set. Proof silver dollar and gold $5	335
4-coin set. One each of Proof and Uncirculated silver dollar and gold $5	730
(2004) Thomas A. Edison	
Edison set. Uncirculated silver dollar and light bulb	38
(2004) Lewis and Clark	
Coin and Pouch set. Proof silver dollar and beaded pouch	125
"Coinage and Currency" set. Uncirculated silver dollar, Sacagawea golden dollar, two 2005 nickels,	
replica 1901 $10 Bison note, silver-plated Peace Medal replica, three stamps, two booklets	60
(2004) Westward Journey Nickel Series™	
Westward Journey Nickel Series™ Coin and Medal set. Proof Sacagawea golden dollar, two 2004 Proof	
nickels, silver-plated Peace Medal replica	35
(2005) Westward Journey Nickel Series™	
Westward Journey Nickel Series™ Coin and Medal set. Proof Sacagawea golden dollar, two 2005 Proof	
nickels, silver-plated Peace Medal replica	32
(2005) Chief Justice John Marshall	
"Coin and Chronicles" set. Uncirculated silver dollar, booklet, BEP intaglio portrait	35
(2005) American Legacy	
American Legacy Collection. Proof Marine Corps dollar, Proof John Marshall dollar, 11-piece Proof set ..	110

a. Packaged in cherrywood box.

COMMEMORATIVES

	Value

(2005) Marine Corps 230th Anniversary
Marine Corps Uncirculated silver dollar and stamp set $42

(2006) Benjamin Franklin
"Coin and Chronicles" set. Uncirculated "Scientist" silver dollar, four stamps, *Poor Richard's Almanack*
replica, intaglio print 40

(2006) American Legacy
American Legacy Collection. Proof 2006P Benjamin Franklin, Founding Father silver dollar; Proof 2006S
San Francisco Old Mint silver dollar; Proof cent, nickel, dime, quarter, half dollar, and dollar 85

(2007) American Legacy
American Legacy Collection. 17 Proof coins for 2007: five state quarters; four Presidential dollars;
Jamestown and Little Rock Central High School Desegregation silver dollars; Proof cent, nickel, dime,
half dollar, and dollar 95

(2007) Little Rock Central High School Desegregation
Little Rock Coin and Medal set. Proof 2007P silver dollar, bronze medal 120

(2008) Bald Eagle
3-piece set. Proof clad half dollar, silver dollar, and gold $5 325
Bald Eagle Coin and Medal Set. Uncirculated silver dollar, bronze medal 32
"Young Collector" set. Uncirculated clad half dollar 10

(2008) American Legacy
American Legacy Collection. 15 Proof coins for 2008: cent, nickel, dime, half dollar, and dollar;
five state quarters; four Presidential dollars; Bald Eagle dollar 100

(2009) Louis Braille
Uncirculated silver dollar in tri-folded package 30

(2009) Abraham Lincoln Coin and Chronicles
Four Proof 2009S cents and Abraham Lincoln Proof silver dollar 110

PROOF COINS AND SETS

Proof coins can usually be distinguished by their sharpness of detail, high wire edge, and extremely brilliant, mirrorlike surface. Proofs are sold by the Mint at a premium.

Proof coins were not struck during 1943–1949 or 1965–1967. Sets from 1936 through 1972 include the cent, nickel, dime, quarter, and half dollar; from 1973 through 1981 the dollar was also included. *Values shown are for original unblemished sets.*

Figures in parentheses represent the total number of full sets minted.

Year	Mintage	Issue Price	Current Value	Year	Mintage	Issue Price	Current Value
1936	(3,837)	$1.89	$5,000.00	1978S	(3,127,781)	$9.00	$5.00
1937	(5,542)	1.89	2,500.00	1979S, Filled S	(3,677,175)	9.00	5.00
1938	(8,045)	1.89	1,200.00	1979S, Clear S	*	9.00	50.00
1939	(8,795)	1.89	1,000.00	1980S	(3,554,806)	10.00	4.00
1940	(11,246)	1.89	900.00	1981S	(4,063,083)	11.00	4.00
1941	(15,287)	1.89	900.00	1982S	(3,857,479)	11.00	2.00
1942, Both nickels	(21,120)	1.89	825.00	1983S	(3,138,765)	11.00	3.00
1942, One nickel	*	1.89	800.00	1983S, Prestige set			
1950	(51,386)	2.10	500.00	(Olympic dollar)	(140,361)	59.00	43.00
1951	(57,500)	2.10	400.00	1984S	(2,748,430)	11.00	4.00
1952	(81,980)	2.10	165.00	1984S, Prestige set			
1953	(128,800)	2.10	140.00	(Olympic dollar)	(316,680)	59.00	15.00
1954	(233,300)	2.10	70.00	1985S	(3,362,821)	11.00	2.90
1955, Box pack	(378,200)	2.10	75.00	1986S	(2,411,180)	11.00	3.00
1955, Flat pack	*	2.10	90.00	1986S, Prestige set (Statue			
1956	(669,384)	2.10	35.00	of Liberty half, dollar)	(599,317)	48.50	15.00
1957	(1,247,952)	2.10	16.00	1987S	(3,792,233)	11.00	3.00
1958	(875,652)	2.10	32.00	1987S, Prestige set			
1959	(1,149,291)	2.10	15.00	(Constitution dollar)	(435,495)	45.00	14.00
1960, With Lg Date cent	(1,691,602)	2.10	13.00	1988S	(3,031,287)	11.00	3.00
1960, With Sm Date cent	*	2.10	20.00	1988S, Prestige set			
1961	(3,028,244)	2.10	10.00	(Olympic dollar)	(231,661)	45.00	16.00
1962	(3,218,019)	2.10	10.00	1989S	(3,009,107)	11.00	4.00
1963	(3,075,645)	2.10	11.00	1989S, Prestige set			
1964	(3,950,762)	2.10	10.00	(Congressional half,			
1968S	(3,041,506)	5.00	3.50	dollar)	(211,807)	45.00	22.00
1969S	(2,934,631)	5.00	4.50	1990S	(2,793,433)	11.00	3.00
1970S	(2,632,810)	5.00	5.00	1990S, With No S cent	(3,555)	11.00	4,200.00
1970S, With Sm Date cent	*	5.00	60.00	1990S, With No S cent			
1971S	(3,220,733)	5.00	2.25	(Prestige set)	*	45.00	4,200.00
1972S	(3,260,996)	5.00	3.00	1990S, Prestige set			
1973S	(2,760,339)	7.00	4.00	(Eisenhower dollar)	(506,126)	45.00	15.00
1974S	(2,612,568)	7.00	5.00	1991S	(2,610,833)	11.00	7.00
1975S, With 1976 quarter,				1991S, Prestige set (Mt.			
half, and dollar	(2,845,450)	7.00	5.00	Rushmore half, dollar)	(256,954)	59.00	35.00
1976S	(4,149,730)	7.00	5.00	1992S	(2,675,618)	11.00	3.00
1976S, 3-piece set	(3,998,621)	15.00	10.00	1992S, Prestige set			
1977S	(3,251,152)	9.00	4.00	(Olympic half, dollar)	(183,293)	56.00	38.00

* Included in number above.

Year	Mintage	Issue Price	Current Value
1992S, Silver . . . .(1,009,586)		$21.00	$10.00
1992S, Silver Premier set . . .(308,055)		37.00	11.00
1993S . . . .(2,409,394)		12.50	6.00
1993S, Prestige set (Bill of Rights half, dollar) . . . .(224,045)		57.00	18.00
1993S, Silver . . . .(570,213)		21.00	16.00
1993S, Silver Premier set . . .(191,140)		37.50	16.00
1994S . . . .(2,308,701)		12.50	6.00
1994S, Prestige set (World Cup half, dollar) . . . . .(175,893)		57.00	25.00
1994S, Silver . . . .(636,009)		21.00	18.00
1994S, Silver Premier set . . .(149,320)		37.50	18.00
1995S . . . .(2,010,384)		12.50	19.00
1995S, Prestige set (Civil War half, dollar) . . . . . .(107,112)		57.00	70.00
1995S, Silver . . . .(549,878)		21.00	48.00
1995S, Silver Premier set . . .(130,107)		37.50	48.00
1996S . . . .(1,695,244)		12.50	8.00
1996S, Prestige set (Olympic half, dollar) . . .(55,000)		57.00	225.00
1996S, Silver . . . .(623,655)		21.00	20.00
1996S, Silver Premier set . . .(151,366)		37.50	21.00
1997S . . . .(1,975,000)		12.50	14.00
1997S, Prestige set (Botanic dollar) . . . .(80,000)		48.00	68.00
1997S, Silver . . . .(605,473)		21.00	31.00
1997S, Silver Premier set . . .(136,205)		37.50	32.00
1998S . . . .(2,086,507)		12.50	7.00
1998S, Silver . . . .(638,134)		21.00	14.00
1998S, Silver Premier set . . .(240,658)		37.50	15.00
1999S, 9-piece set . . . . .(2,543,401)		19.95	24.00
1999S, 5-piece quarter set (1,169,958)		13.95	22.00
1999S, Silver 9-piece set . . .(804,565)		31.95	175.00
2000S, 10-piece set . . . . .(3,082,572)		19.95	7.00
2000S, 5-piece quarter set . .(937,600)		13.95	4.00
2000S, Silver 10-piece set . .(965,421)		31.95	20.00
2001S, 10-piece set . . . . .(2,294,909)		19.95	50.00
2001S, 5-piece quarter set . .(799,231)		13.95	28.00
2001S, Silver 10-piece set . .(889,697)		31.95	70.00
2002S, 10-piece set . . . . .(2,319,766)		19.95	18.00
2002S, 5-piece quarter set . .(764,479)		13.95	10.00
2002S, Silver 10-piece set . .(892,229)		31.95	45.00
2003S, 10-piece set . . . .(2,172,684)		$19.95	$12.00
2003S, 5-piece quarter set (1,235,832)		13.95	7.00
2003S, Silver 10-piece set (1,125,755)		31.95	20.00
2004S, 11-piece set . . . .(1,789,488)		22.95	22.00
2004S, 5-piece quarter set . .(951,196)		15.95	8.00
2004S, Silver 11-piece set (1,175,934)		37.95	23.00
2004S, Silver 5-piece quarter set . . . .(593,852)		23.95	15.00
2005S, 11-piece set . . . .(2,275,000)		22.95	10.00
2005S, 5-piece quarter set . .(987,960)		15.95	7.00
2005S, Silver 11-piece set (1,069,679)		37.95	22.00
2005S, Silver 5-piece quarter set . . . .(608,970)		23.95	17.00
2006S, 10-piece set . . . .(2,000,428)		22.95	20.00
2006S, 5-piece quarter set . .(882,000)		15.95	11.00
2006S, Silver 10-piece set (1,054,008)		37.95	16.00
2006S, Silver 5-piece quarter set . . . .(531,000)		23.95	15.00
2007S, 14-piece set . . . .(1,702,116)		26.95	19.00
2007S, 5-piece quarter set . .(672,662)		13.95	10.00
2007S, 4-piece Presidential set . . . . .(1,285,972)		14.95	11.00
2007S, Silver 14-piece set . .(875,050)		44.95	30.00
2007S, Silver 5-piece quarter set . . . .(672,662)		25.95	15.00
2008S, 14-piece set . . . .(1,405,674)		26.95	65.00
2008S, 5-piece quarter set . .(672,438)		13.95	28.00
2008S, 4-piece Presidential set . . . . . .(869,202)		14.95	15.00
2008S, Silver 14-piece set . .(774,874)		44.95	48.00
2008S, Silver 5-piece quarter set . . . .(429,021)		25.95	20.00
2009S, 18-piece set . . . . .(1,296,853)		29.95	40.00
2009S, 6-piece quarter set . .(574,570)		14.95	20.00
2009S, 4-piece Presidential set . . . . . .(594,864)		14.95	16.00
2009S, Silver 18-piece set . .(581,677)		52.95	55.00
2009S, Silver 6-piece quarter set . . . .(255,532)		29.95	24.00
2009S, 4-piece Lincoln Bicentennial set		7.95	10.00

* Included in number above.

UNCIRCULATED MINT SETS

Official Mint Sets are specially packaged by the government for sale to collectors. They contain uncirculated specimens of each year's coins for every denomination issued from each mint. Sets from 1947 through 1958 contain two examples of each regular-issue coin. No official sets were produced in 1950, 1982, or 1983. Privately assembled sets are valued according to individual coin prices. Only official sets are included in the following list. Unlike the Proof sets, these are normal coins intended for circulation and are not minted with any special consideration for quality.

Year	Mintage	Issue Price	Current Value	Year	Mintage	Issue Price	Current Value
1947 P-D-S	5,000	$4.87	$850.00	1978 P-D	2,162,609	$7.00	$4.00
1948 P-D-S	6,000	4.92	425.00	1979 P-D	2,526,000	8.00	3.75
1949 P-D-S	5,000	5.45	575.00	1980 P-D-S	2,815,066	9.00	4.85
1951 P-D-S	8,654	6.75	550.00	1981 P-D-S	2,908,145	11.00	8.50
1952 P-D-S	11,499	6.14	490.00	1984 P-D	1,832,857	7.00	4.00
1953 P-D-S	15,538	6.14	325.00	1985 P-D	1,710,571	7.00	3.00
1954 P-D-S	25,599	6.19	140.00	1986 P-D	1,153,536	7.00	7.00
1955 P-D-S	49,656	3.57	95.00	1987 P-D	2,890,758	7.00	4.00
1956 P-D	45,475	3.34	90.00	1988 P-D	1,646,204	7.00	3.00
1957 P-D	34,324	4.40	155.00	1989 P-D	1,987,915	7.00	2.50
1958 P-D	50,314	4.43	85.00	1990 P-D	1,809,184	7.00	3.00
1959 P-D	187,000	2.40	31.00	1991 P-D	1,352,101	7.00	5.00
1960 P-D	260,485	2.40	18.00	1992 P-D	1,500,143	7.00	3.50
1961 P-D	223,704	2.40	27.00	1993 P-D	1,297,431	8.00	4.25
1962 P-D	385,285	2.40	15.00	1994 P-D	1,234,813	8.00	3.00
1963 P-D	606,612	2.40	15.00	1995 P-D	1,038,787	8.00	6.00
1964 P-D	1,008,108	2.40	15.00	1996 P-D, Plus			
1965*	2,360,000	4.00	2.50	1996W dime	1,457,949	8.00	12.00
1966*	2,261,583	4.00	3.00	1997 P-D	950,473	8.00	9.00
1967*	1,863,344	4.00	6.00	1998 P-D	1,187,325	8.00	4.00
1968 P-D-S	2,105,128	2.50	3.00	1999 P-D (18 pieces)	1,243,867	14.95	8.00
1969 P-D-S	1,817,392	2.50	3.00	2000 P-D (20 pieces)	1,490,160	14.95	7.00
1970 P-D-S	2,038,134	2.50	9.00	2001 P-D (20 pieces)	1,116,915	14.95	11.00
1971 P-D-S	2,193,396	3.50	2.00	2002 P-D (20 pieces)	1,139,388	14.95	13.00
1972 P-D-S	2,750,000	3.50	2.00	2003 P-D (20 pieces)	1,001,532	14.95	11.00
1973 P-D-S	1,767,691	6.00	9.00	2004 P-D (22 pieces)	842,507	16.95	22.00
1974 P-D-S	1,975,981	6.00	4.00	2005 P-D (22 pieces)	1,160,000	16.95	7.00
1975 P-D	1,921,488	6.00	5.00	2006 P-D (20 pieces)	847,361	16.95	8.00
1776–1976, 3-piece set	4,908,319	9.00	9.00	2007 P-D (28 pieces)	895,628	22.95	17.00
1976 P-D	1,892,513	6.00	4.00	2008 P-D (28 pieces)	745,464	22.95	37.00
1977 P-D	2,006,869	7.00	5.00	2009 P-D (36 pieces)	643,897	27.95	20.00

*Note: Sets issued from 2005 onward have a special Satin Finish that is somewhat different from the finish on Uncirculated coins made for general circulation. * Special Mint Set.*

$1 SILVER EAGLES

Values below are based on spot silver value of $18 per ounce.

	Mintage	Unc.	PF		Mintage	Unc.	PF
$1 1986	5,393,005	$20		$1 1998P	(450,000)		$36
$1 1986S	(1,446,778)		$35	$1 1999	7,408,640	$18	
$1 1987	11,442,335	18		$1 1999P	(549,769)		36
$1 1987S	(904,732)		35	$1 2000(W)	9,239,132	18	
$1 1988	5,004,646	18		$1 2000P	(600,000)		35
$1 1988S	(557,370)		39	$1 2001(W)	9,001,711	18	
$1 1989	5,203,327	18		$1 2001W	(746,398)		36
$1 1989S	(617,694)		35	$1 2002(W)	10,539,026	18	
$1 1990	5,840,210	18		$1 2002W	(647,342)		35
$1 1990S	(695,510)		35	$1 2003(W)	8,495,008	18	
$1 1991	7,191,066	18		$1 2003W	(747,831)		35
$1 1991S	(511,925)		38	$1 2004(W)	8,882,754	18	
$1 1992	5,540,068	18		$1 2004W	(801,602)		35
$1 1992S	(498,654)		35	$1 2005(W)	8,891,025	18	
$1 1993	6,763,762	18		$1 2005W	(701,606)		35
$1 1993P	(405,913)		50	$1 2006(W)	10,021,000	18	
$1 1994	4,227,319	20		$1 2006W, Burnished	198,553	40	
$1 1994P	(372,168)		75	$1 2006W	(843,602)		35
$1 1995	4,672,051	21		$1 2006P, Reverse Proof	(250,000)		125
$1 1995P	(438,511)		65	$1 2007(W)	9,028,036	18	
$1 1995W	(30,125)		2,000	$1 2007 W, Burnished	621,333	19	
$1 1996	3,603,386	30		$1 2007W	(821,759)		35
$1 1996P	(500,000)		45	$1 2008(W)	20,583,000	18	
$1 1997	4,295,004	22		$1 2008W, Burnished	444,558	19	
$1 1997P	(435,368)		50	$1 2008W	(713,353)		35
$1 1998	4,847,549	19		$1 2009(W)	28,766,500	18	

From 2006 to 2008, special American Eagle Uncirculated coins in silver, gold, and platinum have been sold directly from the United States Mint. The term "Uncirculated-burnished" refers to the specialized minting process used to create these coins. Although they are similar in appearance to the ordinary Uncirculated American Eagle bullion coins, the Uncirculated-burnished coins can be distinguished by the addition of a mintmark and by the use of burnished coin blanks. Proof coins, which also have a mintmark, have a highly reflective, mirrorlike surface.

AMERICAN EAGLE GOLD COINS

Bullion values are based on spot gold at $1,100 per ounce.

$5 Tenth-Ounce Gold

	Mintage	Unc.	PF		Mintage	Unc.	PF
$5 MCMLXXXVI (1986)	912,609	$110		$5 1999	2,750,338	$110	
$5 MCMLXXXVII (1987)	580,266	110		$5 1999W	(48,426)		$150
$5 MCMLXXXVIII (1988)	159,500	135		$5 2000	569,153	110	
$5 MCMLXXXVIII (1988)P	(143,881)		$150	$5 2000W	(49,970)		150
$5 MCMLXXXIX (1989)	264,790	110		$5 2001	269,147	110	
$5 MCMLXXXIX (1989)P	(84,647)		150	$5 2001W	(37,547)		150
$5 MCMXC (1990)	210,210	110		$5 2002	230,027	110	
$5 MCMXC (1990)P	(99,349)		150	$5 2002W	(40,864)		150
$5 MCMXCI (1991)	165,200	110		$5 2003	245,029	110	
$5 MCMXCI (1991)P	(70,334)		150	$5 2003W	(46,000)		150
$5 1992	209,300	110		$5 2004	250,016	110	
$5 1992P	(64,874)		150	$5 2004W	(15,636)		150
$5 1993	210,709	110		$5 2005	300,043	110	
$5 1993P	(58,649)		150	$5 2005W	(17,546)		150
$5 1994	206,380	110		$5 2006	270,000	110	
$5 1994W	(62,849)		150	$5 2006W, Burnished	10,439	120	
$5 1995	223,025	110		$5 2006W	(21,946)		150
$5 1995W	(62,673)		150	$5 2007	190,010	110	
$5 1996	401,964	110		$5 2007W, Burnished	15,497	120	
$5 1996W	(56,700)		150	$5 2007W	(24,317)		150
$5 1997	528,266	110		$5 2008	305,000	110	
$5 1997W	(34,984)		150	$5 2008W, Burnished	10,379	120	
$5 1998	1,344,520	110		$5 2008W	(16,083)		150
$5 1998W	(20,000)		150	$5 2009	*270,000*	110	

$10 Quarter-Ounce Gold

	Mintage	Unc.	PF		Mintage	Unc.	PF
$10 MCMLXXXVI (1986)	726,031	$275		$10 1992	59,546	$275	
$10 MCMLXXXVII (1987)	269,255	275		$10 1992P	(46,269)		$300
$10 MCMLXXXVIII (1988)	49,000	275		$10 1993	71,864	275	
$10 MCMLXXXVIII (1988)P	(98,028)		$300	$10 1993P	(46,464)		300
$10 MCMLXXXIX (1989)	81,789	275		$10 1994	72,650	275	
$10 MCMLXXXIX (1989)P	(54,170)		300	$10 1994W	(48,172)		300
$10 MCMXC (1990)	41,000	275		$10 1995	83,752	275	
$10 MCMXC (1990)P	(62,674)		300	$10 1995W	(47,484)		300
$10 MCMXCI (1991)	36,100	290		$10 1996	60,318	275	
$10 MCMXCI (1991)P	(50,839)		300	$10 1996W	(37,900)		300

	Mintage	Unc.	PF
$10 1997 108,805		$275	
$10 1997W . . . .(29,808)			$300
$10 1998 309,829		275	
$10 1998W . . . .(29,733)			300
$10 1999 564,232		275	
$10 1999W . . . .(34,416)			300
$10 2000 128,964		275	
$10 2000W . . . .(36,033)			300
$10 2001 71,280		275	
$10 2001W . . . .(25,630)			310
$10 2002 62,027		275	
$10 2002W . . . .(29,242)			300
$10 2003 74,029		275	
$10 2003W . . . .(31,000)			300

	Mintage	Unc.	PF
$10 2004 72,014		$275	
$10 2004W . . . .(9,344)			$300
$10 2005 72,015		275	
$10 2005W . . . .(7,992)			300
$10 2006 46,000		275	
$10 2006W, Burnished 4,984		350	
$10 2006W . . . .(10,796)			310
$10 2007 34,004		275	
$10 2007W, Burnished 5,762		350	
$10 2007W . . . .(11,953)			300
$10 2008 70,000		275	
$10 2008W, Burnished 6,203		400	
$10 2008W . . . .(15,229)			300
$10 2009 . . . .*110,000*		275	

$25 Half-Ounce Gold

	Mintage	Unc.	PF
$25 MCMLXXXVI (1986) 599,566		$550	
$25 MCMLXXXVII (1987) . . .131,255		550	
$25 MCMLXXXVII (1987)P (143,398)			$700
$25 MCMLXXXVIII (1988) 45,000		575	
$25 MCMLXXXVIII (1988)P . .(76,528)			700
$25 MCMLXXXIX (1989) 44,829		575	
$25 MCMLXXXIX (1989)P . . .(44,798)			700
$25 MCMXC (1990) 31,000		575	
$25 MCMXC (1990)P . . . . . .(51,636)			700
$25 MCMXCI (1991) 24,100		900	
$25 MCMXCI (1991)P . . . . .(53,125)			700
$25 1992 54,404		550	
$25 1992P . . . .(40,976)			700
$25 1993 73,324		550	
$25 1993P . . . .(43,319)			700
$25 1994 62,400		550	
$25 1994W . . . .(44,584)			700
$25 1995 53,474		550	
$25 1995W . . . .(45,442)			700
$25 1996 39,287		550	
$25 1996W . . . .(34,700)			700
$25 1997 79,605		550	
$25 1997W . . . .(26,801)			700
$25 1998 169,029		550	
$25 1998W . . . .(25,549)			700

	Mintage	Unc.	PF
$25 1999 263,013		$550	
$25 1999W . . . .(30,452)			$700
$25 2000 79,287		550	
$25 2000W . . . .(32,027)			700
$25 2001 48,047		550	
$25 2001W . . . .(23,261)			700
$25 2002 70,027		550	
$25 2002W . . . .(26,646)			700
$25 2003 79,029		550	
$25 2003W . . . .(33,000)			700
$25 2004 98,040		550	
$25 2004W . . . .(7,835)			700
$25 2005 80,023		550	
$25 2005W . . . .(7,054)			700
$25 2006 42,000		550	
$25 2006W, Burnished 4,960		650	
$25 2006W . . . .(8,991)			700
$25 2007 47,002		550	
$25 2007W, Burnished 4,451		650	
$25 2007W . . . .(9,789)			700
$25 2008 61,000		550	
$25 2008W, Burnished 5,378		800	
$25 2008W . . . .(14,792)			700
$25 2009 . . . .*110,000*		550	

$50 One-Ounce Gold

	Mintage	Unc.	PF
$50 MCMLXXXVI (1986) . .1,362,650		$1,100	
$50 MCMLXXXVI (1986)W (446,290)			$1,400
$50 MCMLXXXVII (1987) . .1,045,500		1,100	
$50 MCMLXXXVII (1987)W (147,498)			1,400
$50 MCMLXXXVIII (1988) . . .465,000		1,100	
$50 MCMLXXXVIII (1988)W .(87,133)			1,400

	Mintage	Unc.	PF
$50 MCMLXXXIX (1989) 415,790		$1,100	
$50 MCMLXXXIX (1989)W . .(54,570)			$1,400
$50 MCMXC (1990) 373,210		1,100	
$50 MCMXC (1990)W . . . . .(62,401)			1,400
$50 MCMXCI (1991) 243,100		1,100	
$50 MCMXCI (1991)W . . . . .(50,411)			1,400

Chart continued on next page.

	Mintage	Unc.	PF
$50 1992	275,000	$1,100	
$50 1992W	(44,826)		$1,400
$50 1993	480,192	1,100	
$50 1993W	(34,389)		1,400
$50 1994	221,633	1,100	
$50 1994W	(46,674)		1,400
$50 1995	200,636	1,100	
$50 1995W	(46,484)		1,400
$50 1996	189,148	1,100	
$50 1996W	(36,000)		1,400
$50 1997	664,508	1,100	
$50 1997W	(27,554)		1,400
$50 1998	1,468,530	1,100	
$50 1998W	(26,060)		1,400
$50 1999	1,505,026	1,100	
$50 1999W	(31,446)		1,400
$50 2000	433,319	1,100	
$50 2000W	(33,006)		1,400
$50 2001	143,605	1,100	
$50 2001W	(24,580)		1,400

	Mintage	Unc.	PF
$50 2002	222,029	$1,100	
$50 2002W	(27,499)		$1,400
$50 2003	416,032	1,100	
$50 2003W	(33,000)		1,400
$50 2004	417,019	1,100	
$50 2004W	(8,720)		1,400
$50 2005	356,555	1,100	
$50 2005W	(9,784)		1,400
$50 2006	201,500	1,100	
$50 2006W, Burnished	5,708	1,125	
$50 2006W	(11,765)		1,400
$50 2006W, Reverse Proof	(10,000)		1,800
$50 2007	140,016	1,100	
$50 2007W, Burnished	11,602	1,125	
$50 2007W	(17,574)		1,400
$50 2008	710,000	1,100	
$50 2008W, Burnished	9,390	1,125	
$50 2008W	(16,327)		1,400
$50 2009	1,315,500	1,100	

Gold Bullion Sets

	PF
1987 Gold Set. $50, $25	$2,100
1988 Gold Set. $50, $25, $10, $5	2,550
1989 Gold Set. $50, $25, $10, $5	2,550
1990 Gold Set. $50, $25, $10, $5	2,550
1991 Gold Set. $50, $25, $10, $5	2,550
1992 Gold Set. $50, $25, $10, $5	2,550
1993 Gold Set. $50, $25, $10, $5	2,550
1993 Bicentennial Gold Set. $25, $10, $5, $1 silver eagle, and medal	1,225
1994 Gold Set. $50, $25, $10, $5	2,550
1995 Gold Set. $50, $25, $10, $5	2,550
1995 Anniversary Gold Set. $50, $25, $10, $5, and $1 silver eagle	4,600
1996 Gold Set. $50, $25, $10, $5	2,550

	PF
1997 Gold Set. $50, $25, $10, $5	$2,550
1997 Impressions of Liberty Set. $100 platinum, $50 gold, $1 silver	2,850
1998 Gold Set. $50, $25, $10, $5	2,550
1999 Gold Set. $50, $25, $10, $5	2,550
2000 Gold Set. $50, $25, $10, $5	2,550
2001 Gold Set. $50, $25, $10, $5	2,550
2002 Gold Set. $50, $25, $10, $5	2,550
2003 Gold Set. $50, $25, $10, $5	2,550
2004 Gold Set. $50, $25, $10, $5	2,550
2005 Gold Set. $50, $25, $10, $5	2,550
2006 Gold Set. $50, $25, $10, $5	2,550
2007 Gold Set. $50, $25, $10, $5	2,550
2008 Gold Set. $50, $25, $10, $5	2,550

2006 20th Anniversary Sets

2006W $50 Gold Set. Uncirculated, Proof, Reverse Proof	$4,300
2006 Silver Dollars. Uncirculated, Proof, Reverse Proof	200

2006W 1-oz. Gold- and Silver-Dollar Set. Uncirculated	$1,120

AMERICAN BUFFALO .9999 FINE GOLD BULLION COINS

	Mintage	Unc.	PF
$5 2008W, Burnished 12,544		$350	
$5 2008W ....(11,363)			$400
$10 2008W, Burnished 4,117		700	
$10 2008W ....(5,972)			750
$25 2008W, Burnished 3,297		1,000	
$25 2008W ....(4,638)			1,100
$50 2006 337,012		1,100	
$50 2006W ....(246,267)			1,175
$50 2007 136,503		1,100	
$50 2007W ....(58,998)			1,175

	Mintage	Unc.	PF
$50 2008 189,500		$1,100	
$50 2008W ....(11,660)			$2,400
$50 2008W, Burnished 3,124		1,800	
$50 2009 116,500		1,100	
$50 2009W ....(19,468)			1,175
2008W Four-coin set		3,850	4,700
2008W Double Prosperity set. Uncirculated $25 Buffalo gold and $25 American Eagle coins		1,550	

FIRST SPOUSE $10 GOLD BULLION COINS
Half-Ounce 24-Karat Gold

Martha Washington   Abigail Adams   Jefferson's Liberty   Dolley Madison

	Mintage	Unc.	PF
$10 2007W, Martha Washington ....(19,169) 17,661		$550	$560
$10 2007W, Abigail Adams ....(17,149) 17,142		550	560
$10 2007W, Thomas Jefferson's Liberty ....(19,823) 19,823		550	560
$10 2007W, Dolley Madison ....(17,661) 11,813		550	560

Elizabeth Monroe **Louisa Adams** **Jackson's Liberty** **Van Buren's Liberty**

	Mintage	Unc.	PF
$10 2008W, Elizabeth Monroe	(7,933) 4,519	$550	$560
$10 2008W, Louisa Adams	(7,454) 4,223	550	560
$10 2008W, Andrew Jackson's Liberty	(7,454) 4,281	550	560
$10 2008W, Martin Van Buren's Liberty	(6,187) 3,443	550	560

Anna Harrison

Letitia Tyler

Julia Tyler

Sarah Polk

Margaret Taylor

	Mintage	Unc.	PF
$10 2009W, Anna Harrison	(5,801) 2,993	$550	$560
$10 2009W, Letitia Tyler	(4,341) 2,381	550	560
$10 2009W, Julia Tyler	(3,878) 2,188	550	560
$10 2009W, Sarah Polk	(3,512) 1,893	550	560
$10 2009W, Margaret Taylor		550	560

| Abigail Fillmore | Jane Pierce | Buchanan's Liberty | Mary Lincoln |

U.S. Mint artist renderings.

	Unc.	PF		Unc.	PF
$10 2010W, Abigail Fillmore	$550	$560	$10 2010W, James Buchanan's Liberty	$550	$560
$10 2010W, Jane Pierce	550	560	$10 2010W, Mary Lincoln	550	560

MMIX ULTRA HIGH RELIEF GOLD COIN

A modern version of the famous United States 1907 Ultra High Relief double eagle gold pattern was produced in 2009 at the Philadelphia Mint. It was made as a tour de force to demonstrate how technical advances in minting techniques can now accommodate manufacturing such a coin. The original design was never made for commercial use because it was at that time impossible to make it in sufficient quantities.

The design used on these coins was the artistry of Augustus Saint-Gaudens. A version of it in much lower relief was used on double eagle coins minted from 1907 to 1933. In recreating the artist's attempt to mint a stunning coin in ultra high relief, the 2009 version was made in a slightly smaller diameter, and composed of 24-karat gold, thus making it easier to strike and maintain the fidelity of the design. Through 21st-century technology the original Saint-Gaudens plasters were digitally mapped by the Mint and used in the die-making process. The date was changed to 2009, and four additional stars were added to represent the current 50 states. The inscription "In God We Trust" was not used on the 1907 version.

The MMIX Ultra High Relief gold coins are 4 mm thick and contain one ounce of .999 fine gold. All are Uncirculated (business strikes). All are made at the West Point Mint, and packaged by the Mint in a special mahogany box.

MMIX Ultra High Relief Gold Coin
Photographed at an angle to show the edge, lettered E PLURIBUS UNUM, and the depth of relief.

	Mintage	Unc.
MMIX Ultra High Relief $20 Gold Coin	*115,178*	$1,200

AMERICAN EAGLE PLATINUM COINS

The one-ounce American Eagle platinum coin is designated $100 and contains one ounce of pure platinum. Fractional denominations containing 1/2 ounce, 1/4 ounce, or 1/10 ounce are called $50, $25, and $10, respectively.

Bullion values are based on spot platinum at $1,500 per ounce.

Obverse for Bullion and Proof, All Years

Reverse for Bullion, All Years; for Proof in 1997

Vistas of Liberty Reverse Designs

1998, Eagle Over New England

1999, Eagle Above Southeastern Wetlands

2000, Eagle Above America's Heartland

2001, Eagle Above America's Southwest

2002, Eagle Fishing in America's Northwest

$10 Tenth-Ounce Platinum

	Mintage	Unc.	PF		Mintage	Unc.	PF
$10 1997	70,250	$150		$10 2001W	(25,000)		$170
$10 1997W	(37,025)		$170	$10 2002	23,005	$150	
$10 1998	39,525	150		$10 2002W	(12,365)		170
$10 1998W	(19,832)		170	$10 2003	22,007	150	
$10 1999	55,955	150		$10 2003W	(9,249)		170
$10 1999W	(19,123)		170	$10 2004	15,010	150	
$10 2000	34,027	150		$10 2004W	(3,171)		350
$10 2000W	(15,651)		170	$10 2005	14,013	150	
$10 2001	52,017	150		$10 2005W	(2,583)		170

PLATINUM BULLION

	Mintage	Unc.	PF
$10 2006 13,000	$150	
$10 2006W, Burnished 1,555	200	
$10 2006W . . . .(4,899)		$170
$10 2007 13,003	150	
$10 2007W, Burnished 3,080	170	

	Mintage	Unc.	PF
$10 2007W . . . .(3,581)		$170
$10 2008 17,000	$150	
$10 2008W, Burnished 2,465	170	
$10 2008W . . . .(3,052)		190

$25 Quarter-Ounce Platinum

	Mintage	Unc.	PF
$25 1997 27,100	$375	
$25 1997W . . . .(18,661)		$410
$25 1998 38,887	375	
$25 1998W . . . .(14,860)		410
$25 1999 39,734	375	
$25 1999W . . . .(13,514)		410
$25 2000 20,054	375	
$25 2000W . . . .(11,995)		410
$25 2001 21,815	375	
$25 2001W . . . .(8,858)		410
$25 2002 27,405	375	
$25 2002W . . . .(9,282)		410
$25 2003 25,207	375	
$25 2003W . . . .(6,829)		410

	Mintage	Unc.	PF
$25 2004 18,010	$375	
$25 2004W . . . .(2,583)		$825
$25 2005 12,013	375	
$25 2005W . . . .(932)		425
$25 2006 7,800	375	
$25 2006W, Burnished 687	450	
$25 2006W . . . .(2,507)		410
$25 2007 8,402	375	
$25 2007W, Burnished 1,204	375	
$25 2007W . . . .(1,422)		410
$25 2008 22,800	375	
$25 2008W, Burnished 1,736	395	
$25 2008W . . . .(1,293)		550

$50 Half-Ounce Platinum

	Mintage	Unc.	PF
$50 1997 20,500	$750	
$50 1997W . . . .(15,463)		$800
$50 1998 32,415	750	
$50 1998W . . . .(13,821)		800
$50 1999 32,309	750	
$50 1999W . . . .(11,098)		800
$50 2000 18,892	750	
$50 2000W . . . .(11,049)		800
$50 2001 12,815	750	
$50 2001W . . . .(8,268)		800
$50 2002 24,005	750	
$50 2002W . . . .(8,772)		800
$50 2003 17,409	750	
$50 2003W . . . .(6,963)		800

	Mintage	Unc.	PF
$50 2004 13,236	$750	
$50 2004W . . . .(1,073)		$1,400
$50 2005 9,013	750	
$50 2005W . . . .(846)		850
$50 2006 6,600	750	
$50 2006W, Burnished 588	750	
$50 2006W . . . .(2,343)		800
$50 2007 7,001	750	
$50 2007W, Burnished 1,149	750	
$50 2007W . . . .(1,341)		800
$50 2008 14,000	750	
$50 2008W, Burnished 1,257	770	
$50 2008W . . . .(1,056)		825

$100 One-Ounce Platinum

	Mintage	Unc.	PF		Mintage	Unc.	PF
$100 1997	56,000	$1,500		$100 2004	7,009	$1,500	
$100 1997W	(18,000)		$1,600	$100 2004W	(2,017)		$1,650
$100 1998	133,002	1,500		$100 2005	6,310	1,500	
$100 1998W	(14,203)		1,600	$100 2005W	(1,663)		1,650
$100 1999	56,707	1,500		$100 2006	7,000	1,500	
$100 1999W	(12,351)		1,600	$100 2006W, Burnished	1,079	1,500	
$100 2000	10,003	1,500		$100 2006W	(3,846)		1,650
$100 2000W	(12,453)		1,600	$100 2007	7,202	1,500	
$100 2001	14,070	1,500		$100 2007W, Burnished	1,691	1,500	
$100 2001W	(8,990)		1,600	$100 2007W	(3,768)		1,650
$100 2002	11,502	1,500		$100 2008	21,800	1,500	
$100 2002W	(9,834)		1,600	$100 2008W, Burnished	1,905	1,500	
$100 2003	8,007	1,500		$100 2008W	(2,432)		1,750
$100 2003W	(8,106)		1,600	$100 2009W			1,750

Platinum Bullion Sets

1997 Platinum Set. $100, $50, $25, $10	$3,000
1998 Platinum Set. $100, $50, $25, $10	3,000
1999 Platinum Set. $100, $50, $25, $10	3,000
2000 Platinum Set. $100, $50, $25, $10	3,000
2001 Platinum Set. $100, $50, $25, $10	3,000
2002 Platinum Set. $100, $50, $25, $10	3,000
2003 Platinum Set. $100, $50, $25, $10	3,000
2004W Platinum Set. $100, $50, $25, $10	4,250
2005W Platinum Set. $100, $50, $25, $10	3,000
2006W Platinum Set. $100, $50, $25, $10	3,000
2007W Platinum Set. $100, $50, $25, $10	3,000
2008W Platinum Burnished Set. $100, $50, $25, $10	3,325

Prices are for original Uncirculated or Proof pieces with box and papers.

Private coins were circulated in most instances because of a shortage of regular coinage. Some numismatists use the general term *private gold* to refer to coins struck outside of the United States Mint. In the sense that no state or territory had authority to coin money, *private gold* simply refers to those interesting necessity pieces of various shapes, denominations, and degrees of intrinsic worth which were circulated in isolated areas of our country by individuals, assayers, bankers, etc. Some will use the words "Territorial" and "State" to cover certain issues because they were coined and circulated in a territory or state. While the state of California properly sanctioned the ingots stamped by F.D. Kohler as state assayer, in no instance were any of the gold pieces struck by authority of any of the territorial governments.

The stamped ingots put out by Augustus Humbert, the United States assayer of gold, were not recognized at the United States Mint as an official issue of coins, but simply as ingots, though Humbert placed the value and fineness on the pieces as an official agent of the federal government.

TEMPLETON REID
Georgia Gold 1830

The first private gold coinage under the Constitution was struck by Templeton Reid, a jeweler and gunsmith, in Milledgeville, Georgia, in July 1830. To be closer to the mines, he moved to Gainesville, where most of his coins were made. Although weights were accurate, Reid's assays were not, and his coins were slightly short of claimed value. Accordingly, he was severely attacked in the newspapers and soon lost the public's confidence.

	VG	VF
1830, $2.50	$30,000	$50,000
1830, $5	75,000	125,000
1830, TEN DOLLARS	135,000	225,000
(No Date) TEN DOLLARS	120,000	180,000

California Gold 1849

1849, TEN DOLLAR CALIFORNIA GOLD *(unique, in Smithsonian collection)* . . . .

THE BECHTLERS
RUTHERFORD COUNTY, NC, 1831–1852

Two skilled German metallurgists, Christopher Bechtler and his son August, and later Christopher Bechtler, Junior, a nephew of Christopher the elder, operated a private mint at Rutherfordton, North Carolina. Rutherford County, in which Rutherfordton is located, was the principal source of the nation's gold supply from 1790 to 1848.

Christopher Bechtler

	VF	EF	AU	Unc.
ONE DOLLAR CAROLINA, 28.G, N Reversed	$1,000	$1,800	$2,500	$5,000
ONE GOLD DOLLAR N. CAROLINA, 28.G, No Star	2,200	3,250	4,500	9,000
ONE GOLD DOLLAR N. CAROLINA, 30.G.	1,350	2,000	3,000	7,500
2.50 CAROLINA, 67.G., 21 CARATS	3,000	5,000	6,000	11,000
2.50 CAROLINA, 70.G, 20 CARATS	3,200	5,500	6,500	13,000
2.50 GEORGIA, 64.G, 22 CARATS	3,500	6,000	6,750	15,000
2.50 NORTH CAROLINA, 75.G., 20 CARATS. RUTHERFORD in a Circle. Border of Large Beads	9,000	12,000	19,000	30,000
2.50 NORTH CAROLINA, 20 C. Without 75.G.	9,000	13,000	20,000	32,000

Without 150.G.

	VF	EF	AU	Unc.
5 DOLLARS NORTH CAROLINA GOLD, 150.G., 20.CARATS	$9,000	$13,000	$20,000	$35,000
Similar, Without 150.G.		—	—	
5 DOLLARS CAROLINA, RUTHERFORD, 140.G., 20 CARATS				
Plain Edge	3,250	5,000	6,500	11,000
Reeded Edge	8,000	14,000	19,000	29,000
5 DOLLARS CAROLINA GOLD, RUTHERF., 140.G., 20 CARATS,				
AUGUST 1, 1834	3,500	5,000	6,000	11,000
Similar, but "20" Distant From CARATS	3,250	5,500	6,500	13,000
5 DOLLARS CAROLINA GOLD, 134.G., 21 CARATS, With Star	3,000	4,000	5,000	9,000
5 DOLLARS GEORGIA GOLD, RUTHERFORD, 128.G., 22 CARATS	3,250	4,500	7,000	13,000
5 DOLLARS GEORGIA GOLD, RUTHERF, 128.G., 22 CARATS	3,250	4,500	7,000	13,000

August Bechtler

	VF	EF	AU	Unc.
1 DOL.:, CAROLINA GOLD, 27.G., 21.C.	$800	$1,200	$1,600	$2,500
5 DOLLARS, CAROLINA GOLD, 134.G.:, 21 CARATS	2,700	4,000	5,750	16,000

	VF	EF	AU	Unc.
5 DOLLARS, CAROLINA GOLD, 128.G., 22 CARATS	$6,000	$8,000	$12,000	$18,000
5 DOLLARS, CAROLINA GOLD, 141.G., 20 CARATS	5,100	7,500	11,500	19,000

NORRIS, GREGG & NORRIS
SAN FRANCISCO 1849

These pieces are considered the first of the California private gold coins. A newspaper account dated May 31, 1849, described a five-dollar gold coin struck at Benicia City, though with the imprint San Francisco, and the private stamp of Norris, Gregg & Norris.

	F	VF	EF	AU	Unc.
1849, Half Eagle, Plain Edge	$2,500	$3,500	$5,500	$8,000	$16,500
1849, Half Eagle, Reeded Edge	2,500	3,500	5,500	8,000	16,500
1850, Half Eagle, With STOCKTON Beneath Date *(unique, in Smithsonian collection)*					

MOFFAT & CO.
SAN FRANCISCO 1849–1853

The firm of Moffat & Company was perhaps the most important of the California private coiners. The assay office they conducted was semi-official in character, and successors to this firm later sold its facilities to the Treasury Department, which used them to create the San Francisco Mint.

In June or July, 1849, Moffat & Co. began to issue small rectangular pieces of gold in values from $9.43 to $264. The $9.43, $14.25, and $16.00 varieties are the only types known today.

	EF
$9.43 Ingot *(unique, in Smithsonian collection)*	—
$14.25 Ingot *(unique, in Smithsonian collection)*	—
$16.00 Ingot	$50,000

The dies for the $10 piece were cut by Albert Kuner. The words Moffat & Co. appear on Liberty's coronet instead of the word LIBERTY as in regular United States issues.

	F	VF	EF	AU	Unc.
1849, FIVE DOL. *(all varieties)*	$900	$1,400	$1,900	$2,500	$6,000
1850, FIVE DOL. *(all varieties)*	900	1,500	2,000	2,750	6,500
1849, TEN DOL.	1,800	2,750	5,500	9,000	18,000
1849, TEN D.	1,900	2,900	6,000	10,000	20,000

UNITED STATES ASSAY OFFICE
Augustus Humbert
United States Assayer of Gold, 1851

When Augustus Humbert was appointed United States Assayer, he placed his name and the government imprint on the ingots of gold issued by Moffat & Co. The assay office, a provisional government mint, was a temporary expedient to accommodate the Californians until the establishment of a permanent branch mint. The $50 gold piece was accepted as legal tender on a par with standard U.S. gold coins.

Lettered Edge Varieties

	F	VF	EF	AU	Unc.
1851, 50 D C 880 THOUS., No 50 on Reverse. Sunk in Edge: AUGUSTUS HUMBERT UNITED STATES ASSAYER OF GOLD CALIFORNIA 1851	$9,500	$15,000	$20,000	$29,000	$59,000

50 on Reverse

	F	VF	EF	AU	Unc.
1851, 50 D C 880 THOUS, Similar to Last Variety, but 50 on Reverse	$10,500	$20,000	$27,000	$45,000	$80,000
1851, 50 D C, 887 THOUS., With 50 on Reverse	10,000	18,000	23,000	35,000	66,000

Reeded Edge Varieties

	F	VF	EF	AU	Unc.
1851, FIFTY DOLLS, 880 THOUS., "Target" Reverse	$7,000	$9,000	$13,000	$20,000	$35,000
1851, FIFTY DOLLS, 887 THOUS., "Target" Reverse	7,000	9,000	13,000	20,000	35,000
1852, FIFTY DOLLS, 887 THOUS., "Target" Reverse	7,000	9,000	13,000	20,000	37,500

Moffat & Co. proceeded in January 1852 to issue a new ten-dollar piece bearing the stamp MOFFAT & CO.

	F	VF	EF	AU	Unc.
1852, TEN D. MOFFAT & CO. (Close Date)	$1,900	$3,200	$6,500	$15,000	$35,000

	F	VF	EF	AU	Unc.
1852, TEN DOLS., 1852, 2 Over 1	$1,650	$2,750	$4,200	$7,000	$14,500
1852, TEN DOLS.	1,350	2,000	2,750	5,000	12,500

	F	VF	EF	AU	Unc.
1852, TWENTY DOLS., 1852, 2 Over 1	$3,500	$5,200	$10,000	$19,500	$46,000

United States Assay Office of Gold – 1852

The firm of Moffat & Co. was reorganized as Curtis, Perry & Ward, which assumed the government contract to conduct the United States Assay Office of Gold.

	F	VF	EF	AU	Unc.
1852, FIFTY DOLLS., 887 THOUS.	$7,200	$9,500	$15,000	$21,000	$38,000
1852, FIFTY DOLLS., 900 THOUS.	7,500	10,000	16,500	23,000	40,000

	F	VF	EF	AU	Unc.
1852, TEN DOLS., 884 THOUS.	$1,000	$1,650	$2,500	$4,000	$9,000
1853, TEN D., 884 THOUS.	3,500	7,000	13,500	18,000	35,000
1853, TEN D., 900 THOUS.	2,000	3,000	4,500	8,000	12,000
1853, TWENTY D., 884 THOUS.	3,500	5,000	9,000	14,000	25,000
1853, TWENTY D., 900 THOUS.	1,250	1,650	2,500	3,500	6,500

Moffat & Company Gold

The last Moffat issue was an 1853 $20 piece that is very similar to the U.S. double eagle of that period. It was struck after the retirement of John L. Moffat from Moffat & Company.

	F	VF	EF	AU	Unc.
1853, TWENTY D.	$2,000	$2,600	$3,900	$6,750	$16,000

CINCINNATI MINING & TRADING CO. (1849)

The origin and location of this company are unknown. It might have been organized in Ohio, and conducted business in California.

	EF	Unc.
1849, FIVE DOLLARS	—	—
1849, TEN DOLLARS	$350,000	—

MASSACHUSETTS AND CALIFORNIA COMPANY

This company was believed to have been organized in Northampton, Massachusetts, in May 1849.

	F	VF	EF
1849, FIVE D.	$65,000	$95,000	$150,000

MINERS' BANK
SAN FRANCISCO 1849

The institution of Wright & Co., exchange brokers located in Portsmouth Square, San Francisco, was known as the Miners' Bank.

A $10 piece was issued in the autumn of 1849, but the coins were not readily accepted because they were worth less than face value.

	VF	EF	AU	Unc.
(1849) TEN D.	$9,000	$16,500	$25,000	$45,000

J.S. ORMSBY
SACRAMENTO 1849

The initials J.S.O., which appear on certain issues of California privately coined gold pieces, represent the firm of J.S. Ormsby & Co. The firm struck both $5 and $10 denominations, all undated.

	VF
(1849) 5 DOLLS *(unique)*	—
(1849) 10 DOLLS *(4 known)*	$165,000

PACIFIC COMPANY, SAN FRANCISCO 1849

The origin of the Pacific Company is uncertain. All data regarding the firm are based on conjecture.

Edgar H. Adams wrote that he believed that the coins bearing the stamp of the Pacific Company were produced by the coining firm of Broderick and Kohler. The coins were probably hand struck with the aid of a sledgehammer.

	EF
1849, 1 DOLLAR *(2 known)*	—
1849, 5 DOLLARS *(4 known)*	$170,000
1849, 10 DOLLARS *(4 known)*	225,000

F.D. KOHLER
CALIFORNIA STATE ASSAYER 1850

The State Assay Office was authorized on April 12, 1850. That year, Governor Burnett appointed F.D. Kohler, who thereupon sold his assaying business to Baldwin & Co. Kohler served at both the San Francisco and Sacramento offices. The State Assay Offices were discontinued when the U.S. Assay Office was established, on February 1, 1851.

	EF
$36.55 Sacramento	—
$37.31 San Francisco	—
$40.07 San Francisco	—
$45.34 San Francisco	—
$50.00 San Francisco	—
$54.09 San Francisco	—

DUBOSQ & COMPANY
SAN FRANCISCO 1850

Theodore Dubosq, a Philadelphia jeweler, took melting and coining machinery to San Francisco in 1849.

	VF
1850, FIVE D.	$95,000
1850, TEN D.	95,000

BALDWIN & CO.
SAN FRANCISCO 1850

George C. Baldwin and Thomas S. Holman were in the jewelry business in San Francisco and were known as Baldwin & Co. They were the successors to F.D. Kohler & Co., taking over its machinery and other equipment in May 1850.

	F	VF	EF	AU	Unc.
1850, FIVE DOL.	$3,750	$6,200	$12,000	$18,000	$24,000
1850, TEN DOLLARS, Horseman Type	19,000	35,000	50,000	70,000	110,000

	F	VF	EF	AU	Unc.
1851, TEN D.	$5,000	$12,500	$18,000	$29,000	$67,500

	VF	EF	AU	Unc.
1851, TWENTY D.	$100,000	$170,000	—	—

SHULTZ & COMPANY
SAN FRANCISCO 1851

The firm, located in back of Baldwin's establishment, operated a brass foundry beginning in 1851. Judge G.W. Shultz and William T. Garratt were partners in the enterprise.

	F	VF
1851, FIVE D.	$16,000	$33,000

DUNBAR & COMPANY
SAN FRANCISCO 1851

Edward E. Dunbar operated the California Bank in San Francisco. Dunbar later returned to New York and organized the famous Continental Bank Note Co.

	EF
1851, FIVE D.	$150,000

WASS, MOLITOR & CO.
SAN FRANCISCO 1852–1855

The gold-smelting and assaying plant of Wass, Molitor & Co. was operated by two Hungarian patriots, Count S.C. Wass and A.P. Molitor. They maintained an excellent laboratory and complete apparatus for analysis and coinage of gold.

	F	VF	EF	AU	Unc.
1852, FIVE DOLLARS	$2,100	$4,100	$8,500	$15,000	$29,000

Large Head   **Small Head**

	F	VF	EF	AU	Unc.
1852, TEN D., Large Head	$1,400	$2,200	$3,750	$7,250	$12,500
1852, TEN D., Small Head	3,200	4,250	10,000	17,000	37,000
1855, TEN D.	6,100	9,100	12,500	16,000	30,000

Large Head   **Small Head**

	F	VF	EF	AU	Unc.
1855, TWENTY DOL., Large Head	—	—	$175,000	—	—
1855, TWENTY DOL., Small Head	$6,500	$16,000	20,000	$40,000	$75,000

	F	VF	EF	AU	Unc.
1855, 50 DOLLARS	$12,500	$17,000	$20,000	$40,000	$85,000

KELLOGG & CO.
SAN FRANCISCO 1854–1855

When the U.S. Assay Office ceased operations, a period ensued during which no private firm was striking gold. The new San Francisco branch mint did not produce coins for some months after Curtis & Perry took the government contract. The lack of coin was again keenly felt by businessmen, who petitioned Kellogg & Richter to "supply the vacuum" by issuing private coin. Their plea was soon answered, for on February 9, 1854, Kellogg & Co. placed their first $20 piece in circulation.

	F	VF	EF	AU	Unc.	PF
1854, TWENTY D.	$1,500	$2,000	$2,750	$4,500	$11,000	
1855, TWENTY D.	1,500	2,000	3,200	5,000	13,500	
1855, FIFTY DOLLS.						$190,000

OREGON EXCHANGE COMPANY
OREGON CITY 1849
The Beaver Coins of Oregon

On February 16, 1849, the legislature passed an act providing for a mint and specified $5 and $10 gold coins without alloy. Oregon City, the largest city in the territory with a population of about 1,000, was designated as the location for the mint. At the time this act was passed, Oregon had been brought into the United States as a territory by act of Congress. When the new governor arrived on March 2, he declared the coinage act unconstitutional.

	F	VF	EF	AU	Unc.
1849, 5 D.	$15,000	$23,000	$31,000	$66,000	—
1849, TEN.D	37,000	68,000	120,000	175,000	—

MORMON GOLD PIECES
SALT LAKE CITY, UTAH, 1849–1860

Brigham Young was the instigator of the coinage system and personally supervised the mint, which was housed in a little adobe building in Salt Lake City. The mint was inaugurated in 1849 as a public convenience.

	F	VF	EF	AU	Unc.
1849, TWO.AND.HALF.DO.	$5,500	$9,000	$15,000	$26,000	$40,000
1849, FIVE.DOLLARS	4,000	8,000	14,000	16,500	31,000

	F	VF	EF
1849, TEN.DOLLARS	$85,000	$125,000	$160,000
1849, TWENTY.DOLLARS	35,000	70,000	90,000

	F	VF	EF	AU	Unc.
1850, FIVE DOLLARS	$4,750	$8,500	$13,000	$23,000	$45,000
1860, 5.D.	9,000	16,500	22,000	32,500	45,000

COLORADO GOLD PIECES
Clark, Gruber & Co.
Denver 1860–1861

Clark, Gruber & Co. was a well-known private minting firm in Denver, Colorado, in the early 1860s.

	F	VF	EF	AU	Unc.
1860, 2 1/2 D.	$850	$1,250	$2,000	$3,200	$7,000
1860, FIVE D.	950	1,500	2,100	3,750	7,500

	F	VF	EF	AU	Unc.
1860, TEN D.	$4,000	$6,000	$9,000	$16,000	$27,000
1860, TWENTY D.	25,000	40,000	70,000	120,000	250,000

	F	VF	EF	AU	Unc.
1861, 2 1/2 D.	$900	$1,400	$2,100	$3,500	$8,500
1861, FIVE D.	1,200	1,700	2,600	4,700	17,000
1861, TEN D.	1,200	1,800	2,750	4,750	16,000

	F	VF	EF	AU
1861, TWENTY D.	$7,000	$15,000	$26,000	$50,000

John Parsons & Company
Tarryall Mines – Colorado, 1861

Very little is known regarding the mint of John Parsons and Co., although it is reasonably certain that it operated in the South Park section of Park County, Colorado, near the original town of Tarryall, in the summer of 1861.

	VF
(1861) Undated 2 1/2 D.	$90,000
(1861) Undated FIVE D.	100,000

J.J. Conway & Co.
Georgia Gulch, Colorado, 1861

Records show that the Conway mint operated for a short while in 1861. As in all gold mining areas, the value of gold dust caused disagreement among the merchants and the miners. The firm of J.J. Conway & Co. solved this difficulty by bringing out its gold pieces in August 1861.

	VF
(1861) Undated 2 1/2 DOLL'S	$70,000
(1861) Undated FIVE DOLLARS	90,000
(1861) Undated TEN DOLLARS	—

CALIFORNIA SMALL-DENOMINATION GOLD

There was a scarcity of small coins during the California Gold Rush and, starting in 1852, quarter, half, and dollar pieces were privately minted from native gold to alleviate the shortage. The need and acceptability of these pieces declined after 1856 and they then became popular as souvenirs. Authentic pieces all have CENTS, DOLLAR, or an abbreviation thereof on the reverse. The tokens are much less valuable. Modern restrikes and replicas have no numismatic value.

The values in the following charts are only for coins made before 1883 with the denomination on the reverse expressed as CENTS, DOL., DOLL., or DOLLAR.

Quarter Dollar – Octagonal

	EF-40	AU-50	MS-60
Liberty Head	$75	$100	$160
Indian Head	90	125	170
Washington Head	350	550	750

Quarter Dollar – Round

	EF-40	AU-50	MS-60
Liberty Head	$75	$100	$160
Indian Head	80	110	180
Washington Head	350	550	750

Half Dollar – Octagonal

	EF-40	AU-50	MS-60
Liberty Head	$75	$100	$160
Liberty Head / Eagle	375	500	900
Indian Head	85	125	250

Half Dollar – Round

	EF-40	AU-50	MS-60
Liberty Head	$75	$100	$200
Indian Head	75	100	180

Dollar – Octagonal

	EF-40	AU-50	MS-60
Liberty Head	$200	$300	$550
Liberty Head / Eagle	750	1,200	1,850
Indian Head	200	350	500

Dollar – Round

	EF-40	AU-50	MS-60
Liberty Head	$900	$1,350	$2,000
Indian Head	900	1,350	2,150

HARD TIMES TOKENS (1832–1844)

During the financial crises of 1832 to 1844 many government coins were hoarded, and privately made tokens were used out of necessity. The so-called Hard Times tokens of this period were slightly smaller and lighter than normal large cents. They were made of copper or brass and are of two general groups: political tokens whose theme centered on President Jackson's fight against the United States Bank, and tradesmen's cards, issued by merchants. Many different designs and varieties exist.

	VF	EF
Hard Times Tokens, 1832–1844, most common pieces	$12	$24

CIVIL WAR TOKENS (1860s)

Civil War tokens are generally divided into two groups: tradesmen's tokens, and anonymously issued pieces with political or patriotic themes. They came into existence only because of the scarcity of government coins and disappeared as soon as the bronze coins of 1864 met the public demand for small copper change.

These tokens vary greatly in composition and design. A number were more or less faithful imitations of the copper-nickel cent. A few of this type have the word "not" in very small letters above the words ONE CENT.

	F	VF	EF	Unc.
Copper or Brass Tokens	$6	$10	$12	$22
Nickel or German Silver Tokens	18	25	50	90
White-Metal Tokens	20	30	45	70
Copper-Nickel Tokens	30	50	75	115
Silver Tokens	75	125	200	350

Common-date silver coins are valued according to the price of silver bullion. In recent years the price of silver bullion has been subject to extreme fluctuation. Therefore, when you read this it is highly probable that the current bullion price may differ from the prevailing market price used in tabulating valuations of many 19th- and 20th-century silver coins (priced in italics) listed in this edition. The following chart will help to determine the approximate bullion value of these coins at various price levels. Or the approximate value may be calculated by multiplying the current spot price of silver times the content for each coin as indicated below. Dealers generally purchase common silver coins at 15% below bullion value, and sell them at 15% above bullion value.

Bullion Values of Silver Coins

Silver Price Per Ounce	Wartime Nickel .05626 oz.	Dime .07234 oz.	Quarter .18084 oz.	Half Dollar .36169 oz.	Silver Clad Half Dollar .14792 oz.	Silver Dollar .77344 oz.
$8.00	$0.45	$0.58	$1.45	$2.89	$1.18	$6.19
8.50	0.48	0.61	1.54	3.07	1.26	6.57
9.00	0.51	0.65	1.63	3.26	1.33	6.96
9.50	0.53	0.69	1.72	3.44	1.41	7.35
10.00	0.56	0.72	1.81	3.62	1.48	7.73
10.50	0.59	0.76	1.90	3.80	1.55	8.12
11.00	0.62	0.80	1.99	3.98	1.63	8.51
11.50	0.65	0.83	2.08	4.16	1.70	8.89
12.00	0.68	0.87	2.17	4.34	1.78	9.28
12.50	0.70	0.90	2.26	4.52	1.85	9.67
13.00	0.73	0.94	2.35	4.70	1.92	10.05
13.50	0.76	0.98	2.44	4.88	2.00	10.44
14.00	0.79	1.01	2.53	5.06	2.07	10.83
14.50	0.82	1.05	2.62	5.24	2.14	11.21
15.00	0.84	1.09	2.71	5.43	2.22	11.60
15.50	0.87	1.12	2.80	5.61	2.29	11.99
16.00	0.90	1.16	2.89	5.79	2.37	12.38
16.50	0.93	1.19	2.98	5.97	2.44	12.76
17.00	0.96	1.23	3.07	6.15	2.51	13.15
17.50	0.98	1.27	3.16	6.33	2.59	13.54
18.00	1.01	1.30	3.26	6.51	2.66	13.92
18.50	1.04	1.34	3.35	6.69	2.74	14.31
19.00	1.07	1.37	3.44	6.87	2.81	14.70
19.50	1.10	1.41	3.53	7.05	2.88	15.08
20.00	1.13	1.45	3.62	7.23	2.96	15.47
20.50	1.15	1.48	3.71	7.41	3.03	15.86
21.00	1.18	1.52	3.80	7.60	3.11	16.24
21.50	1.21	1.56	3.89	7.78	3.18	16.63
22.00	1.24	1.59	3.98	7.96	3.25	17.02
22.50	1.27	1.63	4.07	8.14	3.33	17.40
23.00	1.29	1.66	4.16	8.32	3.40	17.79
23.50	1.32	1.70	4.25	8.50	3.48	18.18
24.00	1.35	1.74	4.34	8.68	3.55	18.56
24.50	1.38	1.77	4.43	8.86	3.62	18.95
25.00	1.41	1.81	4.52	9.04	3.70	19.34

The value of common-date gold coins listed in this book may be affected by the rise or fall in the price of gold bullion. Nearly all U.S. gold coins have an additional premium value beyond their bullion content, and thus are not subject to the minor variations described for silver coins. The premium amount is not necessarily tied to the bullion price of gold, but is usually determined by supply and demand levels for actual gold coins occurring in the numismatic marketplace. Because these factors can vary significantly, there is no reliable formula for calculating "percentage above bullion" prices that would remain accurate over time. For this reason the chart below lists bullion values based on gold content only. Consult your nearest coin dealer to ascertain current premium prices.

Bullion Values of Gold Coins

Gold Price Per Ounce	$5.00 Liberty Head 1839–1908 Indian Head 1908–1929 .24187 oz.	$10.00 Liberty Head 1838–1907 Indian Head 1907–1933 .48375 oz.	$20.00 1849–1933 .96750 oz.
$800	$193.50	$387.00	$774.00
825	199.54	399.09	798.19
850	205.59	411.19	822.38
875	211.64	423.28	846.56
900	217.68	435.38	870.75
925	223.73	447.47	894.94
950	229.78	459.56	919.13
975	235.82	471.66	943.31
1,000	241.87	483.75	967.50
1,025	247.92	495.84	991.69
1,050	253.96	507.94	1,015.88
1,075	260.01	520.03	1,040.06
1,100	266.06	532.13	1,064.25
1,125	272.10	544.22	1,088.44
1,150	278.15	556.31	1,112.63
1,175	284.20	568.41	1,136.81
1,200	290.24	580.50	1,161.00
1,225	296.29	592.59	1,185.19
1,250	302.34	604.69	1,209.38
1,275	308.38	616.78	1,233.56
1,300	314.43	628.88	1,257.75
1,325	320.48	640.97	1,281.94
1,350	326.52	653.06	1,306.13
1,375	332.57	665.16	1,330.31
1,400	338.62	677.25	1,354.50
1,425	344.66	689.34	1,378.69
1,450	350.71	701.44	1,402.88
1,475	356.76	713.53	1,427.06
1,500	362.81	725.63	1,451.25

Note: The U.S. bullion coins first issued in 1986 are unlike the older regular issues. They contain the following amounts of pure metal: silver $1, 1 oz.; gold $50, 1 oz.; gold $25, 1/2 oz.; gold $10, 1/4 oz.; gold $5, 1/10 oz.

Is it time to sell your coins? Perhaps you've inherited some of them; or maybe you've collected for years, and you want to explore a new pastime or you need to cash in on your investment. In any case, you have some decisions to make. Will you sell your collection privately, or at a public auction—or perhaps sell it yourself on the Internet? Will you sell locally or to dealers nationwide? What are the benefits of each path, and which will bring the greatest profits? To get started, ask yourself:

WHAT AM I SELLING?

Rolls of Modern Coins; Proof Sets; Modern Commemoratives; Bullion; Etc. This includes bulk investment coins, such as American Eagle bullion pieces, bags of common circulated coins, and so on. It also includes modern commemoratives and coin sets, not all of which have increased in value in the secondary market. Such accumulations are best sold privately to a coin dealer or to another collector. Auctioning them yourself, on the Internet, is another route. Consigning them to an auction house is not likely to be your best option; this venue is typically reserved for scarcer coins.

Coins With Sentimental—but Not Necessarily High-Dollar—Value. You might have inherited an accumulation (as opposed to a studiously compiled collection) of coins—for example, a coffee can full of wheat cents. Your local coin dealer can make you an offer, either buying the entire lot or searching through them to "cherrypick" the better pieces. If you have the time, you might sell them yourself, through an Internet auction site. Also, you might donate them to a local Boy Scout troop or similar organization (this may be tax-deductible).

Rare and/or Significant Coins. For rare, valuable, and historically significant coins, public consigned auctions are often the best way to sell—dedicated collectors know they're good sources for scarce coins. A coin consigned to a well-established auction house with numismatic experience will be carefully studied, cataloged, and presented to a serious audience. You save the time and effort of searching for potential buyers. The auction firm makes money by collecting a commission on each sale.

Another option for selling your rare and significant coins is to approach a dealer nationally recognized as an expert in the field—for example, a specialist who focuses on colonial coins. You can also receive tax benefits from donating your coins to the American Numismatic Association (ANA), the American Numismatic Society, or a museum.

SELLING TO A COIN SHOP

Your local coin shop has the advantage of the personal touch. Good coin-shop proprietors are happy to educate and advise their customers. An active coin dealer stays up to date on the hobby and the market, knows about tax and estate laws that might affect your sale, and can study your collection and make educated decisions. Many dealers have a wide audience for selling coins—which provides the leverage to offer you a good price.

A coin shop can be a venue for selling numismatic items of any value. The owner can often make you an offer and write you a check on the spot. Of course, very rare or specialized coins will likely fetch a higher price at public auction.

You should feel comfortable with the integrity of the shop's proprietor and staff. Talk to coin-collector friends, inquire at the local coin club, and check with the Better Business Bureau. Look at the shop's Web site, advertisements, and flyers or publications—do they project fairness and professionalism?

Coin shops can be found in a phone book or online business directory. Call to make sure the owner or a qualified assistant will be there to examine your coins. A busy dealer can schedule a convenient time to meet with you. Solicit at least two quotes before you decide to sell.

SELLING THROUGH THE MAIL

You can ship your coins to a dealer for their offer; again, trust is important. Does the dealer belong to the ANA or the Professional Numismatists Guild? Does he advertise in hobby newspapers such as *Coin World* and *Numismatic News?* Search the dealer's name on the Internet: do you find satisfied customers, or complaints and concerns?

Inquire by mail, email, or phone before shipping any coins. The dealer might request a list beforehand, and should be able to give you a general idea of value without seeing the coins in person. Once you're comfortable and have decided to sell, ask the dealer for advice on shipping and insurance. Keep in mind that the dealer will need to examine your coins before making a firm offer.

Even if you live near a coin shop, you can broaden the playing field if you're open to selling your coins through the mail to established, respected dealers. This is a good option if you have the time. The entire transaction (finding dealers; packing and shipping; waiting for the check) will likely take longer than getting a local offer.

SELLING TO A DEALER AT A COIN SHOW

Between the national coin shows and the hundreds of coin clubs that sponsor city and regional shows, chances are a show is held somewhere near you at least once a year. With dozens or even hundreds of dealers in one venue, you can shop your coins around before you sell; and, as at coin shop, payment is immediate.

Remember, a coin show is a public venue. Be alert; use common sense. Outside the show, do not publicize the fact that you're carrying valuable coins.

Most shows list participating dealers in their programs. Decide in advance the ones you want to approach (e.g., the silver-dollar specialists, if you have Morgan dollars to sell). Or simply stroll the aisles and introduce yourself to dealers who sell items similar to those in your collection. This is all part of the fun of a coin show.

CONSIGNING AT A PUBLIC AUCTION

Numismatic auction firms are often connected to larger retailers that also sell through the mail, online, etc. As always, reputation is important. Study a potential auctioneer's Web site; learn about their staff, past sales results, any media coverage they might receive. Look at their catalogs: are they professionally made? The effort and experience an auction firm brings to its work will affect how much your coins sell for.

SELLING ONLINE

Selling your coins yourself online can be fun, but it requires time and (usually) some skill with scanning or photography. Each auction site has its own rules, policies, and rates; read them carefully. Be security-conscious (e.g., rent a Post Office box instead of using your home address, and insist on full, guaranteed payment before you ship any coins). You can also use the Internet to sell your coins at a fixed price, through a bulletin-board posting or other announcement. Any online sale to the public requires you to take on responsibilities similar to those of a coin shop or auction firm. There is work involved, but the experience can be enjoyable and profitable.

You now have a good, basic understanding of how to sell your coins. For more information, visit your local library or bookstore. *The Expert's Guide to Collecting and Investing in Rare Coins* (Bowers) and the *Whitman Guide to Coin Collecting* (Bressett) are two recommended resources. Best wishes for a successful sale!

INDEX

alloys, 10
  wartime silver, 73
American Buffalo gold bullion coins, 225
American Numismatic Association (ANA), 15
  grading system of, 13–14
American Plantations token, 19
Auctori Plebis tokens, 35

Bar "coppers," 35
Barber (Charles E.) designs
  dimes, 88–89
  half dollars, 124–126
  quarter dollars, 101–103
Bicentennial coins, 107, 130, 142
blanks, 10
branch mints, 11
Brasher doubloons, 30
Brenner, Victor David, 56. See also small cents, V.D.B.
British New World issues, 16–18
British royal patent, coinage authorized by, 19–21
Buffalo bullion coins, 225
Buffalo nickels, 70–72
buffed coins, 14
bullion coins, 221–230
bullion values of common coins, 250–251

cents
  Fugio (1787), 9, 41
  large (see large cents)
  Lincoln (see Lincoln cents)
  small (see small cents)
  Talbot, Allum & Lee, 36–37
Chalmers, John, issues of, 24–25
Civil War tokens (1860s), 249
coin clubs, 15
coin folders, 14–15
coins
  cleaning, 14
  collecting, 9, 14–15
  production of, 9–11
  storing, 14
commemoratives
  classic, 178–195
  government sets, 213–217
  modern, 195–213
Confederatio coppers, 27
Connecticut, early coinage of, 29–30
Continental Currency, 41
coppers. See individual kinds of coppers
copper sou, 25

deniers, nine, 25
die cutting, 9–10
die varieties, identifying, 11–13
dimes
  Barber or Liberty Head (1892–1916), 88–89
  Capped Bust (1809–1837), 83–84
  Draped Bust (1796–1807), 82
  Liberty Seated (1837–1891), 84–87
  Roosevelt (1946 to date), 92–94

Winged Liberty or "Mercury" (1916–1945), 90–91
dollars
  Bicentennial (1976), 142
  Eisenhower (1971–1978), 141–142
  gold (see gold dollars)
  Native American (2009 to date), 144
  Presidential (2006–2016), 144–146
  Sacagawea (2000–2008), 143–144
  silver (see silver dollars)
  Susan B. Anthony (1979–1999), 142–143
double eagles
  Liberty Head (1849–1907), 172–175
  Saint-Gaudens (1907–1933), 175–177

eagles
  Capped Bust to Right (1795–1804), 166
  Indian Head (1907–1933), 170–171
  Liberty Head (1838–1907), 167–170
  silver (see silver eagles)
early American and related tokens, 21–25
Eisenhower, Dwight D., 141
Elephant tokens, 21–22

file marks, 14
First Spouse bullion coins, 225–227
five-cent pieces, nickel
  Indian Head or Buffalo (1913–1938), 70–72
  Jefferson (1938 to date), 72–77
  Liberty Head (1883–1912), 69–70
  Shield (1866–1883), 68
  wartime silver alloy (1942–1945), 73
  Westward Journey Nickel Series™ (2004–2005), 76–77
five-dollar gold pieces. See half eagles
four-dollar gold pieces or Stellas (1879–1889), 157
Franklin, Benjamin, 36. See also Franklin Press tokens; half dollars, Franklin
Franklin Press tokens, 36
French colonies, coinage of, 25
French New World issues, 25
Fugio cents (1787), 9, 41

Gloucester tokens, 22–23
Gobrecht dollars, 134
gold bullion coins, 222–227
gold dollars
  Indian Princess Head (1854–1889), 148–149
  Liberty Head (1849–1854), 147
golden dollars. See dollars, Presidential (2006–2016); dollars, Sacagawea (2000–2008); Native American (2009 to date)
gold, private and territorial (1830–1850s), 231–248
gold. See bullion values; double eagles; eagles; four-dollar gold pieces; gold bullion coins; gold dollars;

gold, private and territorial; half eagles; quarter eagles; three-dollar gold pieces; and individual commemorative coins
grading, 13–14
Granby coppers. See Higley or Granby coppers

half cents
  Braided Hair (1840–1857), 45
  Classic Head (1809–1836), 44–45
  Draped Bust (1800–1808), 43–44
  Liberty Cap (1793–1797), 42–43
half dimes
  Capped Bust (1829–1837), 79
  Draped Bust (1796–1797), 78–79
  Flowing Hair (1794–1795), 78
  Liberty Seated (1837–1873), 79–81
half dollars
  Barber or Liberty Head (1892–1915), 124–126
  Bicentennial (1976), 130
  Capped Bust, Lettered Edge (1807–1836), 117–119
  Capped Bust, Reeded Edge (1836–1839), 120
  Draped Bust (1796–1807), 116–117
  Flowing Hair (1794–1795), 116
  Franklin (1948–1963), 128–129
  Kennedy (1964 to date), 129–131
  Liberty Seated (1839–1891), 120–124
  Liberty Walking (1916–1947), 126–128
half eagles
  Capped Bust to Left (1807–1812), 159
  Capped Bust to Right (1795–1807), 158–159
  Capped Head to Left (1813–1834), 159–160
  Classic Head (1834–1838), 160
  Indian Head (1908–1929), 165
  Liberty Head (1839–1908), 160–165
halfpennies, Virginia, 21
Hard Times tokens (1832–1844), 249
Hibernia coinage, 20
Hibernia–Voce Populi tokens, 23
Higley or Granby coppers, 23
Hogge Money, 16

Immune Columbia pieces, 26–27
ingots, 10

Jefferson, Thomas. See commemoratives, government sets; commemoratives, modern; five-cent pieces, Jefferson

Kennedy, John F. See half dollars, Kennedy
Kentucky tokens, 36

large cents
  Classic Head (1808–1814), 49–50
  Draped Bust (1796–1807), 47–49
  Flowing Hair (1793), 46

large cents *(continued)*
    Liberty Cap (1793–1796), 46–47
    Liberty Head (1816–1857), 50–53
Lincoln Bicentennial One-Cent
        Program, 63–64
Lincoln cents, 56–64
    Shield reverse, 64
lint marks, 14
Lord Baltimore coinage, 18

Mark Newby coinage, 18
Maryland, early coinage of, 18
Massachusetts, early coinage of,
        16–18, 28–29
Matte Proof coins, 11
"Mercury" dimes (1916–1945), 90–91
Mint sets, uncirculated, 220
mintmarks, 11
Morgan dollars, 137–140
Morgan, George T., 137
Mott store cards, 35

Native American dollars (2009 to date),
        144
"New England" coinage (1652), 16
New Hampshire, early coinage of, 28
New Jersey, early coinage of, 18,
        32–33
New York, early coinage of, 30–32
New Yorke in America tokens, 22
Newby, Mark, 18
nickels. *See* five-cent pieces, nickel
North American tokens, 34–35
Nova Constellatio coppers, 26
Nova Eborac coinage for New York, 32

Oak Tree coinage (1660–1667), 17

patterns, speculative pre-federal, 26–28
Peace dollars, 140–141
Pine Tree coinage (1667–1682), 17–18
Pitt tokens, 24
platinum bullion coins, 228–230
Presidential dollars, 144–146
Proof coins and sets, 218–219
Proof coins, the making of, 11

quarter dollars
    50 State Quarters® Program
        (1999–2008), 108–113
    America the Beautiful™ Program
        (2010–2021), 114–115
    Barber or Liberty Head
        (1892–1916), 101–103

Bicentennial (1976), 107
Capped Bust (1815–1838), 96–97
D.C. and Territories Program (2009),
        113–114
Draped Bust (1796–1807), 96
Liberty Seated (1838–1891),
        98–101
Standing Liberty (1916–1930),
        103–104
Washington (1932–1998), 104–115
quarter eagles
    CAL. (1848), 152
    Capped Bust to Left, Large Size
        (1808), 150
    Capped Bust to Right (1796–1807),
        150
    Capped Head to Left (1821–1834),
        150–151
    Classic Head, No Motto on Reverse
        (1834–1839), 151
    Indian Head (1908–1929), 155
    Liberty Head (1840–1907), 151–154
quarters. *See* quarter dollars

reducing lathe, 10
Rhode Island Ship medals, 24
Roosevelt, Franklin D. *See* commemo-
        ratives, modern
Rosa Americana coins, 19–20

Sacagawea, 143
Saint-Gaudens, Augustus, 175
Schlag, Felix, 72
silver bullion coins, 221
silver dollars
    Draped Bust (1795–1804), 132–133
    Flowing Hair (1794–1795), 132
    Gobrecht (1836–1839), 134
    Liberty Seated (1840–1873),
        134–136
    Morgan (1878–1921), 137–140
    Peace (1921–1935), 140–141
    Trade (1873–1885), 136–137
silver eagles, 221
sliders, 14
small cents
    Flying Eagle (1856–1858), 54
    Indian Head (1859–1909), 54–56
    Lincoln (1909 to date), 56–64
    memorial reverse (1959–2008),
        60–63
    Shield reverse (2010 to date), 64
    V.D.B. (1909), 56

wheat-ear reverse (1909–1958),
        56–60
Sommer Islands (Bermuda) issues, 16
sou, copper, 25
speculative issues, tokens, and patterns,
        26–28
St. Patrick coinage, 18
Standish Barry threepence, 36
statehood quarters. *See* quarter dollars,
    50 State Quarters® Program
    (1999–2008)
states, coinage of early American,
        28–34
steel cents, 59
Stellas, 157

Talbot, Allum & Lee cents, 36–37
tarnish, 14
ten-dollar gold pieces. *See* eagles
three-cent pieces
    nickel (1865–1889), 67
    silver ("trimes"; 1851–1873), 66
three-dollar gold pieces (1854–1889),
        156
tokens. *See individual kinds of tokens*
Trade dollars, 136–137
trimes (1851–1873), 66
twenty-cent pieces (1875–1878), 95
twenty-dollar gold pieces. *See* double
    eagles
two-cent pieces (1864–1873), 65

U.S. Mint, establishment of, 9
Ultra High Relief gold bullion coins
        (2009), 227

V.D.B. cents (1909), 56. *See also*
    Brenner, Victor David
Vermont, early coinage of, 33–34
Virginia halfpennies, 21
Vistas of Liberty reverse designs, 228

Washington pieces, 37–40
Washington, George, 37. *See also*
    commemoratives, government
    sets; commemoratives, modern
Westward Journey Nickel Series™,
        76–77
wheat cents (1909–1958), 56–60
"whizzed" coins. *See* buffed coins
Willow Tree coinage (1653–1660), 17
Wood, William, 19